Core Mac OS X and Unix Programming

Mark Dalrymple
Aaron Hillegass

The authors and publisher have taken care in preparation of this book, but make no expressed or implied warranty of any kind and assume no responsibility for errors of omissions. No liability is assumed for incidental or consequential damages in connection with or arising out of the use of the information or programs contained herein.

For more information about this book or the class it is based upon, contact;
Big Nerd Ranch, Inc.
931 Monroe Drive
Suite 102, PMB 254
Atlanta, GA 30030
(678) 595 - 6773
http://www.bignerdranch.com/

Publishers Cataloging-in-Publication Data

Dalrymple, Mark
    Core Mac OS X and Unix Programming / Mark Dalrymple, Aaron Hillegass
        p. cm.
    ISBN 0-9740785-0-6
            1. Mac OS. 2. Operating Systems (Computers) 3.Macintosh
            I. Hillegass, Aaron
    QA76.76.063 D635 2003

ISBN 0-9740785-0-6
First edition, first printing   June 2003

To Glenn, Mary Jo, and Enna — Mark

To my parents, Tom and Suzanna — Aaron

Table of Contents

Acknowledgements

This book is based upon our experiences teaching a five-day class at the Big Nerd Ranch called *Core Mac OS X and Unix Programming* course. The patience and curiousity of our students has made this a more complete and comprehensible introduction to Darwin and the core technologies.

Assisting us through the entire process, Chris Campbell has shown himself to be a great proofreader and DocBook markup master. Chris also helped develop some of the tools that we used to write and improve the book.

Thanks to Mark's associates in the Western Pennsylvania Linux User's group: Zach Paine helped us enormously by doing much of the DocBook markup, James O'Kane and Kolt Loughran provided many suggestions on early drafts of the manuscript after a trial run of some chapters at a WPLUG tutorial. Also thanks go to Curtis Galloway for answering many low-level questions.

Eric Peyton did a technical review of the book. He made many useful corrections and suggestions. Any errors that remain in this book are completely our fault.

Sarah Hillegass did our copyediting. Courtney Garvin designed the cover.

Emily Herman is handling all the marketing for this book.

All the layout for this book was done using OpenJade, TeX, and Norm Walsh's DSSSL stylesheets for the DocBook DTD. We appreciate the efforts of all the volunteers who have worked on these projects.

We also wish to thank our wives, Sharlotte DeVere and Michele Hillegass, for their support, patience and understanding.

Chapter 1. Introduction

Unix: Built to Evolve

Complex systems come into existence in only two ways: through careful planning or through evolution. An airport is an example of something that is planned carefully beforehand, built, and then undergoes only minor changes for the rest of its existence. Complex organisms (like humans) are an example of something that has evolved continually from something simple.

In the end, organisms that are well suited to evolution will always win out over organisms that are less suited to evolve. For example, sexual reproduction helps create smooth and continuous evolution. As a result, nearly all complex organisms reproduce sexually.

An operating system evolves. Of course, the programmer who creates a new operating system designs it carefully, but in the end, an operating system that is well suited to evolution will replace an operating system that is not. It is, then, an interesting exercise to think about what traits make an operating system capable of evolution.

The first version of Unix was developed by Ken Thompson at Bell Laboratories in 1969. It was written in assembly language to run on a PDP-7. Dennis Ritchie, also at Bell Labs, invented the C programming language. Among computer languages, C is pretty low level, but it is still much more portable than assembly language. Together, Thompson and Ritchie completely rewrote Unix in C. By 1978, Unix was running on several different architectures. Portability, then, was the first indication that Unix is well suited to evolution.

In 1976, Bell Labs began giving the source code for Unix to research facilities. The Computer Systems Research Group at UC Berkeley got a copy and began tinkering with it. The design of Unix was exceedingly elegant and was deemed a perfect platform upon which to build two important technologies: virtual memory and TCP/IP networking. By freely distributing the source code, Bell Labs was inviting people to extend Unix. Extensibility was the second indication that Unix is well suited to evolution.

It should be noted here that Berkeley's work on Unix was funded by DARPA. Without the warm glow of government grants for basic research, there would be no internet. These grants would be much more difficult to get in todays political climate. In fact, not so long ago, the NSA discontinued all work to improve the security of Linux because of complaints that it was creating unfair competition for Microsoft.

4.4BSD was the last release of Unix produced by Berkeley. It was used as the basis for FreeBSD, OpenBSD, NetBSD, and Mac OS X. Today, Unix is used as an operating system for cellular phones and supercomputers. It is the most popular operating system for web servers, mail servers, and engineering workstations. The manner in which it has found a home in so many niches is yet another indication that Unix is capable of evolution.

Mac OS X is based upon 4.4BSD, but notice that this new niche, a desktop operating system that your grandmother will love, is very different from Unix's previous purposes. To reach this goal, Apple has made several important additions to its Unix core.

The Unix part of Mac OS X is called *Darwin*. The large additions to Darwin that Apple has made are known as the *core technologies*. Apple, recognizing that Unix must continue to evolve, has released the source code to Darwin and most of the core technologies.

This Book

As Unix has evolved into this new niche, existing books have fallen behind. There is no other introduction to Darwin and the core technologies for programmers. This book is based on our experiences teaching a five-day class entitled *Core and Unix Programming for Mac OS X* at the Big Nerd Ranch.

As someone who develops applications and servers for Mac OS X, there are large chunks of Unix that you probably do not care about. For example, do you need to know how to neatly format your text on a VT100 terminal? We will do our best to steer clear of historical curiosities and focus on technologies that you will actually need to understand.

When you finish this book, you will be able to:

- Create applications that leverage the full power of the Unix APIs.
- Use advanced ideas like multithreading and interprocess communications to increase the performance and reliability of your application.
- Add networking capabilities to event-driven applications.
- Make networked applications Rendezvous-aware.
- Use the keychain and authorization capabilities of the security framework.
- Use distributed objects to create client/server applications.
- Understand and use gcc, the linker, the debugger, cvs, and make.
- Use the performance tools to evaluate and improve the responsiveness of your existing applications.

The ideas in this book can be broken into three basic groups:

Unix APIs

> There are a set of standard Unix APIs that every programmer should know how to use. Even if higher-level abstractions alleviate the need to ever call them directly, understanding these functions and structures will give you a much deeper knowledge of how your system works.

Core APIs

> There is a whole set of daemons and frameworks that Apple has added to its version of Unix. These frameworks are exceedingly powerful and Apple has been slow to document how they work and how they are to be used.

Tools

> Many of the most commonly used developer tools for Mac OS X come straight from its Unix roots: gcc, gdb, the linker, cvs, and make. We have done our best

to give clear, simple examples of how these tools can be used to their full potential. We have also documented some tools that Apple provides for performance analysis.

The majority of the code in this book is ANSI C. Some of the chapters use the Cocoa APIs, so you should have a basic understanding of Cocoa and Objective-C. You can get the necessary expertise by reading the first nine chapters of Aaron Hillegass' *Cocoa Programming for Mac OS X*.

Typographical Conventions

To make the book easier to comprehend, we have used several typographical conventions.

Function names will appear in a bold, fixed-width font. All standard Unix functions are completely lowercase. Functions developed by Apple are often mixed case. To make it clear that it is a function, the name will be followed by a set of parentheses. For example, you might see, "Use **NSLog()** or **printf()** to display the computed value."

In Objective-C, class names are always capitalized. In this book, I have also made them appear in a bold, fixed-width font. In Objective-C, method names start with a lowercase letter. Method names will also appear in a fixed-width, bold font. So, for example, you might see, "The class **NSObject** has the method **dealloc**."

Other literals that you would see in code will appear in a regular fixed-width font. Also, filenames will appear in this same font. Thus, you might see "In `SomeCode.c`, set the variable `foo` to `null`."

Occasionally, there will be an excerpt from a terminal window. What you should type will appear in a bold fixed-width font. The computer's response will appear in a regular fixed-width font. Example:

```
% ls /var
at        cron     empty    mail    named     root    tmp      yp
backups   db       log      msgs    netboot   run     spool    vm
```

Online Materials

The code in this book should be downloaded from http://www.borkware.com/corebook/. This website also includes a message board where you can find errata, suggestions, and comments from other readers. We hope that this website will be a valuable addition to the book.

Chapter 2. A C Refresher, Part 1: The Basics

To fully understand the day-to-day details of programming with the Unix APIs, a good knowledge of C is vital. Most of the popular modern languages like Java, Perl, and C++ have a strong C flavor. If you know any of these languages it should be easy to pick up the details of C. Well, except for pointers, which many many programmers have trouble with. Pointers, along with structures and arrays, will be described in detail in the next chapter.

One of the things that trips up new C programmers is expecting the language to do more than it actually does. At its foundation, C just moves bytes around with little higher-level meaning projected upon those bytes, and with no hidden behaviors. For instance, most languages have a `String` type and programmers (rightfully) expect the equality operator to compare the strings and indicate whether they contain the same characters in the same order. C has no string type, and the equality operator just compares the starting address of two strings (which is an identity rather than a value check). For C to support the "expected" kind of string compare the language would have to do an implicit loop over the characters of the string. This hidden, expensive behavior goes against the spirit of C. In general, when faced with possible behaviors in a given situation ("does string compare result in an identity or value comparison"), think of the simplest possible behavior. That is most likely what C does.

The C Compiler Pipeline

Here is a simple program:

Example 2-1. first.c

```
// first.c -- a simple first C program

/* compile with:
cc -g -Wall -o first first.c
*/

#include <stdio.h>       // for printf
#include <math.h>        // for cos

int main (int argc, char *argv[])
{
    printf ("the cosine of 1 is %g\n", cos(1.0));
    printf ("thank you, and have a nice day\n");
    return (0);

} // main
```

Compile it like this:

```
% cc -g -o first first.c -lm
```

And run it:

```
% ./first
the cosine of 1 is 0.540302
thank you, and have a nice day
```

Be aware that the **main()** function is special. That is where your program starts executing once the operating system has finished loading the program into memory.

The compiling and building of a C program is a multi-stage process:

Figure 2-1. The C Pipeline

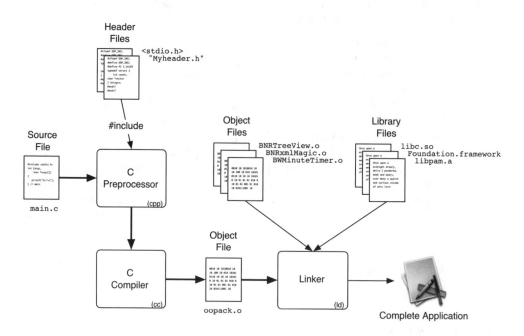

The source file (`first.c` in this case) gets fed into the C preprocessor which does some textual manipulations like file inclusion and macro expansion. The end result gets fed into the C compiler, which translates the program text into binary machine code. If told, it will generate an "object file" containing the machine code (useful if your program is composed of more than one source file). The linker then takes over. The linker takes the object file from the compiler, and includes any other object files or library files (pre-pacakged code supplied by your OS or another vendor) you tell it to so that it can make sure all the features used by the program are available. Once the linking process is done, the completed executable is created and is available for use.

All of that activity is wrapped up in the single cc command. Here is the compilation command:

cc

The program name of the compiler. In this case the GNU C compiler that comes with the developer tools.

-g

Generate debugging symbols (handy if problems develop).

-o first

The name to give to the generated program "first." Otherwise the non-obvious name "a.out" is used.

```
first.c
```

The name of the source file.

```
-lm
```

Link in the math library for the **cos()** function (not strictly needed in Mac OS X, but necessary on most other platforms).

The Preprocessor

The preprocessor is similar to the macro processors of some languages, specifically some of the Lisp languages. C is unique that its preprocessor is a distinct program (which means you can use it for your own uses outside of the C compiler). The preprocessor is a macro processor that performs textual substitutions to the source code before the code goes into the compiler. The preprocessor is pretty dumb, just performing blind substitutions with no idea of the semantics of the C language. Thus it is possible to introduce subtle (and not so subtle) errors through misuse of the preprocessor.

The preprocessor brings three main features to the table: including other files, macro expansion, and conditional compilation.

Including other files

Commands to the preprocessor start with a "#" in the left-most column. (The "#" character is not a comment character like in most scripting languages). For instance, in first.c above, there are these two lines:

```
#include <stdio.h>      // for printf
#include <math.h>       // for cos
```

#include looks for a file and then pastes in the contents of the file. When the file name is surrounded by angled brackets like these, the preprocessor looks in specific directories hard-coded into the compiler such as the directory /usr/include. So, these two lines copy the contents of /usr/include/stdio.h and /usr/include/math.h into our source file. These are just simple text files, so you are welcome to browse around them and see the kind of stuff that is getting included.

The // for printf and // for cos lines are just comments added to show why a particular file has been #included.

If you want to include your own header files, use double quotes instead of angle brackets, like this:

```
#include "myHeader.h"
```

This looks for the include file in the same directory as the source file, and you can add additional paths to the compiler by using the -I command line flag.

Include files (or headers as they are also called) are C's way of importing features that can be used by your program. This is similar to the Java import directive or the Perl use command. C's #include mechanism can be more flexible since the header files can do anything, including defining functions and declaring variables in addition to advertising available features.

It is a good idea to #include all of the headers of the features you need. When you look at a man page for a function, you will see which header file you will need.

For instance:

```
% man 2 open
NAME
      open - open or create a file for reading or writing

SYNOPSIS
      #include <fcntl.h>

      int
      open(const char *path, int flags, mode_t mode);
```

This means you will need to have #include <fcntl.h> before you use the **open()** function.

One common misconception that folks have is that including a header file is all that is necessary to use a feature. Many times that is the case, particularly with functions that live in the standard C library or the Unix API calls. Sometimes you will need to include a specific library (a crypto library or a UI framework) like you did with -lm in the first.c example. The man page for a function often tell you if you need to link in a specific library.

Objective-C adds a #import directive that does the same job as #include, but with one important difference. If you #include the same file twice, it will get evaluated twice. Errors could result if the author of the header file did not account for that. #import will include the file only once, no matter how many #import statements are seen.

Macro expansion

The C preprocessor does simple textual manipulations. You define a sequence of characters to be replaced by another sequence by using #define:

```
#define PI 3.14159
```

will replace the word "PI" with "3.14159" before the file gets shipped off to the compiler. This is handy for making symbolic constants.

Macros can also have arguments, and these arguments get textually substituted. Define macros with arguments like this:

```
#define AVERAGE(x,y)    ((x) + (y) / 2)
```

and you can use it like this:

Table 2-1. Macro Expansion

Code	Expands to
x = AVERAGE (3, 4);	x = (3 + 4) / 2;

Code	Expands to
x = AVERAGE (PI, 23);	x = (PI + 23) /2;
x = (PI + 23) /2;	x = (3.14159 + 23) / 2;

Using all-uppercase for macro names is just a convention. You can make macros using lower case letters, numbers, underscores, etc. Chapter 4 (GCC) chapter will expand on some issues involving macros which can cause problems, and how to fix them.

Some macros in action:

Example 2-2. macros.c

```
// macros.c -- look at C Preprocessor macros

/* compile with:
cc -g -Wall -o macros macros.c
*/

#include <stdio.h>        // for printf

// make some symbolic constants
#define PI              3.14159
#define Version         "beta5"

// make some macros
#define SQUARE(x)               ((x) * (x))
#define AreaOfACircle(r)        (PI * SQUARE(r))

int main (int argc, char *argv[])
{
    printf ("Welcome to version %s of macros\n", Version);
    printf ("The area of a circle with radius 5 is %f\n",
            AreaOfACircle(5));
    return (0);

} // main
```

Note that you can give **printf()** (short for "print formatted") some format indicators that tell it to look for values after the first string in the list of arguments you pass it, like "%f" for a floating point value. Many languages and libraries have adopted **printf**'s format specifiers, so they are not going to be explained here.

Conditional compilation

C is a language that is supported on a huge variety of different computing platforms, from the Apple II up through Crays and iMacs. When writing portable code you are frequently having to write code that is peculiar to a specific platform but you do not want that code to be included on the other platforms.

The preprocessor can conditionally remove chunks of text from your program using the #ifdef, #else, and #endif commands.

For instance:

```
#ifdef SYMBOL_NAME
// first chunk of text
#else
// second chunk of text
#endif
```

If the symbol SYMBOL_NAME has been #defined previously, let the first chunk of text through and delete the second chunk of text. If SYMBOL_NAME has not been #defined, the second chunk remains and the first chunk gets dropped.

If you have a symbol with a numeric value, you can use #if instead of #ifdef. If the symbol (or constant) given to #if is not zero, the first chunk of text survives. If that symbol is zero, the second chunk is what makes it through.

Example 2-3. conditional.c

```
// conditional.c -- look at conditional compilation

/* compile with:
cc -g -Wall -o conditional conditional.c
*/

#include <stdio.h>        // for printf

int main (int argc, char *argv[])
{
#define THING1

#ifdef THING1
    printf ("thing1 defined\n");
#else
    printf ("thing1 is not defined\n");
#endif

#ifdef THING2
    printf ("thing2 is defined\n");
#else
    printf ("thing2 is not defined\n");
#endif

    return (0);

} // main
```

A sample run:

```
% ./conditional
thing1 defined
thing2 is not defined
```

One handy use of #if with constant values (rather than the name of a symbol) is to do a block "comment out" of a big chunk of stuff.

Example 2-4. leaveout.c

```
// leaveout.c -- use the preprocessor to comment out a chunk of code

/* compile with:
cc -g -Wall -o leaveout leaveout.c
*/

#include <stdio.h>        // for printf

int main (int argc, char *argv[])
{
#if 0
    printf ("oh happy day\n");
    printf ("bork bork bork\n");
    we_can even have syntax errors in here
    since the compiler will never see this part
#endif

#if 1
    printf ("this is included.  wheee.\n");
#endif

    printf ("that is all folks\n");

    return (0);

} // main
```

A sample run:

```
% ./leaveout
this is included.  wheee.
that is all folks
```

Constants

Constant values are specified like this in most programming languages:

integer constant:	`1234`
floating point constant:	`3.14159`
single character constant:	`'c'`
string constant:	`"I seem to be a verb"`

With characters there are some variations that indicate to the compiler a special character should be used. The backslash escapes the next character so that it does not get interpreted. For example, this string constant has an embedded double quote:

```
"hello double quote \" you are so cute"
```

Without the escaping you would get a syntax error since the double quote would terminate the string constant, and "you are so cute" would be interpreted as more C code. Escaping also gives special meaning to some characters inside character constants and string constants:

\n

> Newline

\r

> Return character

\t

> Tab

\\

> Backslash

Specific byte values can be given in octal (base-8) by using \###:

\007

> Beep character

\075

> Equals sign

The ascii man page has a list of characters and their numerical value.

Integer constants can be expressed in decimal (base-10), octal (base-8), and hexadecimal (base-16). Octal constants have a leading zero, and hex constants have a leading 0x:

```
octal constant:   0217
hex constant:     0xF33DF4C3
```

Example 2-5. constants.c

```c
// constants.c -- show various constants

/* compile with:
cc -g -o constants constants.c
*/

#include <stdio.h>        // for printf

int main (int argc, char *argv[])
{
    printf ("some integer constants: %d %d %d %d\n",
            1, 3, 32767, -521);
    printf ("some floating-point constants: %f %f %f %f\n",
            3.14159, 1.414213, 1.5, 2.0);
    printf ("single character constants: %c%c%c%c%c\n",
            'W', 'P', '\114', '\125', '\107');
    printf ("and finally a character string constant: '%s'\n",
            "this is a string");

    return (0);

} // main
```

A sample run:

```
% ./constants
some integer constants: 1 3 32767 -521
some floating-point constants: 3.141590 1.414213 1.500000 2.000000
single character constants: WPLUG
and finally a character string constant: 'this is a string'
```

Data Types

C has two fundamental data types: integer and floating point. Everything else is an interpretation of one of these types (such as characters being short integers) or an aggregation of these types (arrays of characters are strings, a group of three pointers can be a tree node).

These are the specific data types available:

Table 2-2. C Data Types

Name	"Usual" Storage Size	"Minimum" Storage Size
char	1 byte	1 byte
short	2 bytes	2 bytes
int	4 bytes	2 bytes
long	4 bytes	4 bytes
long long	8 bytes	8 bytes

So, a `long` being a 4 byte (32 bit) number, can have values between -2,147,483,648 and +2,147,483,467. Which is 31 bits of numerical data and 1 bit to indicate whether the number is positive or negative (called the sign bit).

The header file `<sys/limits.h>` includes `#defined` constants for examining the maximum and minimum values for the basic data types. The constants have names like `INT_MIN`, `INT_MAX`, `SHRT_MIN`, `SHRT_MAX`.

The integer types can also be declared unsigned, meaning that the sign bit is considered to be actual data. An `unsigned long` therefore can have values between 0 and 4,294,967,295. If you want a "byte" data type, use an `unsigned char`.

There are two floating point data types: `float` and `double`, which differ by how many significant bits of storage they have.

You can run this to see what limits your platform has:

Example 2-6. limits.c

```
// limits.c -- show some info about various built-in data types

/* compile with:
cc -g -Wall -o limits limits.c
*/

#include <limits.h>        // for limit constants
#include <stdio.h>         // for printf
#include <stdlib.h>        // for EXIT_SUCCESS
```

```
int main (int argc, char *argv[])
{
    printf ("      type:  bytes %14s %14s %14s\n",
            "min value", "max value", "max unsigned");

    printf ("      char:  %5ld %14d %14d %14u\n", sizeof(char),
            CHAR_MIN, CHAR_MAX, UCHAR_MAX);

    printf ("     short:  %5ld %14d %14d %14u\n", sizeof(short),
            SHRT_MIN, SHRT_MAX, USHRT_MAX);

    printf ("       int:  %5ld %14d %14d %14u\n", sizeof(int),
            INT_MIN, INT_MAX, UINT_MAX);

    printf ("      long:  %5ld %14ld %14ld %14lu\n", sizeof(long),
            LONG_MIN, LONG_MAX, ULONG_MAX);

// not available on all platforms
#ifdef LLONG_MIN
    printf (" long long:  %5ld %20lld %20lld \n"
            "                              %20llu\n", sizeof(long long),
            LLONG_MIN, LLONG_MAX, (long long)ULLONG_MAX);
#endif
    printf ("     float:  %5ld\n", sizeof(float));
    printf ("    double:  %5ld\n", sizeof(double));

    return (EXIT_SUCCESS);

} // main
```

This is what it prints on my machine:

```
% ./limits
      type:  bytes        min value        max value      max unsigned
      char:     1             -128              127               255
     short:     2           -32768            32767             65535
       int:     4      -2147483648       2147483647        4294967295
      long:     4      -2147483648       2147483647        4294967295
 long long:     8 -9223372036854775808  9223372036854775807
                   18446744073709551615
     float:     4
    double:     8
```

The `sizeof` operator evaluates to the number of bytes of the indicated type. Later on when structures are picked up, `sizeof` can be used to figure out how many bytes a structure takes. Note that `sizeof` is a compile time operator, not a run time function.

Predefined Types

Since the standard C types cannot be depended on to have a specific storage size, the standard C library and the Unix API define some more abstract integral types that should be used, like

```
size_t
```

> An unsigned integral value for indicating sizes (in bytes) of data types. Also used as the type of argument for **malloc()**, which dynamically allocates memory. (**malloc()** and memory issues are discussed in Chapter 7 (Memory).)

```
pid_t
```

> An unsigned integral value for representing the process IDs in a Unix system.

```
uid_t
```

> An unsigned integral value for representing the user ID in a Unix. system

There are many more types. The man pages for functions indicate which of these types they use.

Enumerations

Related to the integer types are enums. enums are a way of creating symbolic constants (the other way is using the preprocessor). Unlike C++, enums are just a little syntactic sugar around integer constants. There is no error checking involved, i.e. there is no support to make sure that a function that accepts an enum type will get a predefined enum value.

The syntax for defining an enum is:

```
enum {
    Hearts,
    Moons,
    Stars,
    Clovers
};
```

The first symbol gets a value of zero, and subsequent symbols increment the previous value by one. So the above snippet would have values of:

```
enum {
    Hearts,     // 0
    Moons,      // 1
    Stars,      // 2
    Clovers     // 3
};
```

You can also assign values:

```
enum {
    Doc,                // 0
    Bashful,            // 1
    Dopey = 23,         // 23
    Cranky,             // 24
    Funky,              // 25
```

```
    Shifty = 23,         // 23
    Hungry = 42,         // 42

    Mask1 = 0xFFFF0000,
    Mask2 = 0x00000040
};
```

One nice side effect of using enums (as opposed to just #defining everything) is that sometimes the debugger can map integer values back to the enum name and show you data symbolically.

Variables

Variables are where you store values that can change over the lifetime of your program. C requires you to declare all variables before you use them (unlike Perl or Python), and you have to declare all the variables before any executable lines of code (unlike Java and C++). Newer versions of C and Objective-C restrict this last restriction.

The declaration syntax is:

```
data-type variable-name [ = optional-initializer];
```

Where data-type is one of the predefined data types seen above, or a composite data type defined by you or by the system. Variables can be local to functions or global to the whole file (or even the whole program) depending on where they are defined.

A variable declared inside of a function is local to that function and cannot been seen outside of the function. The storage for the variable goes away when the function exits, and if the function is re-entered, that variable will have a random, uninitialized value.

A variable declared outside of any functions is global.

C also introduces the idea of a "static variable" (one of the many uses of the term static in C). A static variable is a variable that is local to a function, but the value persists from call to call. It is a global variable with local scope.

Example 2-7. variables.c

```
// variables.c -- some simple variable declarations

/* compile with:
cc -g -Wall -o variables variables.c
*/

#include <stdio.h>        // for printf()

int aGlobalInt;           // global
float pi = 3.14159;       // global

void someFunction ()
{
    int aLocalVariable = 0;      // local, random value but
                                 //      initialized to zero
```

```
    static unsigned char aByte; // static, initialized to zero, persists

    myShort = 500 + aLocalVariable;
    aGlobalInt = 5;

    aByte++;

    printf ("aByte: %d, myShort: %d  aGlobalInt: %d\n",
            aByte, myShort, aGlobalInt);

} // someFunction

int main (int argc, char *argv[])
{
    printf ("aGlobalInt before someFunction: %d\n", aGlobalInt);
    someFunction ();

    printf( "aGlobalInt after someFunction: %d\n", aGlobalInt);
    someFunction ();

    aGlobalInt = 23;
    someFunction ();

    return (0);

} // main
```

And the program in action:

```
% ./variables
aGlobalInt before someFunction: 0
aByte: 1, myShort: 500  aGlobalInt: 5
aGlobalInt after someFunction: 5
aByte: 2, myShort: 500  aGlobalInt: 5
aByte: 3, myShort: 500  aGlobalInt: 5
```

You should always initialize variables declared in functions before you use them. Otherwise, they will have undefined (random) values, which if used can cause your program to behave in a random fashion. Note that global variables and static variables are initialized to zero for you.

LValues

You will sometimes hear folks (or compiler messages) refer to the term `lvalue`. That just means something can appear on the left side of an assignment operator. For example:

```
int myVar;
myVar = 5;
```

`myVar` is an `lvalue`, and this is legal code.

But

```
7 = 23;
```

or

```
(i == 3) = 23;
```

is not.

Operators

The C operators, like + - * /, have been adopted by most modern languages and should be familiar. The increment and decrement operators may be new to some:

`x++`

>   Use the value of x, then add 1 to x

`++x`

>   Add 1 to x, then use the value

`x--`

>   Use the value of x, then subtract 1 from x

`--x`

>   Subtract 1 from x, then use the value

Plus there are shorthand assignment operators. `x += y` is the same as `x = x + y`
This idea also generalizes to +, -, *, /, and other operators (like the bitwise operators).

Bitwise Operators

Most languages have adopted C's bitwise operators. Those languages tend not to need to do as much bit banging as C, so the bitwise operators are mentioned in passing and are relegated to the reference chapter nobody reads.

The bitwise operators let you do bitwise AND, OR, XOR, and complement to integral values. You can also shift the bits left or right within an integer value.

The examples below use these two numbers:

Figure 2-2. Binary

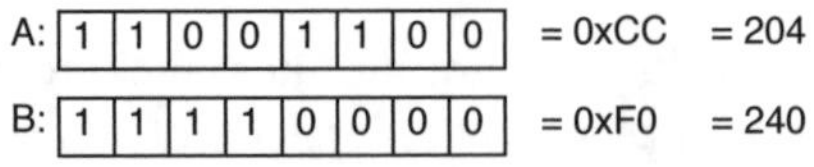

A:	1	1	0	0	1	1	0	0	= 0xCC	= 204
B:	1	1	1	1	0	0	0	0	= 0xF0	= 240

`A & B` has a result that has bits set only if bits are set in both A and B.

Figure 2-3. AND (&)

A:	1	1	0	0	1	1	0	0	= 0xCC	= 204
B:	1	1	1	1	0	0	0	0	= 0xF0	= 240
Result:	1	1	0	0	0	0	0	0	= 0xC0	= 192

A | B has a result that has bits set if bits are set in either A or B.

Figure 2-4. OR (|)

A:	1	1	0	0	1	1	0	0	= 0xCC	= 204
B:	1	1	1	1	0	0	0	0	= 0xF0	= 240
Result:	1	1	1	1	1	1	0	0	= 0xFC	= 252

A ^ B has a result that has bits set if bits are set in either A or B, but not in both. The "or" in this case is like when the wait staff asks, "Would you like soup or salad with that?"

Figure 2-5. XOR (^)

A:	1	1	0	0	1	1	0	0	= 0xCC	= 204
B:	1	1	1	1	0	0	0	0	= 0xF0	= 240
Result:	0	0	1	1	1	1	0	0	= 0x3C	= 60

A ~ flips the bits from zero to 1 and 1 to zero.

Figure 2-6. NOT (~)

A:	1	1	0	0	1	1	0	0	= 0xCC	= 204
Result:	0	0	1	1	0	0	1	1	= 0x33	= 51

A << *n* shifts the bits of A *n* places to the left, filling in zeros in the low-numbered bits.

Figure 2-7. A << 2

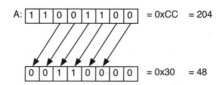

Note that the two high-order 1 bits got shifted out and dropped and zero got shifted in. Note that due to how binary math works, shifting to the left is the same as multiplying by two. Modern processors can shift much faster than they can multiply, which can make for a handy optimization.

A >> *n* shifts the bits of A *n* places to the right.

There is one complication with shift-right. The high-order bit of a piece of signed integer data is the sign bit indicating whether the value is negative or positive. When you shift right, do you preserve the sign bit, or fill it in with zeros? The rule C uses is: if the number is signed and negative, the sign bit fills in with 1:

Figure 2-8. A >> x

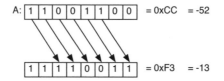

Otherwise, for unsigned integers or positive numbers, the sign bit fills in with zero.

Figure 2-9. Bitwise Shift Right

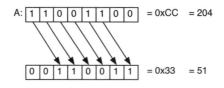

BitMasks

The AND, OR, and NOT operators are handy when dealing with bitmasks. Bitmasking is a technique where information can be compactly stored in small integers by attaching meaning to specific bit positions.

Using bitmasks:

1. Define a constant that matches the bit you wish to deal with.

```
#define MY_BIT_VALUE 8   // 00001000
```

Or use bit shifting.

```
#define MY_BIT_VALUE (1 << 3) // 00001000
```

2. Set the bit with bitwise OR.

```
myFlags |= MY_BIT_VALUE
```

Figure 2-10. Set Flag

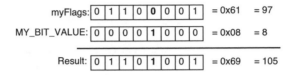

```
      myFlags: 0 1 1 0 0 0 0 1    = 0x61    = 97
 MY_BIT_VALUE: 0 0 0 0 1 0 0 0    = 0x08    = 8

       Result: 0 1 1 0 1 0 0 1    = 0x69    = 105
```

3. Test the bit with bitwise AND.

```
if (myFlags & MY_BIT_VALUE) {
    // do something appropriate
}
```

Figure 2-11. Test Flag

```
      myFlags: 0 1 1 0 1 0 0 1    = 0x61    = 97
 MY_BIT_VALUE: 0 0 0 0 1 0 0 0    = 0x08    = 8

       Result: 0 0 0 0 1 0 0 0    = 0x08    = 8
```

4. Clear the bit with a complement and an AND.

```
myFlags &= ~MY_BIT_VALUE;
```

This is a bit trickier. What is needed is a new mask that will let through all the original values of the bits of the variable you are masking, but leave the masked-out bit behind.

Figure 2-12. Clear Flag

```
       myFlags: 0 1 1 0 1 0 0 1    = 0x69    = 105
 ~MY_BIT_VALUE: 1 1 1 1 0 1 1 1    = 0xF7    = 247

        Result: 0 1 1 0 0 0 0 1    = 0x61    = 97
```

When using a mask with multiple bits set, it is safer to compare against the mask rather than doing a simple logical test:

```
#define MULTI_BITS      0xF0     // 11110000
```

and assuming that `myFlags` is 0x61 (01100001), the statement

```
if (myFlags & MULTI_BITS) {
    // do something if all bits are set
}
```

is bad code. The result of the bitwise-AND is:

Figure 2-13. Result of bitwise-AND

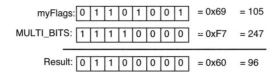

The result is 0x60, which will be treated by the `if` as a true value (everything except zero is considered a true value), even if only a couple of the bits in `MULTI_BITS` is set. It is more correct to do

```
if ((myFlags & MULTI_BITS) == MULTIBITS) {
    // do something if all bits are set
}
```

Example 2-8. bitmask.c

```
// bitmask.c -- play with bitmasks

/* compile with:
cc -g -Wall -o bitmask bitmask.c
*/

#include <stdio.h>        // for printf

#define THING_1_MASK    1         // 00000001
#define THING_2_MASK    2         // 00000010
#define THING_3_MASK    4         // 00000100
#define ALL_THINGS      (THING_1_MASK | THING_2_MASK | THING_3_MASK)
                                  // 00000111

#define ANOTHER_MASK    (1 << 5)  // 00100000
#define ANOTHER_MASK_2  (1 << 6)  // 01000000

#define ALL_ANOTHERS    (ANOTHER_MASK | ANOTHER_MASK_2)    // 01100000
#define ALL_USEFUL_BITS (ALL_THINGS | ALL_ANOTHERS)        // 01100111

void showMaskValue (int value)
{
    printf ("\n"); // space out the output
    printf ("value %x:\n", value);

    if (value & THING_1_MASK) printf ("  THING_1\n");
    if (value & THING_2_MASK) printf ("  THING_2\n");
    if (value & THING_3_MASK) printf ("  THING_3\n");
```

```
        if (value & ANOTHER_MASK) printf ("  ANOTHER_MASK\n");
        if (value & ANOTHER_MASK_2)
                                printf ("  ANOTHER_MASK\n");

        if ((value & ALL_ANOTHERS) == ALL_ANOTHERS)
                                printf ("  ALL ANOTHERS\n");
} // showMaskValue

int setBits (int value, int maskValue)
{
    // set a bit by just OR-ing in a value
    value |= maskValue;
    return (value);

} // setBits

int clearBits (int value, int maskValue)
{
    // to clear a bit, we and it with the complement of the mask.

    value &= ~maskValue;
    return (value);

} // clearBits

int main (int argc, char *argv[])
{
    int intval = 0;

    intval = setBits (intval, THING_1_MASK);    // 00000001 = 0x01
    intval = setBits (intval, THING_3_MASK);    // 00000101 = 0x05
    showMaskValue (intval);

    intval = setBits (intval, ALL_ANOTHERS);    // 01100101 = 0x65
    intval = clearBits (intval, THING_2_MASK);  // 01100101 = 0x65
    intval = clearBits (intval, THING_3_MASK);  // 01100001 = 0x61
    showMaskValue (intval);

    return (0);

} // main
```

A sample run:

```
    % ./bitmask

  value 5:
    THING_1
    THING_3

  value 61:
    THING_1
    ANOTHER_MASK
    ANOTHER_MASK
    ALL ANOTHERS
```

Functions

Functions are C's way of breaking up code into smaller pieces. A function is composed of a declaration of a return type, the name of the function, and any parameters it takes. Following this declaration is a block of code surrounded by braces. Inside of the braces can be variable declarations and executable code. For example:

```
int myFunction (int a, float b, unsigned char c)
{
    int myLocalVar;

    printf ("the character is %c", c);
    myLocalVar = a + floor(b);

    return (myLocalVar * 2);  // ok, so this does nothing useful

} // myFunction
```

The return statement causes the function to exit immediately, and use what is given to it as the return value of the function. Note that the parentheses around the return value are optional, and their use is a personal preference.

You can declare your function for others to use writing just the first declaration line:

```
int myFunction (int a, float b, unsigned char c);
```

This function prototype tells the compiler "if you see someone using **myFunction** it had better take three arguments, an int, a float, and an unsigned char. If someone is using the return value, it should be assigned to an int." With that information the compiler can help error-check your code. Due to C's history, any functions that are used without including the prototype are assumed to return an int and take an arbitrary number of int-sized arguments. Header files are handy places to put these function prototypes.

Even though C has procedures (functions that return no values), they are still called functions. A C function that does not return anything is declared to return void. A function that does not take any parameters has void listed in its argument list:

```
void functionReturnsNothing (void);
```

Note that all parameters to functions are pass by value, that is, the functions get copies of the arguments. You can change the value of your function arguments all you want and the caller will never notice. To achieve pass by reference (where changes to the variable are visible to the caller) you must use pointers, described in the next chapter.

Lastly, functions can be recursive, that is, they can call themselves. The canonical example of a recursive function is calculating factorials. That is, X! is equal to 1 * 2 * 3 ... * X-1 * X

Example 2-9. factorial.c

```
// factorial.c -- calculate factorials recursively

/* compile with:
```

```
cc -g -Wall -o factorial factorial.c
*/

#include <stdio.h>        // for printf

long long factorial (long long value)
{
    if (value == 1) {
        return (1);
    } else {
        return (value * factorial (value - 1));
    }
} // factorial

int main (int argc, char *argv[])
{
    printf ("factorial of 16 is %lld\n", factorial(16));
    return (0);
} // main
```

A sample run:

```
% ./factorial
factorial of 16 is 20922789888000
```

(factorials add up quickly)

Logical Expressions

In C, any expression (even assignment) can be used as a truth value. An expression evaluating to zero is considered a false value. Everything else is considered true. For instance, this is a valid loop:

```
while (result = read(...)) {
    // do stuff with result
    ...
}
```

`read()` reads a number of bytes from an open file. Upon a successful read it returns the number of bytes read. When the end of file is reached, it returns zero. When this loop is executed, the assignment inside of the parentheses is evaluated first.

When end of file is reached `read()` returns zero, result takes the value of zero, and the value of the expression is zero (false), so the loop terminates.

To compare value, use ==. A common, common error is to use a single = (assignment) when you mean to use the == operator. The result of an == expression is a truth value. For instance:

- 5 == 10 results in zero. 5 == 5 results in a non-zero value (you cannot depend on the actual value, just that it is non-zero).

- != is the "not equal" operator.

- 5 != 10 results in a non-zero value, and 5 != 5 results in zero.

You can also use <, >, <=, and >= for inequality tests.

Logical Operators

Expressions can be chained together with the logical operators, && (AND) || (OR), ! (NOT). Unlike their single-character siblings, logical AND and OR deal with the total truth value rather than individual bits. That is:

```
if (a && b) {
    doSomething ();
}
```

doSomething() is only invoked if both a and b are non-zero. Likewise,

```
if (a || b) {
    doSomething ();
}
```

doSomething() is only invoked if either a or b are non-zero.

The "not" operator (!), of course, flips the truth meaning of the expression.

```
if (!var) {
    doSomething ();
}
```

doSomething() is invoked only if var is zero.

Note that && and || short circuit if the value of the total expression can be determined after the evaluation of the first part.

```
if ( (x != 0) && (y = z / x) ) ...
```

is a handy way to check for zero before doing a divide. If x is 0, the first expression will evaluate to false. For a logical AND to be true both sides of the AND need to be true. Since the first part is false, it does not matter what the second part is since there is no way the entire expression can be true, so the second expression is not evaluated.

Likewise, with ||, if the first part is true, the whole expression is true and there is no need to evaluate the second part.

Control Structures

The C control statements have found their way into many of the languages in common use. This will be a very quick overview of what they do.

Where you see expression below you can use any logical expression. Braces are put around the part where you put in code that gets executed. If you have only one line of code, you can omit the braces. Keeping everything fully braced makes adding code to the blocks easier, and it eliminates some classes of errors. (It is also a good idea in any case.)

if

```
if (expression) {
    // true-branch
} else {
    // false-branch
```

```
}
```

Evaluate the expression and execute one of the branches. The `else` part is optional. When you have nested `if` statements, the `else` matches to the closest `if`:

```
if (expression1) {
    if (expression2) {
        // true-true branch
    } else {
        // true-false branch
    }
}
```

This situation can look ambiguous without braces:

```
if (expression1)
    if (expression2)
        // true-true-branch
else
    // something else
```

This is erroneous indentation, but the behavior will be like that of the braced statements.

Related to the `if` statement is the conditional expression (also known as the ternary, trinary, or question-mark operator).

This

```
    x = (expression) ? a : b;
```

is the same as

```
if (expression) {
    x = a;
} else {
    x = b;
}
```

but does it all in one expression.

while

```
while (expression) {
    // executes while expression is true
}
```

`while` executes its code zero or more times, so long as the expression evaluates to a true value. The expression is evaluated every time through the loop, before the body is executed.

for

```
for (initializer; expression; increment) {
    // body
}
```

This is mostly the same as this:

```
initializer;

while (expression) {
    // body
    increment;
}
```

Here is a real `for` loop:

```
for (i = 0; i < 10; i++) {
    printf ("%d\n", i);
}
```

This prints the numbers from zero to 9.

`for` is mostly the same as the `while` loop shown above, except in the face of the `continue` statement. `continue` can be used in any loop to immediately jump to the beginning of the loop, bypassing any subsequent instructions. With the `for` loop, the increment part is performed on a `continue`, while with the `while` loop given above, the increment would not happen.

The `break` statement breaks out of the loop entirely, bypassing the increment stage. `break` can be used to break out of any loop. When nested loops are involved, `break` only breaks out of the innermost one. To break out of multiple loops you need to use a `goto`.

do-while

```
do {
    // body
} while (expression);
```

The body of the loop is executed one or more times. If expression evaluates to zero, the loop terminates.

switch

`switch` is C's case statement. Given an integral value, choose a block of code to execute.

For instance:

```
myChar = getchar();
switch (myChar) {
    case 'a':  printf ("got an a\n");  break;
    case 'e':  printf ("got an e\n");  break;
    case '9':  printf ("got a 9\n");
    case '8':  printf ("got an 8\n");
```

```
    case '7':  printf ("got a 7\n"); break;
    default:   printf ("got something else");
}
```

There are some properties of C's `switch` statement that trip up programmers used to other languages. The first is that the value given to `switch` is an integer value. It cannot be a float or a character string. A single character is OK since a `char` is really an `int` type. The second is that the case labels must also be integer, constant values. You cannot use variables or strings there. In other words, this is very illegal:

```
int x = 5;
switch (someVar) {
    case "hello":  // can't use a string
    case x: // can't use a variable
    case 'x': // this is ok.  it's a constant
}
```

Another bit of odd behavior is that when a case label starts executing, code flow will go straight down until it hits a `break`. In the example above, if `myChar` is 9, the program will print out

```
    got a 9
    got an 8
    got a 7
```

Because execution will start at the `case '9'` label, drop down into the `'8'` label and the `'7'` label before hitting a `break`.

goto

`goto` is an unconditional branch to a label anywhere in the same function the `goto` is used. You can even `goto` the middle of a `for` or a `switch` if you wish.

For instance:

```
for (i = 0; i < 10; i++) {
    for (j = 0; j < 10; j++) {
        if ((i == 5) && (j == 9)) {
            goto bailout;
        }
    }
}

bailout:
printf ("done!\n");
```

For the More Curious: Multiple Source Files

Once a program gets beyond a trivial stage it will require using multiple source files. In C, each file is treated as an independent unit.

Within each file there can be variables global to just that file as well as functions that are only visible in that file. When you precede the variable or function declaration with `static` visibility of the variable or function becomes restricted to only that source file. If you do not declare functions or global variables static, they will be visible to other files.

"Visibility" means visibility to the linker so that the linker can patch up references between files.

Here is an example program composed of 4 files: two source files and two header files.

Example 2-10. file-1.h

```
extern int g_globalVar;
```

Example 2-11. file-1.c

```
// file-1.c -- half of a program split across two files

/* compile with:
cc -g -Wall -c file-1.c
*/

/* link with
cc -o multifile file-1.o file-2.o
*/

// see the stuff file-2 is exporting
#include "file-1.h"
#include "file-2.h"
#include <stdio.h>        // for printf

static int localVar;

int g_globalVar;

static void localFunction ()
{
    printf ("this is file 1's local function. ");
    printf ("No arguments passed.  localVar is %d\n", localVar);

} // localFunction

int main (int argc, char *argv[])
{
    float pi;

    localFunction ();
    pi = file2pi ();

    localVar = 23;
    g_globalVar = 23;

    printf ("g_globalVar before is %d\n", g_globalVar);
    printf ("localVar before is %d\n", localVar);

    file2Function ();

    printf ("g_globalVar was changed to %d\n", g_globalVar);
    printf ("localVar after is still %d\n", localVar);
    return (0);
```

```
} // main
```

Example 2-12. file-2.h

```
// returs the value of Pi
float file2pi (void);

// changes the value of g_globalVar
void file2Function (void);
```

Example 2-13. file-2.c

```
// file-2.c -- second half of a program split across two files

/* compile with:
cc -g -Wall -c file-2.c
*/

#include "file-1.h"
#include "file-2.h"

static double localVar;

static float localFunction (char dummy)
{
    return (3.14159);
} // localFunction

float file2pi (void)
{
    return (localFunction('x'));
} // file2pi

// changes the value of g_globalVar
void file2Function (void)
{
    g_globalVar = 42;
    localVar = 1.2345;
} // file2Function
```

This one is a little more complicated to compile and link:

```
% cc -g -Wall -c file-1.c
% cc -g -Wall -c file-2.c
% cc -o multifile file-1.o file-2.o
```

When you have multiple files like this, you would usually use makefiles or an IDE like `Project Builder` to put things together.

A sample run:

```
% ./multifile
this is file 1's local function. No arguments passed.  localVar is 0
g_globalVar before is 23
localVar before is 23
g_globalVar was changed to 42
```

```
localVar after is still 23
```

Some things of interest to note:

- The use of `extern` in `file-1.h`. That declaration is what will be in `file-2.c`; that is, `file-2.c` knows about the existence of a global variable called `g_globalVar`, but the compiler does not actually allocate any storage for it since the variable was declared `extern`. When the compiler compiles `file-1.c`, it does not have `g_globalVar` declared as `extern`, and so the compiler will allocate some space for it.

- Static variables and functions are truly private to the file. Both of the source files have their own `localVar` and `localFunction` with radically different definitions.

- The header file is the means of communication between the two files. The headers contain the "published API," or set of features that the particular file brings to the table. Implementation details are left to the innards of the file.

This shows who can see and call what:

Figure 2-14. Two-File Scope

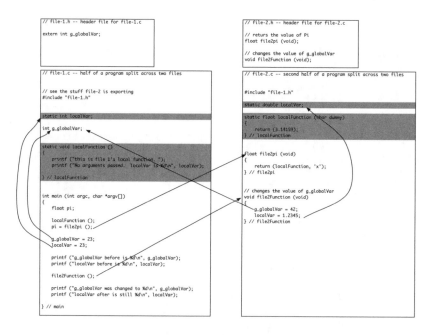

For the More Curious: Common Compiler Errors

The C compiler can be pretty dumb when it encounters errors. Usually a simple mistake will cascade into a huge flurry of syntax errors. In general, when you get a huge pile of errors, fix the first couple and then try compiling again, especially if the errors start looking weird.

For example, consider the program `variables.c`. If you remove a single semicolon (after the constant 3.14159) you will get these errors:

```
% cc -g -o variables variables.c
variables.c:13: illegal external declaration, missing ';' after '3.14159'
cpp-precomp: warning:errors during smart preprocessing, \
retrying in basic mode
variables.c:16: parse error before "void"
variables.c:22: conflicting types for 'myShort'
variables.c:19: previous declaration of 'myShort'
variables.c:22: warning: data definition has no type or storage class
variables.c:23: warning: data definition has no type or storage class
variables.c:25: parse error before '++' token
variables.c:27: parse error before string constant
variables.c:28: warning: conflicting types for built-in function 'printf'
variables.c:28: warning: data definition has no type or storage class
```

For the first error, it is pretty obvious what went wrong (which makes it easy to fix). The subsequent errors and warnings are bogus. Add in that one semicolon back and life will be happy.

Here are some errors you will probably see, and what they (probably) mean. (Do not worry if some of them are gibberish now. Many of the concepts will be explained in the next chapter.)

```
warning: ANSI C forbids newline in string constant
```

Missing double quote from the end of a literal string.

```
structure has no member named 'indData' union has no member named
'shoeSize' 'aGlobalint' undeclared (first use in this function)
```

Using a variable or structure member that has not been declared. Double check the case and spelling (both are significant).

```
warning: control reaches end of non-void function
```

A function is declared as returning a value, but there is no `return` statement.

```
unterminated #if conditional
```

You have an `#if` or `#ifdef` statement, but not the closing `#endif`. Check to make sure you have end `#endif`s when nesting them.

```
illegal function call, found 'blah'
```

Check to see if there is a missing "?" using the `?:` operator. For example, this code: `(*ptrvar) "blah" : "ook";` will generate this error.

```
illegal member declaration, missing name, found '}'
```

This happens if you forget the semicolon at the end of a union declaration.

```
typedef struct Individual {
    int type;
    union {
        Person person;
        Alien  alien;
    } indData
```

```
} Individual;
```

will cause this error.

```
'Alien' redeclared as different kind of symbol
```

Make sure you do not use the same name for different purposes, like having `typedef struct Alien;` **followed by** `enum { Human, Alien }`.

```
undefined type, found 'individual'
```

The type of a parameter in a function declaration does not exist. For instance, this error was caused by

```
void fillAlien (individual *individual)
```

The proper type name is `Individual` (upper case I).

```
warning: comparison between pointer and integer
```

Make sure the types on either side of the `==` or `!=` sign make sense.

Challenge

The Fibonacci number sequence is a sequence that looks like this: 1, 1, 2, 3, 5, 8, 13, 21, 34, 55, ... That is, it starts with 1, 1, then subsequent numbers are the sum of the previous two.

There are two ways of calculating the nth fibonacci number, either iteratively (run a loop and calculate the numbers), or recursively (finding the nth Fibonacci number by calculating the *n-1* and *n-2* Fibonacci number.) For Fibonacci numbers F(1) and F(2), return a value of 1.

Implement both methods of calculating the Fibonacci numbers and compare their performance characteristics.

Chapter 3. A C Refresher, Part 2: Pointers, Structures, and Arrays

The single C feature that seems to cause most programmers a lot of problems are pointers. Pointers are the use of memory addresses to indicate what data to operate on, providing a layer of indirection that becomes handy for solving a lot of problems. Unfortunately the syntax is a bit odd, and it is easy to get confused amongst all the &s and *s flying around.

C structures, the aggregation of individual basic data types, are used to package smaller bits of data into a cohesive whole, so you can abstract data to a higher level. It is easier to tell a function, "Here is a network address," rather than telling it individually, "Here is a machine IP address, here is a port, here is the network protocol to use." Structures and pointers work closely together, allowing structures to reference other structures to build webs of related variables.

Finally, arrays are linear collections of same-type chunks of data. Arrays and pointers are very closely related, and ultimately understanding both arrays and pointers are necessary to fully grasp how C deals with addresses and data.

Pointers

So, what is a pointer? It is nothing more than the address of a byte in memory. What can you do with a pointer? You can read bytes starting from the address and you can write bytes starting at the address. You can also calculate new addresses based on the original one.

Imagine that you like the book *Zen and the Art of Motorcycle Maintenance*. You come across a particular passage that you think your friend would find interesting. You can either mail the book over (which can be expensive), or you can send a postcard that says, "Zen, page 387, starting at the first letter." When he gets the postcard, he knows where to look to find the interesting passage.

A C pointer is like this postcard. It is a small amount of storage (there is only so much you can write on a postcard) that references something larger. It is also a lot cheaper to send around.

Pointer syntax

Pointer syntax involves two special characters, the star (*) and the ampersand (&). The star pulls a double duty; in some cases it is a description, and some cases it is an action. This duality is one of the major causes of confusion.

Here are the fundamental pieces of pointer syntax:

1. Pointer declaration

```
char *ptrvar;
```

ptrvar is the postcard. On the Mac this variable is 4 bytes long and can point to any address the program can access. The star in this case is for declaration. Reading the declaration backwards it says "ptrvar * (is a pointer to) a char value."

Something like

```
int *fooby;
```

says "`fooby *` (is a pointer to) an `int` value."

Just like other variable declarations, if these are found as variables in a function they will have random values, like picking up a postcard from the recycling stack to erase and send again. In any case you should initialize the variable.

2. Getting an address

The ampersand (`&`) yields an address in memory when it is applied to a variable. This gives you the value to write on your postcard.

```
int myVar;
int *pointerToMyVar;
pointerToMyVar = &myVar;
```

Now `pointerToMyVar` contains the address of the first byte of `myVar`. Equivalently, the postcard `pointerToMyVar` has written on it where to find the beginning of the number that `myVar` stores.

3. Getting data from an address

The star is used again, this time as an action. When a star is used on a pointer variable on the right-hand side of an assignment, it means "fetch." It is the same as reading the location in the book from the postcard, opening the book, turning to the page, and then reading at the first letter there.

```
int myVar = 12;
int *pointerToMyVar = &myVar;
int anotherInt;

anotherInt = *pointerToMyVar;
```

Reading from right to left again, you have:

`pointerToMyVar:`	Look at pointerToMyVar. Use the address there.
`*:`	Go fetch an int's worth of bytes from that address.
`=:`	Assign that int's worth of bytes.
`anotherInt:`	To this variable.

Now `anotherInt` has the value 12.

4. Putting data to an address

Once again the star is used. When it is used on a pointer on the left-hand side of an assignment, it means "put". It is like reading the book location from the postcard, opening the book, turning to the page, then erasing the letter there and writing in a new letter.

Using the declarations above, this code:

```
*pointerToMyVar = 42;
```

reading from right to left means:

`42:`	Take this constant value
`=:`	and assign it. To figure out where you want to assign it, look at
`pointerToMyVar:`	for where in memory to start storing the bytes that comprise the value
`*:`	now that you know where to store the data, actually put the bytes the

Without the star on the assignment, you would have `pointerToMyVar = 42;` which would be wrong. That would write "42" onto the postcard, rather than on the pages of the book.

An actual use of pointers: pass by reference

As mentioned in the last chapter, arguments to functions are passed by value, meaning that the values of the arguments are duplicated and then these duplicates are given to the function. The function is free to change them without any impact on the caller.

Sometimes you want to pass arguments by reference and have the function fill in values so that the caller can see the change. This is useful if you are returning more than one result from a function, or you want the function to write into a pre-allocated buffer.

Pointers are used in this case. If you want a function to change an argument, have the function take a pointer argument, and then pass a pointer to your variable. Here is an example:

Example 3-1. pass-reference.c

```
// pass-reference.c -- show pass by reference using pointers

/* compile with:
cc -g -Wall -o pass-reference pass-reference.c
*/

#include <stdio.h>          // for printf

void addemUp (int a, int b, int *result)
{
    *result = a + b;
} // addemUp

int main (int argc, char *argv[])
{
    int answer;

    addemUp (1, 2, &answer);

    printf ("1 + 2 = %d\n", answer);
    return (0);

} // main
```

A sample run:

```
% ./pass-reference
1 + 2 = 3
```

Here is what is happening in memory:

Figure 3-1. Pass By Reference

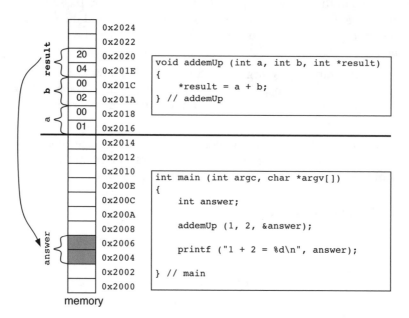

memory

The storage for the variable answer lives at address 0x2004, and extends for 4 bytes through address 0x2007. The **addemUp** function gets called. The numeric values get written to memory (pass by value, remember), and the address of the answer variable (0x2004) gets written to this parameter memory.

When the function executes

```
*result = a + b;
```

This is what it does:

1. Figures out the values of a (1) and b (2).

2. Adds 1 + 2, and stores the result (3) somewhere. probably a processor register.

3. Looks at the value of the result variable (0x2004).

4. Writes the result (a four-byte int value that happens to be 3) starting at address 0x2004, which happens to be the same place the variable answer is stored.

Another use for pointers: strings

C has no string type. There is a convention, though, where a run of characters ending with a zero byte is considered a "string." This is what a string looks like in memory (where the big x is a byte with a value of zero):

Figure 3-2. C String

Starting at any address from `0x100` through `0x11B` will result in a valid C "string." You can use such a string like this:

```
char *myString;
myString = "this is a sequence of chars";
```

Pulling this code apart you have:

`char *myString`

> `myString` is a pointer to a character. This is the postcard where the location of the first letter of a sequence of characters starts.

`"this is..."`

> a sequence of bytes, terminated by a zero byte, that the compiler and linker stick into read-only space. A literal string expression evaluates to the address of the first byte of the sequence.

`=`

> Will assign the address value.

`myString`

> The postcard you are writing on has the location of the first "t" of "this is a sequence of chars"

`myString` now has the value of `0x100`, the address of the first character.

Note the continued pedantry of referring to "the first something of a sequence of somethings." Pointers have no intrinsic knowledge of what they point to. `myString` could point to the beginning of "this is a sequence of chars," or it could be made to point into the middle.

OK, now that you have `myString` pointing to the first byte of the literal string, what can we do with it?

You can get the first letter of the string by doing

```
char charVar = *myString;
```

This assigns the value of "t" to `charVar`.

You can increment the pointer:

```
myString++;
```

That makes `myString` point to the next character. Note that since there is no star attached to this expression, nothing is done with the value being pointed to. There is no star operator to initiate a reading or writing of the pointed-to value. This just changes the location value on the postcard.

`myString` now has the value of `0x101`, the address of the second character.

```
charVar = *myString;
```

assigns the value of "h" to `charVar`.

You can calculate the length of a "string" like this by counting characters until you hit the zero byte at the end. For example:

Example 3-2. strlen1.c

```
// strlen1.c -- calculate the length of a C string

/* compile with:
cc -g -Wall -o strlen1 strlen1.c
*/

#include <stdio.h>          // for printf

int main (int argc, char *argv[])
{
    char *myString = "this is a sequence of chars";
    int length = 0;

    while (*myString != '\0') {
        length++;
        myString++;
    }

    printf ("the length of the string is %d\n", length);
    return (0);

} // main
```

See how it runs:

```
% ./strlen1
the length of the string is 27
```

Things of note: the expression '\0' is a way of signifying a zero byte. You could use just a naked zero in the expression, but using '\0' makes it clear to whomever is reading the code that a character value is being used.

The above idiom, using a pointer to scan through a sequence of data, is very common in C, and it will frequently be abbreviated. This is the same program, but written more idiomatically:

Example 3-3. strlen2.c

```
// strlen2.c -- calculate the length of a C string, idiomatically

/* compile with:
cc -g -Wall -o strlen2 strlen2.c
*/

#include <stdio.h>          // for printf()

int main (int argc, char *argv[])
{
    char *myString = "this is a sequence of chars";
    int length = 0;

    while (*myString++) {
        length++;
    }

    printf ("the length of the string is %d\n", length);
    return (0);

} // main
```

Pull apart the inner loop:

```
    while (*myString++) {
        length++;
    }
```

`*myString++` is the same as `*myString` followed by `myString++`. What does that mean? `*myString` is executed, which looks at the postcard (`myString`), follows the address and fetches a value (the star operator). That value is then used to decide whether the body of the while loop should be evaluated. Then `myString++` is evaluated, which updates the location written on the postcard to indicate the next letter to process.

As an aside, this loop is how the standard library call **strlen()** is implemented. This is an O(N) operation, so it is not a function you would call if you do not have to (like every time in the controlling expression of a `while` loop).

Pointer math

Given a pointer to an address in memory, you can calculate other addresses. Big deal. What is kind of nice is that C takes into account the size of the data the pointer refers to and scales the arithmetic accordingly.

In this example, all the pointers are pointing at the same starting address, but the additions refer to different bytes.

Figure 3-3. Pointer Math

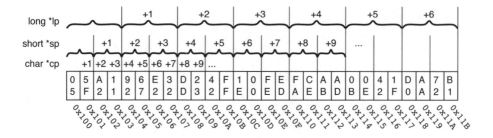

The same sequence of (random) bytes are interpreted with different pointers.

Assume that `lp`, `sp`, and `cp` start off with the same value, `0x100`. When you do something like `sp + 3`, the address `(sp + (3 * sizeof(pointer-base-type)))` is calculated. In the case of a short pointer (where a short is two bytes), `sp` is `0x100`, `sp + 1` is `0x102`, `sp + 2` is `0x104`, and so on.

If `lp` is a long pointer, `lp` is `0x100`, `lp + 1` is `0x104`, `lp + 2` is `0x108`, and so on

You dereference (fetch the value of) a pointer that is being added to like this:

```
long longval = *(lp + 5);
```

Which works like this:

Table 3-1. Play-by-play

Code	Behavior
`lp + 5`	Start with a base address of `lp` (`0x100`). Scale 5 by the `sizeof(long)` so that you get 20 (hex 14). Add them together to get `0x114`. This becomes a a temporary postcard with `0x114` written on it.
`*:`	Go to address `0x114`, and fetch a long's worth of bytes (in this case, it would be `0x0b0e421f`)
`longval =`	Copy the value `0x0b0e421f` into `longval`

Since `++` is the same as adding 1, it too gets scaled by the size of the type.

If you had a loop like this:

```
long *lp = 0x100;
for (i = 0; i < 5; i++) {
    printf ("%d: %x\n", i, *lp);
    lp++;
}
```

You would get output like this:

```
0: 0x055fa211
1: 0x9267e232
2: 0xdd2342ff
3: 0x1e00feed
4: 0xfaceabad
```

For comparison, here it is with a `short` (2 bytes) pointer:

```
short *sp = 0x100;
for (i = 0; i < 5; i++) {
    printf ("%d: %x\n", i, *sp);
    sp++;
}
```

```
0: 0x055f
1: 0xa211
2: 0x9267
3: 0xe232
4: 0xdd23
```

And for completeness, with a `char` (1 byte) pointer:

```
char *cp = 0x100;

for (i = 0; i < 5; i++) {
    printf ("%d: %x\n", i, *cp);
    cp++;
}
```

```
0: 0x05
1: 0x5f
2: 0xa2
3: 0x11
4: 0x92
```

It is the same data in memory, the same starting address, just different pointer types.

The NULL pointer

The NULL pointer, having a zero value, is what you use to say, "This pointer points to nowhere." It is a handy initialization value, which happens automatically for global and static variables. In general, trying to dereference a NULL pointer will crash your program.

Structures

Declaring structures

Structures are C's way of aggregating a bunch of different pieces of data under one name (like a table definition in SQL). For instance:

```
struct Person {
    char    *name;
    int     age;
```

```
    char    gender; // use 'm', 'f'
    double  shoeSize;
};
```

You can then declare instances of `Person` like this:

```
struct Person perfectMate;
```

and set/read the structure field members like this:

```
perfectMate.name = "Brenda";
perfectMate.age = 23;
perfectMate.gender = 'f';
perfectMate.shoeSize = 8.5;

printf ("my perfect mate is named %s, and is %d years old\n",
        perfectMate.name, perfectMate.age);
```

Use a dot between the name of the variable and the name of the field to use.

The layout of the structure in memory looks like this:

Figure 3-4. Structure Layout

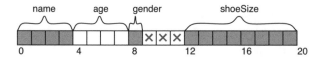

The elements in the structure are laid down in the order they are declared. Note the three bytes that are X'd out. The compiler puts in padding bytes so that types are aligned on byte boundaries that maximize accessing performance. `shoeSize`, being a double, is on a 4-byte boundary. If it were closely packed in against the `gender` byte the CPU would have to do multiple fetches and assemble the data every time it was needed (this is much slower than if it is aligned and the processor can grab it all at once).

One thing to notice is the declaration of `name`. It is `char *name`. This tells the compiler to leave space for a postcard to find the actual name. The name itself will not be stored in the struct, it will just be referenced elsewhere.

Pointers to structs

`sstruct`s and pointers are often used together. `struct`s can become arbitrarily large, so passing them by value (copying all the bytes) can become expensive. Also, it is pretty common to have a function fill in the members of a structure. Pointers come to the rescue here again.

Example 3-4. struct-point.c

```
// struct-point.c -- some structure, pointer stuff

/* compile with:
cc -g -Wall -o struct-point struct-point.c
```

```c
*/

#include <stdio.h>          // for printf

struct Person {
    char    *name;
    int     age;
    char    gender; // use 'm', 'f'
    double  shoeSize;
};

void populatePerson (struct Person *person)
{
    person->name = "Bork";
    person->age = 34;
    person->gender = 'm';
    person->shoeSize = 10.5;
} // populatePerson

void printPerson (struct Person *person)
{
    printf ("name:      %s\n", person->name);
    printf ("age:       %d\n", person->age);
    printf ("gender:    %s\n",
            (person->gender == 'm') ? "male" : "female");
    printf ("shoe size: %f\n", person->shoeSize);
} // printPerson

int main (int argc, char *argv[])
{
    struct Person me;

    populatePerson (&me);
    printPerson (&me);

    return (0);

} // main
```

The output

```
% ./struct-point
name:      Bork
age:       34
gender:    male
shoe size: 10.500000
```

Rather than using a dot to separate a variable from the field you are referencing, you use the cool-looking arrow operator: -> (minus + greater than) An expression like person->name is a shorthand for (*person).name.

One very powerful feature of pointers to structs is that you can employ more interesting data structures like linked lists and trees. The nodes of your data structure can refer to each other via pointers.

Bitfields

C lets you specify bit layout for individual fields in a `struct`.

A `struct` like this:

```
struct PackedPerson {
    char *name;
    unsigned int age : 7;                // enough to hold 127 years
    unsigned int isFemale : 1;           // set if female, clear if male
    unsigned int shoeSize : 4;           // support up to a size 15
    unsigned int padding : 2;            // add breathing room for BigFoot
    unsigned int shoeSizeFraction : 1;   // set if this is a half-size
}
```

would have a memory layout like this:

Figure 3-5. Packed Structure Layout

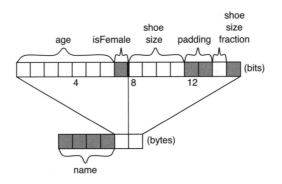

`struct PackedPerson` only takes 6 bytes of storage (vs 20 bytes for just a regular `struct Person`) The access time for the bitfields will be slower since the compiler is generating shifting and masking instructions to pack and unpack the data.

Of course, you can use masks and bitwise operators to do this stuff manually, but sometimes these bitfields can be more convenient.

Typedef

Up in `struct-point.c`, every time you reference the `struct Person` structure in parameter lists and variable declarations you have to include the `struct` keyword. That can get pretty annoying pretty quickly. C allows you to associate an alias name that is easier to deal with, using the `typedef` facility:

```
struct Person {
    char    *name;
    int     age;
    char    gender; // use 'm', 'f'
    double  shoeSize;
};

typedef struct Person Person;
```

Now you can use just `Person` everywhere:

```
void populatePerson (Person *person);
void printPerson (Person *person);
...
    Person me;
```

And given C's love for brevity, you can combine those two:

```
typedef struct Person {
    ...
} Person;
```

Casts

A cast is an operation where you tell the compiler to override the default interpretation of a particular variable. You can use casts to tell the compiler to treat an `int` value as if it were floating point:

```
int thing = 5;
float blah = (float) thing + 3.1415;
```

Here the compiler will convert thing to a floating point value before adding. (The compiler will do this anyway, but you can use the explicit cast to tell the reader what is going on.) Casts can also be used to go between signed and unsigned values. It is a way of telling the compiler, "Hey, I know what I am doing. Go ahead and reinterpret the bits."

Casts are also used to convert between pointer types.

You can have something like this:

```
unsigned char *bytePointer = ....;
```

You have a pointer to a sequence of bytes:

```
int blah = *((int *)bytePointer);
```

The `(int *)bytePointer` cast tells the compiler to treat `bytePointer` as if it were a pointer to `int`s rather than a pointer to `char`s. So, when you dereference `*((int *)bytePointer)`, you will be picking up an `int`'s worth of bytes. If you just did `*bytePointer`, you would only pick up one byte's worth.

Similarly you can use casts on structure pointers:

```
int *blah = ....; // a pointer somewhere
Person *person = (Person *)blah;
```

now `blah` and `person` both point to the same address. You can now do things like

`printf ("name is %s\n", person->name);` and it will pick up the bytes that started where `blah` pointed. In most cases this would probably crash your program by interpreting the bytes in a nonsensical manner, but the compiler lets you do this since it trusts that you know what you are doing.

void *

There are times when you want to say, "Here is a pointer to something. I do not really care what it is, it is just an address in memory." The return values from dynamic memory functions are like this. The C type `void *` is what indicates a pointer-to-anything. When you get a `void *`, you typically assign it to a pointer variable of a particular type and then manipulate it, or you cast it to the type you want.

Function pointers

You can have pointers to code as well as pointers to data. This allows a degree of abstraction by allowing functions to act generically and delegate their work to another function. You can do object-oriented programming in C (polymorphism and dynamic dispatch) using function pointers.

The syntax for declaring function pointers is a bit odd:

```
void (*pointer1)(int, int);
```

which means a pointer to a function that takes two `int`s and returns nothing.

```
int (*pointer2)(void);
```

is a pointer to a function that takes no arguments and returns an integer.

You invoke a function by something like this:

```
(pointer1)(5, 5);
```

or

```
int myvar = (pointer2)();
```

In fact, the parentheses can be omitted too. I like leaving them in that it makes it obvious that a function pointer is being used rather than an explicit function.

This little program invokes a function to print out an integer via a function pointer.

Example 3-5. function-pointer.c

```
// function-pointer.c -- play with function pointers

/* compile with:
cc -g -Wall -o function-pointer function-pointer.c
*/

#include <stdio.h>          // for printf()

void printAsChar (int value)
{
    printf ("%d as a char is '%c'\n", value, value);
} // printAsChar

void printAsInt (int value)
{
    printf ("%d as an int is '%d'\n", value, value);
```

```
} // printAsInt

void printAsHex (int value)
{
    printf ("%d as hex is '0x%x'\n", value, value);
} // printAsHex

void printIt (int value, void (*printingFunction)(int))
{
    (printingFunction)(value);
} // printIt

int main (int argc, char *argv[])
{
    int value = 35;

    printIt (value, printAsChar);
    printIt (value, printAsInt);
    printIt (value, printAsHex);
    return (0);

} // main
```

The program in action:

```
% ./function-pointer
35 as a char is '#'
35 as an int is '35'
35 as hex is '0x23'
```

Unions

Unions are a way of interpreting the bits stored in a structure in two different ways.

Consider this:

```
typedef struct Person {
    char    *name;
    int     age;
    char    gender;    // use 'm', 'f'
    double  shoeSize;
} Person;

typedef struct Alien {
    char    *designation;
    char    bloodType; // use 'Q', 'X', or "@"
    int     hearts;
    short   psiPower;
    short   ducks;      // can be negative
} Alien;

enum { Human, NonHuman };

typedef struct Individual {
    int type;
    union {
        Person person;
```

```
        Alien   alien;
    } indData;
} Individual;
```

The layout of `Individual` looks like this:

Figure 3-6. Layout of `Individual` Union

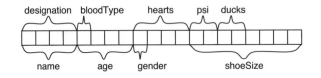

You can store an `Alien`'s worth of data or a `Person`'s worth of data in the same space, but not both at the same time (you will need a second chunk of memory to do that). Unions let you overlay storage like this in order to reduce type proliferation.

Referencing the fields of unions is verbose. You need to specify:

```
variableName.union-name.union-type-name.field;
```

To get the number of hearts for an alien, you need to do:

```
myAlien.indData.alien.hearts;
```

It looks like a lot of extra work to drill down into the union like that. There is not a run-time cost for these, just wear and tear on your keyboard (some `#define`s can come in handy). Internally the compiler calculates the offset from the beginning of the structure and fetches data from there.

Here is a program that uses this union. The `type struct` member tells folks who receive one of these structures what type it is, so they know which side of the union to use.

Example 3-6. union.c

```
// union.c -- play with unions

/* compile with:
cc -g -Wall -o union union.c
*/

#include <stdio.h>          // for printf

typedef struct Person {
    char    *name;
    int     age;
    char    gender;     // use 'm', 'f'
    double  shoeSize;
} Person;

typedef struct Alien {
    char    *designation;
```

```c
    char    bloodType; // use 'Q', 'X', or "@"
    int     hearts;
    short   psiPower;
    short   ducks;      // can be negative
} Alien;

enum { Human, NonHuman };

typedef struct Individual {
    int type;
    union {
        Person person;
        Alien  alien;
    } indData;
} Individual;

void fillAlien (Individual *individual)
{
    individual->type = NonHuman;
    individual->indData.alien.designation = "qwzzk";
    individual->indData.alien.bloodType = 'X';
    individual->indData.alien.hearts = 7;
    individual->indData.alien.psiPower = 2870;
    individual->indData.alien.ducks = 3;
} // fillAlien

void fillPerson (Individual *individual)
{
    individual->type = Human;
    individual->indData.person.name = "Bork";
    individual->indData.person.age = 34;
    individual->indData.person.gender = 'm';
    individual->indData.person.shoeSize = 10.5;
} // fillPerson

void printIndividual (Individual *individual)
{
    if (individual->type == Human) {
        printf ("Human:\n");
        printf ("   name:     %s\n", individual->indData.person.name);
        printf ("   age:      %d\n", individual->indData.person.age);
        printf ("   gender:   %c\n", individual->indData.person.gender);
        printf ("   shoeSize: %f\n", individual->indData.person.shoeSize);

    } else if (individual->type == NonHuman) {
        printf ("NonHuman:\n");

        printf ("   designation: %s\n", individual->indData.alien.designation);
        printf ("   bloodType:   %c\n", individual->indData.alien.bloodType);
        printf ("   hearts:      %d\n", individual->indData.alien.hearts);
        printf ("   psiPower:    %d\n", individual->indData.alien.psiPower);
        printf ("   ducks:       %d\n", individual->indData.alien.ducks);

    } else {
        printf ("oops, bad union qualifier\n");
    }
} // printIndividual
```

```
int main (int argc, char *argv[])
{
    Individual being;

    fillAlien (&being);
    printIndividual (&being);

    fillPerson (&being);
    printIndividual (&being);

    return (0);

} // main
```

Arrays

The last stop on the tour are arrays. Arrays are ordered collections of data of a uniform type, and are similar to arrays in other languages like Java and Pascal.

You can declare an array like this:

```
int intArray[20];
```

This makes an array of 20 elements. You index the array to read and write values like this:

```
intArray[2] = 20;
int intVal = intArray[6];
```

Like all variables, if an array is declared in a function, it will have random values. Global (non-`static` and not declared in a function) or `static` arrays will be initialized to all zeros.

This is how an array looks in memory:

Figure 3-7. Array in Memory

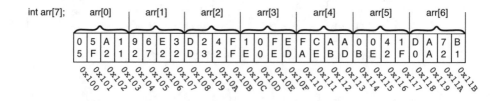

Look familiar? Here is another way to look at it:

Figure 3-8. Array as a Pointer

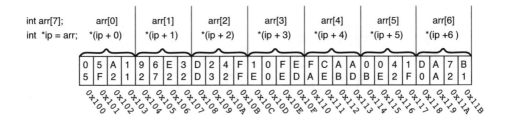

Arrays have a very close relationship with pointers. In general, you can index a pointer with square brackets (just like an array), and you can do pointer math on an array. In fact, pointers are how arrays get passed to functions.

Consider this program, where arrays get passed to the `printArray()` function as a pointer, and indexed as an array:

Example 3-7. array-parameter.c

```
// array-parameter.c

/* compile with:
cc -g -Wall -o array-parameter array-parameter.c
*/

#include <stdio.h>

void printArray (int *array, int length)
{
    int i;

    for (i = 0; i < length; i++) {
        printf ("%d: %d\n", i, array[i]);
    }

} // printArray

int main (int argc, char *argv[])
{
    int array1[5];
    int array2[] = { 23, 42, 55 };
    int i;

    for (i = 0; i < 5; i++) {
        array1[i] = i;
    }

    printf ("array 1:\n");
    printArray (array1, 5);

    printf ("array 2:\n");
    printArray (array2, sizeof(array2) / sizeof(int));

    return (0);
```

```
} // main
```

A sample run:

```
% ./array-parameter
array 1:
0: 0
1: 1
2: 2
3: 3
4: 4
array 2:
0: 23
1: 42
2: 55
```

One thing of interest is the bulk initialization of `array2`. Since there are three elements in that initialization list, the length of `array2` is that of three `int`s , or 12 bytes (3 * 4 = 12). Look at the technique used to calculate the number of elements in the array by dividing the total size (via `sizeof`) by the `sizeof` a single element. This comes in handy when you have tables of stuff defined in your code.

Another thing to note is that the **printArray()** function needs to take a length (or you need to stick some sentinel value) so that the loop knows when to stop. There is no length information encoded in the pointer or array. That is why there exist functions like **strlen()** that have to count characters in a string.

A logical question is, "If that is the case, how come you could do that `sizeof(array2) / sizeof(int)` thing?" Recall that `sizeof` is a compile-time directive. The compiler knows that `array2` has three members because of the initialization list. The function **printArray()** cannot know that since it does not know at compile time which array it is going to be given.

Arrays of pointers

If you've been following along, you've probably noticed a couple dozen of these:

```
int main (int argc, char *argv[])
```

Look at the last argument: what is that?

Here it is taken apart:

argv[]: argv is an array of undetermined length
char *: of character pointers.

In other words, `argv[]` is an array of postcards, and on the postcards are the locations of C strings (zero-terminated sequences of characters). This array (`argv`, for "argument vector") is the set of program arguments given to the program. `argc` (argument count) is the number of elements in `argv`.

For a program started like

```
% myProgram -fish battery -jo2y fund blah.c
```

the resulting `argv` array looks like this:

Figure 3-9. argv

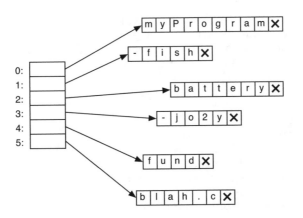

Because of the equivalence of arrays and pointers (they are not identical, but the differences between them are subtle), the declaration for **main()** can also be written as

```
int main (int argc, char **argv)
```

For the More Curious: Data Structures Using Pointers

structs and pointer to structs can be used to build powerful data structures. One of the simpler ones is a binary search tree. Each node of the tree holds a value and a pair of pointers to other nodes. New values less than the value contained in the node get put into the left fork, otherwise they go onto the right fork. If someone is already living on a particular side of the fork, you look at that node and try to place the new value accordingly.

Here is a program that puts some values into a tree, then looks to see if particular values can be found.

Example 3-8. tree.c

```
// tree.c -- use structs and pointers to build a tree of nodes

/* compile with:
cc -g -Wall -o tree tree.c
*/

#include <stdio.h>        // for printf
#include <stdlib.h>       // for malloc

typedef struct TreeNode {
    int value;
    struct TreeNode *left;
    struct TreeNode *right;
} TreeNode;


void addValue (TreeNode *node, int value)
{
```

```
        if (value < node->value) {
            // left side
            if (node->left == NULL) {
                TreeNode *newNode = malloc (sizeof(TreeNode));
                newNode->value = value;
                newNode->left = newNode->right = NULL;
                node->left = newNode;
            } else {
                addValue (node->left, value);
            }
        } else {
            // right side
            if (node->right == NULL) {
                TreeNode *newNode = malloc (sizeof(TreeNode));
                newNode->value = value;
                newNode->left = newNode->right = NULL;
                node->right = newNode;
            } else {
                addValue (node->right, value);
            }
        }
} // addValue

#define TRUE 1
#define FALSE 0

int findValue (TreeNode *node, int value)
{
    if (node == NULL) {
        return (FALSE);
    } else if (node->value == value) {
        return (TRUE);
    } else {
        if (value < node->value) {
            return (findValue(node->left, value));
        } else {
            return (findValue(node->right, value));
        }
    }
} // findValue

int main (int argc, char *argv[])
{
    TreeNode root;

    // put 23 in manually to bootstrap the tree
    root.value = 23;
    root.left = root.right = NULL;

    // now add some stuff

    addValue (&root, 5);
    addValue (&root, 50);
    addValue (&root, 8);
    addValue (&root, 2);
    addValue (&root, 34);
```

```
    if (findValue(&root, 23)) {
        printf ("23 lives in the tree\n");
    } else {
        printf ("23 does not live in the tree\n");
    }

    if (findValue(&root, 42)) {
        printf ("42 lives in the tree\n");
    } else {
        printf ("42 does not live in the tree\n");
    }
    return (0);

} // main
```

A sample run:

```
% ./tree
23 lives in the tree
42 does not live in the tree
```

After the tree is built, it would look something like this in memory:

Figure 3-10. Binary Search Tree

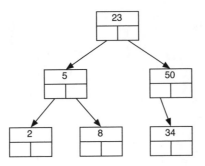

The most interesting part of the code is the declaration of the tree node:

```
typedef struct TreeNode {
    int value;
    struct TreeNode *left;
    struct TreeNode *right;
} TreeNode;
```

You cannot reference the `TreeNode typedef` while you are declaring it, but you can reference `struct TreeNode`.

The other interesting thing is the use of dynamic memory allocation:

```
TreeNode *newNode = malloc (sizeof(TreeNode));
```

This allocates a chunk of memory the size of a `TreeNode` (12 bytes) and gives you a pointer to it. This allows the tree to grow arbitrarily large.

Challenge:

Add a function to `tree.c` to print out the tree.

Chapter 4. The Compiler

The C compiler is probably the central-most tool in the programming arsenal. No matter what editor you use for source code, no matter how you build your programs, the C compiler is involved. The *GNU C compiler* (called gcc, but invoked with the command cc) is what ships with Apple's developer tools. Mac OS X 10.2 ships with gcc 3.1, and subsequent releases of Mac OS X might have newer versions. In addition to the cc program, as of Mac OS X 10.2 you can access the compiler with gcc like on other Unix platforms. The system actually ships with both gcc3 and gcc2 (the compiler used on pre-Jaguar versions of the OS). The older compiler is provided due to newer versions of the compiler tend to be stricter in its error checking, plus gcc 3 changed the C++ ABI. You can switch between the two by running /usr/sbin/gcc_select, giving it an argument of 2 or 3 to choose which compiler you want. Be sure to use this command rather than trying to do it manually since gcc has a lot of moving parts, and it is easy to miss something.

The compiler supports a number of languages, which you can choose from with different file extensions:

.c

> Regular C

.m

> Objective-C

.C

> C++ (but do not use on HFS+ file systems since it is not case sensitive)

.cpp

> C++

.mm

> Objective-C++, a blend of C++ and Objective-C

Handy Flags

Documentation for gcc lives in /Developer/Documentation/DeveloperTools/Compiler/CompilerTOC.html. Beware that gcc is huge, with lots of options, lots of features, lots of flags, and lots of extensions to the language. Also lots of cool stuff. Here are some that I find useful on a regular basis:

-g

> Add debugging symbols.

-E

> See preprocessor output.

-S

> See generated assembly code.

`-save-temps`

> Keep temporary files around.

`-Wall, -Wmost`

> Show more warnings.

`-Werror`

> Treat warnings as errors.

`-DSYMBOL`

> #define from the command line.

`-DSYMBOL=value`

> #define with a value from the command line.

`-O#`

> Set optimization levels.

Debugging

`-g` Turns on debugging symbols, which are chunks of extra data that allow debuggers to map an arbitrary address in your executable code back to the source that generated it. It also contains information on variable names, locations, and types. Having debugging symbols enabled also makes your program bigger (sometimes much bigger), and also may expose some implementation details that you might prefer to be hidden. The `strip` program will remove these symbols. The downside of stripping your executables (or not building your application with `-g`) means that you will not have symbolic stack traces when looking at errors in the field, and you will not be able to easily analyze core files that people email you. Check out the `atos` program that can help map addresses back to program symbols. In general, it is always a good idea to use `-g`. It only adds debugging symbols and does not affect the code generation.

Warnings

I am a big fan of compiler warnings. If the compiler is complaining about something I wrote, most likely the construct is questionable and could lead to errors somewhere down the line. I try to have my code to always compile cleanly without warnings. `-Wall` will show a lot of warnings for most everything the `gcc` developers consider questionable. `-Wmost` is a good middle ground when using the Cocoa frameworks.

Specific warnings can be turned on and off independently depending on your specific coding style. For example, say you are using a library which uses macros that leave unused variables around. Messy, but pretty much harmless since the compiler will not allocate space for them. For example:

Example 4-1. warning.m

```
// warning.m -- show generation of compiler warnings

/* compile with:
cc -Wall -o warning warning.m
*/

int main (int argc, char *argv)
{
    int i;
} // main
```

Then if you build it:

```
% cc -Wall -o warning warning.m
warning.m:2: warning: second argument of 'main' should be 'char **'
warning.m: In function 'main':
warning.m:3: warning: unused variable 'i'
warning.m:4: warning: control reaches end of non-void function
```

Two of those warnings are really interesting since they are actually errors: I messed up the parameters to **main()**, and I did not return anything from **main()**. But (in this case) the unused variable is not a show-stopper. I fix my code otherwise:

```
int main (int argc, char *argv[])
{
    int i;
    return (0);
} // main
```

```
% cc -Wall warning.m
warning.m: In function 'main':
warning.m:3: warning: unused variable 'i'
```

You can turn that warning off with

```
% cc -Wall -Wno-unused warning.m
(no complaints)
```

So you will still get other warnings if you make mistakes. If you wanted to only see unused variables, and no other errors, use -Wunused (drop the no-):

```
% cc -Wunused warning.m
warning.m: In function 'main':
warning.m:3: warning: unused variable 'i'
```

The gcc docs have the full set of warnings described in detail.

It is worth your time to reduce your warning count. If you have a lot of warnings that you "just ignore all the time," useful warnings will get lost in the noise. So either fix them or suppress the ones you consider useless. Another downside with lots of warnings that whiz by is when building a large project, particularly when building from the command line with make or pbxbuild, is that it is easy to miss them and spend some time tracking down a programming error that caused the warning. Setting up projects to give gcc the -Werror flag will make warnings be treated as errors. This halts the build process when using makefiles or Project

Builder. To enable this in Project Builder, you go to the "GCC Compiler Settings" pane of the project Target, and check "Treat all warnings as errors".

And lastly, for a quick syntax check (no code generation), give gcc the -fsyntax-only flag.

Defining Preprocessor Symbols

You can define preprocessor symbols in your code with #define. These set variable values (or just variable existence) in the preprocessor which can then be checked (with #ifdef, #ifndef, or #if), or the values used via substitution or other preprocessor directives. You can define these preprocessor symbols as arguments to the compiler via -D.

Example 4-2. define.m

```
// define.m -- conditional compilation

/* compile with:
cc -g -Wall -o define define.m
*/

#include <stdio.h>

#define THING_3

int main (int arg, char *argv[])
{
#ifdef THING_1
    printf ("thing1\n");
#endif

#if THING_2 == 23
    printf ("thing2\n");
#endif

#ifdef THING_3
    printf ("thing3\n");
#endif

    return (0);

} // main
```

Build it:

```
% cc -g -Wall -o define define.m
```

and run it:

```
% ./define
thing3
```

Defining the other two symbols will get the other two messages printed. You could either add to the code

```
#define THING_2 23
#define THING_1
```

and that will work. You can also tell the compiler to do it for you

```
% cc -g -Wall -o define -DTHING_1 -DTHING_2=23 define.m
```

The definition of `THING_1` just sets the existence of the preprocessor symbol, the second sets a value.

Running it gives all three messages now:

```
% ./define
thing1
thing2
thing3
```

This technique is very handy when you have multiplatform code and you need to turn on or off compatibility features. It also can be used for turning features on or off with a compiler flag. (For instance, a web server communications driver that could include or exclude encryption.)

Be very careful what you decide to `#define`, especially if you define commonly used tokens like `if`. You can run into situations where, for instance, a structure field was `#defined` to another name (presumably to hack around an error in an API), but that could end up clobbering a variable name used elsewhere. Remember that the preprocessor knows nothing about the C language, it just does blind textual replacements.

Seeing Preprocessor Output

Sometimes you get an inscrutable error from the compiler and you have no idea why the compiler is complaining. Or you may have code that looks reasonable and compiles OK, but behaves in a way that defies sanity. At times like this examining the preprocessor output can prove fruitful so you can see exactly what the compiler is seeing. The `-E` flag tells `gcc` to send the preprocessed source code to standard out.

This program looks simple enough. It will read a line from standard in and print it back out.

Example 4-3. preprocTest.m

```
// preprocTest -- a program to show preprocessor output

/* compile with:
cc -g -Wall -o preprocTest preprocTest.m
or
cc -Wall -E preprocTest.m > junk.i
*/

#import <stdio.h>

#define BUFFER_SIZE 2048

int main (int argc, char *argv[])
{
```

```
    char buffer[BUFFER_SIZE];    /* this is a comment */
    char *thing;

    thing = fgets (buffer, BUFFER_SIZE, stdin);
    printf ("%s", thing);

    /* some other comment */
    return (0);

} // main
```

Compile it and run it:

```
% cc -g -Wall -o preprocTest preprocTest.m
% ./preprocTest
hello [return]
hello
%
```

Now let us dig into it with preprocessor output. Compile your program like this now:

```
% cc -g -Wall -E preprocTest.m  > junk.i
```

That is, preprocess the source file and write it to `junk.i` (the `.i` extension is for preprocessed output). `junk.i` will be a couple of hundred lines long, due to the size and complexity of the header files it includes. Open it up in your editor and scroll to the end. You will see something like this:

```
int main ( int argc , char * argv [ ] )
{
char buffer [ 2048 ] ;
char * thing ;

thing = fgets ( buffer , 2048 , ( & __sF [ 0 ] ) ) ;
printf ( "%s" , thing ) ;


return ( 0 ) ;

}
```

It is somewhat recognizable as the original program. Notice that all the comments are gone, as is the indentation. There is also now white space between all of the tokens in the code (presumably to make the actual parsing of the code easier). The `#define BUFFER_SIZE 2048` is gone also, but you can see where 2048 has been substituted into the text stream. Notice that `stdin` has been expanded into the address of the zero element of an array named __sF. What is __sF? Search in `junk.i` for it. About half-way through you will see

```
extern FILE __sF [ ] ;
```

An array of `FILE` structures. Since you will be seeing exactly what the compiler is seeing, you can look at the guts of `FILE` (search for __sFILE). There are all sorts of goodies like function pointers, buffers, and block size variables in there. This is not the kind of stuff you would want your code to depend on, but it can be a big help when tracking down problems. Plus it can be fun to dig into things and see how they work.

Another handy use of preprocessor output is when you are debugging macros. Write your macro, run it through the preprocessor and see if it has the effect you want.

Seeing the Generated Assembly Code

For the real hard-core hackers, you can look at the assembly code generated by the compiler. Sometimes you need this to track down compiler problems, OS problems, or you can browse around just for general amusement and education. To get the assembly code compile with the -S flag, and the results will be put into an .s file based on the name of your source file. For instance, running

```
% cc -g -Wall -S preprocTest.m
```

will create a preprocTest.s. If you want to assemble the resulting file, feed it to the compiler like this:

```
% cc -o preprocTest preprocTest.s
```

You can also use otool to disassemble existing programs if you do not want to muck around with compiler flags. If you want to save all the intermediate elements (including some not covered here), you can use the -save-temps flag.

Preprocessor Hints and Tricks

The C compilation process happens in several stages. The preprocessor performs text substitutions on your source code and strips out comments. The compiler takes the preprocessed output and generates an assembly language file, which is then assembled into the machine code. If you do not tell gcc to just leave the object file sitting around, the linker will also be invoked to complete the build process.

The preprocessor is a pretty simple straight-text substitution mechanism, with some conditional inclusion features. It is not as powerful and full-featured as something like the GNU m4 macro processor, but it has plenty of power.

Predefined Macros

One of the preprocessor features is doing conditional compilation so that you can only include code for particular platforms. How can you tell what platform you are on? Compilers define some built-in macros to let you decide what code to include or not:

__APPLE__

Defined for an Apple Platform, such as OS X.

__APPLE_CC__

This is an integer value representing the version of the compiler.

`__OBJC__`

Defined if the compiler is compiling in Objective-C mode.

`__cplusplus`

Defined if the compiler is compiling in C++ mode.

`__MACH__`

Defined if the Mach system calls are available.

The preprocessor also defines some special macros that expand to the current location in the file being compiled, and the current date and time:

`__DATE__`

The current date.

`__TIME__`

The current time.

`__FILE__`

The name of the file.

`__LINE__`

The line number of the file (before preprocessing).

`__FUNCTION__`

The name of the function or Objective C method being compiled. (This is a `gcc` extension and might not be available on all compilers, if code portability is important to you.)

Example 4-4. predef.m

```
// predef.m -- show compiler pre-defined macros

/* compile with:
cc -g -Wall -o predef predef.m
*/

#import <Foundation/Foundation.h>
#import <stdio.h>

void someFunc (void)
{
    printf ("file %s, line %d, function %s\n",
            __FILE__, __LINE__, __FUNCTION__);
} // someFunc

@interface SomeClass : NSObject { }
+ (void) someMethod;
@end

@implementation SomeClass
+ (void) someMethod
```

```
{
    printf ("file %s, line %d, function %s\n",
            __FILE__, __LINE__, __FUNCTION__);
} // someMethod
@end

int main (int argc, char *argv[])
{
    printf ("__APPLE__: %d,  __APPLE_CC__: %d\n",
            __APPLE__, __APPLE_CC__);
    printf ("today is %s, the time is %s\n",
            __DATE__, __TIME__);
    printf ("file %s, line %d, function %s\n",
            __FILE__, __LINE__, __FUNCTION__);
    someFunc ();
    [SomeClass someMethod];
    return (0);
} // main
```

Compile it with:

```
% cc -g -Wall -o predef -framework Foundation predef.m
```

The `-framework` flag automatically figures out where to find the headers and libraries you need to link against. Most other Unixes do not have frameworks, which can make compiling and linking against sophisticated libraries (like the Foundation kit) more tedious.

Run it:

```
% ./predef
__APPLE__: 1,  __APPLE_CC__: 1151
today is 10/31/02, the time is 15:25:08
file predef.m, line 26, function main
file predef.m, line 10, function someFunc
file predef.m, line 17, function +[SomeClass someMethod]
```

The `__DATE__` and `__TIME__` macros are useful for date and time stamping a program or module when it is compiled. This can be very helpful when you are going through a debug/test cycle with a bunch of plug-ins and it is easy to get confused as to exactly which development version of the code you are working with. It is also handy when diagnosining customer problems in the field to know exactly which version of the code you are dealing with.

Macro hygiene

One of the problems with the C Preprocessor is that it is pretty stupid. It does not have any idea of the context it is working in so it cannot do what you mean, just what you say. So be careful of how you say things.

For instance, say you have a macro like this:

```
#define SQUARE(x)        x*x
```

Pretty simple. `SQUARE(5)` turns into 5*5 which yields the result desired. If someone uses `SQUARE(2+3)`, it will get fed to the compiler as 2+3*2+3, which due to precedence rules is 2 + (3*2) + 3, which is 11. Not 25. If you parenthesize the arguments instead:

```
#define SQUARE(x)        (x)*(x)
```

`SQUARE(2+3)` will turn into (2+3)*(2+3), the correct result.

Also, it is generally a good idea to surround the whole macro result in parentheses as, such as:

```
#define SQUARE(x)        ((x)*(x))
```

to prevent problems if your macro expands into an expression with operators of higher precedence next to it.

Beware of side effects in macros. The preprocessor is strictly textual substitution. Doing `SQUARE(i++)` will expand to `(i++)*(i++)`, which actually is undefined in the C standard, but it could cause `i` to be incremented twice, which probably is not the intended behavior.

Multiline macros

Sometimes you want a macro to be more than one line of code, such as this one which increases a global error count and then displays an error for the user.

```
#define FOUND_AN_ERROR(desc)    \
    error_count++;    \
    fprintf(stderr, "found an error '%s' at file %s, line %n\n", \
        desc, __FILE__, __LINE__);
```

Ideally this macro can be used like:

```
    if (something_bad_happened) {
        FOUND_AN_ERROR("something really bad happened")
    }
```

For example:

Example 4-5. multilineMacro.m

```
// multilineMacro.m -- multi-line macro hygiene

/* compile with:
cc -g -Wall -i multilineMacro multilineMacro.m
*/

#import <stdio.h>

#define FOUND_AN_ERROR(desc)    \
    error_count++;    \
    fprintf(stderr, "found an error '%s' at file %s, line %d\n", \
        desc, __FILE__, __LINE__);

int error_count;

int main (int argc, char *argv[])
```

```
{
    if (argc == 2) {
        FOUND_AN_ERROR ("something bad happened");
    }
    printf ("done\n");
    return (0);
} // main
```

Compile it:

```
% cc -g -Wall -o multilineMacro multilineMacro.m
```

And run it:

```
% ./multilineMacro
done
```

Now run it with an argument (which is considered to be the error condition):

```
% ./multilineMacro bork
found an error 'something bad happened' at file
    multilineMacro.m, line 13
done
```

Looks like it works fine. There is one lurking problem: what if a programmer on your team that does not fully brace the `if` statement uses the macro? The code itself looks innocent enough.

Remove the braces from your `if`:

```
    if (argc == 2)
        FOUND_AN_ERROR ("something bad happened");
```

Build it and run the program without an argument (which is the "non-error" case)

```
% ./multilineMacro
found an error 'something bad happened' at file
    multilineMacro.m, line 13
done
```

Oops! Correct code is now considered to be in error. Take a look at what is happening. The C preprocessor is mutating your code from

```
if (argc == 2)
    FOUND_AN_ERROR ("something bad happened");
```

to

```
if (argc == 2)
    error_count++;
    fprintf(stderr, "found an error '%s' at file %s, line %d\n",
            "something bad happened", "multilineMacro.m", 13);
```

Or, if indented the way that it is actually being executed:

```
if (argc == 2)
    error_count++;
fprintf(stderr, "found an error '%s' at file %s, line %d\n",
```

```
            "something bad happened", "multilineMacro.m", 13);
```

And that is the problem. You need to wrap these multiline macros in curly braces so that they are essentially one statement. It will then become one statement as far as the compiler is concerned.

Change your macro to read:

```
#define FOUND_AN_ERROR(desc)    \
    do {   \
        error_count++;    \
        fprintf(stderr, "found an error '%s' at file %s, line %d\n", \
                desc, __FILE__, __LINE__); \
    } while (0)
```

and recompile (leaving the unbraced if statement). Run it:

```
% ./multilineMacro
done
```

and it works properly. Double-check the error case (just to make sure that did not get broken in the process of making the fix):

```
% ./multilineMacro bork
found an error 'something bad happened' at file
    multilineMacro.m, line 15
done
```

Note that this is wrapped with a `do { } while (0)` statement, which gets executed once. It also has the nice side-effect of turning the operation into a single statement which makes the unbraced `if` behave as expected. (This is a technique also known as "eating the semicolon.") Just plain braces will not work since you will end up with stray semicolons that will confuse the compiler if you have an `else` clase.

Variable Arguments

Functions that take variable arguments are a flexible and powerful interface. The **printf()** family is such an example. One function, an expressive mini command language, and a variable number of arguments leads to an incredibly powerful tool.

The `stdarg` manpage has all the details on using variable arguments.

First declare a variable of type `va_list`, which is like a pointer to argument values in the call stack. Initialize it with **va_start()**, giving it the name of the last declared function argument. Then call **va_arg()**, giving it the type of data you expect. Each call to **va_arg()** will move an internal pointer the next argument on the call stack. Since you give **va_arg** the type (and hence the size), the system knows how much data to give you, as well as how far to advance its pointers when walking the stack.

Figure 4-1. Memory Layout of Variable Arguments

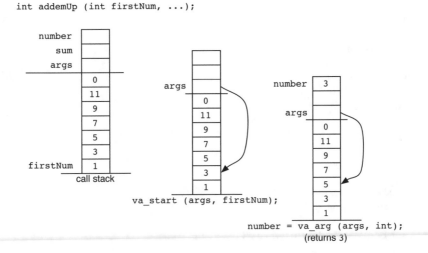

How does **va_arg()** know when to stop? It does not. Your code will need to know when to stop, either by having some kind of pre-supplied format (like **printf()** and friends), or by having some sentinel value (zero or NULL, like with [NSArray arrayWithObjects:]) to signal the end.

va_end cleans up any internal state being used.

Here is a simple program (vararg.m) that provides a function that adds up integers passed to it, using zero as a sentinel value to stop processing:

Example 4-6. vararg.m

```
// vararg.m -- demonstrate variable argument lists

/* compile with:
cc -g -Wall -o vararg vararg.m
*/

#import <stdio.h>     // for printf
#import <stdarg.h>    // varargs stuff

// sum all the integers passed in.  Stopping if it is zero

int addemUp (int firstNum, ...)
{
    va_list args;

    int sum = firstNum;
    int number;

    va_start (args, firstNum);

    while (1) { // just keep spinning until we are done
        number = va_arg (args, int);
```

```
            sum += number;
            if (number == 0) {
                break;
            }
        }

    va_end (args);

    return (sum);

} // addemUp

int main (int argc, char *argv[])
{
    int sumbody;

    sumbody = addemUp (1,2,3,4,5,6,7,8,9,0);
    printf ("sum of 1..9 is %d\n", sumbody);

    sumbody = addemUp (1,3,5,7,9,11,0);
    printf ("sum of odds from 1..11 is %d\n", sumbody);

    return (0);

} // main
```

Build it:

```
% cc -g -Wall -o vararg vararg.m
```

And run it:

```
% ./vararg
sum of 1..9 is 45
sum of odds from 1..11 is 36
```

Another use of variable argument functions is adding value to functions that already take variable arguments. For example, you may want a version of `printf()` that took a debug level and only printed out text if the level is over some globally set value. The technique to use is to write a function to accept the debug level, the format string, the arguments, and then turn around and call `vprintf()`, the varargs-savvy workhorse of `printf()`.

Example 4-7. debuglog.m

```
// deubglog.m -- conditional debug logging

/* compile with:
cc -g -Wall -o debuglog debuglog.m
*/

#import <stdio.h>    // for printf
#import <stdarg.h>   // varargs stuff

int globalLevel = 50;
```

```
void debugLog (int logLevel, const char *format, ...)
{
    if (logLevel > globalLevel) {
        va_list args;
        va_start (args, format);
        vprintf (format, args);
        va_end (args);
    }

} // debugLog

int main (int argc, char *argv[])
{
    debugLog (10, "this will not be seen: %d, %s, %d\n", 10,
              "hello", 23);

    debugLog (87, "this should be seen: %s, %d\n", "bork", 42);

    return (0);

} // main
```

Compile and run it as usual:

```
% cc -g -Wall -o debuglog debuglog.m
% ./debuglog
this should be seen: bork, 42
```

Cocoa programmers can create variable argument functions in Objective-C. It works in exactly the same way. (Be aware you cannot create **NSInvocations** that reference variable argument methods.) Here is describeObjects.m. The **SomeClass** object has a weird little method that takes an arbitrary number of objects (terminated by nil) and prints out their description.

Example 4-8. describeObjects.m

```
// describeObjects -- variable arguments in Objective-C

/* compile with:
cc -g -Wall -o describeObjects \
   -framework Foundation describeObjects.m
*/

#import <Foundation/Foundation.h>

@interface ObjectDescriber : NSObject { }

- (void) describeObjects: (id) firstObject, ...;

@end // ObjectDescriber


@implementation ObjectDescriber

- (void) describeObjects: (id) firstObject, ...
{
```

```
    va_list args;
    id obj = firstObject;

    va_start (args, firstObject);

    while (obj) {
        NSString *string = [obj description];
        NSLog (@"the description is:\n    %@", string);
        // get the next object
        obj = va_arg (args, id);
    }

    va_end (args);

} // describeObjects

@end // ObjectDescriber


int main (int argc, char *argv[])
{
    NSAutoreleasePool *pool = [[NSAutoreleasePool alloc] init];

    ObjectDescriber *describer = [[ObjectDescriber alloc] init];

    NSString *someString = @"someString";
    NSNumber *num = [NSNumber numberWithInt: 23];
    NSDate *date = [NSCalendarDate calendarDate];

    [describer describeObjects:someString, num, date, nil];

    [pool release];

    return (0);

} // main
```

Compile it with this:

```
    % cc -g -Wall -o describeObjects \
-framework Foundation describeObjects.m
    % ./describeObjects
    2003-02-01 21:28:05.200 describeObjects[11890] the description is:
        someString
    2003-02-01 21:28:05.201 describeObjects[11890] the description is:
        23
    2003-02-01 21:28:05.203 describeObjects[11890] the description is:
        2003-02-01 21:28:05 -0500
```

Note that there are also a handful of Cocoa methods that accept va_lists much like
vprintf() did above (like NSString's initWithFormat: arguments, and NSLogv).

Varargs Gotchas

One common mistake is making assumptions on sizes of data that get passed to functions that take varying arguments. For example:

```
size_t mysize = somevalue();
printf ("mysize is %d\n", mysize);
```

This code is making the assumption that `sizeof(size_t) == sizeof(int)`, which could be correct, but also could break in the case if a `size_t` is 8 bytes and an `int` is just 4. The function call here will push 8 bytes of data, but `printf` (having been told to expect an `int`) only pulls off 4 bytes. You will probably crash if there are subsequent arguments: `printf` pulls off the next 4 bytes expecting a character pointer but actually gets the lower 4 bytes of your `size_t` (which is unlikely to be a valid address). The way to fix this is to cast your `size_t` argument to the type specified in the format string. If `size_t` grows in subsequent versions of the OS, you will get a compiler warning about losing precision, which sure beats a crash:

```
size_t mysize = somevalue();
printf ("mysize is %d\n", (int)mysize);
```

For the More Curious: Compiler Optimization

There are two classes of argument flags for controlling optimization, which is how the compiler generates machine code from your C code, as well as how it rewrites your code to behave more optimally. You can use -o with a number or letter to control the optimization level.

-O0

> Means do no optimize.

-O1

> Means do some optimization (also what is used if you use -o without a number).

-O2 and -O3

> Use yet more optimization.

-Os

> Optimize for size. It does the same optimizations as -O2, but does not do function inlining.

Higher optimization levels can make code unstable as more and more mechanical operations happen to it, so be sure to test when changing levels. Sometimes failures that happen at higher levels can actually be indications of memory errors, so if you have the time it may be worthwhile to pursue any failures that happen at higher optimization levels.

If you know of specific optimizations that you want to enable (like strength reduction, or common subexpression evaluation) or disable, you can turn them on or off individually. For example:

`-fstrength-reduce`

> Will enable strength reduction.

`-fno-strength-reduce`

> Will turn off strength reduction, even if the `-O#` setting would have it enabled otherwise.

The `gcc` documentation describes all the available control flags.

Having an optimization level set to `-O1` will issue a warning (when `-Wall` is engaged) if a variable is used before initialization. The compiler needs to do flow analysis to determine if this happens, and that analysis only happens with `-O` levels of 1 or higher.

`gcc` is unique amongst compilers in that it supports both `-g` (debugging) and `-O` (optimization) at the same time. This combination usually is not supported. Although you can use `gdb` on an optimized program, there may be unexpected results because code can be re-ordered and variables may be eliminated. If you are single-stepping through some code in the debugger and your current line is bouncing all over the place, you are most likely dealing with code that has been run through the optimizer.

Apple recommends using `-Os` to optimize for size. It might not produce the best optimization for a specific program, but it gives the best overall system performance since the system working set seems to be a big constraint on performance.

For the More Curious: GCC Extensions

One of the constants of GNU products are large number of features. `gcc` has an incredible number of extensions available. They can help improve your code, but they also destroy portability if you are wanting to target a platform that does not have `gcc` or you are not using `gcc` (if for instance you are using CodeWarrior).

Here are a couple of interesting extensions:

- `long long` and `unsigned long long`: `double` word (e.g. 64 bit) integers, are treated as first class citizens. You can do basic math (+,-,*,/), modular arithmetic, and bitwise operations.

- Complex numbers: in C++ you can create complex numbers as a first class type, but `gcc` C has them built in.

- Variable length automatic arrays: like you can use in C++, declaring the size of a stack-based array at run time:

  ```
  int size = some_function();
  char buffer[size];
  ```

  The array also gets deallocated when the brace level the array was declared in is exited.

- Inline functions (like in C++).

- Macros with variable number of arguments, very handy for wrappers around **printf** and friends.

- Packed structures, which remove any alignment padding the compiler might otherwise include. Add `__attribute((packed_))__` at the end of your structure definition.

A number of these extensions have made their way into `c99` (the most recent version of the ISO C standard), such as variable automatic arrays and complex numbers. Also, Objective-C with the `gcc` compiler lets you declare variables anywhere, just like in C++.

Chapter 5. Libraries

A library is a packaged collection of object files that programs can then link against to make use of the features it provides. Traditional Unix has two kinds of libraries: static libraries where the linker packages the object code into the application, and shared libraries where the linker just stores a reference to a library and the symbols the application needs. Mac OS X brings frameworks to the table also, which package shared libraries with other resources, like header files, documentation, and subframeworks.

Static Libraries

Static libraries are the simplest libraries to work with. Many open source projects that you can download will frequently build static libraries, whether for your programs to link against, or for internal use to simplify the build system where each major module is put into its own static library. All of these libararies are then linked together to make the final executable program. The object code that lives in shared libraries is physically copied into the final executable.

Figure 5-1. Static Libraries

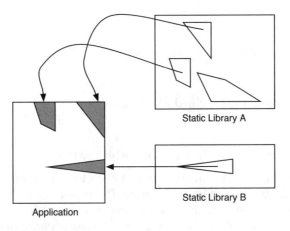

The `ar` program is what is used to create libraries, or in `ar`'s terminology, archives. `ar` can create an archive, add new files to it, and existing files can be extracted, deleted, or replaced. Files are named in the archive by their file name (any files specified with a path just use the file name).

In the materials from the website, you will find five source files that look like this:

Example 5-1. src0.c

```
// src0.c : a simple source file so we can fill a library

/* compile with:
cc -g -Wall -c src0.c
*/

int add_0 (int number)
{
```

```
      return (number + 0);
} // add_0
```

These are little functions that do not actually do anything useful. You can compile them all into object files by this command:

```
% cc -g -c src*.c
```

You can see the source files:

```
% ls *.c
src0.c  src1.c  src2.c  src3.c  src4.c
```

and the associated object files:

```
% ls *.o
src0.o  src1.o  src2.o  src3.o  src4.o
```

And here is a sample creating an archive:

```
% ar crl libaddum.a *.o
```

The flags are:

c

> Create if the archive does not exist.

r

> Replace or add the specified files to the archive.

l

> The next argument is the name of the library file.

After you create or modify an archive, you need to run the `ranlib` command, which builds the table of contents for the archive. The linker needs this table of contents to locate the object files it actually needs to link in. Frequently `ranlib` can be used to "fix" broken libraries. If you get strange linker errors (particularly if you're not using Apple's development tools) when using a static library, run `ranlib` on it and see if it that helps things.

```
% ranlib libaddum.a
```

Figure 5-2. Inside a library

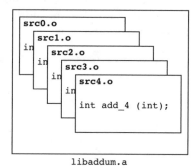

libaddum.a

To actually use a static library in your program, you need to use two compiler flags.
-L tells the linker what directory to look in. -l (lower case Ell) tells the linker what
files to look for. By convention, library file names are of the form libfoo.a, where
foo is some descriptive name for the features the library provides. If you specify
-lfoo, the linker knows to look for libfoo.a.

Here is a program that uses some of the functions from the library:

Example 5-2. useadd.m

```
// useadd.m -- use functions from a library

/* compile with:
cc -g -Wall -o useadd useadd.m -L. -laddum
*/

#import <stdlib.h>      // for EXIT_SUCCESS
#import <stdio.h>       // for printf

int main (int argc, char *argv[])
{
    int i;

    i = 5;
    printf ("i is %d\n", i);

    i = add_1 (i);
    printf ("i after add_1: %d\n", i);

    i = add_4 (i);
    printf ("i after add_4: %d\n", i);

    exit (EXIT_SUCCESS);
} // main
```

If you just try to compile like other programs, you will (understandably) get a
complaint about the missing functions:

```
% cc -g -o useadd useadd.m
/usr/bin/ld: Undefined symbols:
_add_1
```

```
_add_4
```

BSD systems frequently prepend an underscore to symbols during linking. The missing symbol names are actually "add_1" and "add_4" Now add the flags to tell the linker where to look, and what library to use:

```
% cc -g -o useadd useadd.m -L. -laddum
```

A sample run:

```
% ./useadd
i is 5
i after add_1: 6
i after add_4: 10
```

Note that the library stuff is specified after the source file name. If it were the other way around:

```
% cc -g -o useadd -L. -laddum useadd.m
/usr/bin/ld: Undefined symbols:
_add_1
_add_4
```

You still get the errors since the linker scans files left to right. It looks at the library, sees that nobody so far needs those symbols to link, and so discards the file. It then goes on to resolve the symbols for the useadd program itself. Since it already discarded the library, the linker complains about the missing symbols. Depending on the complexity of your libraries (e.g., circular references), you may need to specify a library more than once.

When using libraries provided by other parties, it can be a real hassle figuring out where a symbol lives when you get one of these undefined symbol errors. The nm command can come in handy, since it shows you information about the symbols that live in applications, libraries, and object files.

Compile the program, but generate an object file instead of a program (the -c flag):

```
% cc -g -c  useadd.m
% ls -l useadd.o
-rw-r--r--  1 markd  staff  7532 Aug 25 14:03 useadd.o
```

And now nm it:

```
% nm useadd.o
         U _add_1
         U _add_4
         U _exit
00000000 T _main
         U _printf
         U dyld_stub_binding_helper
```

The U is for "undefined" and the T stands for a defined text section symbol. You can see the two add functions that were used, and **printf**, plus a little housekeeping.

You can nm libraries too:

```
% nm libaddum.a
libaddum.a(src0.o):
```

```
00000000 T _add_0

libaddum.a(src1.o):
00000000 T _add_1

libaddum.a(src2.o):
00000000 T _add_2

libaddum.a(src3.o):
00000000 T _add_3

libaddum.a(src4.o):
00000000 T _add_4
```

Which shows each object file that has been put into the archive, as well as what symbols are present.

Using static libraries in `Project Builder` is really easy. Just drag the `libfoo.a` file into your project. `Project Builder` will automatically link it in.

Shared Libraries

When you use static libraries, the code is linked physically into your executable program. If you have a big library, say 1 megabyte, which is linked into a dozen programs, you will have 12 megabytes of disk space consumed. With today's huge hard drives that is not too big of a deal. You also have the libraries taking up that megabyte of space in each program's memory. This is a much bigger problem. Memory is a scarce shared resource, so having duplicate copies of library code each occupying their own pages in memory can put stress on the memory system and cause paging.

Shared libraries were created to address this problem. Instead of copying the code into the programs, just a reference is included. When the program needs a feature out of a shared library, the linker just includes the name of the symbol and a pointer to the library. When the program is executed, the loader finds the shared libraries, loads them into memory and fixes up the references (resolves the symbols) so that they point to the now-loaded shared library. The shared library code can be loaded into shared pages of memory and shared among many different processes. In the example above, the dozen programs linking to a 1 megabyte shared library will not take up any extra space on disk, plus the library will only appear once in physical RAM and will be shared amongst the dozen processes. Of course, any space for variable data the shared library uses will be duplicated in each process.

Figure 5-3. Shared Libraries

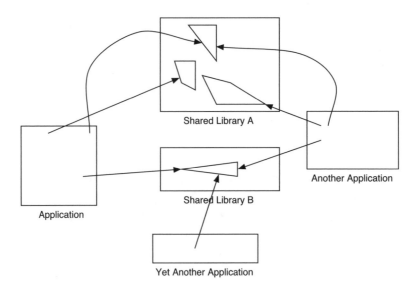

You may have heard the term "two level namespaces" bandied about during the transition from Mac OS X 10.0.x to 10.1.x. All that means is that the name of the library is stored along with the symbol. In the "flat namespace" model just the symbol was stored and the loader would search amongst various libraries for the symbol. That caused problems, for instance, if the `log()` function was defined in a math library and someone else defined a `log()` function to output text to a logfile. The math library function user might get the file logging function instead. The two level namespaces handle this case for you so that the two `log()` can coexist. You can sometimes run into difficulty when building code from other Unix platforms. Adding the flag `-flat_namespace` to the link lines can fix many problems.

To build a shared library, use `ld`, the linker, rather than `ar`. To build the little adder function shared library, use a command like

```
% ld -dynamic -o libaddum.dylib *.o
```

And link it into your program like this:

```
% cc -g -o useadd useadd.m libaddum.dylib
```

As an aside, you can specify a static library like this as well:

```
% cc -g -o useadd useadd.m libaddum.a
```

and you can use the linker search paths with shared libraries:

```
% cc -g -o useadd useadd.m -L. -laddum
```

The linker, when given a choice between a shared library and a static library will choose the shared library.

When you run the program, the loader searches for the shared libraries to load. It looks in a number of default places (like `/usr/lib`), and it also looks at the environment variable LD_LIBRARY_PATH. Any paths specified there (multiple paths can be separated by colons) are searched in order, looking for the library.

By convention on Mac OS X, shared libraries have an extension of .dylib, for Dynamic Library. On most other Unix systems, the extension is .so, for Shared Object, so do not be confused if you go to another system and see lots of .so files lying around.

nm can also be used to see what dynamic libraries an application links against by using -mg flags. In this case, nm is being run against a Cocoa application:

```
% nm -mg BigShow
00000000 (absolute) external .objc_class_name_AppController
         (undefined [lazy bound]) external .objc_class_name_BigElement \
(from BigShowBase)
         (undefined [lazy bound]) external .objc_class_name_NSArray (from \
Cocoa)
         (undefined [lazy bound]) external .objc_class_name_NSBezierPath \
(from Cocoa)
         (undefined [lazy bound]) external .objc_class_name_NSBundle (from \
Cocoa)
         (undefined [lazy bound]) external .objc_class_name_NSColor (from \
Cocoa)
...
         (undefined) external __objcInit (from Cocoa)
         (undefined [lazy bound]) external _abort (from libSystem)
         (undefined [lazy bound]) external _atexit (from libSystem)
         (undefined [lazy bound]) external _calloc (from libSystem)
...
00007008 (__DATA,__data) [referenced dynamically] external _environ
         (undefined) external _errno (from libSystem)
         (undefined [lazy bound]) external _exit (from libSystem)
         (undefined [lazy bound]) external _free (from libSystem)
         (undefined) external _mach_init_routine (from libSystem)
```

Which shows the symbols from Cocoa that are being used (**NSArray, NSBezierPath**, some of the standard C library symbols (**abort(), calloc()**), and some housekeeping calls (_objcInit).

Shared libraries can be loaded on demand after your program has started, and are the standard Unix way for building a plug-in architecture to your program.

If you want to see all the shared libraries a program pulls in, run the program from the command line and set the DYLD_PRINT_LIBRARIES environment variable to 1. You can use this to peek into a program and see how it does some stuff. For instance:

```
% setenv DYLD_PRINT_LIBRARIES 1
% /Applications/iTunes.app/Contents/MacOS/iTunes
loading libraries for image: /Applications/iTunes.app/
Contents/MacOS/iTunes
loading library: /usr/lib/libz.1.1.3.dylib
loading library: /usr/lib/libSystem.B.dylib
loading library: /System/Library/Frameworks/Carbon.framework/
Versions/A/Carbon
loading library: /System/Library/Frameworks/IOKit.framework/
Versions/A/IOKit
...
loading library: /System/Library/QuickTime/\
QuickTimeFirewireDV.component/Contents/MacOS/QuickTimeFirewireDV
loading libraries for image: /System/Library/QuickTime/\
```

```
QuickTimeFirewireDV.component/Contents/MacOS/QuickTimeFirewireDV
loading libraries for image: /System/Library/Extensions/\
IOUSBFamily.kext/Contents/PlugIns/IOUSBLib.bundle/Contents/MacOS/\
IOUSBLib
loading library:/System/Library/Frameworks/\
ApplicationServices.framework/Versions/A/Frameworks/\
CoreGraphics.framework/Resources/libCGATS.A.dylib
```

In all, a total of 136 libraries. It is pretty interesting some of the stuff in there, like Speech Synthesis, a cryptography library, and some of the private frameworks like iPod framework and DesktopServicesPriv.

Frameworks

Shared libraries are nice from a system implementation point of view, but straight shared libraries are a pretty inconvenient way to package and ship a complete product. When you are providing some kind of software library, like database access API, you will want to provide not only the shared library that has the executable code, but also the header files that describe the API provided, the documentation, and any additional resources like images or sounds. With plain old shared libraries (on plain old Unix), you will need to cook up your own packaging format, or use whatever platform specific delivery mechanisms (like RPMs on Red Hat Linux). Even then, the pieces of your product will probably get split up: libraries into `/usr/lib`, header files into `/usr/include`, etc.

Apple came up with the framework idea to address these issues. A framework is a bundle that contains the shared library as well as subdirectories for headers and other resources.

Figure 5-4. A Framework

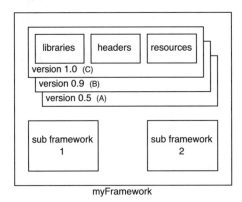

myFramework

Since the framework has a somewhat complex internal structure (including a directory hierarchy for versions and a set of symbolic links to indicate which version is current) which is also being changed by Apple, it is best to just let `Project Builder` do the work.

Building a framework in `Project Builder`:

1. Launch `Project Builder`

2. File > New Project

3. Framework > Cocoa Framework

4. Drag in your source files

5. If you wish, you can remove the Cocoa, Foundation, and AppKit frameworks from the **External Frameworks and Libraries** folder, since you will not need them.

Now make a header file for the adder functions:

Example 5-3. adder.h

```
// adder.h -- header file for the little adder functions we have

int add_0 (int number);
int add_1 (int number);
int add_2 (int number);
int add_3 (int number);
int add_4 (int number);
```

Since it is a public header file, you need to tell `Project Builder` that this header is public so that it will be added to the Headers directory of the framework:

1. Launch `Project Builder`

2. Drag in the header file

3. Targets > Adder > Build Phases > Headers

4. Select `Public`

5. Build.

Figure 5-5. Framework Source Files

Figure 5-6. Exporting the header

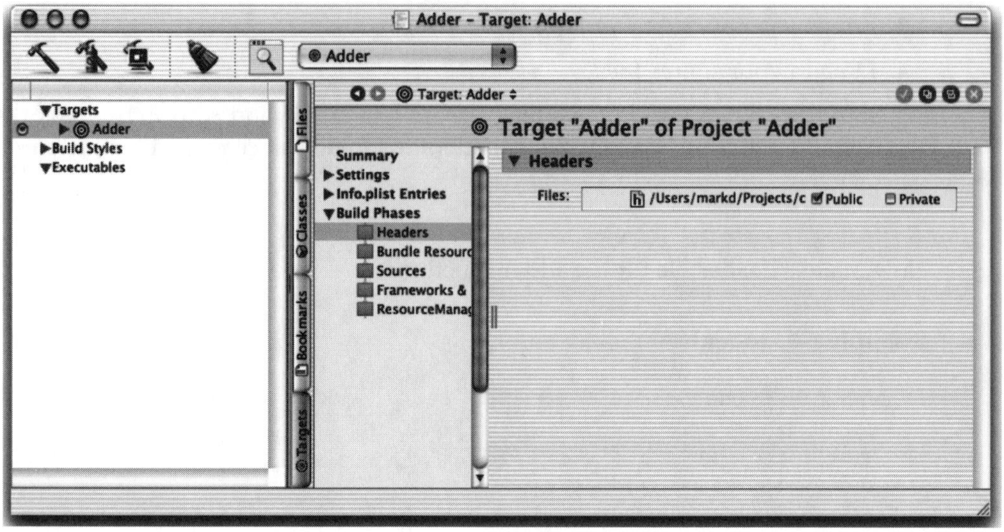

Now to build the `useadd` program:

```
% cc -g -o useadd -F./Adder/build  -framework Adder useadd.m
```

Note the use of `-F` to specify where the linker should search for the framework when linking. It works just like the `-L` flag for static and shared libraries. If you run it now, you will get an error, though:

```
dyld: ./useadd can't open library: /Users/markd/Library/Frameworks/
Adder.framework/Versions/A/Adder (No such file or directory, errno = 2)
```

That is because the `-F` flag only affects compile time behavior (finding the framework so the linker can make sure all the symbols are there). At run time, if the framework is not embedded in the program's bundle, the system looks in these directories in this order:

1. `~/Library/Frameworks`

2. `/Library/Frameworks`

3. `/Network/Library/Frameworks`

4. `/System/Library/Frameworks`

So copy the `Adder.framework` into your `~/Library/Frameworks` (which you may need to manually create), and re-run the program:

```
% ./useadd
i is 5
i after add_1: 6
i after add_4: 10
```

If you turn on `DYLD_PRINT_LIBRARIES`, you can see the program using the new framework:

```
% setenv DYLD_PRINT_LIBRARIES 1
% ./useadd
loading libraries for image: ./useadd
loading library: /Users/markd/Library/Frameworks/Adder.framework/
Versions/A/Adder
loading library: /usr/lib/libSystem.B.dylib
loading libraries for image: /Users/markd/Library/
Frameworks/Adder.framework/Versions/A/Adder
loading libraries for image: /usr/lib/libSystem.B.dylib
loading library: /usr/lib/system/libmathCommon.A.dylib
loading libraries for image: /usr/lib/system/libmathCommon.A.dylib
i is 5
i after add_1: 6
i after add_4: 10
```

You can see the framework being loaded in the beginning.

Framework Versioning

Frameworks include major and minor versioning so that you can update your library and not negatively impact the programs that use the framework. A major version change is one that breaks existing programs that end up usising the newer version, but are linked against an older version. This can happen when an API is removed, a function signature is changed, a method is added to a C++ class, or the size or layout of a class or structure is changed.

A minor version change is one where programs that use newer versions of the library will break when using an older version of the library. This can happen when an API or new structure is added. Older programs can continue to use this newer (minor) version of the library since stuff was only added and nothing removed, but programs that link against this newer version cannot be run against the older library since the new API or structure will not be there.

The inside of a framework is a hierarchy of directories and symbolic links. At the top level is a directory named Versions which contains directories for each of the major versions. Traditionally they're named with letters, like A, B, C, but they can be any name. Inside of the Versions directory is a symbolic link, named Current, which points to the current version (which is usually the newest one, the one wih the highest letter).

Figure 5-7. Inside a framework.

At the top level of the framework are symbolic links to the shared library (without the `.dylib` extension), the `Headers` directory, and the `Resources` directory. These are actually symbolic links to `Current/Headers` and `Current/Resources`. This means that you can just change the `Current` symbolic link to another version and the other symbolic links will automatically point to that other version.

To create a new version directory in `Project Builder`, set the `FRAMEWORK_VERSION` setting of the framework target. When you build the project a new version directory will be added to the framework. This won't update the `Current` symbolic link, though. One thing to watch out for if you end up supporting multiple versions of the framework is to not do a "Clean all;" that will wipe out the older versions, and `Project Builder` will only rebuild the most current version. Or else keep older versions of the framework's guts elsewhere so you can construct the framework for new versions.

Figure 5-8. Setting framework major version

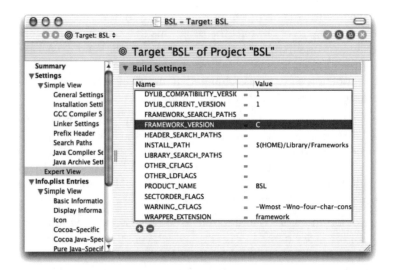

When you link against a framework, the linker will link against the `Current` version. If you want to link against an older version of a framework, you'll need to change the `Current` symbolic link to point to the version you want to link against. At runtime, the loader will choose the correct version of the library. You can see what versions of libraries a program links against by using `otool -Lv`. Here you can see that `iPhoto` links againt the B version of `libSystem`, and uses the A version of the Cocoa frameworks.

```
% otool -Lv /Applications/iPhoto.app/Contents/MacOS/iPhoto
/Applications/iPhoto.app/Contents/MacOS/iPhoto:
    /usr/lib/libSystem.B.dylib
        (compatibility version 1.0.0, current version 55.0.0)
    time stamp 1039863485 Sat Dec 14 05:58:05 2002
    /System/Library/Frameworks/Cocoa.framework/Versions/A/Cocoa
        (compatibility version 1.0.0, current version 7.0.0)
    time stamp 1045684082 Wed Feb 19 14:48:02 2003
    ...
```

For The More Curious

Optimizing the system

You have seen the Apple installers spend an inordinate amount of time "Optimizing your system." What exactly is it doing? It is running the program `update_prebinding` which performs some modifications to shared libraries to make program loading faster.

When a shared library is loaded, the loader picks a place in memory to stick the code. It then calculates the address of all of the symbols exported by the shared library based on the address where it loaded the library (this is also why libraries need to be made out of position indepedent code so that they can be placed at any address). If you have a lot of libraries, or really big libraries, this can take a non-trivial amount of time as the loader chugs through "load at address xyz, calculate address for symbol1, symbol2, symbol3..." for each library.

Prebinding assigns each library a unique address, and when the library is loaded, the system attempts to place the library there. The calculations of symbol addresses can be done just once during the prebinding step and stored in the shared library. Then the loader just has to load the library at the indicated address and the symbols will already have their correct address without any additional work. If there happens to be a conflict (like someone else got loaded at that address), the loader falls back to its default behavior and loads the library at another address and mops up the symbols.

The only thing that gets sped up by this prebinding is application launch times. That is why it is usually OK to interrupt the optimization step, especially if you are doing a lot of individual installs.

Plug-ins

Shared libraries can be loaded on demand after the program has started running. They are the mechanism used to add plug-in features: build a shared library and have the program load it. Generic Unix applications can use the `dyld` functions to load shared libraries and get the addresses of symbols (including function pointers to executable code). Higher-level applications can load bundles at runtime. Cocoa can use the **NSBundle** class, and there are Carbon and Core Foundation bundle loading APIs as well.

Bundles in Cocoa

A bundle is a directory containing some executable code (whether it is a shared library or an executable program) and the various resources that support the code. Cocoa applications are bundles, as are frameworks, screensavers, Interface Builder plug-ins, and a lot of other stuff. Bundles are how Cocoa handles plug-ins that are loaded after the program has launched.

There are two sides to making an application accept plug-ins, namely there is the application doing the loading, and there is the plug-in itself. They both need to agree on some kind of protocol to communicate with each other. There is not any pre-defined protocol for doing this, so you are free to use whatever mechanism you care to. Here is a little foundation tool example that will load plug-ins that return a string, which the main program will print out. Once all the plug-ins have had a chance to print out their stuff, the program exits.

Create three projects in `Project Builder`. First, a `Foundation Tool` called `BundlePrinter`. Then create a `Cocoa Bundle` called `SimpleMessage`, and a `Cocoa Bundle` called `ComplexMessage`.

Add a header file to `BundlePrinter` that looks like this:

Example 5-4. BundlePrinter.h

```
// BundlePrinter.h -- protocol for BundlePrinter plugins to use

@protocol BundlePrinterProtocol

+ (BOOL) activate;
+ (void) deactivate;

- (NSString *) message;

@end
```

A very simple protocol. The class is given an opportunity to do stuff when activated and deactivated (perhaps it needs to create and destroy a big image or load an mp3 file), and then an object method for getting a string message to print.

Add this header file to the two bundle projects. Now go ahead and implement the plug-ins to conform to this protocol. Add a `SimpleMessage.m` file to the `SimpleMessage` project. Also set the `Principal Class` for the project to `SimpleMessage` (go to the Targets pane, select `SimpleMessage` target, select the `Cocoa-Specific` entry under `Info.plist Entries`, and put in `SimpleMessage` for the `Principal Class`).

Here is what `SimpleMessage.m` looks like:

Example 5-5. SimpleMessage.m

```
// SimpleMessage.m -- a simple plug-in that returns a simple,
//                    hard-coded message

#import <Foundation/Foundation.h>
#import "BundlePrinter.h"

@interface SimpleMessage : NSObject <BundlePrinterProtocol>
{
}

@end


@implementation SimpleMessage

+ (BOOL) activate
{
    NSLog (@"SimpleMessage plug-in activated");
    return (YES);
```

```
} // activate

+ (void) deactivate
{
    NSLog (@"SimpleMessage plug-in deactivated");
} // deactivate

- (NSString *) message
{
    return (@"This is a Simple Message");
} // message

@end // SimpleMessage
```

Build it and fix any errors.

Do the same thing for `ComplexMessage` (set the `ComplexMessage` Principal class, and add the `ComplexMessage.m` source file).

Example 5-6. ComplexMessage.m

```
// ComplexMessage -- a plug-in that returns a message
//                   using some stored state

#import <Foundation/Foundation.h>
#import "BundlePrinter.h"
#import <stdlib.h>        // for random number routines
#import <time.h>          // for time() to seed the random generator

@interface ComplexMessage : NSObject <BundlePrinterProtocol>
{
    int randomValue;
}

@end


@implementation ComplexMessage

+ (BOOL) activate
{
    NSLog (@"ComplexMessage plug-in activated");
    return (YES);

} // activate

+ (void) deactivate
{
    NSLog (@"ComplexMessage plug-in deactivated");
} // deactivate

- (id) init
{
    if (self = [super init]) {
        srandom (time(NULL));
        randomValue = random () % 500;
```

```
    }

    return (self);

} // init

- (NSString *) message
{
    return ([NSString stringWithFormat:
                @"Here is a random number: %d", randomValue]);
} // messagee

@end // ComplexMessage
```

This is more complex in that it stores some state at initialization time and uses it later.

Build this and fix any errors.

Now, in the BundlePrinter project, edit main.m so that it looks like this:

Example 5-7. main.m

```
// main.m -- the main BundlePrinter program

#import <Foundation/Foundation.h>
#import "BundlePrinter.h"

NSString *processPlugin (NSString *path)
{
    NSBundle *plugin;
    Class principalClass;
    id pluginInstance;
    NSString *message = nil;

    NSLog (@"processing plug-in: %@", path);

    plugin = [NSBundle bundleWithPath: path];

    if (plugin == nil) {
        NSLog (@"could not load plug-in at path %@", path);
        goto bailout;
    }

    principalClass = [plugin principalClass];

    if (principalClass == nil) {
        NSLog (@"could not load principal class for plug-in at path %@",
                path);
        NSLog (@"make sure the PrincipalClass target setting is correct");
        goto bailout;
    }

    if (![principalClass conformsToProtocol:
            @protocol(BundlePrinterProtocol)]) {
        NSLog (@"plug-in must conform the BundlePrinterProtocol");
    }
```

```
    // tell the plug-in that it's being activated
    if (![principalClass activate]) {
        NSLog (@"could not activate class for plug-in at path %@", path);
        goto bailout;
    }

    // make an instance of the plug-in and ask it for a message
    pluginInstance = [[principalClass alloc] init];

    message = [pluginInstance message];
    [pluginInstance release];


    // ok, we're done with it
    [principalClass deactivate];

 bailout:

    return (message);


} // processPlugin

int main (int argc, const char *argv[])
{
    NSAutoreleasePool *pool = [[NSAutoreleasePool alloc] init];
    NSDirectoryEnumerator *enumerator;
    NSString *path, *message;

    // walk the current directory looking for bundles

    enumerator = [[NSFileManager defaultManager] enumeratorAtPath: @"."];

    while (path = [enumerator nextObject]) {

        if ([[path pathExtension] isEqualToString: @"bundle"]) {
            message = processPlugin (path);

            if (message != nil) { // plugin succeeded
                printf ("\nmessage is: '%s'\n\n", [message cString]);
            }
        }
    }

    [pool release];

    return (0);

} // main
```

main() looks in the directory you invoke the program from searching for entries that end in ".bundle." If it finds one, it attemps to load it and invoke methods on the class it finds there.

Here is a sample run, after copying (or symlinking) the SimpleMessage and ComplexMessage bundles into a directory and run the program. In this case copy them to the BundlePrinter project directory.

```
% build/BundlePrinter
... BundlePrinter[4458] processing plug-in: ComplexMessage.bundle
... BundlePrinter[4458] ComplexMessage plug-in activated
... BundlePrinter[4458] ComplexMessage plug-in deactivated

message is: 'Here is a random number: 198'

... BundlePrinter[4458] processing plug-in: SimpleMessage.bundle
... BundlePrinter[4458] SimpleMessage plug-in loaded
... BundlePrinter[4458] SimpleMessage plug-in unloaded

message is: 'This is a Simple Message'
```

There are a couple of limitations that are glossed over here. One is that you cannot load the same bundle twice. You will get a message from the Objective-C runtime about duplicate classes. The other is you cannot unload an Objective-C bundle. The Objective-C runtime gets its claws into the shared library and refuses to let go.

Bundles With Dylib

If you do not want to use (or cannot use) **NSBundle** for loading plug-ins, you can load a special kind of shared library (also called a bundle, but it is different from the collection of files in a directory meaning) documented in the **NSModule** manpage. (Even though these calls have the NS prefix, they are not part of the Cocoa framework.)

Using shared libraries for plug-ins on Mac OS X is more complicated than most other Unix platforms. The **dlopen()** family of calls is not available (although some groups are working on versions that use the native OS X API).

The various calls to load plug-ins take some flag arguments to tell it how to handle error conditions. It can either print a message to stderr and exit (which is the default), or you can provide some callback functions to try to resolve the problem. Sometimes you can have the call return an error code and use **NSLinkEditError** to get the specifics.

You build a bundle with cc by giving it the -bundle flag:

```
% cc -g -o simplemessage.msg -bundle simplemessage.m
```

(.msg is a suffix just pulled out of the air for this sample.)

Then in the program you wish to load the bundle into, you create an NSObjectFileImage using **NSCreateObjectFileImageFromFile** giving it the path to the shared library. Then **NSLinkModule** to actually have the loader pull in the shared library. **NSLookupSymbolInImage** is used to find the symbol, and then **NSAddressOfSymbol** is used to (finally!) get the address of the symbol.

Here is the same program (printing out messages) but done using shared libraries.

First the plug-ins themselves:

Example 5-8. simplemessage.m

```
// simplemessage.m -- return a malloc'd block of memory to a
//                    simple message
```

```
/* compile with:
cc -g -Wall -o simplemessage.msg -bundle simplemessage.m
*/

#import <string.h>      // for strdup
#import <stdio.h>       // for printf

int BNRMessageActivate (void)
{
    printf ("simple message activate\n");
    return (1);
} // BNRMessageActivate

void BNRMessageDeactivate (void)
{
    printf ("simple message deactivate\n");
} // BNRMessageDeactivate

char *BNRMessageMessage (void)
{
    return (strdup("This is a simple message"));
} // BNRMessageMessage
```

Example 5-9. complexmessage.m

```
// complexmessage.m -- return a malloc'd block of memory
//                     to a complex message

/* compile with:
cc -g -Wall -o complexmessage.msg -bundle complexmessage.m
*/

#import <stdlib.h>      // for random number routines
#import <time.h>        // for time() to seed the random generator
#import <stdio.h>       // for printf
#import <string.h>      // for strdup, and snprintf

static int g_randomValue;

int BNRMessageActivate (void)
{
    printf ("complex message activate\n");

    srandom (time(NULL));
    g_randomValue = random () % 500;

    return (1);

} // BNRMessageActivate

void BNRMessageDeactivate (void)
{
    printf ("complex message deactivate\n");
} // BNRMessageDeactivate

char *BNRMessageMessage (void)
```

```
{
    char buffer[2048];

    snprintf (buffer, 2048, "Here is a random number: %d", g_randomValue);

    return (strdup(buffer));

} // BNRMessageMessage
```

And finally the program to load these plug-ins:

Example 5-10. bundleprinter.m

```
// bundleprinter.m -- dynamically load some plugins and invoke functions
//                    on them

/* compile with:
cc -g -Wall -o bundleprinter bundleprinter.m
*/

#import <mach-o/dyld.h> // for dynamic loading API
#import <sys/types.h>   // for random type definition
#import <sys/dirent.h>  // for struct dirent
#import <dirent.h>      // for opendir and friends
#import <stdlib.h>      // for EXIT_SUCCESS
#import <stdio.h>       // for printf
#import <errno.h>       // for errno/strerror
#import <string.h>      // for strdup

// we need a type to coerce a void pointer to the function pointer we
// need to jump through.  Having a type makes things a bit easier
// to read

typedef int (*BNRMessageActivateFP) (void);
typedef void (*BNRMessageDeactivateFP) (void);
typedef char * (*BNRMessageMessageFP) (void);

// given a module and a symbol, look it up and return the address
// NULL returned if the symbol couldn't be found

void *addressOfSymbol (NSModule *module, const char *symbolName)
{
    NSSymbol    symbol;
    void        *address = NULL;

    symbol = NSLookupSymbolInModule (module, symbolName);

    if (symbol == NULL) {
        fprintf (stderr, "Could not find symbol\n");
        goto bailout;
    }

    address = NSAddressOfSymbol (symbol);

  bailout:
    return (address);
```

```
} // addressOfSymbol

// given a path to a plugin, load it, activate it, get the message,
// deactivate it, and unload it

char *processPlugin (const char *path)
{
    NSObjectFileImage    image;
    NSObjectFileImageReturnCode status;
    NSModule    module = NULL;
    char *message = NULL;

    status = NSCreateObjectFileImageFromFile (path, &image);

    if (status != NSObjectFileImageSuccess) {
        fprintf (stderr, "couldn't load plugin at path %s.  error is %d\n",
                 path, status);
        goto bailout;
    }

        // this will abort the program if an error happens.
        // which we don't want.
        // _OPTION_PRIVATE is necessary so we can use NSLookupSymbolInModule
        // _RETURN_ON_ERROR is so we don't abort the program if a module
        //                  happens to have a problem loading (say undefined
        //                  symbols)

    module = NSLinkModule (image, path,
                           NSLINKMODULE_OPTION_PRIVATE
                           | NSLINKMODULE_OPTION_RETURN_ON_ERROR);

    if (module == NULL) {
        fprintf (stderr, "couldn't load module from plug-in at path %s.",
                 path);
        goto bailout;
    }

        // ok, we have the module loaded.  Look up the symbols and call them
        // if they exist.
    {
        BNRMessageActivateFP activator;
        BNRMessageDeactivateFP deactivator;
        BNRMessageMessageFP messagator;

        activator = addressOfSymbol (module, "_BNRMessageActivate");
        if (activator != NULL) {
            int result = (activator)();
            if (!result) { // the module didn't consider itself loaded
                goto bailout;
            }
        }

        messagator = addressOfSymbol (module, "_BNRMessageMessage");
        if (messagator != NULL) {
            message = (messagator)();
        }
```

```
            deactivator = addressOfSymbol (module, "_BNRMessageDeactivate");
            if (deactivator != NULL) {
                (deactivator)();
            }
        }

    bailout:

        // clean up no matter what
        if (module != NULL) {
            (void) NSUnLinkModule (module, 0);
        }

        // couldn't find a cleanup counterpart to
        // NSCreateObjectFileImageFromFile

        return (message);

    } // processPlugin

    int main (int argc, char *argv[])
    {
        DIR *directory;
        struct dirent *entry;

        // walk through the current directory

        directory = opendir (".");

        if (directory == NULL) {
            fprintf (stderr,
                    "could not open current directory to look for plugins\n");
            fprintf (stderr, "error: %d (%s)\n", errno, strerror(errno));
            exit (EXIT_FAILURE);
        }

        while ( (entry = readdir(directory)) != NULL) {

            // if this is a file of type .msg (an extension made up for this
            // sample), process it like a plug-in

            if (strstr(entry->d_name, ".msg") != NULL) {
                char *message;
                message = processPlugin (entry->d_name);

                printf ("\nmessage is: '%s'\n\n", message);
                if (message != NULL) {
                    free (message);
                }
            }
        }

        closedir (directory);

        return (EXIT_SUCCESS);

    } // main
```

Challenge

Take the Cocoa plug-in example and include it in a GUI program, putting the plug-in name and the message into an `NSTableView`.

Chapter 6. Command Line Programs

Much of the power that Unix brings to the user is in the command line tools, where the user can set up pipelines of independent programs that manipulate data. It is time to take a peek under the hood of a typical command line tool and see how it works, as many of the concepts (handling arguments, checking the environment, handling command line flags) have application to any Unix program. Here you are going to write a program that filters its input by changing any letters it finds to upper or lower case.

Figure 6-1. The Standard File Streams

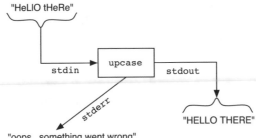

The Basic Program

When you `#import` the `stdio.h` header file, it defines some global symbols that represent the three file streams: `stdin`, `stdout`, and `stderr` (which represent standard In, standard Out, and standard Error).

Use your favorite text editor (`vi`, `emacs`, `TextEdit.app`, `Project Builder`, `BBEdit`) and create a file called `upcase.m`.

First the preliminaries. Import the header files. You will always need some kind of header files:

```
#import <Foundation/Foundation.h>    // for BOOL
#import <stdlib.h>                    // for EXIT_FAILURE/SUCCESS
#import <stdio.h>                     // for standard I/O stuff
```

`Foundation.h` is the Cocoa Foundation Kit which makes available a lot of nice features. For now you are just going to be using the BOOL type.

`stdlib.h` brings in a whole bunch of stuff, in particular the `EXIT_FAILURE` / `EXIT_SUCCESS` macros.

`stdio.h` provides the declarations for the Standard Input/Output types and functions.

Next you need a function to change the case of all the characters in a buffer:

```
void changecaseBuffer (char buffer[], size_t length, BOOL upcase)
{
    char *scan, *stop;

    scan = buffer;
```

```
        stop = buffer + length;

    while (scan < stop) {
        if (upcase) {
            *scan = toupper (*scan);
        } else {
            *scan = tolower (*scan);
        }
        scan++;
    }

} // changecaseBuffer
```

changecaseBuffer() scans over every byte in the buffer and uses the standard C library **toupper()** or **tolower()** functions on each one, and changes a character's case appropriately if it is a letter and leaves it alone if not.

Picking a number out of the air, say 2K, define a buffer size symbolic constant.

```
#define BUFFER_SIZE 2048
```

Finally your main function (which is where program control flow starts when the program is run) reads and processes the input:

```
int main (int argc, char *argv[])
{
    char buffer[BUFFER_SIZE];
    size_t length;
    BOOL upcase = YES;

    while (!feof(stdin)) {
        length = fread (buffer, 1, BUFFER_SIZE, stdin);
        changecaseBuffer (buffer, length, upcase);
        fwrite (buffer, 1, length, stdout);
    }
    return (0);
} // main
```

For now, let us compile this on the command line with:

```
% cc -o upcase upcase.m
```

and run it. (The command is saying to run the c compiler on upcase.m, and generate an executable program with the name upcase. If you did not include the **-o upcase**, the compiler would use the name a.out by default. Not very intuitive.) Invoke your new program with **./upcase**, type some stuff, a return, and press control-D (which is the end of file key sequence). So,

```
%./upcase
HooVeR Ni BOrK
HOOVER NI BORK
^D
```

This program also works in simple pipelines:

```
% echo "HooVeR" | ./upcase
HOOVER
```

It works for more complex pipelines as well:

```
% cat /usr/share/dict/words | ./upcase | grep LENS
ANTILENS
CAMALDOLENSIAN
DECLENSION
...
(and about 18 more LENS-like words).
```

Inside the Central Loop

Take a look at the central loop there:

```
while (!feof(stdin)) {
```

Loop over the body of the `while` loop until you reach the EOF (end of file) for the standard in stream. The end of file happens when you explicitly enter that control-D if you are typing text into the program. When in a pipeline, the standard in stream will be closed when the program ahead exits or decides to close the outgoing pipe on its end.

```
length = fread (buffer, 1, BUFFER_SIZE, stdin);
```

Read in no more than `BUFFER_SIZE` bytes. The arguments look pretty obvious (where to put the data read, how much to read, and where to read it from). What is that "1" hanging around there? This particular family of functions can read uniformly sized blocks of data from a file. (A technique known as record-oriented storage). Say you had a file that had a bunch of 50 byte records that stored people's names, shoe sizes, and blood types. If you wanted to read in a dozen of these records at once, you would have a call like

```
length = fread (buffer, 50, 12, stdin);
```

The system would read 50 * 12 = 600 bytes, and `length` would be 12, signifying the number of records read. The interesting information for the character-case mangling example is the number of bytes read (assuming one byte per character. A pretty safe assumption when dealing with "classic" Unix), you are saying to read `BUFFER_SIZE` records of one byte each, e.g., a maximum of 2048 bytes. If you reversed the order of the arguments, as `BUFFER_SIZE`, 1, that would tell the system to read one record of 2048 bytes. If there were only a dozen bytes available to read, the length would be returned as zero (since there is not enough data for one 2048 byte record) and the code would not do any processing.

```
changecaseBuffer (buffer, length, upcase);
```

Call **changecaseBuffer** to process the buffer. Note that the length is passed as an argument. **fread** will not append a trailing zero (hex `0x00`) terminating character to the string, so the receiving function will not know where to stop processing unless you tell it where to stop.

Finally, write to the standard out pipe:

```
fwrite (buffer, 1, length, stdout);
```

Using the same idea of "writing length records of 1 byte each."

Changing by Name

Now it is time to let the user change the program behavior. One way is to look at the name of the program. There is a Linux utility called BusyBox that implements many of the standard Unix command line programs in one small executable, changing its behavior based on the name. On your system you probably have a /usr/bin/ranlib which is a symbolic link to the libtool program. In this case libtool will work like ranlib when called that.

Here you will choose your behavior if we are run as "upcase" or "downcase". To do this, you need to look at the argv array that gets passed to **main**. argv is the typical contraction of the phrase "argument vector". You could call that parameter anything you wanted to, but typically it will just be argv.

The argv array has all of the command line arguments passed to the program. The shell breaks up the command the user typed in, usually at white space characters (but that can be overridden with quotes). One handy thing is that the program invocation is in the first element of the array, at argv. Note that this is the command as entered by the user. If the program was run with **./upcase**, argv[0] would be "./upcase." If the program was started with **/Users/bork/projects/book/chapter2/upcase**, that is what argv[0] would be. So you cannot really depend on a specific string there. Luckily there is a little convenience function called **fnmatch** that does shell-style filename matching. If the string in argv matches "*upcase" or "*downcase," that will be sufficient to tell the difference.

Example 6-1. upcase.m

```
// upcase.m -- convert text to upper case

/* compile with
cc -g -Wall -o upcase upcase.m
*/
#import <Foundation/Foundation.h>      // for BOOL
#import <stdlib.h>                     // for EXIT_FAILURE
#import <stdio.h>                      // for standard I/O stuff
#import <fnmatch.h>                    // for fnmatch()

#define BUFFER_SIZE 2048

// changecaseBuffer is unchanged

int main (int argc, char *argv[])
{
    char buffer[BUFFER_SIZE];
    size_t length;
    BOOL upcase = YES;

    if (fnmatch ("*upcase", argv[0], 0) == 0) {
        printf ("upcase!\n");
        upcase = YES;
    }
    if (fnmatch ("*downcase", argv[0], 0) == 0) {
        printf ("downcase!\n");
        upcase = NO;
    }
```

```
    while (!feof(stdin)) {
        length = fread (buffer, 1, BUFFER_SIZE, stdin);
        changecaseBuffer (buffer, length, upcase);
        fwrite (buffer, 1, length, stdout);
    }

    return (EXIT_SUCCESS);

} // main
```

Compile your program like before with:

```
% cc -g -Wall -o upcase upcase.m
```

Here is a sample run:

```
% echo "bLaRg" | ./upcase
upcase!
BLARG
```

Now make a symbolic link that points to upcase:

```
% ln -s upcase downcase
```

and run the program like this:

```
% echo "bLaRg" | ./downcase
downcase!
blarg
```

Looking at the Environment

Another way to influence program behavior is through environment variables, which are key/value pairs that are under user control via the shell. The **getenv()** function is used to read the variables the user has set (directly or indirectly) in the environment from which your program has been run.

Figure 6-2. Environment Variables

SHELL	/bin/tcsh
HOME	/Users/markd
USER	markd
LANG	en_US
MACHTPE	powerpc
HOST	ilamp.local.

getenv ("HOME"); ⟶ "/Users/markd"

You give **getenv()** the name of the environment variable you want. If the variable does not exist in the environment you get NULL back. If it does exist you will get a string back with the value. Memory issues like ownership of returned values will be covered in Chapter 7 (Memory). Here, the system owns the memory so you do not need to free it.

To control your case conversion program, you will use the CASE_CONV variable. The value of LOWER will have it massage strings to lower case, and UPPER to massage it to upper case (and if it is not set, it will default to upper case).

You will want to remove the

```
#import <fnmatch.h>
```

The declarations for **getenv()** and family live in stdlib.h, which you already have included.

Also remove the two if blocks that use **fnmatch()** and replace them with:

```
char *envSetting;

envSetting = getenv ("CASE_CONV");

if (envSetting != NULL) {
    if (strcmp(envSetting, "UPPER") == 0) {
        printf ("upper!\n");
        upcase = YES;
    }
    if (strcmp(envSetting, "LOWER") == 0) {
        printf ("lower!\n");
        upcase = NO;
    }
}
```

Recompile it with:

```
% cc -o upcase upcase.m
```

and give it a whirl:

```
% setenv CASE_CONV LOWER
% ./upcase
lower!
GrEEblE
greeble
```

And verify that it works:

```
% setenv CASE_CONV UPPER
% ./upcase
upper!
GrEEblE
GREEBLE
```

Parsing the Command Line

The last way to influence program behavior (outside of reading some configuration files yourself) is by reading command line arguments. This is actually the most common way to do it as well.

Recall earlier that the "choose behavior based on program name" version of your upcase program looked at the first element of argv to get the program name. The `argv` array also has all of the program's arguments in addition to the name used to start the program.

Here is a quick little program that prints out command line arguments:

Example 6-2. dumpargs.m

```
// dumpargs.m -- show program arguments

/* compile with:
cc -g -Wall -o dumpargs dumpargs.m
*/

#include <stdio.h>
#include <stdlib.h>

int main (int argc, char *argv[])
{
    int i;

    for (i = 0; i < argc; i++) {
        printf ("%d: %s\n", i, argv[i]);
    }

    return (EXIT_SUCCESS);

} // main
```

Now feed this program various arguments:

```
% ./dumpargs
0: ./dumpargs
```

As expected, the name of the program lives in the 0th element of the `argv` array.

```
% ./dumpargs -oop -ack -blarg
0: ./dumpargs
1: -oop
2: -ack
3: -blarg
```

You can also see the effect of shell file name globbing, and of quotation marks.

```
% ./dumpargs "dump*" dump*
0: ./dumpargs
1: dump*
2: dumpargs
3: dumpargs.m
```

The first argument, since it is in quotes is given to you explicitly as "`dump*`." The second `dump*` was intercepted by the shell and expanded to be all of the files that start up with `dump` (in this case just the name of the program and the name of the `.m` file).

Now back to `upcase.m`. Use the `-u` flag for uppercase and `-l` (ell) for lowercase.

Remove the code you added for handling the environment variables and add this:

```
    if (argc >= 2) {
        if (strcmp(argv[1], "-u") == 0) {
            printf ("upper!\n");
            upcase = YES;
        }
        if (strcmp(argv[1], "-l") == 0) {
            printf ("lower!\n");
            upcase = NO;
        }
    }
```

Recompile and try it out:

```
% ./upcase -u
upper!
GrEEbLe
GREEBLE

% ./upcase -l
lower!
GrEEbLe
greeble
```

One thing some experienced programmers will notice is the distinct lack of error checking going on. Much of the work of programming Unix is catching and handling errors, whether they are user errors (typing invalid or conflicting command arguments) or system errors (a disk fills up). You may have noticed the return (EXIT_SUCCESS); at the end of each of the **main()** functions. EXIT_SUCCESS is a macro that expands to zero, which when returned, tells the shell that the command succeeded. Any non-zero return value tells the shell that the command failed. The shell uses this return value to decide whether to continue with the work it is doing (whether running a shell script or just a command pipeline). For upcase, you should do a little checking of arguments, such as whether the user entered entered too many, or entered one that is invalid.

EXIT_FAILURE (a macro that expands to the value one) is a handy constant; return it to signal the shell that something went wrong. Here is upcase with some error checking (replace the argv code you entered above with this):

```
    if (argc > 2) {
        fprintf (stderr, "bad argument count.  Must be zero or one\n");
        return (EXIT_FAILURE);

    } else if (argc == 2) {
        BOOL found = NO;

        if (strcmp(argv[1], "-u") == 0) {
            upcase = YES;
            found = YES;
        }
        if (strcmp(argv[1], "-l") == 0) {
            upcase = NO;
            found = YES;
        }
        if (!found) {
            fprintf (stderr, "bad command line argument: '%s'\n",
                    argv[1]);
```

```
            fprintf (stderr, "expecting -u or -l\n");
            return (EXIT_FAILURE);
        }
    }
```

Any time you discover something is wrong, print out a complaint message (to the standard error stream, where errors belong) and bail out with an error code.

In real life programs there is usually some cleanup work that would need to be done, like closing files or freeing memory.

> Personally, I like keeping all of my cleanup code in one place, right before the function ends. I also like to keep a single exit from any function. That means there's a single place to put cleanup code. Therefore I use the venerable and much maligned `goto` statement. If something goes wrong, jump to the bailout point and clean up any messes made, then return.

For example in pseudo-code:

```
{
    my_result = failure;
    blah = allocate_some_memory ();
    if (do_something(blah) == failure) {
        goto bailout;
    }
    ack = open_a_file ();
    if (process_file (blah, ack) == failure) {
        goto bailout;
    }
    hoover = do_something_else ();
    if (have_fun (blah, hoover) == failure) {
        goto bailout;
    }
    // we survived! yay
    my_result = success;

  bailout:
    if (blah) {
        free_the_memory (blah);
    }
    if (ack) {
        close_the_file (ack);
    }
    if (hoover) {
        clean_this_up (hoover);
    }
    return (my_result);
}
```

If you are using C++ you can use exception handling (which is really just a fancy `goto`) and stack-based cleanup objects to simplify cleanup, but in C you have to either have a bunch of nested `if`s or use `goto`.

Here is my final **main()** with error checking of the command line arguments and a single exit point:

```
int main (int argc, char *argv[])
```

```
{
    char buffer[BUFFER_SIZE];
    size_t length;
    BOOL upcase = YES;
    int exitReturn = EXIT_FAILURE;

    if (argc > 2) {
        fprintf (stderr, "bad argument count.  Must be zero or one\n");
        goto bailout;

    } else if (argc == 2) {
        BOOL found = NO;

        if (strcmp(argv[1], "-u") == 0) {
            upcase = YES;
            found = YES;
        }
        if (strcmp(argv[1], "-l") == 0) {
            upcase = NO;
            found = YES;
        }
        if (!found) {
            fprintf (stderr, "bad command line argument: '%s'\n", argv[1]);
            fprintf (stderr, "expecting -u or -l\n");
            goto bailout;
        }
    }

    while (!feof(stdin)) {
        length = fread (buffer, 1, BUFFER_SIZE, stdin);
        changecaseBuffer (buffer, length, upcase);
        fwrite (buffer, 1, length, stdout);
    }

    exitReturn = EXIT_SUCCESS;

 bailout:
    return (exitReturn);

} // main
```

For the More Curious: getopt()

Parsing command line options can be tedious, messy code. Let us say you have a program that takes these command line arguments:

```
% ./myprog
  -f               : run in a fast mode
  -k               : kill other processes with our name
  -t file-name     : twiddle the file named file-name
  -u file-name     : uppercase the file name file-name
  -V               : print out version stuff and exit
```

and then an arbitrary number of additional arguments (file names) to do some other stuff to.

You would have to scan through all of arguments, see if they match the ones you accept, double-check to make sure that -t and -u have a following argument, and complain otherwise. It would also be nice to support the user entering `-fkt oopack` as well as `-f -k -t oopack`.

The `getopt()` function walks through `argv` for you and returns a character for each argument, as well as sets some global variables that contain information on what it has found.

`getopt()` takes a string that describes what arguments you want. If a command line argument takes an additional parameter (like the -u file-name above), put in a colon. So, for this contrived example, you would use the string `"fkt:u:V"`. Order of arguments in the string does not matter. `getopt()` also takes `argc` and `argv`:

```
int getopt (int argc, char * const *argv, const char *optstring);
```

The global `char *optarg` points to the option argument. For instance, upon seeing -u, `optarg` would point to the file name. If `getopt` sees an argument it does not understand, it returns "?". When `getopt` runs out of command line arguments (that is, it finds a "--" argument, or one that does not start with a leading dash), the `optind` global variable has the count of the number of `argv` entries it has looked at. That value can then be used to adjust `argc` and `argv` so that you know what additional arguments there are.

Here is a little program that parses the arguments that you see above. (The code for setting of flags and processing of files has been omitted.)

```
int main (int argc, char *argv[])
{
    int ch;

    while ( (ch = getopt(argc, argv, "fkt:u:V")) != -1) {
        switch (ch) {
          case 'f':
            printf ("found an 'f' flag\n");
            break;
          case 'k':
            printf ("found a 'k' flag\n");
            break;
          case 't':
            printf ("found a 't' flag, and the argument is %s\n",
                    optarg);
            break;
          case 'u':
            printf ("found a 'u' flag, and the argument is %s\n",
                    optarg);
            break;
          case 'V':
            printf ("found a 'V' flag");
            break;
          case '?':
          default:
            printf ("d'oh!  use these flags: f, k, t (file),
                    u(file), V\n");
            return (EXIT_FAILURE);
        }
    }
```

```
    // bias the argv/argc to skip over the processed args
    argc -= optind;
    argv += optind;

    {
        int i;
        for (i = 0; i < argc; i++) {
            printf ("found file argument: %s\n", argv[i]);
        }
    }

    return (EXIT_SUCCESS);

} // main
```

Chapter 7. Memory

Introduction

Many of the Mac OS X marketing buzzwords revolve around the memory management practices of the OS. It employs terms such as "protected memory" and "virtual memory," plus the ability for programs to crash and die in horrible ways and not affect other running programs. Mac OS X typically makes better use of available memory than previous Mac OS versions due to these features.

Virtual Memory

Virtual memory is a way for the computer to fake having more memory than it actually has. For instance, a computer might have 128 megabytes of RAM, but programs can be written that manipulate data several times that amount. The extra memory in question is saved out to disk when not needed, and read back in when the program needs it.

The operating system handles the grungy details of keeping data that is currently being worked on physically in memory, and keeping data that has not been touched in a while saved to the disk, as well as doing the work to bring data from disk and into memory so the program can work on it.

At a fundamental level, the operating system deals with pages, which are 4k chunks of memory that the operating system addresses. As programs request memory, they are given pages. As pages are used, they are kept on a list of recently used pages. As programs request more and more memory from the system, the least recently used pages are written to disk (termed "paging" or "swapping") and the chunk of physical memory is reused.

Pages can be written out and then read back in at different physical addresses. For instance, a 4k page starting at address 0x5000 might be paged out and given to another program. The program that needs the data that was at 0x5000 now needs it again, so the OS reads the page from disk. The chunk of memory at 0x5000 is now in use by the second program. Oops. To fix this, virtual addresses are used. Virtual addresses are the memory addresses a program sees, and each program has its own address space. The virtual address gets mapped by the OS (and hardware in the CPU) to the physical address of a chunk of a page of RAM. In this little example, program A and program B each have a page of data at 0x5000. In physical memory, A's might live at address 0x15020 and B's might live at address 0x3150, but the address translation lets each program live with the fantasy of having their data at address 0x5000.

Figure 7-1. Virtual Memory

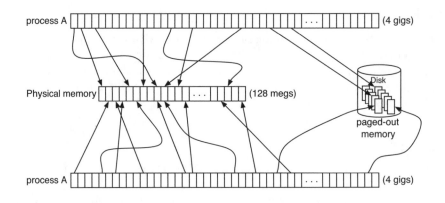

The total amount of memory that a program has allocated to it at a particular time is called its *virtual set*. The amount of memory that is actually located in RAM is called a process' *resident set*. The difference between the virtual set and the resident set is stored out on disk in a swap file (or a dedicated swap partition). "Swap" derives its name from the pages that are swapped for each other when paging happens. You can also lock (a.k.a. "wire") memory down so it does not get swapped out.

Pages can have permissions, such as read-only, read/write, and executable. That helps keep you from scribbling over your own code, as well as helps prevent some exploits that try to execute code from a page that is not marked executable.

Differences From Classic Mac OS Memory Management

The classic Mac memory model presents RAM as one very large (single) address space that is shared between the OS and all the programs that are running. It has a form of virtual memory that uses disk space in addition to physical RAM for all the programs to share (and has the same kinds of virtual address translation working behind the scenes).

Figure 7-2. Classic Mac Memory Map

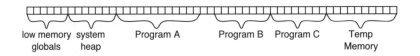

Where classic Mac OS and Mac OS X differ is that the OS and each program live in their own address space. Now, instead of every program sharing the same 32-bit address space (4 gigs), each program now has its *own* 32-bit address space, independent of all the other programs running on the system.

This opens new possibilities with each program having its own 4 gigabytes of independent addressable space. (Well, minus a gigabyte or so of the address space that belongs to the operating system.) You can map files into memory and treat them like any other piece of memory (memory mapped files are discussed in Chapter 10 (Files)). You can also have large but sparse allocations of memory.

(Allocate a a gig of memory but only use a couple of megabytes. Handy for dealing with very large sparse matrices.)

Each program having its own address space also adds a layer of security that does not exist in the classic Mac OS memory model. One program cannot see the memory of another program except under very controlled circumstances, such as with superuser privileges, or through explicit cooperative sharing via shared memory. It becomes impossible for program A to have a pointer error and scribble bad data into program B's memory range. (This is what is known as "protected memory.")

Separate address spaces also removes the need for the user to manually configure memory partitions. The OS, rather than the user, optimizes the amount of physical memory allocated to a particular program based on actual usage, and the user does not have the headache of changing partition sizes or having to quit existing programs to free up enough memory to run a new one.

Some of the curiosities of Mac memory management (hold-overs from the Mac 128K days) such as Handles (pointers to pointers such that the memory ultimately being pointed to can be moved around and free space compacted), the System Heap, and temporary memory are no longer necessary (and in fact are not used in pure Unix programming) because there is no real need to move memory around. Just allocate it and let virtual addressing and paging handle the details.

Program Memory Model

The memory model of individual programs are similar in Classic Mac OS and OS X. There is space for the executable code, a stack, and a heap, although the heaps differ somewhat in the two worlds. Here are the different chunks of memory consumed in a typical program:

Figure 7-3. Unix Program Memory Model

The "Text" Segment

> This is the executable program code. At program launch time the code is mapped into memory from the executable as read-only pages (so no self-modifying code unless you jump through some hoops). Since these pages are read-only they can be easily shared among multiple programs so the pages only have to appear in memory once and can still be shared among multiple users. This is especially handy for shared libraries that are loaded into each program. Since the data is read-only, some Unix operating systems will swap directly from the program's executable file, saving a little space in the swapfile.

Initialized Data Segment

> These are initialized global and static variables. e.g. things like `float pi = 3.1415` outside of any functions, or `static int blah = 25` inside of a function. The initialized data is stored in the data segment itself, which is just copied into memory into a read/write page which the program can then

modify (and this segment is very fast to load and initialize all of the globals. No real explicit initialization happens, just bulk data loads.)

Uninitialized Data Segment

This is all the stuff that lives in global space but is not given an explicit initializer, like `int bork` or `char buffer[5000]` that all gets cleared out to zero on program launch. These are not treated like the initialized data segment (which would mean lots of zero blocks in the executable, and is wasteful of disk space). Just the size of this data segment is stored. On program load, the OS allocates that amount of space and zero-fills it.

This is also referred to as the "bss" segment in man pages and the historical literature. "bss" comes from an assembler instruction that means "block started by symbol."

Heap

The Unix heap is similar to the Classic Mac construct of the same name. It is the area where dynamic (run-time) allocations happen. If you ask for 40K, that 40K will come from the heap. The Unix heap differs from the classic Mac heap is that the Unix heap is just a big arena of memory. There is not any visible auxiliary overhead such as master pointers or handles.

The Program Stack

This is the program call stack. Local (automatic) variables are stored here, as are the stack frames for each function call. When a function calls another function, the processor registers and other assorted bookkeeping need to be stored before the new function is called, and they need to be restored when the new function exits. To support recursion (and an arbitrary depth of function calls) a stack is used.

Memory "allocation" using the program stack is very fast. Internally a pointer is used to indicate where the end of the stack is. Reserving space on the stack is just adding a value to this stack pointer, whether it be five bytes or five thousand. You do not want to store *too* much stuff on the stack (big buffers and whatnot) since some systems have a limit on how big the stack can be. Also when you get into threaded programming, stack space is frequently very limited since each thread has its own chunk of memory to use for a stack. This is discussed in Chapter 22 (Threads).

Since Mac OS X supports Objective-C, there is an additional segment for Objective-C bookkeeping.

The `size` command will show the size of numerous segments of programs. Here is one without any Objective-C stuff:

```
% size /bin/ls
__TEXT        __DATA   __OBJC   others   dec      hex
20480         4096     0        6680     31256    7a18
```

Here is one with Objective-C stuff:

```
% size /Applications/Mail.app/Contents/MacOS/Mail
__TEXT   __DATA   __OBJC   others   dec      hex
671744   24576    57344    37412    791076   c1224
```

(Note that to do a `size` of a Cocoa program, you need to give `size` the actual executable program, not the `*.app` bundle.)

And finally, here is a little program that has 8K of initialized data, and a meg of uninitialized data:

Example 7-1. dataseg.m

```
// dataseg.m -- show size of data segments

/* compile with:
cc -g -Wall -o dataseg dataseg.m
*/

#import <stdio.h>

// about 8K doubles. lives in the initialized data segment.
double x[] = {
    0.0, 1.0, 2.0, 3.0, 4.0, 5.0, 6.0, 7.0, 8.0, 9.0,
    10.0, 11.0, 12.0, 13.0, 14.0, 15.0, 16.0, 17.0, 18.0, 19.0,
    ...
    1010.0, 1011.0, 1012.0, 1013.0, 1014.0, 1015.0,
    1016.0, 1017.0, 1018.0, 1019.0
};

// one meg, all zeros.  Lives in the uninitailzed data segment
char buffer[1048576];

int main (int argc, char *argv[])
{
    printf ("hi!\n");
    return (0);
} // main
```

Running `size` on this program yields:

```
% size dataseg
__TEXT __DATA __OBJC others dec     hex
4096 1060864 0 12288 1077248 107000
```

Here `size` combines the size of initialized and uninitialized data. Note that 1060864 (the data segment size) minus 1048576 (the zero-filled uninitialized data) is 12288, which is 8192 (the 8K of double data) plus 4096 (4K of overhead and bookkeeping).

Note finally that the application size is small:

```
% ls -l dataseg
-rwxr-xr-x  1 markd  staff  17772 Jul 24 22:35 dataseg*
```

`size -m` (which shows some extra stuff from the Mach-O segments) will show some additional details:

```
% size -m dataseg
Segment __PAGEZERO: 4096
Segment __TEXT: 4096
 Section __text: 1084
 Section __picsymbol_stub: 432
 Section __symbol_stub: 0
```

```
    Section __cstring: 164
    total 1680
  Segment __DATA: 1060864
   Section __data: 8192
   Section __la_symbol_ptr: 48
   Section __nl_symbol_ptr: 16
   Section __dyld: 28
   Section __common: 1048640
   total 1056924
  Segment __LINKEDIT: 8192
  total 1077248
```

Memory Lifetime

There are some nuances regarding lifetime of variables and memory in some of the different memory areas of a running Unix process.

Initialized and uninitailzed data segment variables are around during the entire run time of the program. They will not go away. Memory on the heap is explicitly asked for and is explicitly released. Memory here can be deallocated, but it is under program control. Memory on the stack goes away (meaning that it can be reused by someone else) as soon as it goes out of scope (even before a function exits). The stack memory behavior causes errors for some programmers who assume that some memory will be valid longer than it is. A classic error is something like:

```c
char *borkulize (void)
{
    char buffer[5000];

    // work on buffer

    return (buffer);

}
```

buffer is allocated on the stack. Once buffer goes out of scope, that memory becomes available for other functions. Anyone working with the return result of **borkulize()** is taking a chance that someone will clobber the values (potentially much later in time after this function exits).

Dynamic Memory Allocation

Dynamic memory allocation concerns memory that comes from the heap. The heap of the program starts off at an OS-defined default amount of space available for program consumption. As you allocate memory from the heap, it fills up. When it does, your program is given more memory from the OS until the system either runs out of memory or reaches a (configurable) maximum size for allocated memory. You can release memory you have allocated to allow it to be reused by your program. As an aside, memory allocated and subsequently freed is still counted as part of your program. So if you allocate 50 megabytes for temporary workspace and then free it all, your program will still have 50 megabytes of memory allocated to it (which will eventually get swapped out since you might not be using it). The total amount of memory can be considered a high water mark.

The primary functions for allocation and deallocating memory are:

```
void *malloc (size_t size);

void free (void *ptr);

void *realloc (void *ptr, size_t size);
```

These functions give you memory from the heap.

malloc()

malloc() allocates a chunk of memory with the address of the block aligned to the strictest boundary required in the OS. E.g. if an 8-byte double had the strictest alignment, malloc() would return addresses that were evenly divisible by 8. Empirically, on my G4 Titanium PowerBook, OS X returns things 16-byte aligned.

Example 7-2. mallocalign.m

```
// mallocalign.m -- see how malloc aligns its pointers

/* compile with:
cc -g -Wall -o mallocalign mallocalign.m
*/

#import <stdlib.h>
#import <stdio.h>

void allocprint (size_t size)
{
    void *memory;

    memory = malloc (size);
    printf ("malloc(%d) == %p\n", (int)size, memory);
    // intentionally do not free so we get a new malloced block of
    // memory
} // allocprint

int main (int argc, char *argv[])
{
    allocprint (1);
    allocprint (2);
    allocprint (sizeof(double));
    allocprint (1024 * 1024);
    allocprint (1);
    allocprint (1);
    return (0);
} // main
```

has a run of

```
% ./mallocalign
malloc(1) == 0x44400
malloc(2) == 0x44450
malloc(8) == 0x44460
malloc(1048576) == 0xa4000
malloc(1) == 0x44470
malloc(1) == 0x44480
```

which are all addresses evenly divisible by 16. This is good to know when doing Altivec work, since Altivec works best when data is aligned on 16-byte boundaries.

Generally you use the C `sizeof` operator to allocate memory of specific sizes:

```
typedef struct Node {
    int blah; // 4 bytes
    int bork; // 4 bytes
} Node;

Node *mynode = malloc (sizeof(Node));  // 8 bytes
```

and for arrays

```
Node mynode[] = malloc (sizeof(Node) * 100);  // 800 bytes
```

Note that **malloc()** is free to give you a block of memory that is larger than what you ask for. You are only guaranteed of having as much memory that you ask for.

For instance:

Example 7-3. mallocsize.m

```
// mallocsize.m -- see what kind of block sizes malloc is
//                  actually giving us

/* compile with:
cc -g -Wall -o mallocsize mallocsize.m
*/

#import <stdlib.h>      // for malloc()
#import <stdio.h>       // for printf()
#import <objc/malloc.h> // for malloc_size()

void allocprint (size_t size)
{
    void *memory;

    memory = malloc (size);
    printf ("malloc(%d) has a block size of %d\n",
            (int)size, (int)malloc_size(memory));

} // allocprint

int main (int argc, char *argv[])
{
    allocprint (1);
    allocprint (sizeof(double)); // 8 bytes
    allocprint (14);
    allocprint (16);
    allocprint (32);
    allocprint (48);
    allocprint (64);
    allocprint (100);
    return (0);
} // main
```

Yields:

```
% ./mallocsize
malloc(1) has a block size of 14
malloc(8) has a block size of 14
malloc(14) has a block size of 14
malloc(16) has a block size of 30
malloc(32) has a block size of 46
malloc(48) has a block size of 62
malloc(64) has a block size of 78
malloc(100) has a block size of 110
```

Why would this be? Memory allocation algorithms are an interesting area of computer science, and most any operating systems textbook will describe a number of different algorithms for managing dynamic memory. Usually, the system has a bunch of buckets that each contain uniform-sized blocks of memory. The system chooses the smallest block size that will contain the requested amount of memory. Rather than have a whole bunch of 9-byte blocks, and a whole bunch of 10-byte blocks, and a whole bunch of 11-byte blocks (and so on and so on), it will have larger increments. In the above case it has 14 bytes, 30 bytes, 46 bytes, 62 bytes, and so on. Some other allocators have block sizes that are powers of two.

Note that since **malloc_size()** reports sizes (possibly) larger that what was asked for, it cannot be depended on as a way to see "how much memory is allocated to this pointer." That is, if a function is passed a pointer that had been allocated using malloc(8), but you used **malloc_size()** on the pointer and subsequently treaded the pointer like it had come from malloc (14). Doing that would certainly cause problems. **malloc_size()** also won't work for pointers to stack memory. You will still need to pass around sizes of buffers.

Note that the memory returned by **malloc()** has some bookkeeping associated with it (usually stored as a negative offset from the pointer returned to you so that the system can find its bookkeeping information easily). This, along with the previous note on allocation block sizes, means you cannot make any assumptions about memory placement with multiple calls to **malloc()**.

E.g., you cannot depend on this:

```
x = malloc (10);
y = malloc (10);
```

to look like this in memory

Figure 7-4. Incorrect Memory Layout

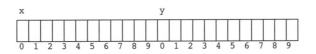

There are actually some web pages out there that assert that this *must* be true. It actually looks something like:

Figure 7-5. How blocks are actually laid out

One last corollary of the above. There is no guarantee of locality of reference (a fancy term meaning data that is frequently used together is near each other in memory, leading to fewer cache misses and less paging activity) either. You could do

```
x = malloc (10);
y = malloc (10);
```

and it is perfectly legal for `malloc()` to give you a pointer to x from one end of your address space and y to be an address way on the other side.

Finally, `malloc()` on Mac OS X is always thread safe, as opposed to `malloc()` on some other Unix variants (like Linux) which is only thread safe if you link in the thread libraries, so there is always going to be a little extra overhead when using `malloc()` and friends on Mac OS X compared to some other Unix operating systems.

free()

`free()` tells the system that you are done with a block of memory and that it can be reused by a subsequent call to `malloc()`. In the above little programs (especially `mallocalign.m`), the allocated memory is purposely never freed since the same block would keep getting returned, and it is hard to draw conclusions about memory alignment if you get the same starting address for a block of memory each time.

Not freeing allocated memory is termed a "memory leak," since the memory just kind of leaks away and is not available for use any more. There is a discussion about memory leaks and memory leak detection tools later on.

Lastly, make sure you only feed `free()` addresses you get from `malloc()`. You will get unpredictable results (crash) if you give `free()` addresses of stack buffers or other memory not allocated by `malloc()`.

realloc()

`realloc()` resizes a chunk of memory that has been previously allocated. Programmers familiar with classic Mac OS memory management will rightfully ask, "How can it resize memory? These are pointers, not handles." Essentially, `realloc()` does something like:

```
void *cheesyRealloc (void *ptr, size_t size)
{
    void *newMem = malloc (size);
    memcpy (newMem, ptr, size);
    free (ptr);
    return (newMem);
```

```
} // cheesyRealloc
```

So these blocks can move in the heap. Handles have the nice property that when they move you do not need to update every one that points to the handle since the double indirection takes care of that for you. In standard Unix memory management you have to do that bookkeeping yourself, usually by just having the pointer be in one place and wrap an API around it, or by using two memory objects: a smaller one that will not move (like a tree node), and a larger one that the smaller one points to (like the user-editable label for the tree node). The larger one can be reallocated and only the tree node needs to update the address change.

As you would expect, `realloc()` has optimizations so that it does not have to do the allocate/copy/free procedure every time a block is reallocated. As noted above, sometimes the block returned from `malloc()` is actually larger than what you asked for. `realloc()` can just say, "OK, you can now use the rest of the block." There are also games `realloc()` can play, like if there is a free block in another bucket that is contiguous with the block of memory you want to reallocate. `realloc()` behind the scenes can glom that second block onto the first and let you use that space.

But in any case, be sure to assign the return value of `realloc()` back to your pointer. (This is a mistake I personally make all too often). E.g., this is a lurking problem:

```
void *blah = malloc (sizeof(Node) * 20);
...
realloc (blah, sizeof(Node) * 40); // this is bad!
...
```

Sometimes it will work, sometimes not. Always do this:

```
blah = realloc (blah, sizeof(Node) * 40);
```

calloc()

`malloc()` does not initialize the memory it returns to you, so you will probably have a bunch of stale junk in the memory you get. A pretty common idiom is to allocate a chunk of memory and zero it out so that it is pretty safe to use:

```
void *memory = malloc (sizeof(Node) * 50);
memset (memory, 0, sizeof(Node) * 50);
```

You can also use `calloc()` to do this in one operation:

```
void *calloc(size_t nelem, size_t elsize);
```

The arguments are a little odd compared to `malloc()` in that it is assuming you are allocating an array. It is just doing a multiplication behind the scenes. So,

```
memory = calloc (sizeof(Node), 50);
```

gives identical results to the two-step sequence above. In general, it is better to use `calloc()` because the OS can do some optimizations behind the scenes (like allowing the kernel to reserve the memory, but not actually allocate it. It can then give you zero-filled pages when it is actually accessed).

alloca()

Even though the man page for **alloca()** says, "This is machine dependent, its use is discouraged," it is still a documented API you can use, which can be useful at times.

```
void *alloca(size_t size);
```

alloca() (for alloc automatic) allocates memory for you on the call stack. This means that allocation is very fast (just some pointer adjustments), and you do not need to perform an explicit **free()** on your memory to release it. When the function ends, the stack frame just goes away and it is the stack frame that contains the alloca memory. As with stuff that appears too good to be true, there is always a catch. Do not go nuts and overflow your stack with lots of local storage, especially if you use lots of recursion, or your code could be run in a threaded environment where stack sizes are much more limited.

Memory Ownership Issues

One of the details involved with dynamic memory is determining who is responsible for a piece of allocated memory and making sure that the memory is freed when nobody else is using it. This is one of those parts of programming that has lots of different solutions, each with their own tradeoffs (as witnessed by Java garbage collection, C++ destructors, and Cocoa's retain/release/autorelease cycles).

There are no real rules for ownership of memory that is passed back and forth between Unix and C function calls, so you pretty much need to check the man page for the calls in question (which is usually a good idea anyway). For instance:

- **getenv()** returns a char *, but you do not need to free it since the environment variables are all stored in a global array and **getenv()** just returns a string contained in that array.

- **strdup()** returns a char *, which you do need to free since it allocates memory on your behalf.

- Some calls take buffers, which you can **malloc** or create on the stack and you are responsible for **free**ing the memory when you are done. A subset of these calls can be given NULL for the buffer argument and they will allocate memory on your behalf. **getcwd()** behaves like this.

- Some other calls will give you reference to memory that they own (usually some kind of global buffer), such as **ctime()** for converting a Unix time into a character constant.

- Finally, there are some APIs that wrap dynamic memory allocation in an API, and depend on you to use that API to create and destroy objects, such as **opendir()** and **closedir()** for iterating through the contents of directories.

And, of course, you can use any of these techniques for modules and APIs that you create, as seems appropriate. It is perfectly fine for you to do your own memory allocation out of a big block if that gives you better behavior. One of my favorite techniques using this is a memory pool, an allocator for vending identically sized objects (handy for tree nodes):

Example 7-4. nodepool.m

```
// nodepool.m -- a simple memory pool for vending like-size pieces of
//                memory.  An example of custom memory management

/* build with:
cc -g -Wall -O1 -framework Foundation -o nodepool nodepool.m
*/

#import <Foundation/Foundation.h>
#import <stdlib.h>
#import <stdio.h>

// this is the free list that gets weaved through all the blocks

typedef struct BWPoolElement {
    struct BWPoolElement *next;
} BWPoolElement;

@interface BWNodePool : NSObject
{
    unsigned char       *memblock; // a big blob of bytes
    BWPoolElement       *freelist;
    size_t               nodeSize;
    size_t               count;
}

- (id)initWithNodeSize:(size_t)nodeSize   count:(size_t)count;
- (void *)allocNode;
- (void)freeNode:(void *)nodePtr;

@end // BWNodePool


@implementation BWNodePool

- (void) weaveFreeListFrom:(unsigned char *)startAddress
                  forCount:(size_t)theCount
{
    unsigned char *scan = startAddress;
    int i;

    for (i = 0; i < theCount; i++) {
        if (freelist == NULL) {
            freelist = (BWPoolElement *) scan;
            freelist->next = NULL;
        } else {
            BWPoolElement *temp = (BWPoolElement*) scan;
            temp->next = freelist;
            freelist = temp;
        }
        scan += nodeSize;
    }

} // weaveFreeListFrom

- (id) initWithNodeSize:(size_t)theNodeSize   count:(size_t)theCount
```

```
    {
        if ((self = [super init])) {
            nodeSize = theNodeSize;
            count = theCount;

            // make sure there's enough space to store the pointers
            // for the freelist

            if (nodeSize < sizeof(BWPoolElement)) {
                nodeSize = sizeof(BWPoolElement);
            }

            // allocate memory for the block
            memblock = malloc (nodeSize * count);

            // walk through the block building the freelist
            [self weaveFreeListFrom:memblock  forCount:theCount];
        }

        return (self);

    } // initWithNodeSize


    - (void)dealloc
    {
        free (memblock);
    } // dealloc


    - (void *)allocNode
    {
        void *newNode = NULL;

        if (freelist == NULL) {
            // out of space. just give up and surrender for now.
            // you can add pool growing by keeping an array of memblocks
            // and creating a new one when the previous block fills up.
            fprintf (stderr, "out of space in node pool.  Giving up\n");
            abort ();
        }

        // take a new node off of the freelist
        newNode = freelist;
        freelist = freelist->next;

        return (newNode);

    } // allocNode


    - (void)freeNode:(void *)nodePtr
    {
        // stick freed node at the head of the freelist
        ((BWPoolElement*)nodePtr)->next = freelist;
        freelist = nodePtr;
    } // freeNode


@end // BWNodePool
```

```
#define NODE_BUF_SIZE 137
typedef struct ListNode {
    int                 someData;
    struct ListNode     *next;
} ListNode;

void haveFunWithPool (int nodeCount)
{
    int i;
    ListNode *head, *node, *prev;
    BWNodePool *nodePool;

    NSLog (@"fun with pool");

    nodePool = [[BWNodePool alloc] initWithNodeSize:sizeof(ListNode)
                                    count:nodeCount];
    head = node = prev = NULL;
    for (i = 0; i < nodeCount; i++) {
        node = [nodePool allocNode];
        node->someData = i;

        // and bookkeeping
        node->next = prev;
        prev = node;
    }
    head = node;

    // clean up the list
    [nodePool release];

} // haveFunWithPool

void haveFunWithMalloc (int nodeCount)
{
    int i;
    ListNode *head, *node, *prev;

    NSLog (@"fun with malloc");

    head = node = prev = NULL;

    for (i = 0; i < nodeCount; i++) {
        node = malloc (sizeof(ListNode));
        node->someData = i;

        // and bookkeeping
        node->next = prev;
        prev = node;
    }
    head = node;

    // now clean it up
    while (head != NULL) {
        ListNode *node = head;
        head = head->next;
        free (node);
```

```
        }

    } // haveFunWithMalloc

    int main (int argc, char *argv[])
    {
        int count;

        if (argc != 3) {
            fprintf (stderr, "usage: %s -p|-m #\n", argv[0]);
            fprintf (stderr, "        program to exercise memory "
                            "allocation\n");
            fprintf (stderr, "          -p to use a memory pool\n");
            fprintf (stderr, "          -m to use malloc\n");
            fprintf (stderr, "          #  number of nodes to play "
                            "with\n");
            return (1);
        }
        count = atoi (argv[2]);

        if (strcmp(argv[1], "-p") == 0) {
            haveFunWithPool (count);
        } else {
            haveFunWithMalloc (count);
        }

        return (0);

    } // main
```

One thing to note is that once the pool is created, allocations and frees are constant time (just a pointer assignment). `malloc()` usually takes longer due to the complexity of its internal data structures. Also note that the pool can free everything at once (handy since these list nodes do not reference any other objects that need to be cleaned up). Here are some timings (in seconds) of runs of the program (from the `time` program):

Count	Pool	`malloc()`
50,000	0.07	0.19
500,000	0.16	1.10
5,000,000	1.35	9.80

This shows there can be, under some circumstances, benefit to doing your own allocation. Generally it is better to test first to find out what your bottlenecks are before implementing your own allocator, but it is nice to have the option when you need it. If you are using C++, you can override the new operator to use a pool for allocations. (Objective-C doesn't give you this kind of control, unfortunately). In one C++ project I worked on, we had a class that supported multiple subscriptings for digging into a compacted dictionary, with access code like
`flavor['page']['sect']['styl'][5]`. Very convenient coding-wise, but this technique caused a lot of temporary objects to be created and destroyed. A pool was put under new and sped things up by an order of magnitude.

One thing to note in the `nodepool.m` code is that it does not handle the pool growing case. You cannot just `realloc()` the memblock since it could move in memory, leaving the freelist pointers dangling (as well as any pointers the objects being allocated might have, such as the linked list pointers). This can be fixed by having an array of memory pointers, when you run out of memory create a new block, add it to the array, and weave the freelist through the new block.

One last note, operations on the nodepool are not thread safe. A challenge is to make it safe in Chapter 22 (Threads).

Debugging Memory Problems

Errors in memory management cause a huge number of problems when programming in C, and can lead to difficult to track down bugs since the manifestation of a problem can happen long after the actual program error happened.

Common API issues

When `malloc()` cannot allocate memory it returns `NULL`. Many programmers tend to ignore `NULL` results from `malloc()`, because if memory is really exhausted the system is in some pretty serious trouble and it is just easier to crash and restart (plus it can be tedious checking the return value of `malloc()` all the time). There is no equivalent of the classic Mac OS `GrowZoneProc` that gets called when the heap is full and lets you free temporary resources. So if you want to do something similar you will need to implement it yourself.

The typical Cocoa idiom of allocation and initialization

```
NSArray *array = [[NSArray alloc] init];
[array addObject: myObject];
```

glosses over allocation problems. If `alloc` returns a `nil` object, and since Objective-C messages to `nil` are legal, in the face of an allocation problem this code will propage this `nil` object without complaint. If you are really paranoid, and/or want to be robust in low memory conditions for your own allocations, you can put a wrapper around `malloc()` (say `mySafeMalloc()`, or use preprocessor tricks to rename `malloc()` itself) that on a `NULL` return from `malloc()` will attempt to free memory and try the allocation again, and perhaps call `abort()` when things are in complete dire straits.

You can get garbage collectors for C and C++ to do automatic cleanup of memory.

Another common API issue is not assigning the return value of `realloc()`. Your program can work fine until the block of memory moves, and then you are pointing to old memory. If that old memory does not get reused right away, things will seem to work fine until the most inconvenient moment, when things will fall apart.

Only free allocated memory once: do not try to free the same pointer twice. That will usually lead to a crash as the `malloc()` data structures get confused. Also do not try to free memory you got from some other API, unless it explicitly says you can call `free()` on it. For instance, `opendir()` allocates a chunk of memory and returns it to you, but do not `free()` that memory, use `closedir()`.

Lastly, do not access memory you have just freed. The old (stale) data may still be there, but that is something you do not want to depend on, especially in a threaded environment.

Memory corruption

Memory corruption happens when a piece of code writes data into the wrong location in memory. At best you will try writing into memory you do not have access to and will crash. At worst you will slightly corrupt some data structure which will manifest itself in an error millions of instructions in the future.

The most common kinds of memory errors in C are buffer overruns and dangling pointers.

Buffer overruns are when you think you have a certain amount of memory at your disposal but you actually have less than that allocated. A classic example is forgetting to account for the trailing zero byte for C string termination.

For instance:

```
char *stringCopy = malloc (strlen(mystring));
strcpy (stringCopy, mystring);
```

You have just written one byte past the end of your allocated block of memory. To correct this, you need to account for that extra byte:

```
char *stringCopy = malloc (strlen(mystring) + 1);
strcpy (stringCopy, mystring);
```

Off-by-one errors (also called "obiwans" or "fence-post errors") can also cause a buffer overrun. For instance:

```
void myFunction ()
{
    int i;
    ListNode mynodes[20];
    char stringBuffer[1024];

    for (i = 0; i <= 20; i++) {
        mynodes[i].stuff = i;
        ...
    }

}
```

Note that the loop runs from 0 through 20, which is 21 times through the loop. The last time through the loop is indexing past the end of the mynodes array and (most likely) has just trashed the beginning of the stringBuffer array. What can make buffer overruns like this so nasty is that **malloc()** stores bookkeeping information in memory immediately before the pointer it gives you. If you overrun a buffer off the beginning of the buffer you will smash that information. If you overrun off the end it could smash the **malloc()** information of another buffer. When you go to free that second piece of memory, you might crash inside of **free()**, and then spend a while on a wild goose chase wondering why some piece of good code just failed.

Another nasty side effect of buffer overruns like this is that malicious data could clobber the stack in such a way that when the function returns, program control will jump to an unexpected place. Many Windows platform exploits work like this.

Dangling pointers are memory addresses stored in pointer variables that do not have any correlation with the memory they should be pointing to. Uninitialized pointers can cause this, as can forgetting to assign the return value of `realloc()`, as well as not propagating the address when memory moves or is changed. For instance:

```
char *g_username;

const char *getUserName ()
{
    return (g_username);
}

void setUserName (const char *newName)
{
    free (g_username);
    g_username = strdup (newName); // performs a malloc
}
```

Now consider this scenario:

```
name = getUserName(); // say it is address 0x1000, "markd"
setUserName ("bork"); // the memory at address 0x1000 has been freed
printf (name);        // using a dangling pointer now
```

The OS X `malloc()` libraries have some built-in tools to help track down some of these conditions. You control it by setting environment variables and then running your program. (If you are debugging a GUI app, you can run it from the command line by doing "`open /path/to/your/AppBundle.app`".)

```
% setenv MallocHelp 1
```

will display help. Note that you can use the `unsetenv` command to remove environment variables. To turn off `MallocHelp` you would execute `unsetenv` `MallocHelp`. The next few sections will cover what some of the different environment variables are and what they do when set. All are case-sensitive.

MallocGuardEdges

For large blocks, puts a 4k page with no permissions before and after the allocation. This will catch buffer overruns before and after the allocated block. The size of a "large block" is undefined, but experimentally 12K and larger seem to be considered large blocks.

Here is a little program to show it in action:

Example 7-5. mallocguard.m

```
// mallocguard.m -- exercise MallocGuardEdges.

/* compile with:
cc -g -Wall -o mallocguard mallocguard.m
```

```
*/

#import <stdlib.h>

int main (int argc, char *argv[])
{
    unsigned char *memory = malloc (1024 * 16);
    unsigned char *dummy = malloc (1024 * 16);

    unsigned char *offTheEnd = memory + (1024 * 16) + 1;

    *offTheEnd = 'x';

    return (0);

} // main
```

The first `malloc()` gets us 16K of memory. The second one is there to provide some more pages of memory that can be clobbered with the bad assignment to offTheEnd.

Running it normally gives us this:

```
% ./mallocguard
%
```

Like nothing happend. Let us turn on the guard:

```
% setenv MallocGuardEdges 1
% ./mallocguard
malloc[20622]: protecting edges
Bus error
```

A program error found for us. gdb can tell us exactly where the error happened.

MallocScribble

This writes over freed blocks with a known value (0x55) which will catch attempts to reuse memory blocks. That is a bad pointer value (an odd address) which will cause addressing errors if it gets used. Judging from experiments, `free()` will always clear the first 8 or so bytes to zero on a free which will catch some errors, but not all.

Here is a little example:

Example 7-6. mallocscribble.m

```
// mallocscribble.m -- exercise MallocScribble

/* compile wth:
cc -g -Wall -o mallocscribble mallocscribble.m
*/

#import <stdlib.h>      // for malloc()
#import <stdio.h>       // for printf()
#import <string.h>      // for strcpy()


typedef struct Thingie {
```

```
    char blah[16];
    char string[30];
} Thingie;

int main (int argc, char *argv[])
{
    Thingie *thing = malloc (sizeof(Thingie));

    strcpy (thing->string, "hello there");
    printf ("before free: %s\n", thing->string);
    free (thing);
    printf ("after free: %s\n", thing->string);

    return (0);

} // main
```

(The 16-character `blah` entry is to work around **free()**'s zeroing of the data so the code can show what it is doing with `MallocScribble` enabled.)

Here is the run without anything set in the environment:

```
% ./mallocscribble
before free: hello there
after free: hello there
```

And after:

```
% setenv MallocScribble 1
% ./mallocscribble
malloc[20701]: enabling scribbling to detect mods to free blocks
before free: hello there
after free: UUUUUUUUUUUUUUUUUUUUUUUUUUUUUUU
```

MallocStackLogging and MallocStackLoggingNoCompact

Records stacks on memory management calls for later use by tools like `malloc_history`.

MallocCheckHeapStart

After *n* dynamic memory operations, start performing sanity checks of the **malloc()** data structures for any signs of corruption.

Example 7-7. malloccheckstart.m

```
// malloccheckstart.m -- play with MallocCheckHeapStart

/* compile wth:
cc -g -Wall -o malloccheckstart malloccheckstart.m
*/

#import <stdlib.h>   // for malloc()
#import <string.h>   // for memset()

int main (int argc, char *argv[])
```

```
{
    int i;
    unsigned char *memory;

    for (i = 0; i < 10000; i++) {
        memory = malloc (10);

        if (i == 3783) {
            // smash some memory
            memset (memory-16, 0x55, 26);
        }
    }
    return (0);
} // main
```

If you just run it, it seems to work OK:

```
% ./malloccheckstart
%
```

But `setenv MallocCheckHeapStart 100` and you get a lot of information:

```
% ./malloccheckstart
malloc[20765]: checks heap after 100th operation and each \
1000 operations
MallocCheckHeap: PASSED check at 100th operation
MallocCheckHeap: PASSED check at 1100th operation
MallocCheckHeap: PASSED check at 2100th operation
MallocCheckHeap: PASSED check at 3100th operation
*** malloc[20765]: invariant broken for 0x52f20 (prev_free=0) this
msize=21845
*** malloc[20765]: Region 0 incorrect szone_check_all() counter=5
*** malloc[20765]: error: Check: region incorrect
*** MallocCheckHeap: FAILED check at 4100th operation
Stack for last operation where the malloc check succeeded:
0x70056c80 0x700042b0 ...
(Use 'atos' for a symbolic stack)
*** Recommend using 'setenv MallocCheckHeapStart 3100;
setenv MallocCheckHeapEach 100' to narrow down failure
*** Sleeping for 100 seconds to leave time to attach
```

Then use `gdb` to attach to the running program and poke around to see what is going on.

These are really handy utilities. They do not pinpoint exactly what went wrong, but they are useful for narrowing down the error possibilities.

Memory Leaks

Another common set of memory-related errors are memory leaks. These are bits of memory that get allocated and never deallocated. Frequently, memory leaks happen when you assign a pointer to a new value but do not free the old value:

```
char *mystring;
mystring = strdup ("hello"); // performs a malloc() and a string copy
mystring = strdup ("there");
```

The first string ("hello") has been leaked. Since the address of that memory was never preserved, it can never be freed. A little memory leaked here or there, aside from being a bit sloppy, is not all that bad in today's systems with gobs of RAM. What is the real killer are leaks that happen often, like inside of a loop, or every time the user does a common operation. Leaking 100 bytes is not too bad. Leaking 100 bytes every time the user presses a key in a word processor can be deadly. Applications in Mac OS X tend to stay running for long periods of time. The user may forget about an app, then click on it in the Dock to do something with it. A small memory leak can really add up when your program can be running for weeks between restarts.

One easy way to tell if your program is leaking is to run the `top` program, find your application in the list, and watch the right-most column. If that number is continually increasing, you probably have a memory leak.

OS X comes with a utility called `leaks` that will grovel around in your program's address space and find unreferenced memory. There is a graphical version of this called `MallocDebug.app` (found in the `/Developer/Applications`). Both of these tools failed to find obvious memory leaks in some trial programs, but give them a whirl and see if they help out with your programs.

Memory Leaks in Cocoa

In addition to **`malloc()`**-related memory leaks, you can also leak memory in Cocoa programs by not being careful with your `retain` and `release` calls.

For instance:

Example 7-8. objectleak.m

```
// objectleak.m -- leak some Cocoa objects

/* compile with:
cc -g -Wall -framework Foundation -o objectleak objectleak.m
*/

#import <Foundation/Foundation.h>

int main (int argc, char *argv[])
{
    NSAutoreleasePool *pool = [[NSAutoreleasePool alloc] init];
    NSMutableArray *array = [[NSMutableArray alloc] init];
    NSNumber *number;
    int i;

    for (i = 0; i < 20; i++) {
        // alloc creates an object with a retain count of 1
        number = [[NSNumber alloc] initWithInt: i];
        [array addObject: number]; // number has retain count of 2
    }

    [array release]; // each of the numbers have retain counts of 1

    [pool release];

    return (0);
```

```
} // main
```

Each of the `NSNumber` objects still has a retain count of one after the array is released, therefore they have been leaked. `MallocDebug.app` can show some information about the leaks. `ObjectAlloc.app`, discussed in Chapter 25 (Performance), can show you Cocoa object leaks as well.

For the More Curious

ps and top

The `ps` command ("process status") command has some features for keeping tabs on your program's memory use. Here is a handy use of `ps`:

```
% ps -auxw | grep something-interesting
```

where `something-interesting` is the PID or program name of interest. So, something like

```
% ps -auxw | grep Finder
```

will show some information about the Finder process:

```
markd   229   0.0 1.9   84160  10096  ??  S   0:43.11 /System/ \
Library/CoreServices/Finder.app/Contents/MacOS/Finder -psn_0_2621
```

In order, the columns are:

1. Owner of the process (markd).
2. Process ID (229).
3. CPU currently taken (0.0%).
4. Real memory in use (1.9%).
5. Virtual size, the total footprint of the program (84160K, or 84 megs).
6. Resident set size, how much is living in RAM right now. (This is 10096K, or about 10 megs, which for a 512 meg machine is about 1.9%. It is nice when those things work out.)
7. Controlling terminal (not important).
8. Process state (more about this in Chapter 15 (Multiprocessing)).
9. Total CPU time consumed by the process (43 seconds).
10. Command with arguments that started the process.

Relating to memory, the fifth and sixth columns are the most interesting. You can look at just those with the command

```
ps -ax -o user,pid,vsz,rss,command
```

Which will show the owner, the PID, the virtual size, the resident size, and the command. ps can show a wealth of information about what is running on your system. Check out the man page for more.

You can run this repeatedly to see if your program (or any other) seems to be growing without bound.

The `top` program, referenced a little earlier, also shows a wealth of information, and it updates stuff in real time.

Here is a sample snapshot during the writing this chapter:

```
Processes: 42 total, 3 running, 39 sleeping. 124 threads        15:00:28
Load Avg: 0.27, 0.18, 0.01 CPU usage: 14.2% user, 12.4% sys, 73.5% idle
SharedLibs: num = 113, resident = 20.7M code, 2.31M data, 5.99M LinkEdit
MemRegions:num = 3733, resident = 52.5M + 3.58M private, 41.7M shared
PhysMem:  44.5M wired, 78.2M active, 81.9M inactive, 205M used, 307M free
VM: 2.19G + 56.0M   59120(0) pageins, 254239(0) pageouts
```

PID	COMMAND	%CPU	TIME	#TH	#PRTS	#MREGS	RPRVT	RSHRD	RSIZE	VSIZE
21013	top	9.7%	0:00.81	1	14	15	212K	372K	468K	1.62M
21007	tcsh	0.0%	0:00.12	1	24	16	488K	700K	960K	5.76M
21001	tcsh	0.0%	0:00.15	1	24	16	488K	700K	956K	5.76M
20467	Mozilla	0.0%	2:32.92	6	87	368	17.7M	21.8M	31.4M	86.4M
20318	tcsh	0.0%	0:00.11	1	16	16	0K	648K	0K	9.46M
19895	BorkPad	0.0%	0:03.03	2	113	99	804K	6.04M	764K	56.0M
18612	TruBlueEn	2.6%	84:27.76	18	177	231	10.7M	3.55M	12.8M	1.05G
17407	tcsh	0.0%	0:00.31	1	16	16	288K	668K	384K	9.46M
6779	tcsh	0.0%	0:00.13	1	16	16	0K	648K	0K	9.46M
1086	tcsh	0.0%	0:01.17	1	16	17	296K	668K	504K	9.71M
327	emacs	0.0%	2:09.06	1	13	558	4.27M	1.72M	5.61M	13.1M
297	SecurityA	0.0%	0:01.34	2	88	86	696K	4.95M	748K	54.2M
270	tcsh	0.0%	0:00.21	1	24	17	0K	648K	0K	5.74M
259	Terminal	3.5%	12:43.40	8	133	582	3.65M	8.28M	7.30M	64.0M
254	automount	0.0%	0:00.04	2	11	19	48K	432K	124K	2.14M

The stuff related to memory is bolded.

```
MemRegions: num = 3733, resident = 52.5M + 3.58M private, 41.7M shared
```

This line tells us the number of memory regions (blocks of allocated memory from the kernel), how much RAM is currently swapped in, how much is private to the kernel, and how much is shared between processes (like for text segments of programs).

```
PhysMem:44.5M wired, 78.2M active, 81.9M inactive, 205M used, 307M free
```

This describes the physical memory:

`wired memory`

> Memory that will not be swapped out to disk.

`active memory`

> Physical memory that is resident and mapped (a process has active use of the memory), and it has been recently accessed.

inactive memory

> Pages currently resident in physical memory, but have not been recently accessed. They contain valid data. These pages are ripe for being swapped out to disk.

used memory

> The sum of wired, active, and inactive memory.

free memory

> Pages no longer containing valid data. The system can use these to cache disk blocks.

The numbers (44.5 + 78.2 + 81.9 + 307) add up to 511.6, which is close enough to the 512M of RAM installed on the machine.

```
VM: 2.19G + 56.0M   59120(0) pageins, 254239(0) pageouts
```

2.19 gigs of cumulative virtual address space are being consumed on machine. Along with 56 megs of virtual address space consumed by the kernel.

There have been 59,120 pageins (bringing pages from swap into memory) and 254,239 pageouts (moving pages from memory into swap). Recently there have not been any pageins or pageouts. (There was a whole lot of virtual memory activity with some sample programs that ran amok allocating huge reams of memory.)

The columns RPRVT, RSHRD, RSIZE, and VSIZE all relate to memory.

RPRVT

> Resident private memory.

RSHRD

> Resident shared memory.

RSIZE

> Total resident memory. Total number of real pages that this process currently has associated with it. Includes pages that may be shared with other processes.

VSIZE

> Total address space currently allocated.

RSIZE and VSIZE are the most interesting ones, especially if they are increasing, or are huge.

ProcessViewer.app (in /Applications/Utilities) shows a much simplified version of top's information, including the VSIZE and RSIZE. (You need to use the Statistics tab under the "More Info" disclosure triangle.)

Resource limits

Since Unix is a a multi-user system, there are safeguards in the OS to keep processes from dominating (and possibly bringing down) the system by consuming too many resources. There are a number of different resources that are controlled:

RLIMIT_DATA

> Maximum size (bytes) of the data segment for a process (that is, the maximum size of the heap plus initialized + uninitialized data segments).

RLIMIT_RSS

> Maximum size (bytes) which a processes resident set may grow (e.g., maximum amount of physical RAM to be given). If memory becomes scare, the system will first take memory away from processes that have exceeded their RSS limit.

RLIMIT_STACK

> Maximum size (bytes) of the stack segment. How deep your program stack can get.

RLIMIT_MEMLOCK

> Maximum size (bytes) which a process can lock (wire) into memory with the **mlock()** function.

There are also resources not related to memory:

RLIMIT_FSIZE

> Maximum size (bytes) of a file that may be created.

RLIMIT_NOFILE

> Maximum number of simultaneously open files.

RLIMIT_NPROC

> Maximum number of simultaneous processes for the current user.

RLIMIT_CPU

> Maximum amount of CPU time (in seconds).

RLIMIT_CORE

> Largest size (in bytes) of core files.

Resource limits are expressed as a soft limit and a hard limit. When the soft limit is exceeded, the program may receive a signal (like a software interrupt. Signals are discussed in depth in Chapter 9 (Exceptions)) but it will be allowed to continue execution until it reaches the hard limit. The soft limits are usually set lower, but you can raise them to the hard limit. You can lower the hard limit, but you can never raise the hard limit unless you are running with superuser privileges.

Here is a little program to show you the hard and soft limits currently in force:

Example 7-9. limits.m

```
// limits.m -- see the resource limits in force

/* compile with:
cc -g -Wall -o limits limits.m
*/

#import <sys/types.h>
#import <sys/time.h>
#import <sys/resource.h>
#import <stdio.h>
#import <string.h>
#import <errno.h>

typedef struct Limit {
    int resource;
    const char *name;
} Limit;

Limit limits[] = {
    { RLIMIT_DATA,      "data segment maximum (bytes)" },
    { RLIMIT_RSS,       "resident size maximum (bytes)" },
    { RLIMIT_STACK,     "stack size maximum (bytes)" },
    { RLIMIT_MEMLOCK,   "wired memory maximum (bytes)" },
    { RLIMIT_FSIZE,     "file size maximum (bytes)" },
    { RLIMIT_NOFILE,    "max number of simultaneously open files" },
    { RLIMIT_NPROC,     "max number of simultaneous processes" },
    { RLIMIT_CPU,       "cpu time maximum (seconds)" },
    { RLIMIT_CORE,      "core file maximum (bytes)" }
};

// turn the rlim_t value in to a string, also translating the magic
// "infinity" value to something human readable
void stringValue (rlim_t value, char *buffer, size_t buffersize)
{
    if (value == RLIM_INFINITY) {
        strcpy (buffer, "infinite");
    } else {
        snprintf (buffer, buffersize, "%lld", value);
    }
} // stringValue

// right-justify the first entry in a field width of 45, then display
// two more strings

#define FORMAT_STRING "%45s: %-10s (%s)\n"

int main (int argc, char *argv[])
{
    struct rlimit rl;
    Limit *scan, *stop;

    scan = limits;
    stop = scan + (sizeof(limits) / sizeof(Limit));

    printf (FORMAT_STRING, "limit name", "soft-limit", "hard-limit");
```

```
      while (scan < stop) {
          if (getrlimit (scan->resource, &rl) == -1) {
              fprintf (stderr, "error in getrlimit for %s: %d/%s\n",
                      scan->name, errno, strerror(errno));
          } else {
              char soft[20];
              char hard[20];

              stringValue (rl.rlim_cur, soft, 20);
              stringValue (rl.rlim_max, hard, 20);

              printf (FORMAT_STRING, scan->name, soft, hard);
          }
          scan++;
      }
      return (0);
} // main
```

And here is the output on my system:

```
                              limit name: soft-limit (hard-limit)
            data segment maximum (bytes): 6291456    (infinite)
            resident size maximum (bytes): infinite    (infinite)
             stack size maximum (bytes): 524288     (67108864)
            wired memory maximum (bytes): infinite    (infinite)
             file size maximum (bytes): infinite    (infinite)
   max number of simultaneously open files: 256        (infinite)
      max number of simultaneous processes: 100        (infinite)
              cpu time maximum (seconds): infinite    (infinite)
             core file maximum (bytes): 0          (infinite)
```

All in all, the system is pretty kind to us.

You read the current resource limits by using **getrlimit()** as shown in the code above, and you can change the resource limits by using **setrlimit()** and passing it an appropriately filled in struct rlimit.

Here is a program that will attempt to open the same file over and over. (It is easier to show resource limits with files than trying to overflow the stack.)

Example 7-10. openfiles.m

```
// openfiles.m -- see what happens when we open a lot of files

/* compile with:
cc -g -Wall -o openfiles openfiles.m
*/

#import <fcntl.h>
#import <stdio.h>

int main (int argc, char *argv[])
{
    int fd, i;
```

```
    for (i = 0; i < 260; i++) {
        fd = open ("/usr/include/stdio.h", O_RDONLY);
        printf ("%d: fd is %d\n", i, fd);
    }

    return (0);

} // main
```

When run, this happens:

```
% ./openfiles
0: fd is 3
1: fd is 4
2: fd is 5
...
250: fd is 253
251: fd is 254
252: fd is 255
253: fd is -1
254: fd is -1
```

Note that the fd variable starts becoming -1 (cannot open the file) after a value of 255 (which correlates with what the result of limits.m up above). There are already the 3 files opened for us, stdin, stdout, stderror, which count as open files against the resource limit.

Here is a modification to openfiles.m to set the soft limit:

Example 7-11. openfiles.m (revised)

```
// openfiles.m -- see what happens when we open a lot of files

/* compile with:
cc -g -Wall -o openfiles openfiles.m
*/

#import <sys/types.h>
#import <sys/time.h>
#import <sys/resource.h>
#import <fcntl.h>
#import <stdio.h>
#import <errno.h>

int main (int argc, char *argv[])
{
    int fd, i;
    int limit;
    struct rlimit rl;

    if (argc != 2) {
        fprintf (stderr, "usage:  %s open-file-rlimit\n", argv[0]);
        exit (1);
    }
    limit = atoi (argv[1]);
    rl.rlim_cur = limit;
    rl.rlim_max = RLIM_INFINITY;
```

```
    if (setrlimit(RLIMIT_NOFILE, &rl) == -1) {
        fprintf (stderr, "error in setrlimit for RLIM_NOFILE: %d/%s\n",
                errno, strerror(errno));
        exit (1);
    }

    for (i = 0; i < 260; i++) {
        fd = open ("/usr/include/stdio.h", O_RDONLY);
        printf ("%d: fd is %d\n", i, fd);
    }

    return (0);

} // main
```

Here are some sample runs:

```
% ./openfiles 10
0: fd is 3
1: fd is 4
2: fd is 5
3: fd is 6
4: fd is 7
5: fd is 8
6: fd is 9
7: fd is -1
8: fd is -1

% ./openfiles 1000000
0: fd is 3
1: fd is 4
2: fd is 5
...
257: fd is 260
258: fd is 261
259: fd is 262
```

Setting lower resource limits can be handy when you are spawning off other programs (which is talked about in Chapter 15 (Multiprocessing)). If you do not trust the other programs, or want to constrain their limits, you can use **setrlimit()** on yourself, then launch your child process who will run under the reduced limits.

Some other tools

The heap tool lists all the **malloc()**-allocated buffers in the heap of a program. Give it the PID of the program to look at.

heap is interesting when pointed at a Cocoa program because it shows Objective-C classes. Here is stuff from objectleak.m (edited down):

```
Process 6999: 4 zones
All zones: 1139 nodes malloced - 103KB
...
All zones: 1139 nodes malloced - Sizes: 32KB[1] 16KB[1]
  4KB[1] 2062[1] 2046[1] 1806[1] 878[1] 862[1] 638[1] 558[1]
  526[2] 398[1] 270[1] 254[2] 238[1] 222[1] 206[1] 190[3]
```

```
174[2] 158[4] 142[3] 126[4] 110[3] 94[9] 78[10] 62[40]
46[186]  30[787] 14[69]
...
Found 232 ObjC classes in process 6999
...
Zone DefaultMallocZone_0x8b1d0: 1139 nodes (105054 bytes)

<not Objective C object>         = 1103 (104438 bytes)
NSshortNumber      = 20 (280 bytes)
NSRandomSpecifier        = 1 (14 bytes)
NSAutoreleasePool        = 1 (30 bytes)
NSPlaceholderValue       = 1 (14 bytes)
NSunsignedIntNumber      = 1 (14 bytes)
NSHTTPURLHandle          = 1 (14 bytes)
NSPlaceholderMutableArray = 1 (14 bytes)
NSCFBoolean              = 1 (14 bytes)
NSPlaceholderNumber      = 1 (14 bytes)
NSMachPort               = 1 (14 bytes)
NSMiddleSpecifier        = 1 (14 bytes)
NSFormatter              = 1 (14 bytes)
NSNotificationCenter     = 1 (62 bytes)
NSValue                  = 1 (14 bytes)
NSMoveCommand            = 1 (14 bytes)
NSThread                 = 1 (62 bytes)
NSTerminologyRegistry    = 1 (14 bytes)
```

All sorts of cool stuff that is lurking under the hood, such as the notification center, a Mach port, a thread, and the 20 NSshortNumbers.

malloc_history will show you a history of memory activity. This requires that you set MallocStackLogging to 1 in your environment before running.

Here is a little program that does some memory manipulations, and then sleeps:

Example 7-12. mallochistory.m

```
// mallochistory.m -- do some mallocation so we can use malloc_history
// be sure to the environment variable MallocStackLogging or
// MallocStackLoggingNoCompact to 1. Then run this program, and while
// it sleeps at the end, run 'malloc_history pid -all_by_size' or
// 'malloc_history pid -all_by_count'

/* compile with:
cc -g -Wall -o mallochistory mallochistory.m
*/

#import <unistd.h>    // for getpid(), sleep()
#import <stdlib.h>    // for malloc()
#import <stdio.h>     // for printf

void func2 ()
{
    char *stuff;
    int i;

    for (i = 0; i < 3; i++) {
        stuff = malloc (50);
        free (stuff);
```

```
    }
    stuff = malloc (50);
    // so we can use the malloc_history address feature
    printf ("address of stuff is %p\n", stuff);

    // intentionally leak stuff

} // func2

void func1 ()
{
    int *numbers;

    numbers = malloc (sizeof(int) * 100);
    func2 ();

    // intentionally leak numbers

} // func1

int main (int argc, char *argv[])
{
    printf ("my process id is %d\n", getpid());
    func1 ();

    sleep (600);
    return (0);
} // main
```

When run, this program does:

```
% setenv MallocStackLogging 1
% ./mallochistory
malloc[7090]: recording stacks using standard recorder
my process id is 7098
address of stuff is 0x45490
```

Then in another terminal, see who has manipulated the block:

```
% malloc_history 7098 0x45490

Call [2] [arg=50]: thread_800013b8 |0xbffffc80 | start | _start
    | main | func1 | func2 | malloc | malloc_zone_malloc
```

You can also see what stuff is currently allocated and who did it. In this case, the stack entries are ordered by size. Stuff that is purely overhead has been removed.

```
% malloc_history 7098 -all_by_size
1 calls for 131072 bytes: thread_800013b8 |0xbffffc80 | start
    | _start | main | printf | vfprintf | __swsetup | __smakebuf
    | malloc | malloc_zone_malloc
```

Looks like `printf()` and friends need a big (128K) buffer to do their work:

```
1 calls for 400 bytes: thread_800013b8 |0xbffffc80 | start | _start
    | main | func1 | malloc | malloc_zone_malloc
```

Here is the numbers array:

```
1 calls for 50 bytes: thread_800013b8 |0xbffffc80 | start | _start
    | main | func1 | func2 | malloc | malloc_zone_malloc
```

And the final `malloc()` from `func2()`.

vm_stat

`vm_stat` shows some Mach virtual memory statistics. Here it is for my system right now:

```
Mach Virtual Memory Statistics: (page size of 4096 bytes)
Pages free:                   62921.
Pages active:                 19655.
Pages inactive:               36597.
Pages wired down:             11899.
"Translation faults":      20246163.
Pages copy-on-write:        1330902.
Pages zero filled:          4738887.
Pages reactivated:           595761.
Pageins:                      60044.
Pageouts:                    254239.
Object cache: 412841 hits of 484419 lookups (85% hit rate)
```

You could run `vm_stat` at different points in time to see if your system is swapping (lots of pageins and pageouts). The man page has information on each of the entries.

vmmap

`vmmap` is like `leaks` and `heap` in that it looks into a running program. In this case, it shows all the mapped pages in memory, including permissions on the pages. There is a lot of output from this command.

Remember earlier when `MallocGuardEdges` considered a "large block" to be 12K? I used `vmmap` to figure that out.

Example 7-13. mallochelp.m

```
// mallochelp.m -- try to figure out the "large" block size

/* compile with
cc -g -Wall -o mallochelp mallochelp.m
*/

#import <sys/types.h>   // for random types
#import <unistd.h>      // for getpid(), sleep()
#import <stdlib.h>      // for malloc()
#import <stdio.h>       // for printf()

int main (int argc, char *argv[])
{
    malloc (1024 * 16);
    printf ("my process ID is %d\n", getpid());
    sleep (30);
    return (0);
```

```
} // main
```

will run, print its process ID, and sleep. I ran vmmap on it and directed its output to a file:

```
% ./mallochelp
my process ID is 7139
```

and in another terminal window:

```
% vmmap 7139 > tmp1
```

Then set the MallocGuardEdges environment variable and run mallochelp again:

```
% setenv MallocGuardEdges 1
% ./mallochelp
malloc[7141]: protecting edges
my process ID is 7141
```

and run in the other terminal window:

```
% vmmap 7141 > tmp2
```

And then diff the two:

```
% diff tmp1 tmp2
```

And the interesting lines are:

```
> GUARD                          84000 [   4K] ---/rwx SM=NUL
> GUARD                          ab000 [   4K] ---/rwx SM=NUL
```

These are two new guard pages of 4K in size, with no user permissions (---) on them. I just kept lowering the amount of memory allocated until these guard pages did not appear.

Challenge

Find all the errors in this program, some of which are memory related (I found nine of them).

Example 7-14. memerror.m

```
// memerror.h -- try to find (and fix!) all the memory-related errors
//                in this program

// Take a string from the command line.  Make a linked-list out of it
// in reverse order. Traverse it to construct a string in reverse.
// Then clean up afterwards.

/* compile with
cc -g -o memerror memerror.m
*/

#import <stdio.h>
#import <stdlib.h>
```

```
typedef struct CharNode {
    char theChar;
    struct CharNode *next;
} CharNode;


// build a linked list backwards, then walk the list.

void reverseIt (char *stringbuffer)
{
    CharNode *head, *node;
    char *scan, *stop;

    // clear out local vars
    head = node = NULL;

    // find the start and end of the string so we can walk it
    scan = stringbuffer;
    stop = stringbuffer + strlen(stringbuffer) + 1;

    // walk the string
    while (scan < stop) {
        if (head == NULL) {
            head = malloc (sizeof(CharNode*));
            head->theChar = *scan;
            head->next = NULL;
        } else {
            node = malloc (sizeof(CharNode*));
            node->theChar = *scan;
            node->next = head;
            head = node;
        }
        scan++;
    }

     // ok, re-point to the buffer so we can drop the characters
    scan = stringbuffer;

    // walk the nodes and add them to the string
    while (head != NULL) {
        *scan = head->theChar;
        free (head);
        node = head->next;
        head = node;
        scan++;
    }

    // clean up the head
    free (head);

} // reverseIt


int main (int argc, char *argv[])
{
    char *stringbuffer;
```

```
    // make sure the user supplied enough arguments.  If not, complain
    if (argc != 2) {
        fprintf (stderr, "usage: %s string.  This reverses the string "
                "given on the command line\n");
        exit (1);
    }

    // make a copy of the argument so we can make changes to it
    stringbuffer = malloc (strlen(argv[1]));
    strcpy (argv[1], stringbuffer);

    // reverse the string
    reverseIt (stringbuffer);

    // and print it out
    printf ("the reversed string is '%s'\n", *stringbuffer);

    return (0);

} // main
```

Chapter 8. Debugging With GDB

What is a Debugger?

A debugger is a program that runs your program and has the power to suspend its execution and poke around in memory, examining and changing memory values. It can catch your program after it runs into trouble so you can investigate the problem. Debuggers know about the data structures you are using and can display those structures in an intellegent way. You can experiment with your program, and you can also step through someone else's code to figure out how it works.

Mac OS X comes with gdb, the GNU project's debugger, which has a long heritage dating back to 1988. It is fundamentally a command-line oriented tool, but it has been extended over the years to make integration into IDEs (like Project Builder and emacs) pretty easy.

To effectively use the debugger, your program needs to be compiled with debugging symbols enabled (usually by giving the -g flag to the compiler). These debugging symbols include lookup tables that map addresses in memory to the appropriate source file and line of code as well as data type information for the program's custom data structures. You can freely mix code which has debug symbols and no debug symbols. gdb will try its best it can to present a reasonable view of the world. Understandably, you will not be able to do much with code that has not been compiled with debug symbols.

Documentation for gdb can be found at /Developers/Documentation/DeveloperTools/gdb/gdb/gdb_toc.html. gdb has a positively huge feature list, but you will hit the highlights here.

Using GDB From The Command Line

First, look at driving gdb from the command line. Why waste time with gdb's command line mode? Historically gdb has been a command line program. You have access to all of gdb's features, both common and esoteric. The GUIs that are layered on top of gdb never export all of the features and so can limit some of the power that is lurking under the hood. Luckily, Project Builder gives you a console pane to interact with gdb's command line, so you have the best of both worlds there. Being comfortable at the gdb command line also makes gdb more useful when you want to do remote debugging (running your program and the debugger on another machine over an ssh connection, for instance) or if you are debugging non-GUI apps like web servers.

A Sample GDB Session

At the end of Chapter 7 (Memory) is a challenge to find all nine errors in the program memerror, which reverses a string given to the program as a command line argument.

Here we will use gdb and track down some of the errors.

Compile the program and make sure the -g flag is used to turn on debug symbols:

```
% cc -g -o memerror memerror.m
```

If you are using `Project Builder`, make sure that no optimizations are turned on. Otherwise, single-stepping will behave erratically.

Trying to run the program gives this:

```
% ./memerror blargle
the reversed string is '(null)'
```

Which is not the desired result.

Start gdb and tell it to use memerror for the target program:

```
% gdb ./memerror
GNU gdb 5.0-20001113 (Apple version gdb-203) (Wed Nov 7 16:28 GMT 2001)
Copyright 2000 Free Software Foundation, Inc.
[...]
(gdb)
```

Here gdb gives you its prompt. Since this is a small program, you will single-step over some code. Set a breakpoint on the **main()** function. A breakpoint is a spot in your code where gdb will halt your program's execution and give control to gdb so you can look around.

Here is how you set a breakpoint at the beginning of a function, which will get triggered before any code in the function gets executed:

```
(gdb) break main
Breakpoint 1 at 0x1d1c: file memerror.m, line 74.
```

and run the program:

```
(gdb) run
Starting program:/Users/markd/BNRunix/gdb-chapter/./memerror
[Switching to thread 1 (process 742 thread 0x1603)]

Breakpoint 1, main (argc=1, argv=0xbffffb44) at memerror.m:74
74          if (argc != 2) {
```

OK, so the breakpoint on **main()** was triggered. You will single-step using the next command to execute code one instruction at a time.

```
(gdb) next
75          fprintf (stderr, "usage: %s string.  This reverses the string "
```

Hmmm, that is interesting. You are on the usage line. You get in this case if argc is not two. What is argc's value?

```
(gdb) print argc
$1 = 1
```

It is a value of one, since you did not specify any arguments to the program (oops). The "$1" printed in the above statement can be ignored. It is a convenience variable you can use to refer to the value later.

So, just single step on out to finish the program:

```
(gdb) next
usage: kmewrkmfijq348tdrnmg8i34jtnragujnttns string. This reverses the
string given on the command line.
```

Wow. A lot of garbage there. Looks like you stumbled across the first bug (bug #1) unexpectedly:

```
fprintf (stderr, "usage: %s string.  This reverses the string "
            "given on the command line\n");
```

Note that **fprintf()** has a %s format specifier in the string, but no corresponding value to plug in there, so it picked up some garbage from the stack. Looks like it is expecting to use the name of the program as specified by the user in the message. That is an easy enough fix:

```
fprintf (stderr, "usage: %s string.  This reverses the string "
            "given on the command line\n", argv[0]);
```

You could quit gdb and run your compilation command again, but you could tell gdb to run a shell command for you to do it.

```
(gdb) shell cc -g -o memerror memerror.m
```

Now restart the program with a command-line argument:

```
(gdb) run blargle
The program being debugged has been started already.
Start it from the beginning? (y or n)
```

and answer y and press return. It will print out:

```
'/Users/markd/BNRunix/gdb-chapter/./memerror' has changed;
    rereading symbols.
```

to let you know that it realizes the program is different and needs to be reloaded.

Since you did not quit gdb, the breakpoint on **main()** is still active.

```
Breakpoint 1, main (argc=2, argv=0xbffffb38) at memerror.m:74
74              if (argc != 2) {
```

And just for paranoia's sake:

```
(gdb) print argc
$1 = 2
```

A value of two. Good. And for fun look at the argument vector:

```
(gdb) print argv
$2 = (char **) 0xbffffb38

(gdb) print argv[0]
$3 = 0xbffffbec "/Users/markd/BNRunix/gdb-chapter/./memerror\000"...

(gdb) print argv[1]
$4 = 0xbffffc16 "blargle\000"...
```

That looks good. So single-step

```
(gdb) next
81              stringbuffer = malloc (strlen(argv[1]));
```

and see how big that is going to be. You can call your program's functions from inside the debugger.

```
(gdb) call (int) strlen(argv[1])
$5 = 7
```

So this will allocate 7 bytes of memory. So single-step over the allocation:

```
(gdb) n
```

You can abbreviate commands so long as they do not become ambiguous. In this case, n is the same as next.

```
(gdb) n
82              strcpy (argv[1], stringbuffer);
```

Hmmm.. wait a minute. Strings in C are null-terminated, meaning that you need an extra byte. The above call to **malloc()** did not allocate enough memory, so this call to **strcpy()** (which you have not executed yet) will clobber an extra byte of memory. That is easy enough to fix in code. You would change

```
stringbuffer = malloc (strlen(argv[1]));
```

to be

```
stringbuffer = malloc (strlen(argv[1]) + 1);
```

Go ahead and change the code (bug #2). No need to recompile and rerun, you can patch this error for this session immediately.

```
(gdb) set var stringbuffer = (void *)malloc ((int)strlen(argv[1]) + 1)
```

Note that there are explicit casts for return values from functions you are calling. That is necessary when you call a function that does not have debug info (like the library functions **strlen()** and **malloc()**).

OK, with that done, execute the next line of code (the **strcpy()**):

```
(gdb) n
85              reverseIt (stringbuffer);
```

Look at stringbuffer to make sure it has a resonable value:

```
(gdb) print stringbuffer
$7 = 0x62c0 "\000"...
```

What? The line of code in question is:

```
strcpy (argv[1], stringbuffer);
```

Checking the man page, it looks like the arguments are reversed. **strcpy()** takes *destination* first, then the source (bug #3). This is also an easy code change to make:

```
strcpy (stringbuffer, argv[1]);
```

Unfortunately, you cannot fix this up as easily as you did with the **malloc()** error, since the bad **strcpy()** clobbered argv[1].

```
(gdb) print argv[1]
$9 = 0xbffffc16 "\000"...
```

So, fix the code, and rebuild:

```
(gdb) shell cc -g -o memerror memerror.m
```

You are reasonably sure now that the code up until the call to **reverseIt()** is pretty good. So add a new breakpoint on **reverseIt()**:

```
(gdb) break reverseIt
Breakpoint 2 at 0x1bb4: file memerror.m, line 30.
```

and rerun the program. You do not need to respecify the arguments given to the program, gdb will remember them.

```
(gdb) run

Starting program:/Users/markd/BNRunix/gdb-chapter/./memerror blargle
[Switching to thread 1 (process 778 thread 0x220b)]

Breakpoint 1, main (argc=2, argv=0xbffffb38) at memerror.m:74
74          if (argc != 2) {
(gdb)
```

Thus, you can see that your first breakpoint is still there. Doing continue will resume execution until the program exits, or a breakpoint is hit.

```
(gdb) continue
Continuing.

Breakpoint 2,reverseIt(stringbuffer=0x62b0 "blargle\000"...)
    at memerror.m:30
30          head = node = NULL;
```

You are in **reverseIt()**. You can ask gdb for a listing to remind yourself what code is involved:

```
(gdb) list
25      {
26          CharNode *head, *node;
27          char *scan, *stop;
28
29          // clear out local vars
30          head = node = NULL;
31
32          // find the start and end of the string so we can walk it
33          scan = stringbuffer;
34          stop = stringbuffer + strlen(stringbuffer) + 1;
```

So you are about ready to execute line 30. So some more single-stepping

```
(gdb) n
33          scan = stringbuffer;
(gdb) n
34          stop = stringbuffer + strlen(stringbuffer) + 1;
(gdb) n
```

```
37              while (scan < stop) {
```

and take a look at the pointer chase variables

```
(gdb) print scan
$1 = 0x62b0 "blargle\000"...

(gdb) print stop
$2 = 0x62b8 "\000"...
```

That looks OK. Looking at the address that stop has, 0x62b8, is 8 bytes past 0x62b0, the contents of scan. "Blargle" is 7 characters, plus the null byte is 8. That looks good. More single stepping:

```
(gdb) n
38              if (head == NULL) {

(gdb) n
39                  head = malloc (sizeof(CharNode*));
```

To sanity check the amount of memory being allocated:

```
(gdb) print sizeof(CharNode*)
$3 = 4
```

4 bytes. Pull apart the types here:

```
(gdb) whatis head
type = CharNode *
```

head is a pointer to a CharNode. What is a CharNode?

```
(gdb) ptype CharNode
type = struct CharNode {
    char theChar;
    CharNode *next;
}
```

A CharNode is a char plus a pointer. That sounds like it should be more than 4 bytes.

```
(gdb) print sizeof(CharNode)
$4 = 8
```

Sure enough, you are not allocating enough memory. Here is the line of code again:

```
        head = malloc (sizeof(CharNode*));
```

It is allocating enough memory for a pointer to a CharNode, not a CharNode itself. To fix this, it should be

```
        head = malloc (sizeof(CharNode));
```

(bug #4). Looking at the code, there is a nearly identical line of code in the else branch. That should be fixed too.

```
        node = malloc (sizeof(CharNode*));
```

becomes

```
node = malloc (sizeof(CharNode));
```

(bug #5).

You will need to recompile and restart things to fix this. Before doing that, clean up the breakpoints. You do not need the one on **main()**, and probably do not need the one at the top of **reverseIt()** since you are pretty sure the beginning of that function is good.

For fun, do the where command to see the call stack.

```
(gdb) where
#0  reverseIt (stringbuffer=0x62b0 "blargle\000"...) at memerror.m:39
#1  0x00001d80 in main (argc=2, argv=0xbffffb38) at memerror.m:85
#2  0x00001ae8 in _start ()
#3  0x00001918 in start ()
```

so you are at line 39 of memerror.m in **reverseIt()**, and at line 85 of memerror.m, inside of **main()**. Do a list to see exactly what gdb thinks is line 39.

```
(gdb) list
34              stop = stringbuffer + strlen(stringbuffer) + 1;
35
36              // walk the string
37              while (scan < stop) {
38                  if (head == NULL) {
39                      head = malloc (sizeof(CharNode*));
40                      head->theChar = *scan;
41                      head->next = NULL;
42                  } else {
43                      node = malloc (sizeof(CharNode*));
```

A good place to break would be on line 37, right before entering the loop.

```
(gdb) break memerror.m:37
Breakpoint 4 at 0x1be8: file memerror.m, line 37.
```

To see all the current breakpoints, info breakpoints will show them and their ID number:

```
(gdb) info breakpoints
Number Type          Disposition Enabled Address WhatStackFrame
    Condition                                IgnoreCount      Commands
1       breakpoint keep        y  0x001d10 in main at memerror.m:74
    breakpoint already hit 1             time
2       breakpoint keep        y  0x001bb4 in reverseIt at memerror.m:30
    breakpoint already hit 1             time
4       breakpoint keep        y  0x001be8 in reverseIt at memerror.m:37
```

Disable the first two.

```
(gdb) disable 1
(gdb) disable 2
```

and double-check that they are disabled:

```
(gdb) info breakpoints
Number Type         Disposition Enabled Address  WhatStackFrame
    Condition                                 IgnoreCount Commands
1       breakpoint keep      n  0x001d10 in main at memerror.m:74
    breakpoint already hit 1           time
2       breakpoint keep      n  0x001bb4 in reverseIt at memerror.m:30
    breakpoint already hit 1           time
4       breakpoint keep      y  0x001be8 in reverseIt at memerror.m:37
```

The "enabled" column now reads n for the first two breakpoints. So, assuming you have fixed the above `mallocs`, rebuild the program

```
(gdb) shell cc -g -o memerror memerror.m
```

and run it

```
(gdb) run
The program being debugged has been started already.
Start it from the beginning? (y or n) y
'/Users/markd/BNRunix/gdb-chapter/./memerror' has changed;
rereading symbols.
Starting program:/Users/markd/BNRunix/gdb-chapter/./memerror blargle
[Switching to thread 1 (process 793 thread 0x1813)]

Breakpoint 4,reverseIt(stringbuffer=0x62b0 "blargle\000"...)
    at memerror.m:37
37              while (scan < stop) {
```

And sure enough, you are at the beginning of the loop. Time to step again.

```
(gdb) n
38                  if (head == NULL) {

(gdb) print head
$1 = (CharNode *) 0x0
```

So you will go into the first branch of the `if`.

```
(gdb) n
39                      head = malloc (sizeof(CharNode));
(gdb) n
40                      head->theChar = *scan;
(gdb) n
41                      head->next = NULL;
(gdb) n
42                  } else {
```

And for fun, print out `head` to make sure it is sane:

```
(gdb) print *head
$2 = {
  theChar = 98 'b',
  next = 0x0
}
```

Looks good. Now step back through the top of the loop:

```
(gdb) n
48                       scan++;
(gdb) n
49              }
```

gdb will frequently stop on close braces, even though there is not really any code there to execute.

```
(gdb) n

Breakpoint 4,reverseIt(stringbuffer=0x62b0 "blargle\000"...)
    at memerror.m:37
37              while (scan < stop) {
```

And you are back at the top. For fun, double-check the value of scan:

```
(gdb) print scan
$3 = 0x62b1 "largle\000"...
```

This is good: you are one character into the string.

```
(gdb) n
38                       if (head == NULL) {
(gdb) n
43                       node = malloc (sizeof(CharNode));
```

Now you are into the else clause (notice the line number jump from 38 to 43).

```
(gdb) n
44                       node->theChar = *scan;
(gdb) n
45                       node->next = head;
(gdb) n
46                       head = node;
(gdb) n
48                       scan++;
```

And sanity check stuff:

```
(gdb) print *node
$4 = {
  theChar = 108 'l',
  next = 0x62c0
}

(gdb) print *node->next
$5 = {
  theChar = 98 'b',
  next = 0x0
}
```

So the linked list looks pretty good.

Step over the scan++:

```
(gdb) n
49              }
```

So you are reasonably sure the loop is good. The gdb command until will resume execution until the line of code after the current one. Since you are sitting on the close brace that terminates the loop, execution will continue until the loop finishes (no need to single-step through everything).

So, disable the breakpoint at the top of the loop (breakpoint 4 above)

```
(gdb) dis 4
```

and do until

```
(gdb) until
52              scan = stringbuffer;
```

Which just so happens to be after the loop.

Take a look at the linked list just to be sure:

```
(gdb) print *head
$8 = {
  theChar = 0 '\000',
  next = 0x6320
}

(gdb) print *head->next
$9 = {
  theChar = 101 'e',
  next = 0x6310
}

(gdb) print *head->next->next
$10 = {
  theChar = 108 'l',
  next = 0x6300
}

(gdb) print *head->next->next->next
$11 = {
  theChar = 103 'g',
  next = 0x62f0
}
```

Looks like a reversed string. That leading zero value at the head looks a bit odd. You might or might not want that in there. So, continuing on:

```
(gdb) n
55              while (head != NULL) {

(gdb) n
56                  *scan = head->theChar;

(gdb) n
57                  free (head);

(gdb) n
58                  node = head->next;
```

Something does not look right there. Print out *head again:

```
(gdb) print *head
$12 = {
  theChar = 0 '\000',
  next = 0x0
}
```

It does not look exactly like it did earlier. Oops. The head gets freed, and then the memory gets used after the **free()** (bug #6). That is pretty bad. So fix it. Change

```
free (head);
node = head->next;
```

to

```
node = head->next;
free (head);
```

Step a couple of times to go back to the top of the loop

```
(gdb) n
59                 head = node;
(gdb) n
60                 scan++;
(gdb) n
61           }
(gdb) n
55           while (head != NULL) {
```

and set a breakpoint here

```
(gdb) break
Breakpoint 5 at 0x1c84: file memerror.m, line 55.
```

Just break by itself sets a breakpoint at the current position.

So, rebuild

```
(gdb) shell cc -g -o memerror memerror.m
```

and restart. (I know I get a little peeved at the "The program being debugged has been started already. Start it from the beginning? (y or n)" messages, so I am going to turn them off, and then restart):

```
(gdb) set confirm off

(gdb) run
'/Users/markd/BNRunix/gdb-chapter/./memerror' has changed;
    rereading symbols.
[Switching to thread 1 (process 815 thread 0x2013)]

Breakpoint 5, reverseIt(stringbuffer=0x62b0 "blargle\000"...)
    at memerror.m:55
55           while (head != NULL) {
```

and then single-step some more, and then finish the loop:

```
55           while (head != NULL) {
(gdb) n
```

```
56                    *scan = head->theChar;
(gdb) n
57                    node = head->next;
(gdb) n
58                    free (head);
(gdb) n
59                    head = node;
(gdb) n
60                    scan++;
(gdb) n
61            }

(gdb) disable 5
(gdb) until
64            free (head);
```

Now take a look at the buffer

```
(gdb) print stringbuffer
$1 = 0x62b0 "\000"...
```

It does not look very promising. Maybe that leading zero byte in the linked list is messing things up. Look at the memory one byte into the string:

```
(gdb) print (char *)(stringbuffer + 1)
$2 = 0x62b1 "elgralb\000"...
```

Sure enough, that is "blargle" spelled backwards. So it looks like bug #7 is that extra zero byte. Where would that have come from? The code is walking the string from beginning to end, and building a reversed linked list, so the *last* character of the string becomes the *head* of the linked list, and it is the head where that zero byte is. So it looks like the first loop is going one byte too far. Revisit this line of code:

```
    stop = stringbuffer + strlen(stringbuffer) + 1;
```

There it is right there! It explicitly includes the trailing zero byte, but you do not want it. Change this line of code to

```
    stop = stringbuffer + strlen(stringbuffer);
```

So, it looks like you found the problem! Fix that code, quit gdb:

```
(gdb) quit
%
```

and rebuild the program:

```
% cc -o memerror memerror.m
```

and run it:

```
% ./memerror blargle
Bus error
```

Oops. You crashed. You were, like most programmers, a little too optimistic. gdb is pretty handy for catching crashes like these. There is usually a smoking gun. So, gdb the program:

```
% gdb ./memerror
[... copyright stuff ...]
```

You have to re specify the command line arguments since you exited gdb earlier.

```
(gdb) run blargle
Starting program:/Users/markd/BNRunix/gdb-chapter/./memerror blargle
[Switching to thread 1 (process 853 thread 0x1603)]

Program received signal EXC_BAD_ACCESS, Could not access memory.
0x70000a50 in strlen ()
```

and look at the stack:

```
(gdb) where
#0  0x70000a50 in strlen ()
#1  0x70001b14 in vfprintf ()
#2  0x700129f0 in printf ()
#3  0x00001d9c in main (argc=2, argv=0xbffffb38) at memerror.m:88
#4  0x00001aec in _start ()
#5  0x0000191c in start ()
```

Looks like something bad is happening at line 88 in memerror.m, stack frame number 3. Go to that frame:

```
(gdb) frame 3
#3  0x00001d9c in main (argc=2, argv=0xbffffb38) at memerror.m:88
88              printf ("the reversed string is '%s'\n", *stringbuffer);
```

What is stringbuffer?

```
(gdb) print stringbuffer
$1 = 0x62b0 "elgralb\000"...
```

That looks OK. Of course, looking closer at the code, why did the programmer dereference the stringbuffer pointer?

```
(gdb) print *stringbuffer
$2 = 101 'e'
```

So printf() is trying to interpret the number 101 as an address of a string. That is not a valid address, so eventually some function deep in the standard library will use that bad address and choke. Generally, if you see standard library functions on the stack, there is not anything really wrong with them. The code calling them has messed something up. This is an easy enough fix. Change

```
    printf ("the reversed string is '%s'\n", *stringbuffer);
```

to

```
    printf ("the reversed string is '%s'\n", stringbuffer);
```

Get out of gdb:

```
(gdb) quit
The program is running.  Exit anyway? (y or n) y
```

Fix the code and rebuild:

```
% cc -g -o memerror memerror.m
```

and run it:

```
% ./memerror blargle
the reversed string is 'elgralb'
```

Hooray! It works! You found eight errors. There are actually nine. The last one does not affect the program's output, but is a little bit of sloppiness. The string buffer gets memory from `malloc()`, but that memory is never explicitly freed.

GDB Specifics

The above walk through hits on the major things you can do with gdb in command-line mode:

- See program listings
- See the stack trace and move around in the stack looking at the variables in various functions
- Set and disable breakpoints
- Display data
- Change data
- Change execution flow

Here is some reference stuff of different commands that could be useful. This is still a very small subset of what gdb is capable of.

Help

gdb has extensive online help. Just doing `help` shows you the top-level classes of help available:

```
(gdb) help
List of classes of commands:

aliases -- Aliases of other commands
breakpoints -- Making program stop at certain points
data -- Examining data
files -- Specifying and examining files
internals -- Maintenance commands
obscure -- Obscure features
running -- Running the program
stack -- Examining the stack
status -- Status inquiries
support -- Support facilities
tracepoints -- Tracing of program execution without
               stopping the program
user-defined -- User-defined commands
```

You can look at a particular class of stuff:

```
(gdb) help breakpoints

Making program stop at certain points.

List of commands:

awatch -- Set a watchpoint for an expression
break -- Set breakpoint at specified line or function
catch -- Set catchpoints to catch events
clear -- Clear breakpoint at specified line or function
[...]
thbreak -- Set a temporary hardware assisted breakpoint
txbreak -- Set temporary breakpoint at procedure exit
watch -- Set a watchpoint for an expression
xbreak -- Set breakpoint at procedure exit
```

as well as help on a particular command:

```
(gdb) help until
Execute until the program reaches a source line greater than the
current or a specified line or address or function (same args as
break command). Execution will also stop upon exit from the current
stack frame.
```

The apropos command lets you search through the help if you do not know the exact name or class of a command.

```
(gdb) apropos thread
catch -- Set catchpoints to catch events
info mach-thread -- Get info on a specific thread
info mach-threads -- Get list of threads in a task
info thread -- Get information on thread
info threads -- IDs of currently known threads
[...]
thread -- Use this command to switch between threads
thread apply -- Apply a command to a list of threads
apply all -- Apply a command to all threads
thread resume -- Resume a thread
thread suspend -- Suspend a thread
```

Stack Traces

You can see a stack trace, that is, all of the currently active functions, with the where command (also backtrace and bt). It will show you the stack frames currently active:

```
(gdb) where
#0  0x70000a50 in strlen ()
#1  0x70001b14 in vfprintf ()
#2  0x700129f0 in printf ()
#3  0x00001d9c in main (argc=2, argv=0xbffffb38) at memerror.m:88
#4  0x00001aec in _start ()
#5  0x0000191c in start ()
```

The bottom-most frame, **start()** in this case is termed the "innermost" stack frame. The top of the stack is the "outermost" frame (good to know for some gdb documentation). You can move up and down the stack using up and down, up being towards the innermost frame, and down being towards the outermost. Unfortunately that is backwards from the way the stack is listed in the backtrace. Specifically, if you were at frame #3 (**main()**), doing down would put you into frame 2, doing up would put you into frame 4.

You can look at the local variables or arguments with a single operation:

info args

> Show all the arguments to the function.

info locals

> Show the local variables and their values.

info catch

> Show any active C++ exception handlers.

Program Listings

You can see around where you are by using the list command. You can see the first 10 lines around the beginning of a function by doing list function-name. To change the number of lines listed, use set listsize:

```
(gdb) set listsize 17
(gdb) list reverseIt
17          char theChar;
18          struct CharNode *next;
19      } CharNode;
20
21
22      // build a linked list backwards, then walk the list.
23
24      void reverseIt (char *stringbuffer)
25      {
26          CharNode *head, *node;
27          char *scan, *stop;
28
29          // clear out local vars
30          head = node = NULL;
31
32          // find the start and end of the string so we can walk it
33          scan = stringbuffer;
```

(Note that gdb lists lines centered on the given line.)

If you are very curious, you can see a disassembly of your code:

```
(gdb) break main
Note: breakpoint 1 also set at pc 0x1d1c.
Breakpoint 3 at 0x1d1c: file memerror.m, line 74.
(gdb) run
Starting program:/Users/markd/BNRunix/gdb-chapter/./memerror blargle
[Switching to thread 1 (process 916 thread 0x2107)]

Breakpoint 1, main (argc=2, argv=0xbffffb38) at memerror.m:74
```

```
74              if (argc != 2) {
(gdb) disassemble
Dump of assembler code for function main:
0x1cf8 <main>:         mflr    r0
0x1cfc <main+4>:       stmw    r30,-8(r1)
0x1d00 <main+8>:       stw     r0,8(r1)
0x1d04 <main+12>:      stwu    r1,-80(r1)
0x1d08 <main+16>:      mr      r30,r1
[...]
0x1d98 <main+160>:     bl      0x1f28 <dyld_stub_printf>
0x1d9c <main+164>:     li      r3,0
0x1da0 <main+168>:     bl      0x1ee0 <dyld_stub_exit>
0x1da4 <main+172>:     lwz     r1,0(r1)
0x1da8 <main+176>:     lwz     r0,8(r1)
0x1dac <main+180>:     mtlr    r0
0x1db0 <main+184>:     lmw     r30,-8(r1)
0x1db4 <main+188>:     blr
End of assembler dump.
```

Breakpoints

Use break to set a breakpoint. You can break on a function name, or you can give a filename:line specification to stop in a specific place.

Breakpoints can have conditions attached to them:

```
(gdb) break memerror.m:74 if argc != 2
Breakpoint 1 at 0x1d1c: file memerror.m, line 74.
```

This breakpoint will only be triggered if argc is not 2. You can also attach conditions after the breakpoint has been created by using the cond command.

```
(gdb) cond 2 (argc != 2)
```

rbreak lets you use a regular expression to stop on a bunch of functions. Very handy for overloaded functions in C++.

```
(gdb) rbreak .*printf.*
(sets about 35 breakpoints for me)
```

info breakpoints will show you all the currently active breakpoints.

You saw the next command previously. That steps one line of code at a time, but does not step into function calls. You can use step to go into function calls.

Breakpoints can be disabled (so they do not fire) or enabled (to wake up a disabled breakpoint). You can set an ignore count on a breakpoint which gets decremented every time the breakpoint is hit by using ignore breakpoint# count. When the ignore count reaches zero the breakpoint will trigger. You would use this when you know that the first 700 pieces of data process OK but item 701 fails.

Displaying Data

`print` can be used to display variables and the result of function calls. You can control the format of the displayed data by adding a format flag after the command:

```
(gdb) print i
$1 = 17263812

(gdb) print/x i
$2 = 0x1076cc4

(gdb) print /o i
$3 = 0101666304

(gdb) print/t i
$4 = 1000001110110110011000100
```

Here are some of the format flags:

/x

Hexadecimal

/d

Signed decimal

/u

Unsigned decimal

/o

Octal

/t

Binary (t for "two")

/c

Print as a character constant

/f

Floating point

You can use these in ad-hoc expressions too:

```
(gdb) print/o 0xfeedface
$5 = 037673375316

(gdb) print/d "help"
$7 = {104, 101, 108, 112, 0}

(gdb) print /x 0644
$8 = 0x1a4
```

These are life saver if your HP-16C calculator is not handy to do base conversions.

You can look at static/global variables in other scopes by qualifiying the variable name with a scope:

by file

```
"file"::variable-name
```

by function

```
function-name::variable-name
```

If you want to see all of the processor's registers, use `info registers`, which shows all registers except the floating point ones. `info all registers` shows all of them, including the AltiVec registers.

For Objective-C programs, there are a couple of commands:

`info classes`

Show all classes that have debugging symbols.

`info selectors`

Show all selectors.

If you are looking at a variable, `whatis variable-name` will show you the type of the variable name. `ptype type-name` will show you the datastructure for that type.

Lastly, you can call functions in your program with `call function-name`, independent of the main flow of execution that `gdb` currently has interrupted. This is nice if you have a complex data structure - you can write a program to look at the data structure and return a string that presents it in a more readable form. This is pretty much what the `po` (print object) command does. It invokes the **-description** method for the given object. One thing to look out for is that this function could crash `gdb` itself if the program state is bad or your function generates an access exception.

Changing Data

This is really easy. Use `set var varname = expression`, where `expression` can include standard C operators (+, -, |, &, etc) and can call functions in your program.

Changing Execution Flow

You can bail out of a function early with `return`. For functions that return values, you can also specify a return value. This is very useful if you know the function is going to return a bad value and you know what it should be returning.

`finish` will continue execution `until` the current function ends, then the program will break back in again. `until` will resume execution and break after the next instruction when `until` was invoked. This is useful (as seen above) for letting a loop finish.

Handy Tricks

Sometimes you are running and you get an error like this:

```
*** malloc[1064]: Deallocation of a pointer not malloced: 0x442b0;
This could be a double free(), or free() called with the
middle of an allocated block; Try setting environment
variable MallocHelp to see tools to help debug
```

But usually by the time you can react, your program has moved far past that. You can set a breakpoint on **malloc_printf()**, which is what generates that particular message.

Another even more common occurence in Cocoa programming is this error:

```
2002-08-20 18:33:04.545 badmessage[1082] ***-[NSCFArray frobulate:]:selecto
not recognized
2002-08-20 18:33:04.545 badmessage[1082] *** Uncaught exception:
<NSInvalidArgumentException> ***-[NSCFArray frobulate:]:selector not
recognized
```

And by the time you see this, your program is long past the point of the error. You can set a breakpoint on -**[NSException raise]** to break every time this happens.

It would be really handy to have a breakpoint put on -**[NSException raise]** every time you run gdb. You could add it to your Project Builder project and to the project templates. But that would not help you if you get someone else's project and they have this error. When gdb starts up, it looks for a file in your home directory called .gdbinit. It will read each line and execute it as if you had typed it in yourself. My .gdbinit contains:

Example 8-1. .gdbinit

```
fb -[NSException raise]
fb malloc_printf
```

fb stands for future break. gdb attempts to set the breakpoint whenever it loads a shared library or a framework. Eventually it will load the framework that contains -**[NSException raise]** or **malloc_printf** and set the breakpoint there.

What's nice is that this sets stuff for every gdb session you have no matter what is or is not set in the project.

Lastly, you can debug programs remotely, meaning that you do not have to physically be at the machine where the program being debugged is running. For embedded systems and kernel programming, you can set up a network connection or a serial line. For ordinary, every day programs, it is much easier to just ssh into the box (which means you need a login) and run the program. You can also attach gdb to a program that is already running. This is very useful for the user who always has some kind of bad problem but it never happens when you are around watching. In this case, ssh into their machine, attach to the program, set some breakpoints, do a continue, and leave it. Eventually the problem will manifest itself and you can poke around and see what is going wrong.

For The More Curious

Core files

Core files are a Unixism where a program that has crashed (usually by trying to read or write into memory it does not have access to) will write out its address space to disk. You can then poke around this core file with gdb and see what was happening when the program crashed, kind of like a software autopsy.

By default on Mac OS X, core files are not dropped when your program crashes. Core files take a *long* time to write on OS X, and on machines with less-than-stellar disk throughput, it can hose your machine for a fair number of seconds while the core file is being written. So in general you will not get core files unless you ask for them.

Here is a program that can generate errors that can drop core files:

Example 8-2. assert.m

```
// assert.m -- invoke assert, thereby dropping a core file

/* compile with:
cc -g -Wall -o assert assert.m
*/

#import <assert.h>        // for assert
#import <stdio.h>         // for printf() and friends
#import <string.h>        // for strlen()
#import <stdlib.h>        // for EXIT_SUCCESS

void anotherFunction (char *ook)
{
    assert (strlen(ook) > 0);

    printf ("wheeee! Got string %s\n", ook);

} // anotherFunction


void someFunction (char *blah)
{
    anotherFunction (blah);
} // someFunction


int main (int argc, char *argv[])
{
    someFunction (argv[1]);
    return (EXIT_SUCCESS);
} // main
```

If you run this with no arguments, you will get a bus error (since `anotherFunction()` tries to print a NULL pointer). If it is run with an argument of "", an assertion will be raised that causes a core dump. If run with a non-empty argument, it will get printed out.

If you run it using the default environment, no core file is dropped. You can tell your shell to allow programs to drop cores:

```
% limit
cputime         unlimited
filesize        unlimited
datasize        6144 kbytes
stacksize       4335 kbytes
coredumpsize    0 kbytes
memoryuse       unlimited
descriptors     256
memorylocked    unlimited
maxproc         100
```

Note that `coredumpsize` is zero kbytes. You can up the limit with

```
% limit coredumpsize unlimited
```

Now, if you run the program

```
% ./assert ""
assert.m:13: failed assertion 'strlen(ook) > 0'
Abort (core dumped)
```

core files get dropped in the `/cores` directory with the name `core.process-id`.

Then you can look at it in gdb:

```
% gdb ./assert /cores/core.1104
[... copyright stuff ...]
warning: core file may not match specified executable file.
#0  0x7001a70c in kill ()
```

So the program terminated in the **kill()** function. Look at the whole stack trace:

```
(gdb) where
#0  0x7001a70c in kill ()
#1  0x7006f990 in abort ()
#2  0x00001df0 in __eprintf ()
#3  0x00001d00 in anotherFunction(ook=0xbffffc85 "\000"...)
        at assert.m:13
#4  0x00001d48 in someFunction (blah=0xbffffc85 "\000"...)
        at assert.m:21
#5  0x00001d84 in main (argc=2, argv=0xbffffbec) at assert.m:27
#6  0x00001bf8 in _start ()
#7  0x00001a28 in start ()
```

Move to the third stack frame:

```
(gdb) up 3
#3  0x00001d00 in anotherFunction(ook=0xbffffc85 "\000"...)
        at assert.m:13
13                  assert (strlen(ook) > 0);
```

This is the assert. The smoking gun, so you know exactly what happened.

You can turn off core dumps by doing

```
% limit coredumpsize 0
```

One place where core files are very useful is for crashes that happen out in the field, where the user can send you the core file for later dissection. However, having them run a shell and set limits might not be practical. You can programmatically tell the system you want to drop a core file even if the shell limit is zero. Recall from Chapter 7 (Memory) about process resource limits. One of the resource limits is RLIMIT_CORE, the largest size (in bytes) of core files. You can manaully use the resource limit calls to increase the coredump size. Here is a modified assert.m:

Example 8-3. assert2.m

```
// assert2.m -- invoke assert, thereby dropping a core file

/* compile with:
cc -g -Wall -o assert2 assert2.m
*/

#import <assert.h>          // for assert()
#import <stdio.h>           // for printf() and firends
#import <sys/types.h>       // for random types
#import <sys/time.h>        // for random types
#import <sys/resource.h>    // for setrlimit()
#import <errno.h>           // for errno
#import <string.h>          // for strlen()
#import <stdlib.h>          // for EXIT_SUCCESS


void anotherFunction (char *ook)
{
    assert (strlen(ook) > 0);

    printf ("wheeee! Got string %s\n", ook);

} // anotherFunction


void someFunction (char *blah)
{
    anotherFunction (blah);
} // someFunction

void enableCoreDumps ()
{
    struct rlimit rl;

    rl.rlim_cur = RLIM_INFINITY;
    rl.rlim_max = RLIM_INFINITY;


    if (setrlimit (RLIMIT_CORE, &rl) == -1) {
        fprintf (stderr, "error in setrlimit for RLIMIT_CORE: %d (%s)\n",
                errno, strerror(errno));
    }

} // enableCoreDumps
```

```
int main (int argc, char *argv[])
{
    enableCoreDumps ();

    someFunction (argv[1]);
    return (EXIT_SUCCESS);
} // main
```

If you run it now, you get a core file:

```
% ./assert2 ""
assert2.m:19: failed assertion 'strlen(ook) > 0'
Abort (core dumped)
```

To use this in a real program, you might want to put in some secret way that the user can execute that function to allow core dumping. Like, "Command-click the about box OK button and you will get a debug panel. Check the core dump check box, then do whatever it is that crashes the program."

Stripping

Debugging symbols are pretty big and can bloat up your executable. A simple Cocoa application of mine weighs in at 262K with debug symbols, whereas without the symbols it is about 30K. Depending on the application, keeping debug symbols around might not be a bad thing. For a high-traffic web server application, we kept the debug symbols to make diagnosing production problems easier (and it really came in handy sometimes). If your program has 500 megs of graphics and support files, a couple of hundred K of debug symbols probably is not too bad. On the other hand, if you are writing smaller downloadable applications, the extra hundred K or a meg could be a significant barrier to your program being used. You can either rebuild your program using the **Deployment** target in `Project Builder`, or you can just run the `strip` program against the executable. For instance:

```
% ls -l BorkPad
-rwxr-xr-x  1 markd  staff  262780 Aug 19 21:10 BorkPad
% strip BorkPad
% ls -l BorkPad
-rwxr-xr-x  1 markd  staff  30608 Aug 20 21:37 BorkPad
```

So what happens then if your program crashes out in the field? If you can get a core file, you can load the core file into a `gdb` session with an unstripped version of your executable and be able to debug symbolically. For example, use the `assert2` program, make a stripped copy, and generate a core file:

```
% cp assert2 stripped
% strip stripped
% ./stripped ""
assert2.m:19: failed assertion 'strlen(ook) > 0'
Abort (core dumped)
```

If you `gdb` the stripped program, thestack traces are not very useful:

```
% gdb stripped /cores/core.2342
```

```
...
(gdb) where
#0   0x9001b52c in kill ()
#1   0x9005ceec in abort ()
#2   0x00001d18 in dyld_stub_exit ()
#3   0x00001c20 in ?? ()
#4   0x00001c64 in ?? ()
#5   0x00001ca4 in ?? ()
#6   0x00001978 in ?? ()
#7   0x000017f8 in ?? ()
```

But if you use the original, unstripped file, you have good stack traces:

```
% gdb assert2 /cores/core.2342
...
(gdb) where
#0   0x9001b52c in kill ()
#1   0x9005ceec in abort ()
#2   0x00001d18 in dyld_stub_exit ()
#3   0x00001c20 in anotherFunction (ook=0xbffffb87 "\000"...)
     at assert2.m:19
#4   0x00001c64 in someFunction (blah=0xbffffb87 "\000"...)
     at assert2.m:27
#5   0x00001ca4 in main (argc=2, argv=0xbffffadc) at assert2.m:37
#6   0x00001978 in _start (argc=2, argv=0xbffffadc, envp=0xbffffae8)
     at /SourceCache/Csu/Csu-45/crt.c:267
#7   0x000017f8 in start ()
```

If you do not want to mess with gdb, or the user emails you a stack trace from the crash reporter, you can use atos to map the address to a symbol to see what function and line caused the problem.

```
% atos -o assert2 0x00001ca4
_main (assert2.m:38)

% atos -o assert2 0x00001c20
_anotherFunction (assert2.m:21)
```

More Advanced GDB Commands

Threads

gdb supports debugging threaded programs (we have lots to say about threading isses in Chapter 22 (Threads)) but here are some useful commands relating to threads.

info threads

Shows information about all the currently active threads. Here is something from a simple Cocoa program while the **Page Setup** dialog is active:

```
(gdb) info threads
  3 process 1208 thread 0x2123 0x70000978 in mach_msg_overwrite_trap ()
  2 process 1208 thread 0x1f07 0x70000978 in mach_msg_overwrite_trap ()
* 1 process 1208 thread 0x1603 0x70000978 in mach_msg_overwrite_trap ()
```

You can change between threads with the `thread` command, and then poke around and see what it is doing:

```
(gdb) thread 3
[Switching to thread 3 (process 1208 thread 0x2123)]
#0  0x70000978 in mach_msg_overwrite_trap ()

(gdb) where
#0  0x70000978 in mach_msg_overwrite_trap ()
#1  0x70005a04 in mach_msg ()
#2  0x7017bf84 in __CFRunLoopRun ()
#3  0x701b70ec in CFRunLoopRunSpecific ()
#4  0x7017b8cc in CFRunLoopRunInMode ()
#5  0x7061be08 in XIOAudioDeviceManager::NotificationThread ()
#6  0x706141c0 in CAPThread::Entry ()
#7  0x7002054c in _pthread_body ()
```

`thread apply`

Run a command for every thread.

```
(gdb) thread apply all where

[... took out the same stack trace as above ...]

Thread 2 (process 1208 thread 0x1f07):
#0  0x70000978 in mach_msg_overwrite_trap ()
#1  0x70005a04 in mach_msg ()
#2  0x70026a2c in _pthread_become_available ()
#3  0x70026724 in pthread_exit ()
#4  0x70020550 in _pthread_body ()


Thread 1 (process 1208 thread 0x1603):
#0  0x70000978 in mach_msg_overwrite_trap ()
#1  0x70005a04 in mach_msg ()
#2  0x7017bf84 in __CFRunLoopRun ()
#3  0x701b70ec in CFRunLoopRunSpecific ()
#4  0x7017b8cc in CFRunLoopRunInMode ()
...
#23 0x7938bed0 in NSApplicationMain ()
#24 0x000036b4 in _start ()
#25 0x000034e4 in start ()
#0  0x70000978 in mach_msg_overwrite_trap ()
```

When debugging, one thread is always the focus for the debugging, known as the current thread. You can break in particular threads if you wish, using `thread apply # break ...`. When the program stops, all threads stop, and when the program starts (even just doing a step), all threads potentially start as well. Note that during the time of the single-step, the other threads will run full bore. The single-stepping only applies to the current thread.

Chapter 9. Exceptions, Error Handling, and Signals

One of the grisly facts of programming life is that errors can happen and program code must react to those errors and deal with them appropriately. With the Unix APIs, there are two primary ways that exceptional conditions are communicated to programs. One is through return codes from function calls plus a global variable that describes the error in more detail. The other is through signals sent to the program from the OS. The Cocoa framework in Mac OS X also provides an exception-handling architecture that programs can take advantage of.

errno

Most of the library functions and system calls provided by Mac OS X have a return value that signifies that an error happened during the execution of the call. The global integer variable `errno` will be set to a value to indicate what went wrong.

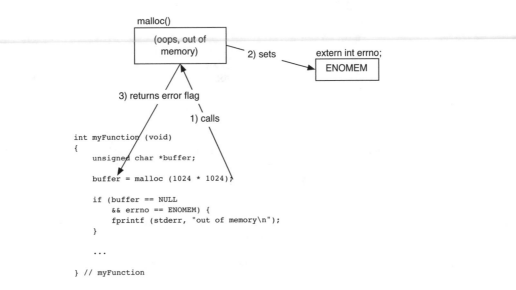

You can use the function **strerror()** to get a human description of the error. It is necessary to #include <errno.h> to get the definition of errno. The prototype for **strerror()** lives in <string.h>. You can look in /usr/include/sys/errno.h for the complete set of errno values. It is important to include errno.h rather than providing your own extern int errno, since errno is implemented in a thread-safe manner that is more than just a simple global int.

The man pages for Unix calls spell out in detail what the error code is and what specific errno values are set. For example, from the open(2) man page:

```
OPEN(2)                 System Calls Manual                 OPEN(2)

NAME
     open - open or create a file for reading or writing

SYNOPSIS
     #include <fcntl.h>
```

```
int
open (char *path, int flags, mode_t mode);
```

DESCRIPTION
The file name specified by path is opened for reading and/or
writing as specified by the argument flags and the file
descriptor returned to the calling process. The flags argument
may indicate the file is to be created if it does not exist (by
....
If successful, open() returns a non-negative integer, termed a
file descriptor. It returns -1 on failure. The file pointer
used to mark the current position within the file is set to the
beginning of the file.

ERRORS
The named file is opened unless:

[ENOTDIR]   A component of the path prefix is not a
                     directory.

[ENAMETOOLONG]   A component of a pathname exceeded
                     {NAME_MAX} characters, or an entire path
                     name exceeded {PATH_MAX} characters.

[ENOENT]   O_CREAT is not set and the named file does not
                     exist.

[ENOENT]   A component of the path name that must exist
                     does not exist.

...

[EFAULT]   Path points outside the process's allocated
                     address space.

[EEXIST]   O_CREAT and O_EXCL were specified and the file
                     exists.

[EOPNOTSUPP]   An attempt was made to open a socket (not
                     currently implemented).

The symbols in square brackets are the errno value. Here is some code that looks
for specific errors, and presumably would handle them as appropriate. This is an
example of detecting the errors.

Example 9-1. open.m

```
// open.m -- try opening files and getting different errors.


/* compile with:
cc -g -Wall -o open open.m
*/

#import <fcntl.h>        // for open()
#import <unistd.h>       // for close()
```

```
#import <sys/stat.h>     // for permission flags
#import <stdlib.h>       // for EXIT_SUCCESS, etc
#import <stdio.h>        // for printf() and friends
#import <errno.h>        // for errno
#import <string.h>       // for strerror()

// given a path and access flags, try to open the file.
// if an error happens, write it out to standard error.

void tryOpen (const char *path, int flags)
{
    int result;

    result = open (path, flags, S_IRUSR | S_IWUSR | S_IRGRP | S_IWGRP);

    if (result == -1) {
        fprintf (stderr, "an error happened opening %s\n", path);

        switch (errno) {

          case ENOTDIR:
            fprintf (stderr, "    part of the path is not a directory\n");
            break;

          case ENOENT:
            fprintf (stderr, "    something doesn't exist, "
                     "like part of a path, or O_CREAT is not set and "
                     "the file doesn't exist\n");
            break;

          case EISDIR:
            fprintf (stderr, "    tried to open directory for writing\n");
            break;

          default:
            fprintf (stderr, "    another error happened:  "
                     "errno %d, strerror: %s\n",
                     errno, strerror(errno));
        }

    } else {
        close (result);
    }

    fprintf (stderr, "\n");

} // tryOpen

int main (int argc, char *argv[])
{
    // trigger ENOTDIR
    tryOpen ("/mach.sym/blah/blah", O_RDONLY);

    // trigger ENOENT, part of the path doesn't exist
    tryOpen ("/System/Frameworks/bork/my-file", O_RDONLY);

    // trigger ENOENT, O_CREAT not set and file doesn't exist
```

```
    tryOpen ("/tmp/my-file", O_RDONLY);

    // trigger EISDIR
    tryOpen ("/dev", O_WRONLY);

    // trigger EEXIST
    tryOpen ("/private/var/log/system.log", O_CREAT | O_EXCL);

    return (EXIT_SUCCESS);

} // main
```

In most cases it is not possible to handle *every* possible error condition (like ENFILE: System file table is full). But in general try to handle what error makes sense and have a catch-all case that will log the error. The main downside with this error reporting technique is that it is necessary to check the result code of every function call which can get tedious pretty quickly. Plus all of the error-handling code obscures the flow of control.

With that caveat, you are free to use this convention (special error value, assign errno to a result code) for your own code, which can be nice when you are supplying a library to programmers familiar with the Unix conventions. There is no standard way to add your own error strings to **strerror()**, unfortunately.

setjmp, longjmp

Languages like C++ and Java have exception-handling features built in. This is where code can happily go about its business, but if something goes wrong, an exception can be thrown which will terminate the current flow of code. Control resumes execution at a previously registered exception handler which can then decide how best to recover from the problem and resume the work.

C has a primitive form of exception handling that can be used in a similar manner. The **setjmp** and **longjmp** functions are used like a super-goto:

```
int setjmp(jmp_buf env);

void longjmp(jmp_buf env, int val);
```

The jmp_buf is a data structure that holds the current execution context (the current program counter, stack pointer, etc). You **setjmp** where you want execution to return (equivalent to your exception handler), and call **longjmp** when you want to branch back to that point (equivalent to throwing an exception).

Here is a sample:

Example 9-2. longjmp.m

```
// longjmp.m -- use setjmp, longjmp

/* compile with:
cc -g -Wall -o longjmp longjmp.m
*/

#import <setjmp.h>      // for setjmp / longjmp
#import <stdio.h>       // for printf
```

```
#import <stdlib.h>        // for EXIT_SUCCESS

static jmp_buf handler;

void doEvenMoreStuff ()
{
    printf ("        entering doEvenMoreStuff\n");
    printf ("        done with doEvenMoreStuff\n");

} // doEvenMoreStuff

void doMoreStuff ()
{
    printf ("    entering doMoreStuff\n");
    doEvenMoreStuff ();
    longjmp (handler, 23);
    printf ("    done with doMoreStuff\n");
} // doMoreStuff

void doStuff ()
{
    printf ("entering doStuff\n");
    doMoreStuff ();
    printf ("done with doStuff\n");
} // doStuff

int main (int argc, char *argv[])
{
    int result;

    if ( (result = setjmp(handler)) ) {
        printf ("longjump called, result of %d\n", result);
    } else {
        doStuff ();
    }

    return (EXIT_SUCCESS);

} // main
```

A sample run:

```
% ./longjmp
entering doStuff
    entering doMoreStuff
        entering doEvenMoreStuff
        done with doEvenMoreStuff
longjump called, result of 23
```

Note that the "done with" statements for two of the functions never get executed. They just get jumped over.

The interesting piece here is the `if` statement. When **setjmp()** is called, it returns zero so the second branch of the `if` is taken. When **longjmp()** is called, that `if` statement is essentially evaluated again and execution begins again at that point. The argument to **longjmp()** is what is returned from **setjmp()** the second time it returns.

Any number of `setjmp()` calls can be active at any point in time, so long as they use different memory locations for their `jmp_bufs`. You can maintain a stack of `jmp_bufs` so that `longjmp` knows to jump to the closest `setjmp()`. This is what Cocoa uses for its exception handling mechanism (discussed after Signals).

There is one rule to remember when using `setjmp()` and `longjmp()`. Any local variables in the function that calls `setjmp()` and that might be used after a `longjmp()` must be declared `volatile`. That will force the compiler to read the variables from memory each time rather than using processor registers. `setjmp` saves some processor state, but it does not save every register. When `longjmp()` branches back to its matching `setjmp()`, any garbage in the registers can give you wrong values in variables.

Signals

Signals are like software interrupts, they can be delivered to your program at any time due to a number of well-defined conditions, like when you write out of your memory you will get sent a `SIGBUS` (bus error) or a `SIGSEGV` (segmentation violation) signal. If a subprocess of yours terminates you will get a `SIGCHLD` (child stopped) signal. If your controlling terminal goes away, there is `SIGHUP` (terminal hung up), and if you use the `alarm()` function, you will get sent `SIGALRM` when the time expires. The system defines about 31 different signals, many of which deal with job control or specific hardware issues.

A Signal is delivered to your program asynchronously whenever it enters the operating system, whether it be via a system call or just regular process scheduling. This means that your code can be interrupted at pretty much any time to handle the signal.

As seen above, signals are named with SIG plus an abbreviation of what the signal does. (These are defined in `<sys/signal.h>` if you are curious as to what is there.) The `signal()` function (which is a simplified form of `sigaction`, which will be discussed shortly) is used to provide a handler for a signal.

Handling A Signal

Use the `signal` function to register a signal handler.

```
typedef void (*sig_t) (int);

sig_t signal (int sig, sig_t func);
```

where `sig` is the signal number (e.g., `SIGHUP`) and `func` is the handler function. If you do not call `signal()` for a particular signal, the system default handler is used. Depending on the signal, the default handler will either ignore the signal or terminate the process. Check the `signal(2)` man page for details on which is which.

Here is a simple program that will catch some signals and either print out that the signal was caught (`SIGHUP` and `SIGUSR1`), or exit (`SIGUSR2`). By the way, `SIGUSR1` and `SIGUSR2` are signals that your program can use for its own purposes. The OS will not send those signals unless explicitly told to.

Example 9-3. catch.m

```
// catch.m -- catch some signals

/* compile with:
cc -g -Wall -o catch catch.m
*/

#import <signal.h>       // for signal functions and types
#import <stdio.h>        // printf and friends
#import <stdlib.h>       // for EXIT_SUCCESS
#import <unistd.h>       // for sleep
#import <string.h>       // for strlen

static void writeString (const char *string)
{
    int length = strlen (string);
    write (STDOUT_FILENO, string, length);
} // writeString

void handleHUP (int signo)
{
    writeString ("got a HUP!\n");
} // handleHUP

void handleUsr1Usr2 (int signo)
{
    if (signo == SIGUSR1) {
        writeString ("got a SIGUSR1\n");

    } else if (signo == SIGUSR2) {
        writeString ("got a SIGUSR2. exiting\n");
        exit (EXIT_SUCCESS);
    }

} // handleUsr1Usr2

int main (int argc, char *argv[])
{
    int i;

    // register our signal handlers

    (void) signal (SIGHUP, handleHUP);
    (void) signal (SIGUSR1, handleUsr1Usr2);
    (void) signal (SIGUSR2, handleUsr1Usr2);

    // now do our Real Work

    for (i = 0; i < 500000; i++) {
        printf ("i is %d\n", i);
        sleep (1);
    }

    return (EXIT_SUCCESS);

} // main
```

And a sample run. Here two terminals are used: one to see the output, and the other to run the `kill` command, which sends signals to programs.

```
Terminal 1                        Terminal 2
% ./catch &
[1] 7429   (this is the process ID)
1
2
3
4
5
6
7                                 kill -HUP 7429
got a HUP!
8
9
10
11
12                                kill -USR1 7429
got a SIGUSR1
13
14
15
16
17
18                                kill -USR2 7429
got a SIGUSR2, exiting
[1]   Done   ./catch
```

Some things to note: A signal handler can handle more than one signal; also, the return value of **signal()** is the previously registered function. If you are adding a signal handler to a library, or know that more than one handler will be registered for a signal, you should hang on to that return value and call that when your handler is invoked. If you want to register the same function for a bunch of signals, you will need to call **signal()** a bunch of times.

To ignore a signal, use the constant SIG_IGN instead of a function address. To restore the default behavior, use SIG_DFL. You cannot ignore or block the SIGKILL or SIGSTOP. That gives system adminstrators the ability to kill any process that has run amok.

Also, if you want to send yourself a signal, use the **raise()** system call

```
int raise (int sig);
```

where `sig` is a signal number. You can terminate yourself by raising SIGKILL.

Blocking Signals

Sometimes it is inconvenient to have a signal handled during a critical piece of code. For instance you are using a signal to interrupt a long-running process but you do not want to stop in the middle of a complex data structure change and leave your program's environment in an inconsistent state.

Every running program has a signal mask associated with it. This is a bitmask that specifies what signals are blocked from delivery. When a signal is blocked like this, the kernel keeps track of which blocked signals have been sent to the application (but not how many times a signal has been sent). The signal gets delivered when it gets unblocked.

Figure 9-1. Blocking Signals

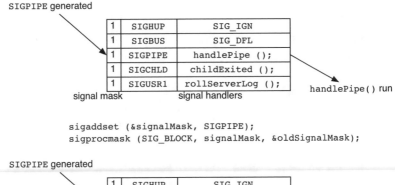

You use **sigprocmask()** to control the signal mask:

```
int sigprocmask (int how, const sigset_t *set, sigset_t *oset);
```

how is one of

SIG_BLOCK

Add the given signals to the program's signal mask (union).

SIG_UNBLOCK

Remove the signals from the program's signal mask (intersection).

SIG_SETMASK

Replace the program's signal mask with the new one.

sigset_t is an abstract type that represents the signal mask. set is the set of signals you want to add or remove, and oset is the original set. (handy for feeding back into **sigprocmask** with SIG_SETMASK). You manipulate sigset_t with these functions (defined in man sigsetops(3)).

```
int sigemptyset (sigset_t *set);
```

Clear a signal set to all zeros (no signals).

```
int sigfillset (sigset_t *set);
```

Fill it with all 1s (all signals).

```
int sigaddset (sigset_t *set, int signo);
```

Add a specific signal to the set.

```
int sigdelset (sigset_t *set, int signo);
```

Remove a specific signal from the set.

```
int sigismember (const sigset_t *set, int signo);
```

Test membership

Here is a variation of the catch program above, but instances in which i is not a multiple of five are considered a critical section.

Example 9-4. catchblock.m

```
// catchblock.m -- catch and block some signals

/* compile with:
cc -g -Wall -o catchblock catchblock.m
*/

#import <signal.h>      // for signal functions and types
#import <stdio.h>       // printf and friends
#import <stdlib.h>      // for EXIT_SUCCESS
#import <unistd.h>      // for sleep
#import <string.h>      // for strlen

static void writeString (const char *string)
{
    int length = strlen (string);
    write (STDOUT_FILENO, string, length);

} // writeString

void handleHUP (int signo)
{
    writeString ("got a HUP!\n");

} // handleHUP

void handleUsr1Usr2 (int signo)
{
    if (signo == SIGUSR1) {
        writeString ("got a SIGUSR1\n");

    } else if (signo == SIGUSR2) {
        writeString ("got a SIGUSR2. exiting\n");
        exit (EXIT_SUCCESS);
    }

} // handleUsr1Usr2

int main (int argc, char *argv[])
{
    int i;
    sigset_t signalMask, oldSignalMask;
```

```
    // register our signal handlers

    (void) signal (SIGHUP, handleHUP);
    (void) signal (SIGUSR1, handleUsr1Usr2);
    (void) signal (SIGUSR2, handleUsr1Usr2);

    // construct our signal mask.  We don't want to be bothered
    // by SIGUSR1 or SIGUSR2 in our critical section.
    // but we will leave SIGHUP out of the mask so that it will get
    // delivered

    sigemptyset (&signalMask);
    sigaddset (&signalMask, SIGUSR1);
    sigaddset (&signalMask, SIGUSR2);

    // now do our Real Work

    for (i = 0; i < 500000; i++) {
        printf ("i is %d\n", i);

        if ( (i % 5) == 0) {
            printf ("blocking at %i\n", i);
            sigprocmask (SIG_BLOCK, &signalMask, &oldSignalMask);
        }

        if ( (i % 5) == 4) {
            printf ("unblocking at %i\n", i);
            sigprocmask(SIG_SETMASK, &oldSignalMask, NULL);
        }

        sleep (1);
    }

    return (EXIT_SUCCESS);

} // main
```

A sample run:

```
Terminal 1                              Terminal 2
./catchblock &
[1] 7533
i is 0
blocking at 0
i is 1
i is 2
i is 3
i is 4
unblocking at 4
i is 5
blocking at 5
i is 6                                  kill -HUP 7533
got a HUP!
i is 7
i is 8                                  kill -HUP 7533
got a HUP!
```

```
i is 9
unblocking at 9
i is 10
blocking at 10
i is 11                                        kill -USR1 7533
i is 12
i is 13
i is 14
unblocking at 14
got a SIGUSR1
i is 15
blocking at 15
i is 16                                        kill -USR1 7533
i is 17                                        kill -USR1 7533
i is 18                                        kill -USR1 7533
i is 19
unblocking at 19
got a SIGUSR1
i is 20
blocking at 20
i is 21
i is 22                                        kill -USR2 7533
i is 23
i is 24
unblocking at 24
got a SIGUSR2. exiting
```

It works as expected: HUPs make it through immediately, and USR1 and USR2 are only handled once at the unblocking no matter how many times they are sent.

You can use **sigpending()** to see if a signal of interest is pending:

```
int sigpending (sigset_t *set);
```

Which returns a mask of the pending signals.

Handling signals with *sigaction()*

sigaction() is the full-featured way of handling signals:

```
struct sigaction {
    void     (*sa_handler)();
    sigset_t sa_mask;
    int      sa_flags;
};
```

```
int sigaction (int sig, const struct sigaction *act,
                         struct sigaction *oact);
```

Instead of just passing in a handler function, you pass in a structure containing the handler function, the set of signals that should be added to the process signal mask, and some flags. Usually you just set them to zero. The **sigaction()** man page describes them (mainly used for some SIGCHLD signals, or for controlling which stack is used when signals are handled).

Like **signal()**, the previous setting is returned, this time in the oact parameter if it is non-NULL.

Signal Issues

Reentrancy

There are a number of difficult programming issues involved with signals which sometimes make them more difficult to deal with than they are worth. The first is reentrancy, and the second concerns race conditions.

A reentrant function is one that will work if there are two execution streams active in it at one time. This can happen even without threads. For example, consider this code:

```
...
ptr = malloc (50);
...
```

The program is in the middle of calling `malloc()` and `malloc()` is messing with its internal data structures and is in an inconsistent state. Then a signal happens. Since signals happen asynchronously, your program is interrupted and the signal handler runs:

```
...
tempPtr = malloc (20);
...
```

Since `malloc()` is in the middle of its previous work you will most likely crash.

In your signal handlers you should only use reentrant functions. Unfortunately the `sigaction()` man page in Mac OS X 10.2 does not list the known system and library functions that are reentrant (even though the `signal()` man page says it should).

In general, these are safe:

- `longjmp()`
- Reentrant versions of functions, like `strtok_r()`
- Program terminators like `abort()` and `exit()`
- Unbuffered I/O (`read()`, `write()`, `open()`, etc)
- Interrogative functions (`getgid()`, `getpid()`, `getuid()`)
- Signal functions (`sigaction()`, `sigprocmask()`)
- Any of your own reentrant functions

These are unsafe:

- Buffered I/O printf and friends. That is why a custom writeString function was used earlier
- `malloc()` and `free()`
- Anything using static buffer space, like `strtok()`
- Any of your non reentrant functions

You do not need to make your signal handler reentrant. When a signal handler is entered, the signal that triggered the handler is automatically added to the process signal mask. The handler will not get triggered again until it returns. Note that if a handler is registered for more than one signal using **signal()** or **sigaction()**, you will need to make it reentrant.

You may notice that **longjmp()** is on the set of safe functions. You are free to **longjmp()** out of a signal handler to wherever the matching **setjmp()** was placed. This is a way of handling the interruption of a long running process. You may wonder about the process signal mask. If you **longjmp()** out of a handler, is the signal still being blocked? **longjmp()** automatically restores the signal mask when jumping out of a signal handler. If you do not want this behavior (like what exists on some other Unixes) you can use the **_setjmp()** and **_longjmp()** functions.

Here is an example of breaking out of a long-running process.

Example 9-5. interrupt.m

```
// interrupt.m -- show interruption of a long-running process

/* compile with:
cc -g -Wall -o interrupt interrupt.m
*/

#import <signal.h>      // for signal functions and types
#import <unistd.h>      // for sleep
#import <string.h>      // for strerror
#import <setjmp.h>      // for setjmp / longjmp
#import <stdio.h>       // for printf
#import <stdlib.h>      // for EXIT_SUCCESS
#import <errno.h>

static jmp_buf handler;

void handleSignal (int signo)
{
    longjmp (handler, 1);
} // handleSignal

void doLotsOfWork ()
{
    int i;

    for (i = 0; i < 50000; i++) {
        printf ("i is %d\n", i);
        sleep (1);
    }

} // doLotsOfWork

int main (int argc, char *argv[])
{
    volatile int handlerSet = 0;

    struct sigaction action;

    sigemptyset (&action.sa_mask);
    sigaddset (&action.sa_mask, SIGTERM);

    action.sa_handler = handleSignal;
```

```
    action.sa_flags = 0;

    if (sigaction (SIGUSR1, &action, NULL) == -1) {
        fprintf (stderr, "error in sigaction: %d / %s\n",
                errno, strerror(errno));
        return (EXIT_FAILURE);
    }

    while (1) {

        if (!handlerSet) {
            if (setjmp (handler)) {
                // we longjmp'd to here.  Reset our handler
                // next time around
                handlerSet = 0;
                continue;
            } else {
                handlerSet = 1;
            }
        }

        printf("starting lots of work\n");
        doLotsOfWork ();
    }

    return (EXIT_SUCCESS);

} // main
```

A sample run:

```
Terminal 1                              Terminal 2
% ./interrupt &
[1] 7625
starting lots of work
i is 0
i is 1
i is 2
i is 3
i is 4
i is 5
i is 6                                  kill -USR1 7625
starting lots of work
i is 0
i is 1
i is 2                                  kill -USR1 7625
starting lots of work
i is 0
i is 1
i is 2
i is 3
i is 4                                  kill 7625

[1]    Terminated                     ./interrupt
```

The last kill sends a SIGTERM, which terminates the process if not handled.

Race conditions

The other bugaboo with signals are race conditions (a subject revisited in Chapter 22 (Threads)). A race condition happens when two different streams of execution hit an ambiguous area of code and the code's behavior changes depending on the order in which the two streams execute.

A piece of code as simple as

```
i = 5;
i = i + 7;
```

can be subject to race conditions. Depending on order of operations, you can get different results:

```
thread 1                     thread 2
  i = 5
  copy i to register
  add 7 to 5
  store 12 into i
                             i = 12
                             copy i to register
                             add 7 to 12
                             store 19 into i


Final value: 19
```

```
thread 1                     thread 2
  i = 5
  copy i to register
                             i = 5
                             copy i to register
                             add 7 to 5
                             store 12 into i
  add 7 to 5
  store 12 into i

Final value : 12
```

The `interrupt.m` program has a couple of race conditions in it. The first happens after you register the signal handler but before the call to `setjmp()` on the `jump_buf`. If a SIGUSR1 signal happens any time after the **`sigaction()`** and **`setjmp()`**, you will crash by trying to **`longjmp()`** with an invalid jump buffer.

Likewise, if a SIGUSR1 signal happens between the time that the code returns from **`setjmp()`** and you call **`setjmp()`** again, you will crash from using an out-of-date `jmp_buf`. You can use **`sigprocmask()`** to block the signals during these vulnerable times.

Exception-Handling in Cocoa

Cocoa provides an exception-handling mechanism similar to what C++ and Java offer. You wrap a body of code in an NS_DURING clause. Any exceptional conditions will raise an exception which can then be caught by an NS_HANDLER.

The way you work it is:

```
NS_DURING
```
... code that might throw an exception
```
NS_HANDLER
```
... code to examine the exception and possibly handle it
```
NS_ENDHANDLER
```

If any code between `NS_DURING` and `NS_HANDLER` raises an exception, execution immediately resumes with the first instruction after `NS_HANDLER`.

Figure 9-2. Exception flow of control

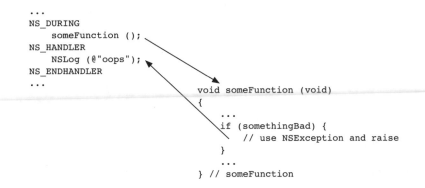

Handlers can be arbitrarily nested, so you could call a function that is in an `NS_DURING` handler, and it can set up its own `NS_DURING` handler. When someone finally raises an exception, flow of control will jump to the closest `NS_HANDLER`.

The macro for `NS_HANDLER` declares a local variable called `localException` that you can query for details about the exception - specifically, its name and the reason it happened. You can also use `localException` to "rethrow" the exception, y using `[localException raise]`.

Here is a little foundation tool to show exception-handling in action. `-[NSString characterAtIndex:]` will raise an exception if you try to get a character that is beyond the length of the string.

Example 9-6. exception.m

```
// exception.m -- show simple exception handling in Cocoa

/* compile with:
cc -g -Wall -o exception -framework Foundation exception.m
*/

#import <Foundation/Foundation.h>
#import <stdlib.h>                      // for EXIT_SUCCESS

int main (int argc, char *argv[])
{
    NSAutoreleasePool *pool = [[NSAutoreleasePool alloc] init];
    NSString *string = @"hello";

    NS_DURING
```

```
        NSLog (@"character at index 0: %c",
               [string characterAtIndex:0]);
        NSLog (@"character at index 1: %c",
               [string characterAtIndex:1]);
        NSLog (@"character at index 2000: %c",
               [string characterAtIndex: 2000]);
        NSLog (@"character at index 2: %c",
               [string characterAtIndex:2]);

    NS_HANDLER
        NSLog (@"inside of exception handler.");
        NSLog (@"name is : %@", [localException name]);
        NSLog (@"reason is : %@", [localException reason]);
        NSLog (@"userInfo dict: %@", [localException userInfo]);

    NS_ENDHANDLER

    [pool release];

    return (EXIT_SUCCESS);

} // main
```

A sample run:

```
% ./exception
2002-09-03 16:17:31.433 exception[7700] character at index 0: h
2002-09-03 16:17:31.433 exception[7700] character at index 1: e
2002-09-03 16:17:31.435 exception[7700] inside of exception handler.
2002-09-03 16:17:31.435 exception[7700] name is : NSRangeException
2002-09-03 16:17:31.435 exception[7700] reason is:
    [NSConstantString characterAtIndex:]: Range or index out of bounds
2002-09-03 16:17:31.435 exception[7700] userInfo dict: (null)
```

The first two **characterAtIndex** method calls succeed, and the third raised an exception, terminating the code in the NS_DURING section of code.

Specific Cocoa methods document whether they raise exceptions. Unfortunately there is not a list of all methods that can raise exceptions.

Cocoa exception-handling is based on **setjmp()/longjmp()**, so you again must use volatile variables if they might be used after the **longjmp()** to your NS_HANDLER. Also, there is no automatic cleanup of allocated objects when exceptions happen (like with stack objects in C++). Also, there are some restrictions in what you can do during the NS_HANDLER portion. Specifically, you should not **goto** or **return** out of an exception-handling domain (anywhere between NS_DURING and NS_HANDLER), otherwise the exception handler stack will be left in a bad state. Also, **setjmp()/longjmp()** should not be used if it crosses an NS_DURING statement. In general, if you are using Cocoa exception handling, you will not need to use **setjmp()/longjmp()**.

Cocoa exception-handling is a heavy-weight operation, so do not use it for normal flow of control. For instance, test a string's length when processing characters rather than falling off the end and depending on an exception to terminate your processing.

There is an **NSException** object that you can allocate and this is what is used to raise your own exceptions. You can supply your own name and reason strings or use some of the built-in ones.

Here is a foundation tool that raises a custom exception:

Example 9-7. raise.m

```
// raise.m -- raise an exception

/* compile with:
cc -g -Wall -o raise -framework Foundation raise.m
*/

#import <Foundation/Foundation.h>
#import <stdlib.h>                      // for EXIT_SUCCESS

void doSomethingElse ()
{
    NSDictionary *userInfo;
    userInfo = [NSDictionary dictionaryWithObjectsAndKeys:
                                        @"hello", @"thing1",
                                        @"bork", @"thing2",
                                        nil];
    NSException *exception;
    exception = [NSException exceptionWithName: @"MyException"
                        reason: @"doSomethingElse raised MyException"
                    userInfo: userInfo];
    [exception raise];

    NSLog (@"after the raise.  This will not be executed");

} // doSomethingElse

void doSomething ()
{
    doSomethingElse ();
} // doSomething

int main (int argc, char *argv[])
{
    NSAutoreleasePool *pool = [[NSAutoreleasePool alloc] init];

    NS_DURING
        doSomething ();

    NS_HANDLER
        NSLog (@"inside of exception handler.");
        NSLog (@"name is : %@", [localException name]);
        NSLog (@"reason is : %@", [localException reason]);
        NSLog (@"userInfo dict: %@", [localException userInfo]);

    NS_ENDHANDLER

    [pool release];

    return (EXIT_SUCCESS);
```

```
} // main
```

A sample run:

```
% ./raise
... raise[7736] inside of exception handler.
... raise[7736] name is : MyException
... raise[7736] reason is : doSomethingElse raised a MyException
... raise[7736] userInfo dict: <CFDictionary 0x94d00 [0xa01303fc]>
{type = immutable, count = 2, capacity = 2, pairs = (
        1 : thing1 = hello
        2 : thing2 = bork
)}
```

The Cocoa exception-handling mechanism is fundamentally string based, in that there is not a hierarchy of exception classes like there is in Java and C++. When someone throws a built-in exception (like **NSGenericException**), that is just an NSString that gets put into an **NSException** object.

You can use gdb to halt execution when exceptions are thrown. Put a breakpoint on **-[NSException raise]**.

Subclassing NSApplication to catch exceptions

In some applications, Project Builder for example, when an exception falls through the stack all the way to the run loop, the user is shown the exception in a panel. (Often, the panel just says something like "Something has gone wrong. You may want to save what you are working on and restart this application.") How is this done?

When an exception falls through the stack all the way to the run loop, the instance of **NSApplication** gets sent the following message:

- (void)**reportException:**(NSException *)theException

This method simply logs the exception using **NSLog()** and the run loop begins again. If you would like to alter this behavior, you must subclass **NSApplication** and override **reportException:**.

If you do this, make sure that you also alter the Info.plist for your application so that it uses your subclass instead of **NSApplication**:

```
<key>NSPrincipalClass</key>
<string>MyExceptionReportingApplication</string>
```

Note that this only works if your Objective-C code is in a Cocoa application. If you have written a tool, you will call **NSSetUncaughtExceptionHandler()** and supply it with a pointer to a function with this signature:

```
void MyHandler(NSException *e);
```

Logging

In our development careers at one time or another we have all done "caveman debugging", putting in lots of print statements to see program flow and to see what values our variables have. Putting in **fprintf()** and **NSLog()** to print to the terminal and using the stuff from Chapter 10 (Files) you can redirect those print statements to log files.

There are times too when you are logging and it is not debugging related, like server programs keeping a log of connections or printing information that may be of interest to administrators (such as that the disk is filling up). Most Unix systems have a daemon running called syslogd, the system logging daemon. System administrators can configure syslogd to log to a file or to send the log information from many machines to a central location (very useful if you have a lot of machines to keep an eye on). Our programmatic interface to syslogd, the **syslog()** function, is:

```
void syslog (int priority, const char *message, ...);
```

The message is a **printf()**-style string. You can use any **printf()** token in there you want. There is also an added format string, "%m", to put in the current error message from strerror(). **syslog()** also adds a trailing newline if one is not already specified in the message string.

The priority controls if the logging will be seen or not. Here is their order high to low

LOG_EMERG

A panic condition. This is normally broadcast to all users.

LOG_ALERT

A condition that should be corrected immediately, such as a corrupted system database.

LOG_CRIT

Critical conditions, e.g., hard device errors.

LOG_ERR

Errors.

LOG_WARNING

Warning messages.

LOG_NOTICE

Conditions that are not error conditions, but should possibly be handled specially.

LOG_INFO

Informational messages.

LOG_DEBUG

Messages that contain information normally of use only when debugging a program.

The configuration file for `syslogd`, `/etc/syslogd.conf`, contains the controls for setting the threshold where logging will occur. By default, `LOG_DEBUG` messages are not shown, but everything else is.

You can control some of the syslog behavior of the logging output by using **openlog()**.

```
void openlog (const char *ident, int logopt, int facility);
```

`ident` is the name to use for the program in the log. By default, the executable name is used. `logopt` is any one of these flags bitwise-OR'd together.

`LOG_CONS`

> If **syslog()** cannot pass the message to `syslogd`, it will attempt to write the message to the console (`/dev/console`).

`LOG_NDELAY`

> Open the connection to **syslogd(8)** immediately. Normally the open is delayed until the first message is logged. This is useful for programs that need to manage the order in which file descriptors are allocated.

`LOG_PERROR`

> Write the message to standard error output as well as to the system log.

`LOG_PID`

> Log the process ID with each message; this is useful for identifying instantiations of daemons.

The facility parameter tells `syslogd` that the program is a member of a standard facility, like being a daemon, or are part of the security subsystem. For example, if you were writing a daemon that was part of the mail system, you would call **openlog()** with a facility of `LOG_MAIL`. These constants are listed in the man page.

Here is a sample that logs to `syslog`, which by default gets written locally to `/private/var/log/system.log`. This is the same log that the `Console.app` looks at.

Example 9-8. syslog.m

```
// syslog.m -- use the syslog functions

/* compile with:
cc -g -Wall -o syslog syslog.m
*/

#import <syslog.h>      // for syslog and firneds
#import <stdlib.h>      // for EXIT_SUCCESS
#import <errno.h>       // for errno

int main (int argc, char *argv[])
{
    syslog (LOG_WARNING, "this is a warning message");
    errno = EINVAL;
    syslog (LOG_ERR, "this is an error, %m", errno);
```

```
                                          ;

                         )G_NDELAY | LOG_CONS,
```

```
                                     Tue Sep  3 20:27:53 2002...

                                 is a warning message
                                 is an error, Invalid argument
                             P!! WHOOP!!
                           _7855]: Notice message
```

Here you can see the LOG_EMERG getting broadcast to all the open terminals, then the various syslog messages. You can call **openlog()** at anytime. You can see how the LOG_PID and "BNRsyslogTest" settings appear.

For The More Curious

Assertions

Assertions are a programming technique where tests are put in for conditions that cannot happen. If the program does get into such a state, the program kills itself, dropping a core file if it is configured to do so.

The assert macro

```
assert(expression);
```

evaluates the expression. If the expression is false, the process is terminated, a diagnostic message is written to the standard error stream, and the **abort()** function is called, which terminates the program by raising the signal SIGABRT. Since most programmers use asserts for debugging purposes, you can compile them out of a production program by using the preprocessor flag -DNDEBUG. Personally, I am the sort that likes to leave that stuff in (so long as it is not computationally expensive) since we are much more likely to run into problems with our programs out in the field where disabled assertions will not do us much good, but that is an individual decision.

Cocoa also has an assertion mechanism, **NSAssertionHandler**. There you use macros like **NSAssert** (when in a method) and **NSCAssert** (when in a regular old C function) to evaluate a condition. If it evalutes to false, the message is passed to an **NSAssertionHandler** (one associated with each thread). When invoked, this object prints an error message, and raises an NSInternalInconsitencyException, which can be caught using NS_DURING/NS_HANDLER.

Challenges

1. Fix the race conditions in `interrupt.m` by using **`sigprocmask()`**. Is the behavior of **`longjump()`** appropriate, or should **`_setjmp()`** and **`_longjmp()`** be used instead?

2. Tweak `/etc/syslogd.conf` to display the debug message from `syslog.m` in the `system.log` file.

Chapter 10. Files, Part 1: I/O and Permissions

Files are the permanent storage for the data that your programs generate. The semantics of handling files are similar to most every other common platform (open, read, write, seek to a particular location, close), with some added nuances that live in the details.

The idea of a file is a fundamental Unix concept. Pretty much everything is treated as a file. Ordinary "write the bits for a jpeg graphic" go to files in the file system. Network connections are treated as files. Accessing physical devices is done with file operations. Interacting with the terminal is done with file operations. This has the nice side effect of using the same API for reading and writing data to all of these disparate machine entities. The downside is that there is some additional complexity in the API to handle the different corner cases involved with accessing all of these OS features.

Unbuffered I/O

The unbuffered I/O APIs are the fundamental system calls (function calls that go into the kernel) upon which other APIs (like the buffered I/O ones) can be built.

Opening a file

`open` opens a file:

```
int open (const char *path, int flags, mode_t mode);
```

The `mode` argument deals with default permissions on newly created files (which person has authority to read and write to the file), the details of which will be talked about a little later. The `flags` field is used to control the behavior of the file. Bitwise-OR in one of these flags

`O_RDONLY`

> Open read-only

`O_WRONLY`

> Open write-only

`O_RDWR`

> Open read/write

and any of these flags:

`O_APPEND`

> Append on every write. This does an implicit seek to the end before writing, but is atomic.

`O_NONBLOCK`

> Do not block for an open, and do not block when waiting for data.

`O_CREAT`

> Create the file if it does not exist.

O_TRUNC

> Truncate the file to zero bytes when opening it.

O_EXCL

> Generate an error if the file already exists.

O_SHLOCK

> Obtain a shared lock.

O_EXLOCK

> Obtain an exclusive lock (more on locks later).

If there was an error, **open()** returns -1 and sets the errno global variable to the appropriate value. This "returning -1 and setting errno on an error" is common to most of the file I/O functions (unfortunately not all).

If **open()** was successful, the return value is a non-negative integer called a *file descriptor*, frequently shortened to just fd. This integer value is the index into a per-process table that references open files. This file descriptor is used as a handle to the file for subsequent calls.

The three standard streams that shells establish for programs are located at file descriptor values zero (for standard in), one (for standard out), and two (for standard error). You can pass these numbers to the **read()** and **write()** functions, or you can use the symbolic constants STDIN_FILENO, STDOUT_FILENO, or STDERR_FILENO.

Figure 10-1. File Descriptors

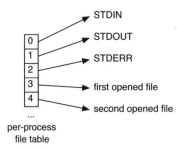

One piece of trivia, when you open a file, the file descriptor returned is guaranteed to be the lowest numbered unused descriptor. This can be useful when you are reopening a file on one of the standard streams (although the **dup2()** call is better for that).

Here is a little program that closes stdout and reopens it to a logfile, set in append-only mode. Note that **printf()** writes to the standard out.

Example 10-1. append.m

```
// append.m -- show an opening of a logfile, replacing a
//              standard stream.
```

```
/* compile with:
cc -g -Wall -o append append.m
*/

#import <unistd.h>      // for STDOUT_FILENO
#import <stdlib.h>      // for EXIT_SUCCESS
#import <fcntl.h>       // for OPEN
#import <stdio.h>       // for printf() and friends
#import <errno.h>       // for errno
#import <string.h>      // for strerror()
#import <sys/stat.h>     // for permission constants

int main (int argc, char *argv[])
{
    int fd;

    close (STDOUT_FILENO);

    // open a log file, write only, and to always automatically append.
    // oh, and create the file if it does not exist already
    fd = open ("/tmp/logthingie.txt", O_WRONLY | O_CREAT | O_APPEND,
               S_IRUSR | S_IWUSR);

    if (fd == -1) {
        fprintf (stderr, "cannot open log file.  Error %d (%s)\n",
                 errno, strerror(errno));
        exit (EXIT_FAILURE);
    }

    printf ("wheee, we have a log file open\n");

    exit (EXIT_SUCCESS);

} // main
```

Here are some runs of the program:

```
% ls -l /tmp/logthingie.txt
ls: /tmp/logthingie.txt: No such file or directory


% ./append

% ls -l /tmp/logthingie.txt
-rwxr-xr--  1 markd  wheel  31 Aug 10 11:55 /tmp/logthingie.txt*

% cat /tmp/logthingie.txt
wheee, we have a log file open

% ./append
% ./append

% cat /tmp/logthingie.txt
wheee, we have a log file open
wheee, we have a log file open
wheee, we have a log file open
```

Some things to note about the code. That is a lot of header files to include for such a small program. Things are pretty scattered about in the headers, but the man pages usually tell you what files to include to use particular features. For others, (like finding where STDOUT_FILENO live) you can resort to just grepping the files:

```
% cd /usr/include
% grep STDOUT_FILENO *.h
unistd.h:#define STDOUT_FILENO 1 /* standard output file */
```

Another thing to note is the manual writing to standard error. Since standard out was closed you could not use **printf()** to complain about the error opening the file. After all, the file opening failed.

Lastly, note the file permissions of the file:

```
-rwxr-xr--  1 markd  wheel  31 Aug 10 11:55 /tmp/logthingie.txt*
```

Plain old text files should not be executable. This can be fixed by explicitly setting the file permissions (described later).

Writing to a file

The **write()** system call is what is used to move bytes from memory to the disk:

```
ssize_t write (int fd, const void *buf, size_t nbytes);
```

Give it an address and a number of bytes to write, and the bytes will make it out to the file.

The return value is -1 in the case of an error (in which errno is set to whatever complaint the system is having), or else the number of bytes written. Note that the number of bytes written could be less than nbytes, such as in the case of writing a whole lot of data to a network connection or to a pipe (you could be filling up kernel buffers). The samples here will just call **write()** without a loop. Chapter 13 (Networking) will demonstrate the paranoid way of calling **write()**.

Each open file has an offset associated with it. This is the location within the file where writing and reading happen. This offset is automatically updated on each read or write, and can be explicitly set by **lseek()**. The O_APPEND flag overrides this and forces all writing to happen at the end of the file.

Here is a little program that uses **write()** to create a file that contains a string the user passed in when invoking the program. To add a little interest, you will write out the length of the string first, and not have the traditional trailing zero byte that terminates string:

Example 10-2. writestring.m

```
// writestring.m -- take argv[1] and write it to a file,
//                  prepending the length of the string

/* compile with:
cc -g -Wall -o writestring writestring.m
*/

#import <fcntl.h>        // for open()
#import <sys/stat.h>     // for permission flags
```

```
#import <stdlib.h>        // for EXIT_SUCCESS et. al.
#import <stdio.h>         // for printf() and friends
#import <errno.h>         // for errno
#import <string.h>        // for strerror()
#import <unistd.h>        // for write()

int main (int argc, char *argv[])
{
    int fd;
    int stringLength;
    ssize_t result;

    if (argc != 2) {
        fprintf (stderr, "usage:  %s string-to-log\n", argv[0]);
        exit (EXIT_FAILURE);
    }

    fd = open ("/tmp/stringfile.txt", O_WRONLY | O_CREAT | O_TRUNC,
               S_IRUSR | S_IWUSR);

    if (fd == -1) {
        fprintf (stderr, "cannot open file.  Error %d (%s)\n",
                 errno, strerror(errno));
        exit (EXIT_FAILURE);
    }

    // write the length
    stringLength = strlen (argv[1]);
    result = write (fd, &stringLength, sizeof(stringLength));

    if (result == -1) {
        fprintf (stderr, "cannot write to file.  Error %d (%s)\n",
                 errno, strerror(errno));
        exit (EXIT_FAILURE);
    }

    // now write the string
    result = write (fd, argv[1], stringLength);

    if (result == -1) {
        fprintf (stderr, "cannot write to file.  Error %d (%s)\n",
                 errno, strerror(errno));
        exit (EXIT_FAILURE);
    }

    close (fd);

    exit (EXIT_SUCCESS);

} // main
```

Here it is in action:

```
% ./writestring "I seem to be a fish"
%
```

Looking at the size of the file:

```
% ls -l /tmp/stringfile.txt
-rw------- 1 markd  wheel  23 Aug 10 12:24 /tmp/stringfile.txt
```

Note that the permissions are much more reasonable. That is what the S_IRUSR | S_IWUSR did. The file is 23 bytes, which is the exact size it should be: 4 bytes for the length, plus 19 for the text.

The hexdump program is useful for seeing inside of files:

```
% hexdump -C /tmp/stringfile.txt
0000  00 00 00 13 49 20 73 65  65 6d 20 74 6f 20 62 65
          |....I seem to be|
0010  20 61 20 66 69 73 68
          | a fish|
0017
```

How to parse the output: The left-hand column is the number of bytes into the file that the particular line starts on. The bytes of hex are the contents of the file, 16 bytes per line. The right-hand column shows the ASCII interpretation, with unprintable characters replaced by periods.

So, the first couple of bytes:

```
00000000  00 00 00 13
```

Starting at offset zero are four bytes of 00000013, which is decimal 19 (the length of the string). Following that are 19 bytes of the actual string data.

Reading From a File

Reading is the inverse of writing: it moves bytes from the file into memory. The prototype is nearly identical to **write()**:

```
ssize_t read (int d, void *buf, size_t nbytes);
```

Note that buf is not a const void *, but just a void *, meaning that the function could change the contents of the buffer. Of course, that is the whole point of the function call.

Like the other calls around here, **read()** returns -1 on an error (setting errno as appropriate). For a successful read, it will return the number of bytes actually read, and return zero on end of file (EOF). When run from an interactive terminal, some magic happens under the hood and **read()** reads entire lines. Note that **read()** can return fewer bytes than asked for, such as when it reaches EOF, or due to networking buffering, reading from the terminal, or when dealing with record-oriented devices like tape drives. Like **write()**, **read()** also updates the current location.

Here is the counterpart to writestring, which takes the specially formatted file and reads it back in.

Example 10-3. readstring.m

```
// readstring.m -- open /tmp/stringfile.txt and write out
//                 its contents

/* compile with:
cc -g -Wall -o readstring readstring.m
```

```
*/

#import <fcntl.h>        // for open()
#import <stdlib.h>       // for EXIT_SUCCESS et. al.
#import <stdio.h>        // for printf() and friends
#import <errno.h>        // for errno and strerror()
#import <string.h>       // for strerror()
#import <unistd.h>       // for close() and read()

int main (int argc, char *argv[])
{
    int fd;
    int stringLength;
    ssize_t result;
    char *buffer;

    fd = open ("/tmp/stringfile.txt", O_RDONLY);

    if (fd == -1) {
        fprintf (stderr, "cannot open file.  Error %d (%s)\n",
                errno, strerror(errno));
        exit (EXIT_FAILURE);
    }

    result = read (fd, &stringLength, sizeof(stringLength));

    if (result == -1) {
        fprintf (stderr, "cannot read file.  Error %d (%s)\n",
                errno, strerror(errno));
        exit (EXIT_FAILURE);
    }

    buffer = malloc (stringLength + 1);  // account for trailing 0 byte

    result = read (fd, buffer, stringLength);

    if (result == -1) {
        fprintf (stderr, "cannot read file.  Error %d (%s)\n",
                errno, strerror(errno));
        exit (EXIT_FAILURE);
    }

    buffer[stringLength] = '\000';

    close (fd);

    printf ("our string is '%s'\n", buffer);

    free (buffer); // clean up our mess

    exit (EXIT_SUCCESS);

} // main
```

And the program in action:

```
% ./readstring
```

```
our string is 'I seem to be a fish'
```

Closing files

To close a file, you use `close()`:

```
int close (int fd);
```

This removes the file descriptor from the per-process file table and frees up system resources associated with this open file. This has a return value of -1 to indicate error, otherwise it returns a zero on successful completion. In the above samples, the return value from `close()` is not checked. That is primarily just laziness, since errors should not happen on close, and if they do, there is not a lot you can do about it.

When a process exits, all open files are automatically closed, and any blocks waiting in kernel buffers are queued for writing.

Changing the Read/Write Offset

The read/write offset is the number of bytes from the beginning of the file where the next read or write operation will take place. This offset is an attribute of the open file, so if you open the same file twice you will get two file descriptors, each with an independent file offset. The offset starts at zero unless O_APPEND was used to open the file.

The `lseek()` call is what is used to change the offset:

```
off_t lseek (int fd, off_t offset, int whence);
```

`offset`, in combination with `whence`, is used to locate a particular byte in the file. `whence` can have one of three values:

SEEK_SET

    Offset is an absolute position.

SEEK_CUR

    Offset is a delta from the current location.

SEEK_END

    Offset is relative off the end of the file.

The offset can be negative for SEEK_CUR and SEEK_END. So, if you wanted to start writing five bytes from the end of the file, you would do something like:

```
blah = lseek (fd, -5, SEEK_END);
```

Note that the offset itself can never go negative. It will get pinned to zero.

Figure 10-2. lseek()

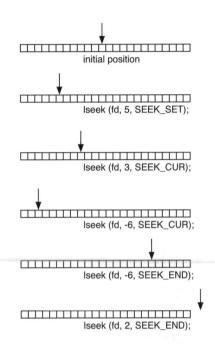

The return value from **lseek()** is the resulting offset location in bytes from the beginning of the file. Otherwise a -1 return value and `errno` are used to communicate back the error.

You are quite welcome to seek off the end of the file. Any bytes not explicitly written will default to zero. Note also that some devices are incapable of seeking, like a pipe or a network connection.

lseek() is a logical operation, not a physical one. It is just updating a value in the kernel, so no actual I/O takes place until you perform a read or write.

To get the current offset, do:

```
off_t offset = lseek (fd, 0, SEEK_CUR);
```

This will also tell you if the device is capable of seeking. If you get an error, you know you cannot seek with this kind of file.

Why is it called **lseek()**? Back in the misty past, the function to perform this work was originally called just seek, but it took an `int` parameter, which could be 16 or 32 bit. When seek was extended to support larger files, a long argument was used, hence the "L."

Atomic operations

In man pages (and around this chapter), you will see references to "atomic operations." These are operations that do multiple things, but all happen within one system call, thereby preventing race condition errors with other programs.

For example, **open()** has the `O_APPEND` flag, which makes the append be an atomic operation. You just **write()** to the file descriptor and the output happens in the end.

Without O_APPEND, you would have to do two operations:

```
lseek (fd, 0, SEEK_END); // seek to the end
write (fd, buffer, datasize);
```

The race condition happens if your program gets pre-empted by the kernel after the **lseek()**, but before the **write()**, and someone else happens to be writing to the file as well.

Figure 10-3. Race condition start

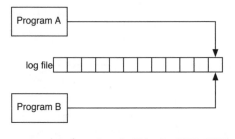

each performs lseek (fd, 0, SEEK_END);

Figure 10-4. Program A writes its data

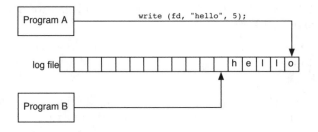

Figure 10-5. Program B clobbers it

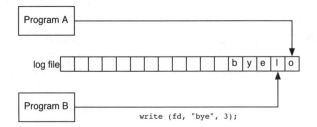

So say the file log.txt looks like

```
finished frobulating the bork\nadded a hoover\n
```

and the last position is at offset 50,000.

- Program A does the lseek to 50,000, and gets pre-empted.
- Program B does an `lseek()` to 50,000, and writes `"removed the wikkit\n"`.
- Program A is scheduled again, and writes `"ack ack\n"`.

The file now looks like

```
finished frobulating the bork\nadded a hoover\nack ack\nhe wikkit\n
```

in short, it is been trashed. Atomic operations were introduced to prevent such errors.

Another example of an atomic operation is doing an open with O_CREAT and O_EXCL. The open will fail if the file exists. This is a handy way to check whether your program is already running, if you only want one copy to be active, like many internet server programs.

Scatter / gather I/O

Frequently when writing, you will be doing multiple `write()` calls for a logical piece of data. For instance, in the `writestring.m` program above, there were two writes: one for a size and one for the string. Web server software has two distinct chunks of data involved when responding to any request: the reply headers and the actual data, which are usually kept in distinct data structures. In these cases you can do multiple writes (which have the overhead of multiple system calls), or copy all the data into a different buffer and then write it in one call (which has data copying overhead, and possibly involves dynamic memory, which is another performance hit). Or you can use the scatter/gather read functions `readv()` and `writev()` to package up your data and have the kernel write it all in one operation. From the receiver's point of view (whether the bytes are from a file or from the program on the other end of a network connection), all three are equivalent.

```
ssize_t readv (int fd, const struct iovec *iov, int iovcnt);

ssize_t writev (int fd, const struct iovec *iov, int iovcnt);
```

Rather than taking a buffer, these two take an array of `struct iovec`

```
struct iovec {
    void *iov_base;
    size_t iov_len;
};
```

where `iov_base` is the buffer location and `iov_len` is how much data to read and write.

Figure 10-6. Scatter / Gather I/O

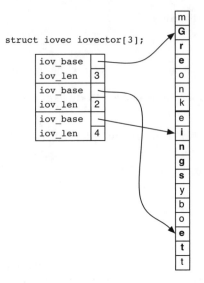

```
struct iovec iovector[3];
```

iov_base	–
iov_len	3
iov_base	–
iov_len	2
iov_base	–
iov_len	4

```
writev (fd, iovector, 3);
```
will write the bytes

"Greetings"

Here are `writestring` and `readstring` updated to use scatter/gather I/O:

Example 10-4. writevecstring.m

```
// writevecstring.m -- take argv[1] and write it to a file, prepending
//                     the length of the string.  and using
//                     scatter/gather I/O

/* compile with:
cc -g -Wall -o writevecstring writevecstring.m
*/

#import <sys/types.h>    // for ssize_t
#import <sys/uio.h>      // for writev() and struct iovec
#import <fcntl.h>        // for open()
#import <sys/stat.h>     // for permission flags
#import <stdlib.h>       // for EXIT_SUCCESS et. al.
#import <stdio.h>        // for printf() and friends
#import <errno.h>        // for errno
#import <string.h>       // for strerror()
#import <unistd.h>       // for close()

int main (int argc, char *argv[])
{
    int fd;
    int stringLength;
    ssize_t result;
    struct iovec vector[2]; // one for size, one for string

    if (argc != 2) {
        fprintf (stderr, "usage:  %s string-to-log\n", argv[0]);
        exit (EXIT_FAILURE);
    }
```

```
fd = open ("/tmp/stringfile.txt", O_WRONLY | O_CREAT | O_TRUNC,
           S_IRUSR | S_IWUSR);

if (fd == -1) {
    fprintf (stderr, "cannot open file.  Error %d (%s)\n",
             errno, strerror(errno));
    exit (EXIT_FAILURE);
}

stringLength = strlen (argv[1]);
vector[0].iov_base = (void *) &stringLength;
vector[0].iov_len = sizeof(stringLength);
vector[1].iov_base = argv[1];
vector[1].iov_len = stringLength;

result = writev (fd, vector, 2);

if (result == -1) {
    fprintf (stderr, "cannot write to file.  Error %d (%s)\n",
             errno, strerror(errno));
    exit (EXIT_FAILURE);
}

close (fd);

exit (EXIT_SUCCESS);

} // main
```

Note the cast here:

```
vector[0].iov_base = (void *) &stringLength;
```

Unfortunately, the man page and the header file do not always agree. In the header file `sys/uio.h` is this:

```
/*
 * XXX
 * iov_base should be a void *.
 */
struct iovec {
    char    *iov_base;      /* Base address. */
    size_t  iov_len;        /* Length. */
};
```

So in this case you need to cast (`int *`) to something that is compatible with a (`char *`).

Here is the equivalent on the read side:

Example 10-5. readvecstring.m

```
// readvecstring.m -- open /tmp/stringfile.txt and write out
//                    its contents using scatter/gather reads

/* compile with:
cc -g -Wall -o readvecstring readvecstring.m
```

```
*/

#import <sys/types.h>    // for ssize_t
#import <sys/uio.h>      // for readv() and struct iovec
#import <fcntl.h>        // for open()
#import <sys/stat.h>     // for permission flags
#import <stdlib.h>       // for EXIT_SUCCESS et. al.
#import <stdio.h>        // for printf() and friends
#import <errno.h>        // for errno
#import <string.h>       // for strerror()
#import <unistd.h>       // for close()

int main (int argc, char *argv[])
{
    int fd;
    int stringLength;
    ssize_t result;
    char buffer[4096];
    struct iovec vector[2];

    fd = open ("/tmp/stringfile.txt", O_RDONLY);

    if (fd == -1) {
        fprintf (stderr, "cannot open file.  Error %d (%s)\n",
                errno, strerror(errno));
        exit (EXIT_FAILURE);
    }

    vector[0].iov_base = (void *) &stringLength;
    vector[0].iov_len = sizeof(stringLength);
    vector[1].iov_base = buffer;
    vector[1].iov_len = 4096;

    result = readv (fd, vector, 2);

    if (result == -1) {
        fprintf (stderr, "cannot read file.  Error %d (%s)\n",
                errno, strerror(errno));
        exit (EXIT_FAILURE);
    }

    buffer[stringLength] = '\000'; // need to zero-terminate it

    close (fd);

    printf ("our string is '%s'\n", buffer);

    exit (EXIT_SUCCESS);

} // main
```

Unfortunately, the reading side of things is not as pretty as the writing side. Since the size of the string is unknown, a guess was made at the maximum size of the string. Hard-coded limits like this will be the source of errors in the future (as soon as someone writes a 4K+1 string to one of these files). In general the **writev()** will be the most convenient way to write scattered data like this, but you will still do multiple reads to pull apart the data - either that or read a lot of stuff into a buffer and process the data.

creat()

Just a historical note, there is also a the **creat()** function which you might see in your travels through other people's code:

```
int creat (const char *path, mode_t mode);
```

This creates files, and has been superceded by **open()**. creat(path, mode) is equivalent to

```
open(path, O_CREAT | O_TRUNC | O_WRONLY, mode);
```

Blocking I/O

By default, file I/O is blocking. The function call will wait until the I/O completes. If you open with the O_NONBLOCK flag, reads will return immediately with an error (errno of EAGAIN). You can also use the **select()** or **poll()** functions (discussed in detail in Chapter 13 (Networking)) to see if I/O is possible for a particular file descriptor.

Buffered I/O

The preceeding calls are generally considered "unbuffered I/O". There is a little bit of buffering that happens the kernel (probably no more than a couple of disk blocks) so that a physical I/O is not performed for every byte read, but for the most part what you read is what you get in terms of physical I/O. If you want to read in large blocks of data and process the data out of that buffer, you will have to do the work yourself (refilling the buffer when it gets low, remembering your place in the buffer, handling reading and writing, etc). It is not hard work, just kind of tedious.

The Standard C I/O functions are known as buffered I/O. The library handles the details of buffer allocation I/O in optimally sized chunks, only doing real physical I/O when the buffer is empty (for reading) or is full (for writing), or is explicitly flushed to the disk.

Rather than passing file descriptors around, buffered I/O has an opaque type called FILE (also known as a stream), and you pass pointers to FILEs around. Wrapped in that FILE is the file descriptor, the buffer, and other pieces of housekeeping.

There are three kinds of buffering that buffered I/O can use:

Fully Buffered

> Actual I/O only happens when the buffer gets full, and is the default for files associated with non-interactive devices.

Line Buffered

> I/O happens when a newline character is encountered on input or output. You can use a function to write one character at a time to a stream, but the actual I/O only happens on a newline (or when the buffer is getting full).

Unbuffered

> No buffering happens, calls just turn around and invoke **read()** or **write()**. The Standard Error stream is usually unbuffered so that error messages appear instantly. The other two standard streams are either fully or line buffered, depending on whether they are attached to an interactive device (like a terminal).

You can use **setbuf()** or **setvbuf()** to change the buffering behavior.

Opening files

The buffered I/O functions (with a few exceptions) begin with "f." So, for instance, opening files is done with **fopen()**:

```
FILE *fopen (char *path, char *mode);
```

fopen() returns a pointer to newly allocated FILE structure (you do not need to worry about allocating it, but be sure to dispose of it with **fclose()**). It is an opaque type, but you can look at it anyway (hint: stdio.h, or print out a FILE structure in gdb).

There are buffered I/O versions of the three standard streams, called stdin, stdout, stderr, and you can pass any of these to the buffered I/O functions.

Back to **fopen()**. It takes a pathname to the file, and a mode, which is a character string.

Here are the modes:

"r"

> Open file for reading.

"r+"

> Open for reading and writing.

"w"

> Truncate file to zero length, or create if it does not exist, and then open for writing.

"w+"

> Truncate file to zero length, or create if it does not exist, and then open for reading and writing.

"a"

> File is created if it does not exist, then open it for writing in append mode.

"a+"

> File is created if it does not exist, then open it for reading, and writing in append mode.

Or, put another way,

"r"   Open for reading, file must exist.

"w" Truncate or create if necessary, file does not need to exist.

"a" Create if necessary, file does not need to exist. Append mode.

And stick on a "+" to have both reading and writing possible.

There are some subtleties with "+" modes. Output cannot be followed by input without an explicit **fflush()** or something that flushes the buffer (like an **fseek()**, **fsetpos()**, **rewind()**). Similarly input cannot be directly followed by output without calling of the above calls.

Since buffered I/O comes from the portable standard C library, it has support for a distinction between binary files and text files because some operating systems have that distinction. Unix makes no such distinction, so any special binary flags (sticking a "b" onto a/a+/w/w+, etc.) passed for the mode are ignored.

Files created with **fopen()** have permissions rw-rw-rw-. You cannot change that directly with **fopen()**, but instead use the **chmod()** or **fchmod()** system calls.

There are two companion calls to **fopen()**:

```
FILE *fdopen (int fd, char *mode);

FILE *freopen (char *path, char *mode, FILE *stream);
```

fdopen() takes an existing file descriptor (gotten from **open()**, or from a networking call) and wraps a FILE stream around it.

freopen() closes and reopens a given file pointer, but using the new path instead of what was used before. **freopen()** is very handy if you are redirecting the standard streams. You can do something like stdin = freopen ("/my/new/stdin.file", "w+", stdin); to redirect standard in.

Closing Files

```
int fclose (FILE *stream);
```

Dissociates the stream from its underlying file. Any buffered data is queued to the kernel using **fflush()** and the enclosed file descriptor is closed. If the program terminates abnormally, any buffered data will not be flushed to the kernel, and will be lost.

Text I/O

The buffered I/O API has two concepts of I/O when it comes to reading and writing: one is text oriented, the other is binary oriented.

Text I/O can be done a character-at-a-time, or a line at a time. Here are the character at a time functions:

```
int getc (FILE *stream);

int getchar ();

int fgetc (FILE *stream);
```

Each will try to get the next input character from the given stream (or from stdin for **getchar()**). It is interesting that these functions return an int rather than a char. The return value is overloaded so that it returns both the function data or a status value. Since char's useful values cover the entire expressible range of values, some other extra bits are needed to store a unique result values. If end of file or a read error occurs, the return returns the constant EOF (usually -1). You need to use the routines **feof()** and **ferror()** to distinguish between end of file and an error. In the case of error, errno is set like in the unbuffered I/O function. On a successful read, the return value is the character data. You can use the function **clearerr()** to clear the end of file and error indicators on the FILE stream.

The implementation of **getc()** and **fgetc()** are defined by the ANSI C standard. **getc()** is implemented by a macro, and **fgetc()** is implemented as a function. The implications of this specification are that the argument to **getc()** should not have any side effects since it could get evaluated more than once by the macro. It also means that if you want to stash something in a function pointer, you can use **fgetc()**. The actual time difference between **getc()** and **fgetc()** is negligible, so just use **fgetc()**, unless you can measure that the function call overhead is a problem.

Here is how to check for EOF, and discriminate between error and end of file:

Example 10-6. buffread.m

```
// buffread.m -- show how to read using buffered I/O, including
//                error / eof handling

/* compile with:
cc -g -Wall -o buffread buffread.m
*/

#import <stdlib.h>      // for EXIT_SUCCESS, etc
#import <stdio.h>       // all the buffered I/O API
#import <errno.h>       // for errno
#import <string.h>      // for strerror()

int main (int argc, char *argv[])
{
    FILE *file;
    int result;

    file = fopen ("/etc/motd", "r");

    while (1) {
        result = fgetc (file);
        if (result == EOF) {
            if (feof(file)) {
                printf ("EOF found\n");
            }
            if (ferror(file)) {
                printf ("error reading file: %d (%s)\n",
                        errno, strerror(errno));
            }
            break;
        } else {
            printf ("got a character: '%c'\n", (char) result);
        }
    }
```

```
    fclose (file);

    return (EXIT_SUCCESS);

} // main
```

Not only can you read characters from the stream, you can push them back onto the stream with **ungetc()**:

```
int ungetc (int c, FILE *stream);
```

ANSI C only guarantees one character of pushback, but the OS X man pages says you can push back an arbitrary amount. Being able to push back characters is handy in some parsers. You can peek a character ahead to see if this particular chunk of text is interesting. If not, push that character back and let some other piece of code handle the parsing. **ungetc()** clears the EOF flag so you can unget a character on an EOF and then read it later. Note that calls to a positioning function (**fseek()**, **fsetpos()**, or **rewind()**) will discard the pushed-back characters.

So those are the character-at-a-time read functions. To actually write to a stream character-wise, use one of these:

```
int fputc (int c, FILE *stream);

int putchar(int c);

int putc (int c, FILE *stream);
```

These are exactly analogous to the reading functions. **fputc()** is a function, **putc()** is a macro, **putchar()** implicitly uses stdout.

For line-at-a-time I/O, use these functions:

```
char *fgets (char *str, int size, FILE *stream);

char *gets (char *str); // do not use this one

int fputs (const char *str, FILE *stream);

int puts (const char *str);
```

You give **fgets()** and **gets()** an already allocated character buffer. The functions will return when they see an end of line character, or they fill up the buffer. Note that **gets()** does not accept a size so there is no way to really control how much will get put into the buffer, making buffer overflows really easy (so do not use it). **fgets()** stores the newline character in the buffer, while **gets()** does not. If an end of file or an error occurs they return NULL, and you need to check **feof()** and **ferror()** to see what happened. In both cases, a zero byte is appended to the end of the string.

puts() writes to standard out. **fputs()** does not automatically put a newline to the stream, while **puts()** does.

Binary I/O

Binary I/O is not limited to just binary data: you can use it for blocks of text too. (block I/O would probably be a better name). These calls are handy for writing arrays of structures to disk. Beware of portability problems when blindly writing structures like this. If any of the data types should change size you can end up breaking your file format.

```
size_t fread (void *ptr, size_t size, size_t nmemb, FILE *stream);

size_t fwrite (const void *ptr, size_t size, size_t nmemb, FILE *stream);
```

Each function has a pointer to memory, the size of the struct, and the number of elements in an array of these structs. The return value is the number of actual *elements* written, not the number of bytes written. Internally it is just doing the multiplication and writing that number of bytes. These functions do not stop at zero bytes or newlines like the text I/O functions do. If the number of elements read or written is less than expected, check **ferror()** and **feof()**.

Here is a little sample:

Example 10-7. fbinaryio.m

```
// fbinaryio.m -- do some binary reading and writing using buffered I/O

/* compile with:
cc -g -Wall -o fbinaryio fbinaryio.m
*/

#import <stdlib.h>      // for EXIT_SUCCESS, etc
#import <stdio.h>       // for the buffered I/O API
#import <errno.h>       // for errno and strerror()
#import <string.h>       // for strerror()

typedef struct Thing {
    int         thing1;
    float       thing2;
    char        thing3[8];
} Thing;

Thing things[] = {
    { 3, 3.14159, "hello" },
    { 4, 4.29301, "bye" },
    { 2, 2.14214, "bork" },
    { 5, 5.55556, "elf up" }
};

int main (int argc, char *argv[])
{
    size_t thingCount = sizeof(things) / sizeof(Thing); // how many we have
    size_t numWrote;
    FILE *file;

    file = fopen ("/tmp/thingfile", "w");

    if (file == NULL) {
        fprintf (stderr, "error opening file: %d (%s)\n",
                errno, strerror(errno));
        exit (EXIT_FAILURE);
    }
```

```
numWrote = fwrite (things, sizeof(Thing), thingCount, file);

if (numWrote != thingCount) {
    fprintf (stderr, "incomplete write (%d out of %d). Error %d (%s)\n",
             (int)numWrote, (int)thingCount, errno, strerror(errno));
    exit (EXIT_FAILURE);
}

fclose (file);

// now re-open and re-read and make sure everything is groovy
file = fopen ("/tmp/thingfile", "r");

if (file == NULL) {
    fprintf (stderr, "error opening file: %d (%s)\n",
             errno, strerror(errno));
    exit (EXIT_FAILURE);
}


{
    // we know we are reading in thingCount, so we can go ahead and
    // allocate that much space
    Thing readThings[sizeof(things) / sizeof(Thing)];
    ssize_t numRead;

    numRead = fread (readThings, sizeof(Thing), thingCount, file);
    if (numRead != thingCount) {
        fprintf (stderr, "short read.  Got %d, expected %d\n",
                 (int)numRead, (int)thingCount);
        if (feof(file)) {
            fprintf (stderr, "we got an end of file\n");
        }
        if (ferror(file)) {
            fprintf (stderr, "we got an error: %d (%s)\n",
                     errno, strerror(errno));
        }
    } else {
        // just for fun, compare the newly read ones with the ones
        // we have statically declared
        int i;
        for (i = 0; i < thingCount; i++) {
            if (   (things[i].thing1 != readThings[i].thing1)
                || (things[i].thing2 != readThings[i].thing2)
                || (strcmp(things[i].thing3, readThings[i].thing3)
                    != 0)) {
                fprintf (stderr, "mismatch with element %d\n", i);
            } else {
                printf ("successfully compared element %d\n", i);
            }
        }
    }
}

fclose (file);

exit (EXIT_SUCCESS);
```

```
} // main
```

Here is a sample run:

```
% ./fbinaryio
successfully compared element 0
successfully compared element 1
successfully compared element 2
successfully compared element 3
```

And just for fun, look at the file itself:

```
% hexdump -C /tmp/thingfile
0000  00 00 00 03 40 49 0f d0  68 65 6c 6c 6f 00 00 00
            |....@I..hello...|
0010  00 00 00 04 40 89 60 57  62 79 65 00 00 00 00 00
            |....@.'Wbye.....|
0020  00 00 00 02 40 09 18 d2  62 6f 72 6b 00 00 00 00
            |....@...bork....|
0030  00 00 00 05 40 b1 c7 26  65 6c 66 20 75 70 00 00
            |....@..&elf up..|
```

You can see that there are 4 bytes of integer, 4 bytes of float, and 8 bytes of character data. It just so happens to line up with the `struct Thing` definition.

Positioning

Like unbuffered I/O, the buffered I/O FILE streams have a current position.

```
long ftell (FILE *stream);

int fseek (FILE *stream, long offset, int whence);
```

`ftell()` returns the current location in the file. `fseek()` is like `lseek()`. It has the same use of offset and whence (SEEK_SET, SEEK_CUR, SEEK_END). The return value of `fseek()` is zero on successful completion, otherwise -1 is returned and errno is set appropriately. Note that the offset type of these functions are longs, which can limit file sizes. There are also versions that take off_t types, which could be larger than longs:

```
off_t ftello(FILE *stream);

int fseeko(FILE *stream, off_t offset, int whence);
```

An alternate interface is

```
int fgetpos(FILE *stream, fpos_t *pos);

int fsetpos(FILE *stream, const fpos_t *pos);
```

using the opaque fpos_t type. On some platforms it is the same as an off_t. On other platforms it is an 8-byte array.

```
void rewind (FILE *stream);
```

will reset the current location in the file to the very beginning, also clearing the error flag.

Formatted I/O

The `printf` family of calls live under standard / buffered I/O since they write out to FILE streams, either explicitly or implicitly (or in the case of `s[n]printf` which writes to a buffer, but it has the same syntax as its I/O companions).

```
int printf (const char *format, ...);

int fprintf (FILE *stream, const char *format, ...);

int sprintf (char *str, const char *format, ...);

int snprintf (char *str, size_t size, const char *format, ...);

int asprintf (char **ret, const char *format, ...);
```

`printf()` writes to the stdout file. `fprintf()` writes to any FILE. `sprintf()` writes into a buffer, and `snprintf()` writes into a buffer but it is given the size of the buffer. Always use `snprintf()` instead of `sprintf()`. There is no prevention of buffer overruns in `sprintf()`, especially if any user-entered data gets fed into the function. With `snprintf()` buffer overruns will not happen. `asprintf()` takes `snprintf()` to the next level by automatically allocating a buffer for you that is the correct size (which you will need to `free()` once you are done with it).

The specifics of the `printf`-style of formatting are covered in opaque detail in the man page, and in most every C-101 book out there.

You can do formatted input as well, using

```
int scanf (const char *format, ...);

int fscanf (FILE *stream, const char *format, ...);

int sscanf (const char *str, const char *format, ...);
```

These take format strings like `printf()`, but instead of just regular arguments in the ... section of the parameter list, you need to provide pointers to appropriate-sized areas of memory. The `scanf()` functions will not allocate memory for you. There is not much in the way of error detection or recovery when using the functions. Outside of toy programs, you will probably want to write your own parsing code, use lex/yacc, or use a regular expression library.

Misc Functions

Here are miscellaneous buffered I/O functions.

```
int fileno(FILE *stream);
```

Returns the file descriptor that the stream is wrapped around. This is handy if you need to use `fcntl()`, `fchmod()`, `fstat()`, or the `dup()` functions.

```
int getw(FILE *stream);
```

```
int putw(int w, FILE *stream);
```

These are like `getc()`/`putc()`, but read or write an integer. The integers are not written in a canonical form (discussed in Chapter 13 (Networking)), so if you want to be portable, you will need to put the bytes into a known byte order.

Buffered I/O vs. Unbuffered I/O

With buffered I/O, there is a lot of data copying happening:

program structures -> FILE buffer -> kernel buffer -> disk.

With unbuffered I/O, the copy to the `FILE` buffer is avoided, and with scatter/gather I/O, the kernel might be able to avoid a copy into its own buffers.

Since `read()`/`write()` are not buffered (save for a disk block or two in the kernel data structures) they can be slow when dealing with lots of smaller reads and writes. Buffered I/O would be a win here.

When doing big reads and writes (dozens of K of image data, for instance), there is a win to using plain `read()` and `write()` calls to avoid the buffering step in between.

Fundamentally everything boils down to the file descriptor. Even `FILE`s have a file descriptor at their heart. Be careful when mixing buffered and unbuffered I/O with the same file descriptor. The `FILE` part of the world does not get notified if you do I/O with the file descriptor, leading to some confusing synchronization errors.

In both the buffered and unbuffered I/O cases, there is some magic that happens when input or output are going to a terminal device. `read()` takes on per-line semantics, and the buffered I/O calls take on line buffering behavior.

Lastly, when both buffered and unbuffered I/O perform a write operation, the data does not necessarily end up on disk immediately. The kernel will buffer the writing to reduce the number of physical I/O operations it has to do. This means that you can dutifully write your data, have the OS crash, and your data is lost. If you are truly paranoid about having data written to disk (like in a database system), you can use one of the sync calls:

```
void sync (void);
```

This forces the queuing of modified buffers in the block buffer for I/O. This call will return immediately and the kernel will write the blocks at its leisure. This will force writing for all modified blocks system wide.

```
int fsync (int fd);
```

causes all modified data and metadata for a file to be flushed out to the physical disk. This is applies to just one file. The call will block for all I/O to complete before returning.

Removing Files

Removing files is pretty easy. Use the `unlink()` system call:

```
int unlink (const char *path);
```

This returns zero on successful completion or -1 if there was an error (with errno set to the error that actually happened). A file can have multiple references to itself (hard links, which will be discussed in a bit), and a file is removed when all references to it have been eliminated.

There is one subtly when unlinking files that are currently open. The directory entry for the file is removed immediately (so if you do an ls on the directory you will not see the file), but the file's contents still exist on the disk, still consume space, and are still available to the program that has the file open. The actual space is reclaimed by the OS once all programs close the file. This is useful for temporary files, ones you do not want to hang around after the program goes away. By unlinking the temporary file immediately after opening it, you do not need to worry about deleting the file once your program is over. The space occupied by the file will be reclaimed even if your program crashes.

This behavior can occasionally lead to puzzling system administration issues. Imagine the scenario where a web server has a 100-meg log file open and the disk it is on is filling up. Someone deletes the file hoping to reclaim the space. Since the log file is still open, those 100 megs are still being used, but they will not show up using any command (like du).

Rather than deleting the file, you can truncate it with the command:

```
% sudo cp /dev/null /the/log/file/name
```

If you have already deleted the file, you can use the command lsof, to "ls Open Files" and see what is there. lsof is pretty handy anyway to peek inside the system and see what is going on.

```
% sudo lsof
(Huge amount of output.  Here are a couple lines.)

pbs    266 markd  cwd  VDIR   14,9      1486       2 / (/dev/disk0s9)
pbs    266 markd   0u  VCHR    0,0    0t4015 26234628 /dev/console
pbs    266 markd   1u  VCHR    0,0    0t4015 26234628 /dev/console
pbs    266 markd   2u  VCHR    0,0    0t4015 26234628 /dev/console
```

This is the pasteboard server, process ID 266, owned by user markd. It has three files open on fd 0, 1, 2, all open for read/write, and all going to /dev/console. It also has the directory / (the unix root directory) open, as the current working directory.

```
Adium   1269 markd   7u  inet 0x0240d7bc    0t0      TCP
10.0.1.142:49249->toc-m04.blue.aol.com:9898 (ESTABLISHED)
```

Adium, an AIM client that is running with pid 1269, has fd 7 being an internet connection. On the local side the IP address 10.0.1.142 port 49249, is connected to toc-m04.blue.aol.com, port 9898.

```
lsof   1361 markd   3r  VCHR   3,0         0t0 26234372 /dev/mem
lsof   1361 markd   4r  VCHR   3,1 0t26432612 26234244 /dev/kmem
lsof   1361 markd   5r  VREG  14,9     3169824    66862 /mach_kernel
```

Finally, this run of lsof has file descriptors 3, 4, 5 open, reading /dev/mem, /dev/kmem (kernel memory), and also has the mach_kernel file open, so it can resolve the data it finds in the memory devices.

Temporary Files

Temporary files, as the name implies, are files that are used by a program as it is running and then are not useful once the program goes away. Unix systems typically store temp files in a well known location so that people know where to clean out files that are left over accidentally, and some systems will clear out the directory that holds the temp files on startup.

When a program wants to create a temporary file it, needs a unique name so that it does not clash with what is already in the temp directory. If two programs ended up using the same temporary file, they would both probably fail in weird and wonderful ways.

Where is this temporary directory? There is an algorithm used when determining where the temp directory is. First, the environment variable TMPDIR is used (if it exists). Then, the directory P_tmpdir defined in /usr/include/stdio.h (which on OS X is /var/tmp), and then the directory /tmp is tried.

Here are the functions for dealing with temporary file names.

These functions generate the file name:

```
char *tmpnam (char *str);

char *tempnam (const char *tmpdir, const char *prefix);

char *mktemp (char *template);
```

And these functions will open the file for you automatically:

```
int mkstemp (char *template);

FILE *tmpfile (void);
```

First the file name generation functions.

tmpnam() returns a pointer to a file name in the P_tmpdir (a global variable declared in stdio.h) directory. If you pass NULL for the str argument the file name will be returned out of a static buffer (not very good for thread safety). You can also pass in a buffer and **tmpnam()** will write into that.

tempnam() is similar to **tmpnam()**, but lets you specify the directory to put the file into, as well as a prefix to the name. This function will allocate memory, which you will need to **free()**. If the prefix is NULL, the P_tmpdir value will be used instead.

mktemp() uses a template you supply, replacing any X characters with something unique. The passed in template gets modified, so keep a copy of your template if you want to use it again.

Here are all of them in action:

Example 10-8. tempfun.m

```
// tempfun.m -- see how different temp file names are generated

/* compile with:
cc -g -Wall -o tempfun tempfun.m
*/
```

```
#import <stdlib.h>        // for EXIT_SUCCESS, etc
#import <stdio.h>         // for the temp name functions
#import <unistd.h>        // for mk[s]temp
#import <string.h>        // for strcpy()

int main (int argc, char *argv[])
{
    char *name;
    char buffer[1024];

    printf ("my process ID is %d\n", getpid());

    name = tmpnam (NULL);
    printf ("tmpnam(NULL) is '%s'\n", name);

    name = tmpnam (buffer);
    printf ("tmpnam(buffer) is '%s'\n", buffer);

    name = tempnam ("/System/Library", "my_prefix");
    printf ("tempnam(/System/Library, my_prefix) is '%s'\n", name);
    free (name);

    name = tempnam ("/does/not/exist", "my_prefix");
    printf ("tempnam(/does/not/exist, my_prefix) is '%s'\n", name);
    free (name);

    strcpy (buffer, "templateXXXXXX");
    name = mktemp (buffer);
    printf ("mktemp(templateXXXXXX) is '%s'\n", name);

    return (0);

} // main
```

And some output:

```
% ./tempfun
my process ID is 1482
tmpnam(NULL) is '/var/tmp/tmp.0.001482'
tmpnam(buffer) is '/var/tmp/tmp.1.001482'
tempnam(/System/Library, my_prefix) is
                '/System/Library/my_prefix001482'
tempnam(/does/not/exist, my_prefix) is '/var/tmp/my_prefix001482'
mktemp(templateXXXXXX) is 'template001482'
```

Note that the temporary file name is related to the process ID of the running program.

Some of the calls do take precautions if a file name already exists:

```
% sudo touch /var/tmp/tmp.0.001505 /var/tmp/tmp.1.001505 \
/System/Library/my_prefix001505 /var/tmp/my_prefix001505 \
template001505

% ./tempfun
my process ID is 1505
tmpnam(NULL) is '/var/tmp/tmp.0.a01505'
tmpnam(buffer) is '/var/tmp/tmp.1.a01505'
```

```
tempnam(/System/Library, my_prefix) is
                    '/System/Library/my_prefixa01505'
tempnam(/does/not/exist, my_prefix) is '/var/tmp/my_prefixa01505'
mktemp(templateXXXXXX) is 'templatea01505'
```

The functions plugged in an extra "a" for the file names.

Remember the discussion a little earlier on atomic operations and race conditions? Unfortunately they can happen here. You generate the temporary name with one function call, then another call to open the file. In the intervening time, a rogue program could create a file of the same name, which could prevent your program from running, or entice it to operate on bad data.

The other two functions, **mkstemp()** and **tmpfile()** generate the temp file name and open the file for you. **mkstemp()** uses the same template idea that **mktemp()** uses, and creates the file with permission mode rw-------, and returns a file descriptor for it.

tmpfile() uses **mkstemp()** and opens a buffered I/O stream to a new file. This file is automatically unlinked so you do not need to worry about cleaning up after it.

File Permissions

The classic Macintosh has a one user, one computer mindset. The user at the computer is pretty much free to do what they want, whether it be simply copying files around or mucking around in the system folder. All of that has changed in OS X. Because OS X has the Unix heritage, it has a multi-user permission model on the file system, and as users and developers, you need to get used to it.

Users and groups

Every user on the system has a user ID (an integer). Each user belongs to one or more named groups and each group has an ID. For instance:

```
% ls -l chapter.txt
-rw-r--r--  1 markd   staff   48827 Aug 11 14:14 chapter.txt
```

The user is markd, the group is staff.

```
% ls -l /bin/ls
-r-xr-xr-x  1 root   wheel   27160 Dec  8  2001 /bin/ls*
```

ls is owned by the user root, the group wheel.

You can see what users and groups are configured on your machine with nidump. On my PowerBook G4, I have

```
% nidump passwd .
nobody:*:-2:-2::0:0:Unprivileged User:/dev/null:/dev/null
root:*:0:0::0:0:System Administrator:/var/root:/bin/tcsh
daemon:*:1:1::0:0:System Services:/var/root:/dev/null
unknown:*:99:99::0:0:Unknown User:/dev/null:/dev/null
www:*:70:70::0:0:World Wide Web Server:/Library/WebServer:/dev/null
markd:39.dxiwzIfvlU:501:20::0:0:markd:/Users/markd:/bin/tcsh
smmsp:*:25:25::0:0:Sendmail User:/private/etc/mail:/dev/null
bork:EB0mNxAcVD2wY:502:20::0:0:bork:/Users/bork:/bin/tcsh
```

The accounts `markd` and `bork` are accounts that were added to the machine. The rest come with the OS. The order of the fields (separated by colons above, are):

- username
- one-way hashed password, "*" if there is no password
- user id (in this case, the user ID is 501)
- group id (20 is `staff`)
- The next three are esoteric (password change time, user access class, and the Gecos field which can be used for general information)
- the full name of the user
- the user's home directory
- the user's login shell

You can see groups with `nidump` also:

```
% nidump group .
(edited)
wheel:*:0:markd,bork
. . .
staff:*:20:root
. . .
admin:*:80:root,markd,bork
```

The fields here are the group name, the group's password (which rarely gets used), the group's ID (gid), and any group members. This way a user can be in more than one group. The user's primary group is what is listed in the `nidump passwd` listing, then they can be added to other groups here. Groups are a way to aggregate users that should have similar access permissions on sets of files. For instance, you would want your developers to be able edit files on a shared documentation tree. Specifically, the user `markd` is in group `staff` (due to the passwd entry), and is also a member of the group `wheel` and `admin`.

On other systems that do not use `NetInfo` (which would be just about every other flavor of Unix out there), the files `/etc/passwd` and `/etc/group` have the above information.

You use the `chown` command line program to change the ownership of a file. You must have superuser privilege to give away one of your own files to another user (otherwise you could use that to defeat disk space quotas).

For instance:

```
% touch spoon

% ls -l spoon
-rw-r--r--  1 markd   staff   0 Aug 11 14:40 spoon

% chown bork spoon
chown: spoon: Operation not permitted

% sudo chown bork spoon
```

```
% ls -l spoon
-rw-r--r--   1 bork   staff   0 Aug 11 14:40 spoon
```

You can change groups with `chgrp`:

```
% chgrp wheel spoon
chgrp: spoon: Operation not permitted

% sudo chgrp wheel spoon

% ls -l spoon
-rw-r--r--   1 bork   wheel   0 Aug 11 14:40 spoon
```

You can combine these two operations into one `chmod` command if you wish:

```
% sudo chown markd:staff spoon

% ls -l spoon
-rw-r--r--   1 markd   staff   0 Aug 11 14:40 spoon
```

There are system calls for manually changing the owner and group of a file:

```
int chown (const char *path, uid_t owner, gid_t group);

int lchown (const char *path, uid_t owner, gid_t group);

int fchown(int fd, uid_t owner, gid_t group);
```

chown() changes the owner and group of a file, **lchown()** changes it for a symbolic link, and **fchown()** operates on a file that is already open.

If you need to look up the owner and group IDs:

```
struct passwd *getpwent (void);

struct passwd *getpwnam (const char *login);

struct passwd *getpwuid (uid_t uid);
```

There are equivalent operations (like **getgrent()**, **getgrnam()**, **getgrgid()**) for getting group information.

`struct passwd` has all of the elements seen in the `passwd` entries above, like pw_name (login name), pw_uid (their user id), pw_gid (their group id), and others. **getpwent()** can be used to iterate through the password list. **getpwnam()** maps a login name to the `passwd` entry. **getpwuid()** maps a numeric userID to the appropriate `passwd` entry.

File permissions

Associated with each file and directory are a number of bits of information. The nine most important of those bits are the file permissions. When you `ls -l` a file, you will see them:

```
% ls -l chapter.txt
-rw-r--r--   1 markd   staff   52655 Aug 11 15:11 chapter.txt
```

In particular, look at rw- r-- r-- three sets of three bits. The first set are permissions for the user who owns the file (markd, who can read from and write to the file). The second set are permissions for the group of the file (staff, who can read the file). Anyone who is a member of the staff group can read this file. The last set of bits are the permissions for all the others (anyone who is not markd and is not in the staff group)

Each of owner, group, and world can have these bits set:

r

Read

w

Write

x

Execute

The clue to the OS that a file is actually an executable program is that the execute bit is set. There is not a magic file name suffix (like .EXE) that tells the OS that this file is executable.

Here are the permissions from some arbitrarily picked files from my file system:

```
% ls -l /bin/ls
-r-xr-xr-x  1 root  wheel  27160 Dec  8  2001 /bin/ls*
```

The user (root) group (wheel), and others can all read and execute the file. Nobody can write to it. (The wheel group is used to designate system administrators on BSD systems)

```
% ls -l /Developer/Documentation/Cocoa/helpviewericon.gif
-rw-rw-r--  1 root  admin  631 Jul 19  2001 \
/Developer/Documentation/Cocoa/helpviewericon.gif
```

The user (root), group (admin) can each read and write the file. All the others can only read it.

```
% ls -l /var/tmp/console.log
-rw-------  1 markd  wheel  39093 Aug 11 15:04 /var/tmp/console.log
```

The user (markd) can read and write the file. Neither the group nor anyone else can do anything to it.

You will sometimes see file permissions expressed numerically. Since each chunk of permissions is three bits, octal is how numbers are usually expressed.

```
r : 100
w : 010
x : 001
```

So a permission of rw is binary 110, which is octal value of 6. A permission of rwx is binary 111, which is octal value of 7.

rwx rw- r-- is the same as 111 110 100, which is 764 in octal.

Figure 10-7. Permission Bits

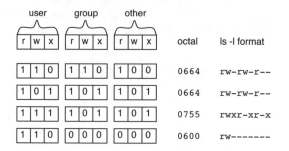

The `chmod` command lets you change these permission bits, either in octal or symbolically.

For instance:

```
% touch test
% ls -l test
-rw-r--r--   1 markd   staff   0 Aug 11 15:23 test

% chmod 775 test
% ls -l test
-rwxr-xr-x   1 markd   staff   0 Aug 11 15:23 test

% chmod 400 test
% ls -l test
-r--------   1 markd   staff   0 Aug 11 15:23 test
```

Most people do not tend to think in octal, so you can use symbols instead.

u

　　Modify user permissions.

g

　　Modify group permissions.

o

　　Modify other permissions.

+

　　Set the bits that follow.

−

　　Clear the bits that follow.

r

　　Read.

w

   Write.

x

   Execute.

```
% chmod ugo+rw test
```

(For user, group, other, turn on the read and write bits.)

```
% ls -l test
-rw-rw-rw-  1 markd  staff  0 Aug 11 15:23 test
```

```
% chmod +x test
```

(This is shorthand for everything.)

```
% ls -l test
-rwxrwxrwx  1 markd  staff  0 Aug 11 15:23 test*
```

```
% chmod g-wx test
```

(Turn off write and execute for group.)

```
% ls -l test
-rwxr--rwx  1 markd  staff  0 Aug 11 15:23 test*
```

There is also an API for affecting the permission bits:

```
int chmod (const char *path, mode_t mode);
```

```
int fchmod (int fd, mode_t mode);
```

where `chmod()` affects a file in the file system, and `fchmod()` changes the permissions on a file you already have open.

There is a whole slew of unpronounceable constants for specifying the mode:

```
#define S_IRWXU 0000700     /* RWX mask for owner */
#define S_IRUSR 0000400     /* R for owner */
#define S_IWUSR 0000200     /* W for owner */
#define S_IXUSR 0000100     /* X for owner */

#define S_IRWXG 0000070     /* RWX mask for group */
#define S_IRGRP 0000040     /* R for group */
#define S_IWGRP 0000020     /* W for group */
#define S_IXGRP 0000010     /* X for group */

#define S_IRWXO 0000007     /* RWX mask for other */
#define S_IROTH 0000004     /* R for other */
#define S_IWOTH 0000002     /* W for other */
#define S_IXOTH 0000001     /* X for other */
```

So, to specify rwxrw-r--, you would do something like this:

```
      user              group              other
      rwx               rw-                r--
```

```
      7                   6                   4
  S_IRWXU |    (S_IRGRP | S_IWGRP)   | S_IROTH
```

There is one more complication that gets thrown into the mix, the umask set by the user. The user has control over what permissions get used when creating new files by using the umask command to specify a numeric (octal) value to specify the bits that should be left unset.

Figure 10-8. umask

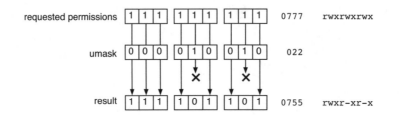

For example:

```
% umask
22
% touch test
% ls -l test
-rw-r--r--  1 markd  staff  0 Aug 11 15:47 test
```

The umask of "22" is binary 000 010 010. The middle bit is the "w" write bit. So a umask of 22 will remove the write bit for group and others. If I change my umask

```
% umask 002
% umask
2
% rm test
% touch test
% ls -l test
-rw-rw-r--  1 markd  staff  0 Aug 11 15:48 test
```

now only the "other" group of permissions has the write bit stripped out. If you are truly paranoid, you can use something like this:

```
% umask 077
% umask
77
% rm test
% touch test
% ls -l test
-rw-------  1 markd  staff  0 Aug 11 15:49 test
```

The 77 (all bits set for group and other) causes all of those permission bits to be stripped out, so now only the user has any access to the files.

If you are using groups to control permissions, a umask of 002 is most friendly. You will not be creating files that cannot be written to by the group (which can temporarily mess up your project tree if you are using CVS).

There is also a **umask()** system call where you can change the umask used on the fly.

```
mode_t umask (mode_t numask);
```

The umask is inherited by child processes, which is handy if you want to make the umask more restrictive before spawning off a subprocess.

One interesting implementation detail in the Unix file system is that if you chmod a file, the modification date does not change. The file itself is not affected, just the metadata.

There is one last commonly used permission bit associated with files, the "set-uid" bit. There are some operations that can only be performed with the permission of root, the superuser, such as modifying the password file. But some of these operations (like changing a password) you want ordinary mortals to be able to do. The way Unix works around this problem is by having a bit that says, "when you run this program, run it as if the user were the same user as the file's owner, rather than running the program as the logged in user."

If you look at /usr/bin/passwd:

```
% ls -l /usr/bin/passwd
-r-sr-xr-x  1 root  wheel  29756 Dec  8  2001 /usr/bin/passwd*
```

Notice the "s" in the user execute bit. That means when /usr/bin/passwd is run, it runs as root rather than as the logged-in user markd.

If you look something like one of the program files in the Oracle database:

```
% cd $ORACLE_HOME/bin
% ls -l oracle
-rwsr-s--x  1  oracle  oinstall 23389261 May 13 1997 oracle*
```

This is suid-oracle. When you run this program, it runs as if the logged in user were oracle. Also notice the second "s" in the group execute bit. That means the program will run as the group oinstall.

When a program runs, there are actually 6 (or more) IDs associated with it:

The real user ID and real group ID.

> This is who you really are, who you were when you logged in. These typically do not change during the life of a running program.

The effective user ID, effective group ID, supplementary group IDs.

> These are used for file permission checks. When you run an suid-root binary, your effective user ID is root.

The saved set-group-ID and saved set-user-ID

> These are used by the exec functions, which will be discussed in Chapter 15 (Multiprocessing).

Example 10-9. uid.m

```
// uid.m -- experiment with user and group ids.
//          run as normal, then change this to be suid, and run again
```

```
/* compile with:
cc -g -Wall -o uid uid.m
*/

#import <sys/types.h>    // for struct group/struct passwd
#import <grp.h>          // for getgrgid()
#import <pwd.h>          // for getpwuid()
#import <stdio.h>        // for printf() and friends
#import <stdlib.h>       // EXIT_SUCCESS
#import <unistd.h>       // for getuid() and friends

int main (int argc, char *argv[])
{
    uid_t user_id;
    uid_t effective_user_id;
    gid_t group_id;
    gid_t effective_group_id;
    struct group *group;
    struct passwd *user;

    user_id = getuid ();
    effective_user_id = geteuid ();

    group_id = getgid ();
    effective_group_id = getegid ();

    user = getpwuid (user_id);
    printf ("real user ID is '%s'\n", user->pw_name);

    user = getpwuid (effective_user_id);
    printf ("effective user ID is '%s'\n", user->pw_name);

    group = getgrgid (group_id);
    printf ("real group is '%s'\n", group->gr_name);

    group = getgrgid (effective_group_id);
    printf ("effective group is '%s'\n", group->gr_name);

    exit (EXIT_SUCCESS);

} // main
```

Here is a run just as markd:

```
% ls -l uid
-rwxrwxr-x  1 markd  staff  16692 Aug 11 16:35 uid*
% ./uid
real user ID is 'markd'
effective user ID is 'markd'
real group is 'staff'
effective group is 'staff'
```

Now make it suid root:

```
% sudo chown root:wheel uid
% sudo chmod ug+s uid
```

```
% ls -l uid
-rwsrwsr-x  1 root   wheel   16692 Aug 11 16:37 uid*
(note the s bits)
% ./uid
real user ID is 'markd'
effective user ID is 'root'
real group is 'staff'
effective group is 'wheel'
```

So now this program is running with privileges of root.

Finally, let is try it as another ordinary user:

```
% sudo chown bork:admin uid
% ls -l uid
-rwsrwsr-x  1 bork   admin   16692 Aug 11 16:37 uid*

% ./uid
real user ID is 'markd'
effective user ID is 'bork'
real group is 'staff'
effective group is 'admin'
```

One thing to note is that the setuid bits get cleared if a non-privileged program writes to the setuid file.

```
% ls -l uid
-rwsrwsr-x  1 bork   admin   16692 Aug 11 16:37 uid*
% cat >> uid
1 [control-D for end of file]
% ls -l uid
-rwxrwxr-x  1 bork   admin   16694 Aug 11 16:40 uid*
```

That is a security measure to keep some malicious program from replacing a setuid program and running hostile code with root privileges.

Directory Permissions

Directories have the same permission bits as files (rwx for user, group, and other), but with slightly different interpretations. Because you cannot run directories as programs, the execute bit takes on a different meaning: it acts like a search bit. When opening any type of file by name, the user in question must have execute permission on every directory mentioned in the path (whether they match the user, group, or are other). Read permission is different from the execute/search permission. Read permission lets you read the directory itself, like with the ls command, to obtain a list of all the file names in the directory. Execute just means that you can pass through, or execute programs in that directory. You do not need read permissions along the way.

As an example, you create a directory, and copy a program into it

```
% mkdir permtest
% cp /bin/hostname permtest
% chmod -rw permtest
% ls -ld permtest
d--x--x--x  3 markd   staff   58 Aug 11 16:52 permtest/
```

Now you have turned off everything but the search bits.

```
% ls permtest
ls: permtest: Permission denied
```

No read permission, so you get an error.

```
% ./permtest/hostname
localhost
```

But you can still run programs in there.

Permission-Check Algorithms

Here is the quick overview of how permissions interact with the file operations discussed earlier:

- Must have read permission to open a file for reading with O_RDONLY or O_RDWR.
- Must have write permission to open a file for writing with O_WRONLY and O_RDWR.
- Must have write permission to O_TRUNCate a file.
- Must have write and execute permission on a directory to create a new file (write permission so you can modify the directory entry, and execute permission so the file can be searched).
- Must have write and execute permission on a directory to delete a file. You do not actually need read/write permissions on the file itself since the operation is actually just on the directory data structures.
- Must have the execute bit set to run a file program as a program.
- For accessing a file:
  - If the effective user ID is zero (root), access is allowed.
  - If the effective user ID is the same as the owner ID of the file, check the appropriate permission bit and allow access.
  - If the effective group ID or supplementary group ID is the same as the group ID of the file, check the appropriate permission bit and allow access.
  - If the appropriate access permission bit is set, allow access.
  - Otherwise do not allow access.

The whole effective user ID and real user ID brings up some interesting questions regarding file permissions. What if the user is running a setuid program but that program does not want to modify any files the user could not ordinarily be able to modify. The **access()** system call comes to the rescue:

```
int access (const char *path, int mode);
```

This checks the accessibility of the file named by the path, using the mode, and as the *real* userID and groupID of the user. The mode is the bitwise OR of the permissions to check:

R_OK

Read permission.

W_OK

Write permission.

X_OK

Execute/search permission.

F_OK

The file exists.

All components of the path are checked for access permissions.

Example 10-10. access.m

```
// access.m -- use the access() call to check permissions
//              run this as normal person, then make suid-root and try again

/* compile with:
cc -g -Wall -o access access.m
*/

#import <unistd.h>      // for access()
#import <stdio.h>       // for printf()
#import <stdlib.h>      // for EXIT_SUCCESS
#import <errno.h>       // for errno
#import <string.h>      // for strerror()

int main (int argc, char *argv[])
{
    int result;

    result = access ("/etc/motd", R_OK);

    if (result == 0) {
        printf ("read access to /etc/motd\n");
    } else {
        printf ("no read access to /etc/motd: %d (%s)\n",
                errno, strerror(errno));
    }

    result = access ("/etc/motd", W_OK);

    if (result == 0) {
        printf ("write access to /etc/motd\n");
    } else {
        printf ("no write access to /etc/motd: %d (%s)\n",
                errno, strerror(errno));
    }

    return (EXIT_SUCCESS);

} // main
```

Run as just `markd`:

```
% ./access
read access to /etc/motd
no write access to /etc/motd: 13 (Permission denied)
```

Run as root:

```
% sudo ./access
read access to /etc/motd
write access to /etc/motd
```

Run setuid-root:

```
% sudo chown root:wheel access
% sudo chmod ug+s access
% ls -l access
-rwsrwsr-x  1 root  wheel  9644 Aug 11 17:10 access*

% ./access
read access to /etc/motd
no write access to /etc/motd: 13 (Permission denied)
```

So it works as expected.

For the More Curious: Memory-Mapped files

Memory-Mapped Files

Memory mapped files are a blend of the virtual memory system and the file system, where a file's contents are mapped onto a range of bytes in memory. When you get bytes from that range of memory, you are reading from the file. When you change bytes in that range of memory, you are writing to the file. In essence you are doing I/O without using `read()` and `write()`. The virtual memory system gets to do the work of buffering, reading, and writing, only bringing in the blocks from disk that are actually used. To use memory-mapped files, you need to open the file, then call

```
caddr_t mmap (caddr_t addr, size_t len, int prot, int flags, int fd,
            off_t offset);
```

The return value is the address where the mapped file starts. Otherwise -1 is returned and `errno` is set.

Here are the arguments:

`addr`

> If non-zero, it is used as a hint to the system where in memory to start mapping to the file. `mmap()` is free to use or ignore this value. Usually you just pass in zero.

`len`

> How many bytes to map from the file. If you have a huge file, you can map just a portion of it to make things a little faster. Plus, it looks like there is a 1 gig limit to the amount of address space that will be mapped with this call.

prot

> Protection on the mapped memory. Pass a bitwise OR of one or more of these values:
>
> PROT_EXEC
>
> > Code may be executed on the mapped pages.
>
> PROT_READ
>
> > You can read from the pages.
>
> PROT_WRITE
>
> > You can write to the pages.
>
> These flags need to match the open mode of the file. For instance, you cannot PROT_WRITE a read-only file.

flags

> specifies various options. Here are the commonly used flags:
>
> MAP_FIXED
>
> > Return value must equal addr. If that is not possible an error is returned.
>
> MAP_SHARED
>
> > Storing bytes in memory will modify the mapped file. Be sure to set this if you expect your memory writes to be reflected back in the file.
>
> MAP_PRIVATE
>
> > Storing bytes in memory causes a copy of the mapped pages to be made, and all subsequent references reference the copy.
>
> MAP_FILE
>
> > Map from a regular file or a character special device. This is the default and does not need to be specified.
>
> MAP_INHERIT
>
> > Permit mapped regions to be mapped across **exec()** system calls so you can pass the mapped regions onto child processes.

fd

> The file descriptor for the open file.

offset

> The number of bytes into the file to start mapping. Usually you just pass in zero.

To unmap pages, use

```
int munmap (caddr_t addr, size_t len);
```

Returns zero on success, -1/setting `errno` on error. If you try to access this memory after the `munmap()`, you will generate invalid memory references. Note that `close()` does not unmap pages, but pages will get unmapped when your program exits.

`addr` and `offset` should be multiples of the system's virtual memory page size (use `sysconf()` to figure it out).

To flush modified pages back to the file system, use `msync()`:

```
int msync (void *addr, size_t len, int flags);
```

If `len` is zero, all modified pages will be flushed. Possible flag values are

MS_ASYNC

Return immediately and let the write happen at the kernel's convenience.

MS_SYNC

Perform synchronous writes.

MS_INVALIDATE

Invalidate all cached data (presumably to force a re-read from the file).

Some rules to remember:

- You can memory-map regular files, not networked file descriptors or device files.
- You need to be careful if the size of the underlying file could change after it gets mapped, otherwise memory access errors might be triggered.
- You cannot use `mmap()` and memory writes to memory to extend files. You will need to seek and write to accomplish that.

Here is a program that opens files, `mmap()`s them, then walks the memory performing the "rot-13" encryption on them. Rot-13 (short for "rotate 13") is a simple letter substitution cypher. It replaces letters with those that are 13 positions head of it in the alphabet. rot-13 is reversible. If you rot-13 text, you can rot-13 it again to get the original text back.

Example 10-11. mmap-rot13.m

```
// mmap-rot13.m -- use memory mapped I/O to apply the rot 13 'encryption'
//                 algorithm to a file.

/* compile with:
cc -g -Wall -o mmap-rot13 mmap-rot13.m
*/

#import <sys/fcntl.h>    // for O_RDWR and open()
#import <sys/stat.h>     // for fstat() and struct stat
#import <sys/mman.h>     // for mmap, etc
#import <stdio.h>        // printf, etc
#import <errno.h>        // for errno
#import <stdlib.h>       // EXIT_SUCCESS, etc
#import <ctype.h>        // for isalpha()
#import <string.h>       // for strerror()
```

```
#import <unistd.h>        // for close()

// walk the buffer shifting alphabetic characters 13 places
void rot13 (caddr_t base, size_t length)
{
    char *scan, *stop;

    scan = base;
    stop = scan + length;

    while (scan < stop) {
        // there are tons of implementations of rot13 out on the net
        // much more compact than this
        if (isalpha(*scan)) {
            if (    (*scan >= 'A' && *scan <= 'M')
                || (*scan >= 'a' && *scan <= 'm')) {
                *scan += 13;
            } else if (   (*scan >= 'N' && *scan <= 'Z')
                || (*scan >= 'n' && *scan <= 'z')) {
                *scan -= 13;
            }
        }
        scan++;
    }

} // rot13

void processFile (const char *filename)
{
    int fd = -1;
    int result;
    caddr_t base = (caddr_t) -1;
    size_t length;
    struct stat statbuf;

    // open the file first
    fd = open (filename, O_RDWR);
    if (fd == -1) {
        fprintf (stderr, "could not open %s: error %d (%s)\n",
                  filename, errno, strerror(errno));
        goto bailout;
    }

    // figure out how big it is
    result = fstat (fd, &statbuf);
    if (result == -1) {
        fprintf (stderr, "fstat of %s failed: error %d (%s)\n",
                  filename, errno, strerror(errno));
        goto bailout;
    }
    length = statbuf.st_size;

    // mmap it
    base = mmap (NULL, length, PROT_READ | PROT_WRITE, MAP_SHARED, fd, 0);
    if (base == (caddr_t) -1) {
        fprintf (stderr, "could not mmap %s: error %d (%s)\n",
                  filename, errno, strerror(errno));
```

```
            goto bailout;
        }


        // actually perform the rot13 algorithm
        rot13 (base, length);

        // flush the results
        result = msync (base, length, MS_SYNC);
        if (result == -1) {
            fprintf (stderr, "msync failed for %s: error %d (%s)\n",
                     filename, errno, strerror(errno));
            goto bailout;
        }

    bailout:
        // clean up any messes we have made
        if (base != (caddr_t) -1) {
            munmap (base, length);
        }
        if (fd != -1) {
            close (fd);
        }

} // processFile

int main (int argc, char *argv[])
{
    int i;

    if (argc == 1) {
        fprintf (stderr, "usage: %s /path/to/file ... \n"
                 "rot-13s files in-place using memory mapped I/O\n",
                 argv[0]);
        exit (EXIT_FAILURE);
    }

    for (i = 1; i < argc; i++) {
        processFile (argv[i]);
    }

    exit (EXIT_SUCCESS);

} // main
```

And of course, a sample run or two:

```
% cat > blorf
Blorf is the name of a bunny rabbit.

% ./mmap-rot13 blorf
% cat blorf
Oybes vf gur anzr bs n ohaal enoovg.

% ./mmap-rot13 blorf
% cat blorf
Blorf is the name of a bunny rabbit.
```

Chapter 11. Files, Part 2: Directories, File Systems, and Links

Directories are the counterparts to files. They are the locations that store the files and give a hierarchical structure to the file system. The file system itself is built upon inodes and data blocks, which are both used by files and directories to store their data. Links (hard links and symbolic links) use features of the file system implementation to give indirect access to files.

Directories

Compared to files, there is comparatively very little that can be done to them. You can create directories, remove them, and iterate through their contents.

Creation and destruction

```
int mkdir (const char *path, mode_t mode);
```

mkdir() creates a new directory at the path. The permissions on the directory arespecified in mode (using the S_I* constants discussed back with chmod()). The umask is applied (clearing bits in the mode that are set in the umask). Do not forget to set the execution bits! This returns zero on success, -1 on error with errno set as appropriate.

```
int rmdir (const char *path);
```

This will remove the directory at the path. The directory must be empty of any files or subdirectories, otherwise an error will be removed. Like mkdir(), zero is returned on success, -1 on error, and errno is set.

Directory iteration

These are the functions you use to iterate through the contents of a directory:

```
DIR *opendir (const char *filename);

struct dirent *readdir(DIR *dirp);

long telldir (const DIR *dirp);

void seekdir (DIR *dirp, long loc);

void rewinddir(DIR *dirp);

int closedir(DIR *dirp);
```

The usual use of this API is to use opendir() on a path. opendir() returns an opaque DIR handle whose resources will be freed when closedir() is called. Call readdir() in a loop until it returns NULL. telldir() lets you know what location you are in a directory stream. seekdir() will move the position of the directory stream to the indicated location, and rewinddir() will reset the position to the beginning of the directory. The struct dirent returned from readdir() looks like:

```
struct dirent {
```

```
    u_long  d_fileno;        /* file number (inode) of entry */
    u_short d_reclen;        /* length of this record */
    u_short d_namlen;        /* length of string in d_name */
    char    d_name[MAXNAMLEN + 1];  /* maximum name length */
};
```

Usually the d_name is the piece of information that is most interesting.

Note that there is no guarantee of the order in which the files will be returned by readdir(). On HFS+ file systems, they seem to be returned in alphabetical order, but you shouldn't assume that this is always the case.

Here is a little program that acts like a cheap version of ls, without any features:

Example 11-1. cheapls.m

```
// cheapls.m -- a cheap-o ls program using the directory
//              iteration functions

/* compile with:
cc -g -Wall -o cheapls cheapls.m
*/

#import <sys/types.h>    // for random type definition
#import <sys/dirent.h>   // for struct dirent
#import <dirent.h>       // for opendir and friends
#import <stdlib.h>       // for EXIT_SUCCESS
#import <stdio.h>        // for printf
#import <errno.h>        // for errno
#import <string.h>       // for strerror()

int main (int argc, char *argv[])
{
    DIR *directory;
    struct dirent *entry;
    int result;

    if (argc != 2) {
        fprintf (stderr, "usage:  %s /path/to/directory\n", argv[0]);
        exit (EXIT_FAILURE);
    }

    directory = opendir (argv[1]);
    if (directory == NULL) {
        fprintf (stderr, "could not open directory '%s'\n", argv[1]);
        fprintf (stderr, "let's see if errno is useful: %d (%s)\n",
                 errno, strerror(errno));
        exit (EXIT_FAILURE);
    }

    while ( (entry = readdir(directory)) != NULL) {
        long position = telldir (directory);
        printf ("%3ld: %s\n", position, entry->d_name);
    }

    result = closedir (directory);
    if (result == -1) {
        fprintf (stderr, "error closing directory: %d (%s)\n",
```

```
                    errno, strerror(errno));
        exit (EXIT_FAILURE);
    }
    return (0);
} // main
```

And some sample runs (edited):

```
% ./cheapls .
  1: .
  2: ..
  3: #uid.m#
  4: .#chapter.txt
  5: .#uid.m
  6: .DS_Store
  7: .gdb_history
  8: access
  9: access.m
 10: access.m~
 11: append
 12: append.m
    ...
 49: writestring.m
 50: writevecstring
 51: writevecstring.m

% ./cheapls /Developer/Applications
  1: .
  2: ..
  3: .DS_Store
  4: Apple Help Indexing Tool.app
  5: AppleScript Studio
  6: DebugNubController.app
  7: Extras
    ...
 23: Quartz Debug.app
 24: Sampler.app
 25: Thread Viewer.app
```

Current working directory

There is a piece of global state in every program which is the current working
directory. If you try to do any file operations without specifying a full path, the
operation constructs a path by appending the arguments to open(), etc., with the
current working directory. You use this concept all the time in the shell when you cd
to a directory and perform operations without specifying a full path (that is, a path
beginning with a slash character).

```
int chdir (const char *path);

int fchdir (int fd);
```

The chdir() function sets your current working directory to the given path, while
fchdir() uses a file descriptor of an open directory. On success it returns zero, and
it returns -1 on error with errno set appropriately.

Use

```
char *getcwd (char *buf, size_t size);
```

to get the current directory. Pass it in a buffer and the size of the buffer. You should make sure that buf is MAXPATHLEN bytes or larger. On successful completion, the address buf is returned, NULL in case of error (with errno set) The **getcwd()** man page warns not to use **getcwd()** to save a directory for the purpose of returning to it (like when using the shell's pushd command). Instead you should open the current directory ("."), stash away the file descriptor, and then use **fchdir()** to return to it.

Note that the current working directory is not a thread-safe concept. One thread could change the working directory and then get pre-empted by another thread, which then changes the working directory. When the first thread gets control, the current working directory will be wrong. If you are going to be dealing with multiple directories in a threaded app, use full path names. (More on similar issues in Chapter 15 (Multiprocessing).)

Inside The File System

The physical disk is divided up into partitions:

Figure 11-1. Partitions

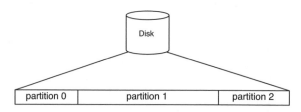

And when you make a filesystem on a particular partition, it looks something like this:

Figure 11-2. Filesystem

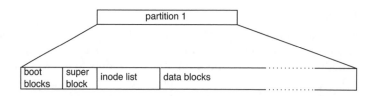

The superblock is a block in a known location that has pointers to the rest of the on-disk data structures. Frequently there are redundant copies of the superblock in case the primary superblock gets destroyed.

An inode (an indirect block) is the handle used to hold onto an individual file. Each file has an inode, and that inode has in it the metadata for the file (the size, modification dates, etc.), as well as a list of datablocks that compose the file. The inode also has a link count, which is a reference count of the number of directory entries that point to the inode. The file is only deleted when the count goes to zero, as noted with `unlink()`.

Figure 11-3. inodes

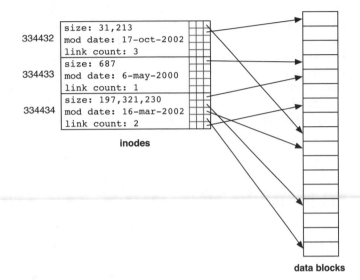

The data blocks can contain either file data or they can be directory blocks (a data block with a flag saying it is a directory). A directory is a list of file names and inode numbers. (The number of an inode is the inode's address. The directory does not actually store a copy of the inode itself.) When you iterate through a directory, it picks up the filename from the directory and can then find the actual file by using the inode.

Figure 11-4. Directory Structure

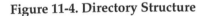

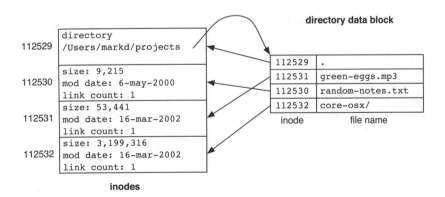

The special files in directories are just inode numbers. For instance, "." is the inode that references the directory, and ".." is the directory's parent. Since the inode points within a particular file system, you cannot have a directory with files that cross file system boundaries. This has the side effect of that if you move a file on to a new place on the same file system, the move is just a couple of directory block manipulations. No data is actually copied.

There are some points to be taken from this. Since files are referenced by their inode number (which you can see when you do an `ls -i`), a file can physically appear in more than one place (known as hard links, which are talked about in a bit). It also means that there is a finite pool of inodes available. You can use `df -i` to see the number of inodes in use and free. If you run out of inodes you will not be able to create any more files on that file system even if there is plenty of space. When you create new file systems from scratch (via the `newfs` command), you need to decide on the inode density. For a file system that will primarily be storing digital video, you do not need a whole lot of inodes since you will have relatively few individual files. If you are creating a file system to store a usenet newsfeed, you will want to have a much higher density of inodes, since newsfeeds tend to have a huge number of tiny files.

Unlike most other Unix systems, you can work around some of these problems by creating disk images with the `DiskCopy`. When mounted, the disk images are treated just like disk devices. You can even `newfs` a mounted disk image to have the inode density you need.

There are some hard-coded limits regarding the filesystem, particularly things like file names and path names. Path names are limited to the constant `PATH_MAX`, which is defined as 1024 bytes. This can really stink for languages like Korean with 3-byte characters in UTF-8. Likewise, the maximum size for a file name is 1024 bytes.

Standard Unix file systems are not journaled (in a journaled filesystem, the metadata on the disk is always consistent). In the event of an abnormal reboot, the program `fsck` does a disk consistency check and cleans up any erroneous metadata. There exists an add-on that turns HFS+ into a journaled file system.

Links

Unix has two kinds of links: hard links and symbolic links. OS X brings the classic Mac concept of an alias to the table as well. Links are ways of referencing a file from more than one place, which can be handy when you are faced with software that makes assumptions about what path something lives in, or when you want a particular file to live in multiple places (say a README placed in each users home directory), but to only occupy disk space for one copy.

Hard links

As mentioned earlier in the brief overview of the file system, hard links are entries in multiple directories that all refer to the same inode. The file appears in multiple places at once. Use the `ln` command to create a hard link:

```
% mkdir linktest
% cd linktest
% touch spoon
(create a new file)

% ln spoon spoon2
(make a hard link)

% ls -li
```

```
total 0
571668 -rw-rw-r-- 2 markd  staff  0 Aug 12 11:52 spoon
571668 -rw-rw-r-- 2 markd  staff  0 Aug 12 11:52 spoon2
```

The left-hand column shows the inode of the file. Note that the inodes are the same.
Also notice the third column. It says that there are two hard links to this file.

```
% ln spoon spoon3
% ls -li
total 0
571668 -rw-rw-r-- 3 markd  staff  0 Aug 12 11:52 spoon
571668 -rw-rw-r-- 3 markd  staff  0 Aug 12 11:52 spoon2
571668 -rw-rw-r-- 3 markd  staff  0 Aug 12 11:52 spoon3
```

Now there are three hard links to the same file.

Since hard links refer to inodes, they cannot cross file system boundaries. If you `mv` a
hard linked file to another file system, the data will get copied, the original
removed, and the link count will go down by one.

Users cannot create hard links to directories. On some file systems the superuser can
make hard links to directories, but in general that is not advisable because hard links
can form cycles in the directories, which the kernel really is not designed to handle.

Symbolic links

A symbolic link is a file that contains the path to another file, and this path can be
relative or absolute. Symbolic links are not included in the reference count of a file,
and in fact do not have to actually point to a real file at all (in which case they
become dangling links). Use `ln -s` to create a symbolic link:

```
% mkdir symlinktest
% cd symlinktest
% touch spoon
(make an empty file)

% ln -s spoon spoon2
(make a relative symbolic link)

% ls -l
total 8
-rw-rw-r-- 1 markd  staff  0 Aug 12 12:08 spoon
lrwxrwxr-x 1 markd  staff  5 Aug 12 12:08 spoon2@ -> spoon

% ln -s 'pwd'/spoon spoon3
(use the backtick shell operator to run pwd, then paste that into the
command, which will give us a full path)

% ls -l
total 16
-rw-rw-r-- 1 markd  staff   0 Aug 12 12:08 spoon
lrwxrwxr-x 1 markd  staff   5 Aug 12 12:08 spoon2 -> spoon
lrwxrwxr-x 1 markd  staff  49 Aug 12 12:08 spoon3 -> /Users/markd/\
BNRUnix/files2-chap/symlinktest/spoon
```

Note the size column. It is the number of characters in the symlink. Also notice the leading character over there in the permissions - a lower case L, signifying this is a link.

If you add the -F flag, you can see some extra symbols attached to file names:

```
% ls -F
spoon    spoon2@ spoon3@
```

The at sign says it is a symbolic link. Additional character suffixes that -F brings are "/" for directories, and "*" for executable files. A trick is to alias ls to be ls -F so that you can see these little clues.

Symlinks are like pointers to files. They were created to work around some of the problems with hard links, such as crossing file systems and making links to directories. You can make a symbolic link to a directory and not cause problems. You can generate loops with symlinks, but function calls that try to resolve them will generate an error.

Figure 11-5. Hard and Symbolic Links

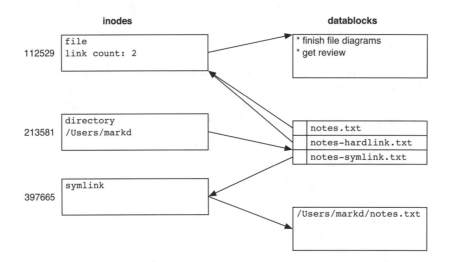

The real power of symbolic links comes in when you are moving things around in the file system. Say your webserver log files in /home/nsadmin/logs/borkware is filling up your drive. You can copy all the log files to another place, like /Volumes/BigDisk/logs/borkware, and then point the first path to the second. No need to change any configuration files, and existing paths to the logs still work. Granted, things can get out of hand and can become unmaintainable if you have too many layers of symlink indirection.

Most of the file API you have seen so far will follow symbolic links automatically, like chmod(), chown(), open(), and stat() (discussed a bit later).

There are some function calls that let you manipulate the link directly.

```
int lchown (const char *path, uid_t owner, gid_t group);
```

This changes the owner

```
int readlink (const char *path, char *buf, int bufsiz);
```

places the contents of the symbolic link path into the buffer. This does not append the terminating zero byte. It returns the number of characters it wrote into the buffer, or -1 on error (with `errno` set appropriately).

And other functions `lstat()`.

And finally, some API will deal with the link directly, like `rename()` and `unlink()`.

This reading through of links (like with `open()`) can lead to some confusion:

```
% ln -s /no/such/file oopack
% ls oopack
oopack
(It is there)
% cat oopack
cat: oopack: No such file or directory
(no, it is not there.  huh?)
```

```
% ls -l oopack
lrwxr-xr-x  1 markd  staff  13 Aug 12 12:30 oopack@ -> /no/such/file
(oh, it is a symlink that points to nowhere)
```

This is another reason to alias `ls` to include the `-F` flag.

```
% ls -F oopack
oopack@
```

This makes it obvious `oopack` is a symlink.

Mac OS aliases

Users can create aliases in the `Finder` by explicitly making an alias or performing some mouse dragging operations. Like symbolic links, aliases are not included in a file's reference count, and they can dangle, pointing nowhere. On HFS+, an alias contains the file's file number (similar to an inode number), so the alias can find the file anywhere on the disk. The path to the file is also stored in case the file is deleted and replaced with a new one.

Differences between the kinds of links:

- Hardlinks always point to valid files.
- Symlinks do not track file moves, but aliases do.
- Symlinks survive file deletions, aliases do not always.
- Symlinks can make loops.

API for links

```
int link (const char *name1, const char *name2);
```

```
int symlink (const char *name1, const char *name2);
```

This creates a hardlink (or symlink) with name2 referring to the same file as name1. Zero is returned on success, -1 on error with errno set appropriately. When making a symlink, use **readlink()** to get the file name stored in the link.

You will need to use the Carbon API if you want to deal with aliases.

File Metadata

File Metadata is data about the file, but is not the file's data itself. This includes stuff like the file's size, the file's type, the last access times, etc.

Three functions can be used to access the metadata:

```
int stat (const char *path, struct stat *sb);

int lstat (const char *path, struct stat *sb);

int fstat (int fd, struct stat *sb);
```

stat() gets information about the file at a path, following any intervening symbolic links. lstat() gets information about the symbolic link itself. fstat() gives you metadata about open files. As with most Unix file functions, a return value of zero indicates success, a value of -1 indicates an error and errno is set appropriately.

You do not need read, write, or execute permissions on a file to **stat()** it, but all directories listed in the path name need to be searchable.

struct stat is the focal point for all of the data returned by these calls. You allocate a struct stat either on the stack or dynamically, and pass that to the function.

```
struct stat {
    dev_t     st_dev;     /* device inode resides on */
    ino_t     st_ino;     /* inode's number */
    mode_t    st_mode;    /* inode protection mode */
    nlink_t   st_nlink;   /* number or hard links to the file */
    uid_t     st_uid;     /* user-id of owner */
    gid_t     st_gid;     /* group-id of owner */
    dev_t     st_rdev;    /* device type, for special file inode */
    struct timespec st_atimespec;  /* time of last access */
    struct timespec st_mtimespec;  /* time of last data modification */
    struct timespec st_ctimespec;  /* time of last file status change */
    off_t     st_size;    /* file size, in bytes */
    quad_t    st_blocks;  /* blocks allocated for file */
    u_long    st_blksize; /* optimal file sys I/O ops blocksize */
    u_long    st_flags;   /* user defined flags for file */
    u_long    st_gen;     /* file generation number */
};
```

Here is a breakdown of the more common fields:

st_mode contains the file type and permissions. The lower nine bits have the user, group, and other permissions. You can focus in on those by using the mask ACCESSPERMS (0777). You can also bitwise-and things using the macros listed back when **chmod()** was discussed (S_IRWXU, S_IRUSR, etc.).

There are also bits for determining the type of file being looked at.

Table 11-1. File Types

Mask	Convenience Macro	What it is
S_IFIFO	S_ISFIFO()	FIFO (named pipe, an IPC mechanism)
S_IFCHR	S_ISCHR()	character special device (like terminals and serial lines)
S_IFDIR	S_ISDIR()	directory
S_IFBLK	S_ISBLK()	block special device (like disks and tapes)
S_IFREG	S_ISREG()	plain old regular file
S_IFLNK	S_ISLNK()	symbolic link
S_IFSOCK	S_ISSOCK()	socket (network communication)

The `st_uid` and `st_gid` fields tell you the user that owns the file, as well as the group associated with the file.

`st_size` has the file size in bytes.

There are three file times associated with each file:

`st_atime`

> The last access time. That is, the last time the file was opened for reading. You can see this with `ls -lu`.

`st_mtime`

> The last modification time. This is the date displayed by `ls -l`.

`st_ctime`

> Last change in inode status, like by using `chmod` or `chown`. `ls -lc` shows this time.

These file times are of type `time_t`, which is the number of seconds since midnight, Jan 1, 1970 (the start of the Unix epoch)

The `utimes()` system call can be used to change access and modification times of a file. This is handy if you are writing something like `tar` and need to preserve access times when you expand an archive.

Here is a little program that will print out a whole bunch of stuff from `struct stat`:

Example 11-2. permtype.m

```
// permtype.m -- use stat to discover the type and permissions
//                for a file

/* compile with:
cc -g -Wall -o permtype permtype.m
*/
```

```
#import <sys/stat.h>      // for stat() and struct stat
#import <stdlib.h>        // for EXIT_SUCCESS
#import <stdio.h>         // for printf
#import <errno.h>         // for errno
#import <grp.h>           // for group file access routines
#import <pwd.h>           // for passwd file access routines
#import <sys/time.h>      // for struct tm, localtime, etc
#import <string.h>        // for strerror


// cheesy little lookup table for mapping perm value to the
// familiar character string
static const char *g_perms[]  = {
    "---", "--x", "-w-", "-wx", "r--", "r-x", "rw-", "rwx"
};

typedef struct StatType {
    unsigned long     mask;
    const char        *type;
} StatType;

static StatType g_types[] = {
    { S_IFREG, "Regular FIle" },
    { S_IFDIR, "Directory" },
    { S_IFLNK, "Symbolic Link" },
    { S_IFCHR, "Character Special Device" },
    { S_IFBLK, "Block Special Device" },
    { S_IFIFO, "FIFO" },
    { S_IFSOCK, "Socket" },
};

void displayInfo (const char *filename)
{
    int result;
    struct stat statbuf;
    StatType *scan, *stop;

    result = lstat (filename, &statbuf);

    if (result == -1) {
        fprintf (stderr, "error with stat(%s) :  %d (%s)\n",
                 filename, errno, strerror(errno));
        return;
    }

    printf ("%s:\n", filename);

    printf ("  permissions: %s%s%s\n",
            g_perms[(statbuf.st_mode & S_IRWXU) >> 6],
            g_perms[(statbuf.st_mode & S_IRWXG) >> 3],
            g_perms[(statbuf.st_mode & S_IRWXO)]);

    // figure out the type
    scan = g_types;
    stop = scan + (sizeof(g_types) / sizeof(StatType));
```

```
    while (scan < stop) {
        if ((statbuf.st_mode & S_IFMT) == scan->mask) {
            printf ("  type: %s\n", scan->type);
            break;
        }
        scan++;
    }

    // any special bits sets?
    if ((statbuf.st_mode & S_ISUID) == S_ISUID) {
        printf ("  set-uid!\n");
    }
    if ((statbuf.st_mode & S_ISGID) == S_ISUID) {
        printf ("  set-group-id!\n");
    }

    // file size
    printf ("  file is %ld bytes (%f K)\n",
            (long)statbuf.st_size,
            (float) (statbuf.st_size / 1024.0));

    // owning user / group
    {
        struct passwd *passwd;
        struct group *group;

        passwd = getpwuid (statbuf.st_uid);
        group = getgrgid (statbuf.st_gid);

        printf ("  user: %s (%d)\n", passwd->pw_name, statbuf.st_uid);
        printf ("  group: %s (%d)\n", group->gr_name, statbuf.st_gid);
    }

    // now the dates
    {
        char buffer[1024];
        struct tm *tm;

        tm = localtime (&statbuf.st_atime);
        strftime (buffer, 1024, "%m/%d/%Y", tm);
        printf ("  last access: %s\n", buffer);

        tm = localtime (&statbuf.st_mtime);
        strftime (buffer, 1024, "%m/%d/%Y", tm);
        printf ("  last modification: %s\n", buffer);

        tm = localtime (&statbuf.st_ctime);
        strftime (buffer, 1024, "%m/%d/%Y", tm);
        printf ("  last inode change: %s\n", buffer);
    }

    // double-space output
    printf ("\n");

} // displayInfo

int main (int argc, char *argv[])
```

```
{
    int i;

    if (argc == 1) {
        fprintf (stderr, "usage:  %s /path/to/file ... \n", argv[0]);
        exit (EXIT_FAILURE);
    }

    for (i = 1; i < argc; i++) {
        displayInfo (argv[i]);
    }

    exit (EXIT_SUCCESS);

} // main
```

A sample run

```
% ./permtype permtype / oopack /dev/kmem /usr/bin/passwd
(where oopack is a symbolic link)

permtype:
  permissions: rwxrwxr-x
  type: Regular FIle
  file is 23924 bytes (23.363281 K)
  user: markd (501)
  group: staff (20)
  last access: 08/12/2002 15:04:30
  last modification: 08/12/2002 15:04:11
  last inode change: 08/12/2002 15:04:11

/:
  permissions: rwxrwxr-x
  type: Directory
  file is 1452 bytes (1.417969 K)
  user: root (0)
  group: admin (80)
  last access: 08/12/2002 15:04:30
  last modification: 08/10/2002 22:41:04
  last inode change: 08/10/2002 22:41:04

oopack:
  permissions: rwxr-xr-x
  type: Symbolic Link
  file is 13 bytes (0.012695 K)
  user: markd (501)
  group: staff (20)
  last access: 08/12/2002 15:03:24
  last modification: 08/12/2002 15:04:28
  last inode change: 08/12/2002 15:04:28

/dev/kmem:
  permissions: rw-r-----
  type: Character Special Device
  file is 0 bytes (0.000000 K)
  user: root (0)
  group: kmem (2)
```

```
    last access: 08/12/2002 14:37:36
    last modification: 08/08/2002 21:44:32
    last inode change: 08/08/2002 21:44:32

/usr/bin/passwd:
   permissions: r-xr-xr-x
   type: Regular FIle
   set-uid!
   file is 29756 bytes (29.058594 K)
   user: root (0)
   group: wheel (0)
   last access: 07/06/2002 11:37:31
   last modification: 12/08/2001 13:58:34
   last inode change: 06/19/2002 15:40:57
```

Now, just to make life a little more complicated, both Cocoa and Carbon have different kinds of metadata they bring to the table, including things like the HFS+ Creator and Type code for files, and whether the file extension should be hidden.

`NSFileManager` has a number of constants for use in the attribute dictionary returned by `-[NSFileManager fileAttributesAtPath: traverseLink:]`. There is some overlap with what you get from `struct stat`:

- `NSFileSize`

- `NSFileModificationDate`

- `NSFileOwnerAccountName`

- `NSFileGroupOwnerAccountName`

- `NSFileReferenceCount` (# of hard links)

- `NSFileIdentifier`

- `NSFilePosixPermissions`(the rwx permissions)

- `NSFIleExtensionHidden`

- `NSFileHFSCreatorCode`

- `HSFileHFSTypeCode`

- `NSFileType` (This is a string that says whether it is of type Directory, Regular, Symbolic Link, etc.)

In Carbon, you can use calls like `FSGetCatalogInfo()` to get an `FSCatalogInfo` structure that has information like AppleShare sharing flags, the creation date, the backup date, `Finder` information, the logical and physical size of the data and resource fork, as well as a text encoding hint.

So if you want to get *all* of the metadata associated with a file, you will need to `stat()`, use `NSFilemanager`, as well as call `FSGetCatalogInfo()`.

Mac OS X Specific Weirdness

Since OS X is a hybrid between classic Mac OS and Unix, there are some peculiarities unique to OS X.

Resource forks

The first regards resource forks, the additional stream files have that store structured data. At the file system level, this is really just two files that happen to share a name. Most Unix command line utilities do not know resource forks are there and so it is possible for the resource fork to get lost or corrupted. `cp` and `tar`, for instance, do not preserve the fork. You can get replacement programs (like `hfstar`) that will preserve them.

In the command line environment, you cannot really see the resource fork unless you use a pretty neat hack: if you append a file name with `/rsrc`, the commands will look at the resource fork.

The outline processor used to outline big chunks of this book is a 1990's version of More running in Classic. Here is a look at More:

```
% cd /Applications
% ls -l MORE
-rw-r--r--   1 markd   unknown   0 Jun 23 12:18 MORE
```

Hmmm, nothing there.

Back in the Old Days, almost nothing was put into an application's data fork. Everything went into the resource fork:

```
% ls -l MORE/rsrc
-rw-r--r--   1 markd   unknown   607251 Jun 23 12:18 MORE??? 3.1/rsrc
```

All of the calls looked at so far in this chapter do not pay any attention to the resource fork, they just affect the data fork. If you need to support resource fork reading and writing, you will need to use the Carbon libraries.

.DS_Store

If you `ls -a` in directories, you will probably find a file named `.DS_Store`. This is a cache file the `Finder` writes that contains file names and icon placement. When mounting network volumes, the `Finder` will scribble the files into any directory the user visits, which can sometimes lead to friction with the people who run the file servers.

Disk I/O and sleep

A programmer on one of the mailing lists was describing a problem he was having with a program that was doing something akin to `tail -f`, monitoring a log file and reading any new stuff that came across. Much to his horror, machines that were running this program would never go to sleep. It turns out that if a lot of I/O happens (say more than one physical disk I/O every couple of seconds) the computer will think it is still busy and will not go to sleep. In this particular case he was seeking to the end and attempting to read. The suggestion was to use `stat()` instead to see if the file changed size. `stat()` does not cause physical I/O once the inode for a file is cached in memory.

For The More Curious

Differences between HFS+ and UFS

The Apple engineers did a masterful job of integrating HFS+ (the default disk format) into the world of Unix. The above discussion about inodes is more accurate for UFS (the Unix file system, also known as the Berkeley Fast File System), but the general concepts apply to both worlds.

In HFS+, file name encoding is in unicode rather than ASCII. File names are also case preserving, but case insensitive. Traditional Unix file systems are case sensitive. The Apple teams originally thought this case preserving / case sensitive difference would cause lots of problems, but it turns out to be not so bad. There are not many examples in the real world where the case of letters in filenames are used to discriminate. Unfortunately, with the make command, makefile and Makefile are different beasts, as are some parts of the CPAN Perl archive. A way around this is to create a UFS partition for these malcontents, or else use DiskCopy to create a UFS disk image.

The path separator for UFS is /, but in HFS+ is :. This is addressed by the HFS+ file system implementation converting colons to slashes and vice versa. The file system sees colons, but everything above that is slashes. Carbon does another transform back into colons since that is the path separator used.

HFS+ lacks support for hard links. It is actually implemented by a kernel-level symbolic link visible only to the HFS+ file system. The behavior is very similar to hard links when viewed from above the kernel, but they are relatively inefficient in comparison.

UFS does not support file IDs. File IDs are persistent handles to files similar to inodes, and can be used similar to path names in Unix. The nice thing about file IDs is that once the ID is obtained, the file can be renamed or moved anywhere on disk and still be found and opened. Also, in HFS+, access by ID is faster than by path (since it avoids path parsing and lookup). These file IDs are part of how aliases do their thing.

HFS+ also allows for arbitrarily named file attributes (similar to the Be File System), but neither OS 9 or OS X support this.

HFS+ filenames are at most 255 characters long, or 512 bytes. Files have a maximum size of 2^{63} bytes.

From running experiments, it does not look like HFS+ supports holes in files. In traditional Unix file systems, if you write a byte, seek 100 megs, then write another byte, your file will only occupy two disk blocks. The intervening zero-filled blocks will not actually be consuming space in the file system. This is a disk space optimization for files that could have large ranges of zeros in them (like core files).

There are differences in deletion semantics between classic Mac OS and OS X. In Mac OS, if you try to delete a file someone else currently has open, the delete fails. This is opposed to traditional Unix where the delete happens but the disk blocks do not get reclaimed until the file is closed. This behavior led some Mac developers to use open files as semaphores, controlling behavior among multiple programs. This difference is in part due to the implementation of the different file systems. In UFS, metadata is in the inode, stored separately from the data. In HFS+, the metadata is stored in with the file data, and there is no real inode. In either case, the kernel caches the metadata so that the stat() call will not cause physical I/O.

The differences in permission semantics are important. OS 9 totally ignores the Unix permission bits. Someone can boot into OS 9 and have free reign over a disk, bypassing all security. This is not a problem in Classic since Classic is just another program running as the current user.

Also, files that are created in OS 9 do not have these permission bits. If a file created in OS 9 is then looked at under OS X, the system plays some games. The owner, group, and mode are shown as some reasonable default (by looking at the permissions on the directory node on which the file system is mounted). The actual permission bits on disk remain unset unless the user sets them explicitly.

There are some cultural differences regarding file names. Mac OS users are used to spaces and special characters in their file names while Unix folks are not. This can lead to really bad situations like the `iTunes` installer wiping out entire disks because it did not consider that a volume name might have a space in it. So if you are doing any file name manipulations (especially in shell scripts), be sure to keep this in mind.

System directories that Unix folks are familiar with (`/etc`, `/usr`, `/tmp`, `/var`) are hidden at the application level, and some are hidden behind symlinks, so that casual Mac users will not need to worry about them.

The usual Unix software install paradigm (put library files into `*/lib`, program files into `*/bin`, documentation int `*/share`) does not work that well with individually administered systems like personal computers. One program can end up scattering junk everywhere, making uninstalling a pain. The NeXT-style bundles (directories that behave like files) address a lot of problems here. The OS folks liked bundles so much, they followed the same scheme for system-wide libraries. Rather than put stuff into `/usr/include` and `/usr/lib`, it goes into framework bundles.

File locking

Multiple processes can have the same file open for reading and writing. Without some kind of synchronization mechanism, these processes can clobber each other's data. Mac OS X supports advisory (cooperative) file locking either of an entire file, or of specific byte ranges within a file. Note that these advisory locks require the cooperation of all programs that access the file. It would be possible for someone to write a rogue program that could scribble data into the file, ignoring any advisory locks that might have been set.

These locks are on files, not file descriptors. This can have some interesting side effects if you have the file open on two different descriptors. The locks are cleared when the first file descriptor gets closed, which could lead to an unexpected release of a lock.

To lock and unlock an entire file, use

```
int flock (int fd, int operation);
```

Where `operation` is one of

LOCK_SH

    Shared lock.

LOCK_EX

> Exclusive lock.

LOCK_NB

> Do not block when attempting to lock.

LOCK_UN

> Unlock.

Multiple shared locks can be applied, but only one exclusive lock can be taken out. There cannot be both exclusive and shared locks in existence at the same time.

`flock()` returns zero if the locking operation is successful, on errors -1 is returned and `errno` is set with the appropriate error value.

A lock with `flock()` semantics can be obtained at `open()` time by setting O_SHLOCK (to get a shared lock) or O_EXLOCK (for an exclusive lock) in with the open flags.

To lock byte ranges, use `fcntl()`: `int fcntl (int fd, int cmd, int arg);`

The commands related to locking are F_GETLK, F_SETLK, F_SETLKW. The `arg` argument for these commands is a `struct flock`:

```
struct flock {
    off_t   l_start;    /* starting offset */
    off_t   l_len;      /* len = 0 means until end of file */
    pid_t   l_pid;      /* lock owner */
    short   l_type;     /* lock type: read (F_RDLCK)/write (F_WRLCK),
                           unlock (F_UNLCK)etc. */
    short   l_whence;   /* type of l_start */
};
```

You should allocate on the stack or in dynamic memory (like allocating a `struct stat`). In all cases, fill out the `l_start`, `l_len`, `l_type`, and `l_whence` fields to indicate what part of the file to lock. F_GETLK will fill in the structure with the information of whomever has a lock on that area. F_SETLK will acquire or release a byte-range lock. If the lock cannot be acquired, the call returns immediately with `errno` having a value of EACCES. If you want to wait for the lock, use F_SETLKW for the command. The function will return when the request can be satisfied, or the program has received a signal (so be sure to check the return value).

Note that the Mac OS X frameworks (Java, Cocoa, Carbon) treat locks as if they were mandatory locks (blocking I/O until they are released). Under the hood they are still advisory locks. The reason why the BSD designers chose advisory locks over mandatory locks were to prevent denial of service attacks, where a rogue program opens a file with a mandatory lock, and blocks everyone out at the kernel level.

Other random calls

Here are some system calls that did not fit in well anyplace else.

`int rename (const char *from, const char *to);`

This causes `from` to be renamed to `to`. This is just inode/directory manipulation, so both `from` and `to` must live on the same file system, in which case you will need to copy the data. This returns zero on success, -1 / `errno` on error.

```
int dup (int fd);

int dup2 (int fd, int newfd);
```

These functions duplicate an existing file descriptor, as if you opened the file again. The return value of `dup()` is a file descriptor that is guaranteed to be the lowest numbered available (or -1 on error). The original file is not closed. A use for `dup()` is for reassigning one of the standard streams. You can close the file descriptor zero (standard in), open another file (say a log file), and then `dup()` that descriptor so that you get `fd` zero.

`dup2()` has slightly different semantics. It will create a duplicate file descriptor at a particular file descriptor value. If there is already a file open using that descriptor, it is closed first. This is another way of replacing the standard streams. Since it does a `close()` and `dup()` in one operation, it is atomic.

Note that duplicated file descriptors share the same reference in the per-process file table. So a write to one `fd` will move the current location of the second `fd`. If you want a true independent reference, reopen the file.

Earlier, `fcntl()` was mentioned in the file locking section. You can also use `fcntl()` with different commands:

F_DUPFD

> Duplicate a file descriptor. The new `fd` is the lowest numbered descriptor that is not open that is greater than or equal to the third argument (as an integer).

F_GETFD / F_SETFD

> Get/set per-processor file descriptor flags (currently the only flag is FD_CLOEXEC, to close the file automatically in child processes).

F_GETFL / F_SETFL

> Get/set kernel status flags: Such as O_RDONLY / O_WRONLY / O_APPEND, etc.

F_GETOWN / F_SETOWN

> Get/set async i/o ownership.

Duplicating descriptors low with `dup()` and `dup2()` makes sense when redirecting streams. Why the F_DUPD behavior, then, of duplicating things higher? This actually came in really handy with AOLserver on older versions of IRIX. AOLserver had an embedded Tcl interpreter that used buffered I/O FILEs for certain commands. Unfortunately, IRIX just used 8 bits to store the file descriptor value in these structures, so you could have at most 253 of these FILEs. Whenever a non-FILE fd was created (by networking, or opening a file to be returned to the web browser), the `fd` was duplicated to a value greater than 256 using `fcntl(F_DUPFD)`, leaving the lower values free.

```
int truncate (const char *path, off_t length);

int ftruncate (int fd, off_t length);
```

These truncate a file (whether by path or an open file descriptor) to be at most the given length. Extra data is lost, but the file is not grown.

```
long pathconf (const char *path, int name);

long fpathconf (int fd, int name);
```

These provide applications a way to determine the current value of some system limits or options. Here are some possible names:

_PC_LINK_MAX

> The maxiumum file link count.

_PC_NAME_MAX

> The maximum number of bytes in a file name.

_PC_PATH_MAX

> The maximum number of bytes in a pathname.

_PC_PIPE_BUF

> The maximum number of bytes that will be written atomically to a pipe.

If the call fails, -1 is returned and errno is set. If the given variable does not have a limit, -1 is returned and errno is not modified. Otherwise, the current value is returned.

```
int sysctl (int *name, u_int namelen, void *oldp, size_t *oldlenp,
            void *newp, size_t newlen);
```

This retrieves system information and lets processes (with appropriate privileges) set system information. There are all sorts of information you can get from this, like kernel debug values, machine model, cpu count, native byte order, amount of physical memory, the kernel page size, etc. Check out the man page for more details.

Other random programs

You saw lsof earlier, which shows open files system wide.

The chflags program is similar to the linux chattr program. It lets you set some attributes on the file. Of particular interest are the [no]schg and [no]uchg flags, which set the system and user immutable flags. When these are set, the files cannot be modified even if their file permissions would allow it. This is handy for hardening a file system against attackers. Most "script kiddie" system crackers are not prepared for immutable files. This is also the flag that the Finder sets when you select the Locked attribute of a file.

/Developer/Tools/SetFile sets attributes of HFS+ files, which include whether a file is an alias, it is a bundle, has a custom icon, is on the desktop, is locked, or is invisible. You can also use it to set the file type and creator.

Cocoa APIs of interest

The equivalent of getcwd() in Cocoa is [[NSFileManager defaultManager] currentDirectoryPath]. You do not need to worry about hardcoded MAXPATHLEN issues.

NSFileManager's **movePath: toPath:** is a single function call to move and rename files. This will copy across file system boundaries. Note that this always does a copy, even on the same file system. In general, try **rename()** first. If that returns an errno of EXDEV, use this **NSFileManager** call. If you are worried about preserving the resource fork, ignore **rename()** and just use this.

Challenge

Using the directory enumeration and metadata functions, write a Cocoa program to descend into a directory hierarchy and build an **NSOutlineview** or **NSBrowser** view of the contents.

Chapter 12. NSFileManager

NSFileManager is a class in the Foundation framework that acts as a convenient wrapper for **stat()**, **unlink()**, **dirent()**, **stat()**, and **mkdir()**. In this chapter, you are going to create a simple file browser using **NSFileManager**.

NSFileManager

Without going into too much detail, here are the basic types of methods that are in **NSFileManager**:

The method for getting the shared instance of **NSFileManager**:

- (NSFileManager *)**defaultManager**

Wrappers for **stat()**:

- (NSDictionary *)**fileAttributesAtPath:**(NSString *)path
                               traverseLink:(BOOL)yorn

- (BOOL)**fileExistsAtPath:**(NSString *)path

- (BOOL)**fileExistsAtPath:**(NSString *)path **isDirectory:**(BOOL *)isDirectory

- (BOOL)**isReadableFileAtPath:**(NSString *)path

- (BOOL)**isWritableFileAtPath:**(NSString *)path

- (BOOL)**isExecutableFileAtPath:**(NSString *)path

- (BOOL)**isDeletableFileAtPath:**(NSString *)path

Change the file attributes:

- (BOOL)**changeFileAttributes:**(NSDictionary *)attributes
                      atPath:(NSString *)path

Linking, copying, and deleting files and directories:

- (BOOL)**linkPath:**(NSString *)src **toPath:**(NSString *)dest **handler:**handler

- (BOOL)**copyPath:**(NSString *)src **toPath:**(NSString *)dest **handler:**handler

- (BOOL)**movePath:**(NSString *)src **toPath:**(NSString *)dest **handler:**handler

- (BOOL)**removeFileAtPath:**(NSString *)path **handler:**handler

Wrappers for `dirent`:

- (NSArray *)**directoryContentsAtPath:**(NSString *)path

- (NSDirectoryEnumerator *)**enumeratorAtPath:**(NSString *)path

- (NSArray *)**subpathsAtPath:**(NSString *)path;

Wrapper for **mkdir**:

- (BOOL)**createDirectoryAtPath:**(NSString *)path
                    attributes:(NSDictionary *)attributes

Reading a file:

- (NSData *)**contentsAtPath:**(NSString *)path

Creating a file:

- (BOOL)**createFileAtPath:**(NSString *)path
                contents:(NSData *)data
            attributes:(NSDictionary *)attr

The display name (In Mac OS X, the display name and the filename may be different):

- (NSString *)**displayNameAtPath:**(NSString *)path

Compare two files:

- (BOOL)**contentsEqualAtPath:**(NSString *)path1 **andPath:**(NSString *)path2

As you can see, **NSFileWrapper** has several very convenient methods. For example, **removeFileAtPath:handler:** will remove directories and their contents, thus it is often easier to use than **rmdir()** which only works on empty directories.

NSBrowser

You will also use **NSBrowser** for this project. The delegate of the browser will supply it with data by implementing the following methods:

- (int)**browser:**(NSBrowser *)sender **numberOfRowsInColumn:**(int)column

Like a table view's data source, the browser delegate will respond to this method with the number of items to be displayed in each column. Note that this is usually called because the user has changed selection.

- (void)**browser:**(NSBrowser *)sender **willDisplayCell:**(id)cell
        atRow:(int)r **column:**(int)c

The browser delegate is passed the cell to be displayed in row r and colum c. The delegate packs the cell with data, marks it as a leaf or branch, and flags it as loaded.

Make a File Browser

Create a new "Cocoa Application" project called **Remover**. (Besides browsing, your app will allow the user to delete files and directories.)

Open the nib file. Create a subclass of **NSObject** called **AppController**. **AppController** needs one action called **deleteSelection:** and one outlet of type **NSBrowser** called browser.

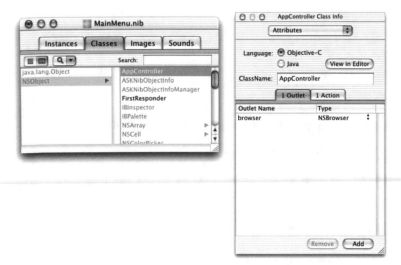

Create the files AppController.h and AppController.m.

Instantiate **AppController**. Drop an **NSBrowser** and an **NSButton** on the window. Make the **AppController** the target of the button and the delegate of the **NSBrowser**.

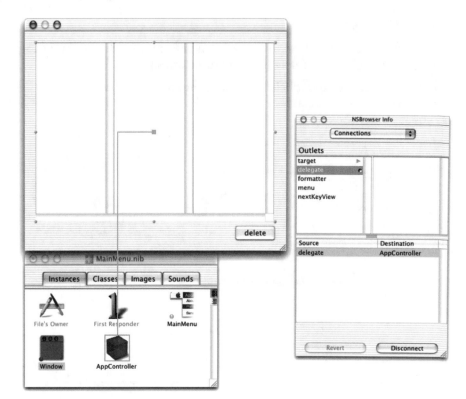

Also, set the browser outlet of **AppController** to point to the **NSBrowser**.

Create the DirEntry class

The file system is essentially a tree; each node of the tree is a directory or a file. We are going to create a class to hold onto the information about one node, so create a class called **DirEntry**.

Each instance of **DirEntry** will know its parent, its file attributes, and its filename. If it is a directory, it will know how to create an array containing **DirEntrys** representing its children. Thus, make DirEntry.h look like this:

Example 12-1. DirEntry.h

```
#import <Foundation/Foundation.h>

@interface DirEntry : NSObject {
    NSDictionary *attributes;
    DirEntry *parent;
    NSString *filename;
}
// Returns an array containing the DirEntrys in the directory p
+ (NSMutableArray *)entriesAtPath:(NSString *)p withParent:(DirEntry *)d;

// The init method is only used by entriesAtPath:withParent:
- (id)initWithFilename:(NSString *)fn parent:(DirEntry *)p;

// fullPath is the full path,  filename is just the filename
- (NSString *)fullPath;
- (NSString *)filename;
```

```
// Returns an array of the components of the path that make up
// the DirEntry's fullPath.
- (NSMutableArray *)components;

- (BOOL)isDirectory;

- (DirEntry *)parent;
- (NSArray *)children;

@end
```

Now to implement these methods:

Example 12-2. DirEntry.m

```
#import "DirEntry.h"

@implementation DirEntry

+ (NSMutableArray *)entriesAtPath:(NSString *)p withParent:(DirEntry *)d
{
    int max, k;
    DirEntry *newEntry;
    NSString *currentFilename;
    NSFileManager *manager = [NSFileManager defaultManager];
    NSArray *filenames;
    NSMutableArray *result = [NSMutableArray array];
    NSLog(@"reading %@", p);
    filenames = [manager directoryContentsAtPath:p];

    // Was the filemanager unable to read the directory at the path?
    if (filenames == nil) {
        NSLog(@"Unable to read %@", p);
        return result;
    }
    max = [filenames count];
    for (k = 0; k < max; k++) {
        currentFilename = [filenames objectAtIndex:k];
        newEntry = [[DirEntry alloc] initWithFilename:currentFilename
                                        parent:d];
        [result addObject:newEntry];
        [newEntry release];
    }
    return result;
}

- (id)initWithFilename:(NSString *)fn parent:(DirEntry *)p
{
    [super init];

    // No need to retain parent
    parent = p;
    filename = [fn copy];
    return self;
}
```

```objc
// Get the array of components using recursion
- (NSMutableArray *)components
{
    NSMutableArray *result;
    if (!parent) {
        result = [NSMutableArray array];

        // Add an empty string at the beginning of the
        // array to represent the "/" entry.
        [result addObject:@""];
    } else {
        result = [parent components];
    }
    [result addObject:[self filename]];
    return result;
}

// Take advantage of the components method to create the fullPath
- (NSString *)fullPath
{
    return [NSString pathWithComponents:[self components]];
}

- (NSString *)filename
{
    return filename;
}

- (BOOL)isDirectory
{
    // Is this the first time we have been asked?
    if (!attributes) {
        NSString *path = [self fullPath];
        attributes = [[NSFileManager defaultManager]
                              fileAttributesAtPath:path
                              traverseLink:YES];

        [attributes retain];
    }
    return [[attributes fileType] isEqual:NSFileTypeDirectory];
}

- (NSArray *)children
{
    NSString *path = [self fullPath];
    return [DirEntry entriesAtPath:path withParent:self];
}

- (DirEntry *)parent
{
    return parent;
}

- (void)dealloc
{
    [attributes release];
    [filename release];
```

```
    [super dealloc];
}

@end
```

Notice that there is a category on **NSDictionary** that enables you to easily read information from the attributes dictionary. Here is the interface for that category:

```
@interface NSDictionary (NSFileAttributes)

- (unsigned long long)fileSize;
- (NSDate *)fileModificationDate;
- (NSString *)fileType;
- (unsigned long)filePosixPermissions;
- (NSString *)fileOwnerAccountName;
- (NSString *)fileGroupOwnerAccountName;
- (BOOL)fileExtensionHidden;
- (OSType)fileHFSCreatorCode;
- (OSType)fileHFSTypeCode;
- (BOOL)fileIsImmutable;
- (BOOL)fileIsAppendOnly;
- (NSDate *)fileCreationDate;
- (NSNumber *)fileOwnerAccountID;
- (NSNumber *)fileGroupOwnerAccountID;
@end
```

Using NSBrowser and DirEntry

Now open `AppController.h`. You will need an array of arrays to hold the **DirEntry** objects.

Example 12-3. AppController.h

```
#import <Cocoa/Cocoa.h>

@interface AppController : NSObject
{
    IBOutlet NSBrowser *browser;

    // 'directories' is an array of arrays of DirEntry
    // Each array represents the entries in one column
    NSMutableArray *directories;
}
- (IBAction)deleteSelection:(id)sender;

@end
```

In the `AppController.m` file, implement these methods:

Example 12-4. AppController.m

```objc
#import "AppController.h"
#import "DirEntry.h"

@implementation AppController

- (id)init
{
    [super init];
    directories = [[NSMutableArray alloc] init];
    return self;
}

// Begin Private Methods

// This method causes the browser to be completely cleared,  and only
// the left-most column gets reloaded
- (void)reload
{
    NSMutableArray *root;

    // Clear the columns
    [directories removeAllObjects];

    // Create the left-most column
    root = [DirEntry entriesAtPath:@"/" withParent:nil];
    [directories addObject:root];
}

// This gets called to ensure that 'directories' is loaded with the
// the data for the selected row and column.
// If column == -1,  no selection
- (void)updateDirectoriesForSelectedRow:(int)row column:(int)column
{
    NSArray *items;
    DirEntry *dirEntry;

    // No selection?  Reload the left-most column
    if (column == -1) {
        [self reload];
        return;
    }

    // Discard the arrays of entries to the right of the selection
    while ([directories count] > column + 1) {
        [directories removeLastObject];
    }

    // Look up the selected dirEntry
    items = [directories objectAtIndex:column];
    dirEntry = [items objectAtIndex:row];

    // If the selection is a directory,  load its children
    if ([dirEntry isDirectory]){
        NSArray *newItems = [dirEntry children];
        [directories addObject:newItems];
```

```objc
        }
}

// Returns the last item in the selection array
- (DirEntry *)selectedDirEntry
{
    int row, col;
    NSArray *items;

    // What row and column are currently selected?
    col = [browser selectedColumn];
    row = [browser selectedRowInColumn:col];

    // Is there no selection?
    if (col < 0) {
        return nil;
    }

    // Get the selected DirEntry
    items = [directories objectAtIndex:col];
    return [items objectAtIndex:row];
}
// End of Private Methods


- (void)awakeFromNib
{
    [self reload];
}

// You will implement deletion later
- (IBAction)deleteSelection:(id)sender
{
    NSLog(@"deleteSelection not implemented");
}


// Begin NSBrowser Delegate Methods

- (int)browser:(NSBrowser *)sender numberOfRowsInColumn:(int)column
{
    int selectedRow, selectedCol;

    // What is currently selected in the browser?
    selectedCol = [browser selectedColumn];
    selectedRow = [browser selectedRowInColumn:selectedCol];

    // If the column being asked about is to the right of the selected
    // column, then the user has clicked on a directory.
    // Thus we need to load the selectedEntry's children into the
    // directories array
    if (column == selectedCol + 1) {
        [self updateDirectoriesForSelectedRow:selectedRow
                                       column:selectedCol];
    }

    // If we are being asked about something beyond the directories
```

```
        // array,  just return zero
        if (column < [directories count]) {
            return [[directories objectAtIndex:column] count];
        } else {
            return 0;
        }
    }

    - (void)browser:(NSBrowser *)sender willDisplayCell:(id)cell
             atRow:(int)row column:(int)column
    {
        NSArray *items = [directories objectAtIndex:column];
        DirEntry *dirEntry = [items objectAtIndex:row];
        [cell setLeaf:![dirEntry isDirectory]];
        [cell setStringValue:[dirEntry filename]];
        [cell setLoaded:YES];
    }

    - (void)dealloc
    {
        [directories release];
        [super dealloc];
    }
@end
```

Build and run the app. You should be able to browse, but not delete. Add these methods to enable deletion:

```
// An action method that tries to delete the selected directory entry
// from the file system and updates the selection in the browser
// accordingly

- (IBAction)deleteSelection:(id)sender
{
    int response;
    BOOL successful;
    DirEntry *dirEntry, *parent;
    NSString *path;
    NSMutableArray *items;
    int selectedRow, selectedColumn;

    // What DirEntry is the user trying to delete?
    dirEntry = [self selectedDirEntry];

    // Is nothing selected?
    if (dirEntry == nil) {
        NSRunAlertPanel(@"Delete", @"Nothing selected", nil, nil, nil);
        return;
    }

    // Get the path of what we are about to delete
    path = [dirEntry fullPath];

    // Show an alert panel to confirm delete
    response = NSRunAlertPanel(@"Delete", @"Really delete %@?", @"Yes",
                               @"No", nil, path);
```

```
        // Did the user choose NO?
        if (response == NSAlertAlternateReturn){
            return;
        }

        // Use the browser to find out what the row and column of the
        // selected entry is.
        selectedColumn = [browser selectedColumn];
        selectedRow = [browser selectedRowInColumn:selectedColumn];

        // The parent will be selected after successful delete
        parent = [dirEntry parent];

        NSLog(@"will delete %i, %i, %@",selectedRow,selectedColumn, path);

        // Try to delete it.
        successful = [[NSFileManager defaultManager] removeFileAtPath:path
                                                    handler:self];

        // Did the delete work?
        if (successful) {

            // Figure out the new selected column and row
            selectedColumn--;

            // Is any column selected?
            if (selectedColumn >= 0) {

                // Figure out the selected row
                items = [directories objectAtIndex:selectedColumn];
                selectedRow = [items indexOfObject:parent];

                // Change the browser's selection and reload
                [browser selectRow:selectedRow inColumn:selectedColumn];
            } else {

                // Unselect everything
                [[browser matrixInColumn:0] deselectAllCells];

                // Reload the left-most column
                [browser loadColumnZero];
            }
        } else {
            NSRunAlertPanel(@"Delete", @"Delete was not successful",
                            nil, nil, nil);
        }
    }

// This gets called if something goes wrong with the delete
- (BOOL)fileManager:(NSFileManager *)manager
        shouldProceedAfterError:(NSDictionary *)errorInfo
{
    NSLog(@"error = %@", errorInfo);
    return NO;
}
```

Build and test this carefully. It really will delete entire directories.

NSWorkspace

On Mac OS X, many file-related activities are handled by the Finder. In the AppKit framework, **NSWorkspace** is an elegant interface to the Finder. For example, if you wanted to get the icon that would be displayed for a particular file, you would use **NSWorkspace**. Also, the **NSWorkspace** posts notifications when Finder-related activities occur. For example, when a device is mounted or unmounted, **NSWorkspace**'s notification center posts a notification.

Here are a few interesting methods in **NSWorkspace**:

+ (NSWorkspace *)**sharedWorkspace**

> Returns the shared instance.

- (BOOL)**openFile:**(NSString *)fullPath

> Opens the file at fullPath with its default application. The application is started if necessary. This method returns YES if the file was successfully opened.

- (BOOL)**openURL:**(NSURL *)url

> Opens a URL with the user's default browser. Returns YES if successful.

- (BOOL)**launchApplication:**(NSString *)appName

> appName is the name of the app or the full path to it. You can include .app or not. Returns YES if the app launches or is currently running.

- (void)**noteFileSystemChanged:**(NSString *)path

> After you create, delete, or rename a file, you should call this method so that Finder will update what is being displayed.

- (NSNotificationCenter *)**notificationCenter**

> Returns the notification center for the **NSWorkspace**. To receive notifications listed below, you will want to register with *this* notification center.

- (NSImage *)**iconForFile:**(NSString *)fullPath;

> Returns the icon for the file at fullPath.

NSWorkspace posts the following notifications:

- NSWorkspaceWillLaunchApplicationNotification

- NSWorkspaceDidLaunchApplicationNotification

- NSWorkspaceDidTerminateApplicationNotification

- NSWorkspaceWillPowerOffNotification

- NSWorkspaceDidMountNotification (The device being mounted or unmounted is in the userInfo dictionary under NSDevicePath.)

- NSWorkspaceWillUnmountNotification

- NSWorkspaceDidUnmountNotification

- NSWorkspaceDidPerformFileOperationNotification (Only notifies app about the completion of its own file operations performed using the **NSWorkspace** object!)

To be a good citizen, when your application performs a deletion, it should inform the Finder. In **deleteSelection:** add the following line:

```
// Try to delete it.
successful = [[NSFileManager defaultManager] removeFileAtPath:path
                                                handler:self];


// Tell Finder
[[NSWorkspace sharedWorkspace] noteFileSystemChanged:path];

// Did the delete work?
if (successful) {
```

Build and run your app. Delete a directory with Remover while browsing the same directory in Finder.

As an educational exercise, register for all notifications from the workspace in **init** and log them as they arrive:

```
- (void)logThis:(NSNotification *)note
{
    NSLog(@"received: %@", note);
}
- (id)init
{
    [super init];
    directories = [[NSMutableArray alloc] init];
    NSNotificationCenter *nc;
    nc = [[NSWorkspace sharedWorkspace] notificationCenter];
    [nc addObserver:self
            selector:@selector(logThis:)
            name:nil
            object:nil];
    return self;
}
```

Build and run the app. Start other applications. Insert and eject a CD. Note that you are informed of these activities.

Historical trivia: On NeXTSTEP, the equivalent of Finder was an application called Workspace. That is why this class is called **NSWorkspace**.

Challenge

1. Use the **NSDirectoryEnumerator** to calculate the size of the selected directory.

2. Use **NSWorkspace** to find and display the appropriate icon in each browser cell.

3. If the user double-clicks a file, open it. (This also uses **NSWorkspace**.)

Chapter 13. Network Programming With Sockets

The native Mac OS X networking API is Berkeley sockets, variants of which are available on just about every platform available today. The sockets API is both elegant (such as just needing a couple of calls to set up network communications) and ugly. The data structures are a bit awkward in that there are few `typedefs` so you have to use the `struct` keyword frequently and a lot of casting is required. One of the problems with networking in general, and sockets in particular, is that there is a lot of documentation and a lot of features of varying levels of obscurity. It is easy to get lost in the details and be unable to get the basics working. Here you are primarily going to be concerned with basic stream-oriented network communication.

The Address Data Structures

Before getting into the API that actually sets up communication, have a look at the various data structures and function calls involved in managing network addresses.

The fundamental data structure (which you will not actually use) is `struct sockaddr`:

```
struct sockaddr {
    u_char        sa_len;
    u_char        sa_family;
    char          sa_data[14];
};
```

The important parts are `sa_len`, the size of the address structure, and `sa_family`, which is the kind of address represented, whether it be an IP address, a local address for Unix sockets, X.25, or any other kind of address. `struct sockaddr` can be considered almost like an abstract base class if this were expressed in an OO way.

The address structure that is actually used for sockets over TCP/IP is `struct sockaddr_in`, where `_in` is for Internet:

```
struct sockaddr_in {
    u_char        sin_len;
    u_char        sin_family;
    u_short       sin_port;
    struct        in_addr sin_addr;
    char          sin_zero[8];
};
```

The first two entries match `struct sockaddr`, so given any address derived from `struct sockaddr` you can look at those first two elements to know what you are dealing with. The last element, `sin_zero`, is padding so that `struct sockaddr` matches the size of `struct sockaddr`. It should be cleared to zero.

TCP/IP communication deals with addresses and ports. You have seen the familiar "dotted-quad" format for IP addresses: 127.0.0.2. Each IP address has 65535 ports associated with it. Communication happens between address/port pairs. For instance, getting to the web server on bignerdranch.com involves going to address 63.151.112.139 and connecting to port 80, and locally your web browser will be communicating from a port on your local IP address. The `sin_port` field indicates which port should be used. The actual address is in `sin_addr`.

The `struct in_addr` is one of the annoying parts of the sockets API:

```
struct in_addr {
    in_addr_t s_addr;
};
```

Which is a structure with only a single element. The actual address type (`in_addr_t`) is actually an unsigned 32 bit integer.

There is one detail: both the port (2 bytes) and the address (4 bytes) need to be in network byte order.

Network Byte Order

The way bytes are ordered in multi-byte values can vary from platform to platform. The integer value of 0x12345678 could be stored as it is written in memory (termed big endian), or stored as 0x78563412 (termed little endian). Macs store their integers in big endian byte order while x86 machines store things in little endian byte order. When transferring integers like this between machines over the network, both parties must agree on what order the specific bytes will have. Most folks just use the "network byte order," which is big endian. What that means to Mac developers is that you do not really have to worry about network byte order, but given that networking stuff tends to be cross platform, and you never know where you will need to port your networking code, it is good to get into the habit of using the functions to ensure that your data is in the network byte order. Here are some useful functions:

```
uint16_t htons (uint16_t hostshort);

uint32_t htonl (uint32_t hostlong);

uint16_t ntohs (uint16_t netshort);

uint32_t ntohl (uint32_t netlong);
```

A hint on parsing the names:

h

  Host

n

  Network

s

  Short

l

  Long

So, `htonl()` is "host to network long,", and the converse is `ntohl()` "network to host long." You do not need to worry about network byte order when sending text data or single bytes.

Address Conversions

Sometimes you will receive an address from the user in the form of dotted quads. Sometimes you have the address in the form of a 4-byte integer. Other times you have the name of a machine (e.g., www.bignerdranch.com). There exist functions to move between these forms.

int **inet_aton** (const char *quadString, struct in_addr *address);

> Converts between an ascii representation of a dotted quad and returns the numeric address (hence a-to-n). It returns 1 if the conversion was successful, or 0 if the string is invalid.

char ***inet_ntoa** (struct in_addr address);

> Converts from the numeric address to an ascii representation. The string returned resides in a static memory area, so it will be clobbered on the next call to **inet_ntoa()**.

When looking up hostnames to resolve the address (via DNS, or local name resolution using configuration files or NetInfo), the struct hostent is used:

```
struct hostent {
    char        *h_name;
    char        **h_aliases;
    int         h_addrtype;
    int         h_length;
    char        **h_addr_list;
    #define     h_addr  h_addr_list[0]
};
```

The element of the structure are:

h_name

> Official name of the host.

h_aliases

> A NULL-terminated array of alternate names for the host.

h_addrtype

> The type of address being returned. AF_INET for internet addresses.

h_length

> The length, in bytes, of the address.

h_addr_list

> A NULL-terminated array of network addresses for the host, network byte order.

h_addr

> The first address in h_addr_list. Here for backward compatibility.

The `gethostbyname()` call looks up a hostname and returns a filled-in `hostent`, which like `inet_ntoa` is allocated in static space, so it will get clobbered on the next call.

Note that `gethostbyname()` does not return an error in `errno`. It provides its own variant of `errno` called `h_errno`, and you can use `hstrerror()` to get a human-readable message.

Here is a program that exercises the address conversion functions:

Example 13-1. addresses.m

```
// addresses.m -- play around with addressing API

/* compile with:
cc -g -Wall -o addresses addresses.m
*/

#import <sys/types.h>    // random types
#import <sys/socket.h>   // for AF_INET
#import <netinet/in.h>   // constants and types
#import <arpa/inet.h>    // for inet_ntoa and friends
#import <stdlib.h>       // for EXIT_SUCCESS
#import <stdio.h>        // for fprintf
#import <unistd.h>       // for hostname
#import <sys/param.h>    // for MAXHOSTNAMELEN
#import <errno.h>        // for errno
#import <string.h>       // for strerror
#import <netdb.h>        // for gethostbyname

int main (int argc, char *argv[])
{
    struct in_addr address;
    const char *asciiAddress = "127.0.0.2";
    const char *translatedAddress;

    // convert to and from an ascii dotted quad

    if (inet_aton(asciiAddress, &address) != 1) {
        fprintf (stderr, "could not inet_aton '%s'\n", asciiAddress);
    } else {
        printf ("address value of %s is %x\n", asciiAddress, address.s_addr);
    }

    translatedAddress = inet_ntoa (address);
    printf ("and translated back is '%s'\n", translatedAddress);

    // see what our hostname is
    {
        char hostname[MAXHOSTNAMELEN];
        if (gethostname(hostname, MAXHOSTNAMELEN) == -1) {
            fprintf (stderr, "error getting hostname.  error is %d / %s\n",
                    errno, strerror(errno));
        } else {
            printf ("our hostname is '%s'\n", hostname);
        }
    }
```

```
    // look up host names
    {
        struct hostent *hostinfo;

        hostinfo = gethostbyname ("www.apple.com");
        if (hostinfo == NULL) {
            fprintf (stderr, "error wtih gethostbyname / apple.  error %s\n",
                    hstrerror(h_errno));
        } else {
            char **scan;

            printf ("gethostbyname www.apple.com\n");
            printf ("    official name: %s\n", hostinfo->h_name);

            if (hostinfo->h_aliases[0] != NULL) {
                scan = hostinfo->h_aliases;
                printf ("    aliases:\n");
                while (*scan != NULL) {
                    printf ("          %s\n", *scan);
                    scan++;
                }
            } else {
                printf ("    no aliases\n");
            }

            printf ("    h_addrtype: %d (%s)\n",
                    hostinfo->h_addrtype,
                    (hostinfo->h_addrtype == AF_INET)
                        ? "AF_INET" : "unknown");

            if (hostinfo->h_addr_list[0] != NULL) {
                printf ("    addresses:\n");

                scan = hostinfo->h_addr_list;

                while (*scan != NULL) {
                    printf ("          %s\n",
                            inet_ntoa(*((struct in_addr *)*scan)));
                    scan++;
                }
            } else {
                printf ("    no addresses\n");
            }
        }
    }

    exit (EXIT_SUCCESS);

} // main
```

and a sample run:

```
% ./addresses
address value of 127.0.0.2 is 7f000002
and translated back is '127.0.0.2'
our hostname is 'borkopolis.local.'
```

```
gethostbyname www.apple.com
    official name: www.apple.com.akadns.net
    aliases:
        www.apple.com
    h_addrtype: 2 (AF_INET)
    addresses:
        17.254.0.91
```

There are two interesting things to note. The hostname of the machine this was on (returned by **gethostname()**) is "borkopolis.local." That is the Rendezvous name for the machine.

The other is that weird official name for www.apple.com. akadns.net is the Akamai service to find the closest host to you when it serves up the page. The aliases entry of www.apple.com has the name that (for instance) a web browser would display when you go to the site.

Simple Network Programming

Server coding

Here is the set of calls and actions used when writing a server program:

1. Get a **socket()**.

2. Construct an address + port that the server will listen to.

3. **bind()** the address to the socket.

4. Tell the socket to start **listen()**ing for new connections.

5. **accept()** new connections.

6. Use **read()** and **write()** to receive and send data.

```
int socket (int domain, int type, int protocol);
```

This creates a socket and returns a file descriptor (just like the file descriptors from Chapter 10). You will not actually read or write through this particular file descriptor for a server, but instead use it as the focus for other networking calls. The **accept()** call described later will give us a file descriptor you can read and write through.

For the domain, use AF_INET for an internet socket. For type use SOCK_STREAM for a reliable connection, which means the bytes you send will be received in the same order you sent them and without error.

For protocol, just pass zero.

This returns -1 on errors and sets errno appropriately.

Constructing an address

To construct the address, create a struct sockaddr_in on the stack and fill out the various fields:

```
struct sockaddr_in address;
```

```
address.sin_len = sizeof (struct sockaddr_in);
address.sin_family = AF_INET;
address.sin_port = htons (2342);
address.sin_addr.s_addr = htonl (INADDR_ANY);
memset (address.sin_zero, 0, sizeof(address.sin_zero));
```

The family for Internet communications is AF_INET (AF for "address family"). INADDR_ANY means that any IP address can be used. This will cause the server program to listen on the network address of your machine. If you have multiple network addreseses, it will listen on all of them. If you have a specific address you want to use, it can be specified here as well.

Note the port and address are put into network byte order, and the sin_zero portion of the structure is zeroed out.

bind

bind() brings together the address and the socket. The socket then owns that address/port pair.

```
int bind (int socket, const struct sockaddr *address, int addresslen);
```

Note that this takes a pointer to a struct sockaddr, not a struct sockaddr_in, so you need to cast. The addresslen parameter is the size of your struct sockaddr_in.

If the address/port pair is already in use **bind()** will return an error. This can be frustrating if your program has crashed but the previously bound socket still exists in the kernel (until a timeout of a couple of minutes). You should tell the socket to reuse the address using this **setsockopt()** call before the **bind()** will do that:

```
int yes = 1;
result = setsockopt (socket, SOL_SOCKET, SO_REUSEADDR, &yes, sizeof(int));
```

setsockopt() is a generic interface for tweaking different socket parameters.

Both **setsockopt()** and **bind()** return -1 on errors and set errno.

listen

The **listen()** system call informs the kernel to start accepting connections to the address and port specified in the address passed to **bind()**.

```
int listen (int socket, int backlog);
```

The backlog parameter is the maximum length of the queue of pending connection requests. Once the queue fills any subsequent attempts to connect to the socket, it will get a "connection refused" error. The system will put a cap on the size of the backlog queue.

accept

The **accept()** call will wait for a new incoming connection. When a new connection is made, **accept()** will return with a file descriptor that can be read and write through. This file descriptor is just like any other. You can use functions like **read()**,

write(), **send()**, **readv()**, and you can wrap it in a standard I/O FILE if you so desire. Some file operations (like seeking) will result in errors since you really cannot seek with a network connection.

```
int accept (int socket, struct sockaddr *address, int *addreslength);
```

Upon a successful **accept()**, the address parameter will be the address and port of the client making the request. This returns -1 on errors and sets errno appropriately.

Note that **accept()** will block until an incoming connection happens or an error happens. The socket can be set into a non-blocking mode so that accept does not block. You will read about that later with multiplexing connections.

Here is a simple server that binds to port 2342 and listens for incoming connections. You can make such a connection using the telnet command. When a connection is made, the data from the other program is read and printed. Then it waits for another connection.

Example 13-2. simpleserver.m

```
// simpleserver.m -- listen on a port, and display any bytes
//                   that come through

/* compile with:
cc -g -Wall -o simpleserver simpleserver.m
*/

#import <sys/types.h>    // random types
#import <netinet/in.h>   // for sockaddr_in
#import <sys/socket.h>   // for socket(), AF_INET
#import <arpa/inet.h>    // for inet_ntoa
#import <errno.h>        // for errno
#import <string.h>       // for strerror
#import <stdlib.h>       // for EXIT_SUCCESS
#import <stdio.h>        // for fprintf
#import <unistd.h>       // for close

#define PORT_NUMBER 2342

int main (int argc, char *argv[])
{
    int fd = -1, result;
    int programResult = EXIT_FAILURE;

    // get a socket
    result = socket (AF_INET, SOCK_STREAM, 0);

    if (result == -1) {
        fprintf (stderr, "could not make a socket.  error: %d / %s\n",
                 errno, strerror(errno));
        goto bailout;
    }
    fd = result;

    // reuse the address so we do not fail on program launch
    {
        int yes = 1;
```

```
    result = setsockopt (fd, SOL_SOCKET, SO_REUSEADDR, &yes, sizeof(int));
    if (result == -1) {
        fprintf (stderr, "could not setsockopt to reuseaddr. %d / %s\n",
                errno, strerror(errno));
        goto bailout;
    }
}


// bind to an address and port
{
    struct sockaddr_in address;
    address.sin_len = sizeof (struct sockaddr_in);
    address.sin_family = AF_INET;
    address.sin_port = htons (PORT_NUMBER);
    address.sin_addr.s_addr = htonl (INADDR_ANY);
    memset (address.sin_zero, 0, sizeof(address.sin_zero));

    result = bind (fd, (struct sockaddr *)&address, sizeof(address));
    if (result == -1) {
        fprintf (stderr, "could not bind socket.  error: %d / %s\n",
                errno, strerror(errno));
        goto bailout;
    }
}

result = listen (fd, 8);

if (result == -1) {
    fprintf (stderr, "listen failed.  error: %d /  %s\n",
            errno, strerror(errno));
    goto bailout;
}

while (1) {
    struct sockaddr_in address;
    int addressLength = sizeof(address);
    int remoteSocket;
    char buffer[4096];

    result = accept (fd, (struct sockaddr*)&address, &addressLength);
    if (result == -1) {
        fprintf (stderr, "accept failed.  error: %d / %s\n",
                errno, strerror(errno));
        continue;
    }
    printf ("accepted connection from %s:%d\n",
            inet_ntoa(address.sin_addr), ntohs(address.sin_port));
    remoteSocket = result;

    // drain the socket
    while (1) {
        result = read (remoteSocket, buffer, 4095);

        if (result == 0) {
            // EOF.
            break;
        } else if (result == -1) {
```

```
                    fprintf (stderr, "could not read from remote socket.  "
                             "error %d / %s\n", errno, strerror(errno));
                    break;
                } else {
                    // null-terminate the string and print it out
                    buffer[result] = '\000';
                    printf ("%s", buffer);
                }
            }

            close (remoteSocket);

            printf ("\n------------------------------------------------\n");
        }

        programResult = EXIT_SUCCESS;

bailout:
    close (fd);
    return (programResult);

} // main
```

A sample run:

In one terminal window run `simpleserver`:

```
% ./simpleserver
```

And in another run `telnet`:

```
% telnet 10.0.1.142 2342
Trying 10.0.1.142...
Connected to 10.0.1.142.
Escape character is '^]'.
Here is some text I typed in.
Here is some more text.
(press control-] to get a telnet prompt)
telnet> quit
%
```

If you've not used `telnet` before, it makes a connection to the address indicated (the local machine at 10.0.1.142, but you can also use a domain name) and a port (2342 in this case). `telnet` will then send any text you enter to the program on the other side, and it will display any returned text (in this case there is not any). Here are the results from `simpleserver`:

```
% ./simpleserver
accepted connection from 10.0.1.142:50605
Here is some text I typed in.
Here is some more text.

------------------------------------------------
```

You can `telnet` again to the server and enter more text. To make the server exit, interrupt it with `control-C`.

Client Coding

Code on the client is very similar to the server:

1. Figure out the address information of the server.

2. Construct a `struct sockaddr_in` address.

3. Get a `socket()`.

4. `connect()` to the server.

5. Use `read()` and `write()` to receive and send data.

Note there is no `bind()` or `listen()` step for a client, but you do `connect()`.

connect

This is how a connection is made to the server. The file descriptor you got from `socket()` is what you will read and write with.

```
int connect (int socket, const struct sockaddr *name, int namelen);
```

Give it the address to connect to and it returns zero if the connection succeeds, or -1 for an error, with `errno` set.

Here is a client that is a little more convenient than `telnet`:

Example 13-3. simpleclient.m

```objc
// simpleclient.m -- read from stdin and send to the simpleserver

/* compile with:
cc -g -Wall -o simpleclient simpleclient.m
*/

#import <sys/types.h>     // random types
#import <netinet/in.h>    // for sockaddr_in
#import <sys/socket.h>    // for socket(), AF_INET
#import <netdb.h>         // for gethostbyname, h_errno, etc
#import <errno.h>         // for errno
#import <string.h>        // for strerror
#import <stdlib.h>        // for EXIT_SUCCESS
#import <stdio.h>         // for fprintf
#import <unistd.h>        // for close

#define PORT_NUMBER 2342

int main (int argc, char *argv[])
{
    int programResult = EXIT_FAILURE;
    int fd = -1, result;
    struct sockaddr_in serverAddress;
    struct hostent *hostInfo;

    if (argc != 2) {
        fprintf (stderr, "usage: client hostname\n");
        goto bailout;
    }
```

```
hostInfo = gethostbyname(argv[1]);

if (hostInfo == NULL) {
    fprintf (stderr, "could not gethostbyname for '%s'\n", argv[1]);
    fprintf (stderr, " error: %d / %s\n", h_errno, hstrerror(h_errno));
    goto bailout;
}
serverAddress.sin_len = sizeof (struct sockaddr_in);
serverAddress.sin_family = AF_INET;
serverAddress.sin_port = htons (PORT_NUMBER);
serverAddress.sin_addr = *((struct in_addr *)(hostInfo->h_addr));
memset (&(serverAddress.sin_zero), 0, sizeof(serverAddress.sin_zero));

result = socket (AF_INET, SOCK_STREAM, 0);

if (result == -1) {
    fprintf (stderr, "could not make a socket.  error: %d / %s\n",
             errno, strerror(errno));
    goto bailout;
}
fd = result;

// no need to bind() or listen()

result = connect (fd, (struct sockaddr *)&serverAddress,
                  sizeof(serverAddress));

if (result == -1) {
    fprintf (stderr, "could not connect.  error: %d / %s\n",
             errno, strerror(errno));
    goto bailout;
}

do {
    char buffer[4096];
    size_t readCount;
    readCount = fread (buffer, 1, 4096, stdin);

    result = write (fd, buffer, readCount);

    if (result == -1) {
        fprintf (stderr, "error writing: %d / %s\n",
                 errno, strerror(errno));
        break;
    }

    // check EOF
    if (readCount < 4096) {
        if (ferror(stdin)) {
            fprintf (stderr, "error reading: %d / %s\n",
                     errno, strerror(errno));
        } else if (feof(stdin)) {
            fprintf (stderr, "EOF\n");
        }
        break;
    }
```

```
    } while (1);

    programResult = EXIT_SUCCESS;

bailout:
    close (fd);
    return (programResult);

} // main
```

Compile this, start the server running in one terminal window, then run the client in another.

```
% ./simpleclient 10.0.1.142
hello
there
bork
bork
bork
(type control-D to send an EOF to the client)
```

When you send EOF to the client, the **fread()** will return, and the text will get written to the server.

On the server side you will see something like

```
accepted connection from 10.0.1.142:50610
hello
there
bork
bork
bork


-------------------------------------------------
```

You can do more than just type text. You can send the contents of a file too.

```
% ./simpleclient 10.0.1.142 < /usr/share/dict/words
```

will send about 2 megs of words across the network to the server.

More Advanced Issues

Multiplexing connections

A one-connection-at-a-time server like simpleserver is OK for some applications, but to truly leverage the power of networking it is better to have a single server support many connections simultaneously. To do this, you need a way to multiplex multiple input and output streams, and to not block unless there is no work to be done.

The **select()** call is the Berkeley sockets way of doing this multiplexing. You give **select()** a set of file descriptors. If there is any data to be read, or if there is the ability to write on any of the descriptors, **select()** will tell you so. Otherwise it will block (with an optional time out) until network activity is possible.

```
int select (int nfds, fd_set *readfds, fd_set *writefds, fd_set *exceptfds,
                struct timeval *timeout);
```

nfds

>One more than the largest file descriptor number.

readfds

>A set of file descriptors to see if you can read data from without blocking.

writefds

>A set of file descriptors to see if you can write data to without blocking.

exceptfds

>A set of file descriptors to see if there are any error conditions.

timeout

>How long to wait for activity before breaking out of the select call. pass NULL for no timeout.

The fd_sets are modified by select(). You set the file descriptors you are interested in before calling select(), then examine the fd_sets to see which ones are interesting afterward.

What are fd_sets? They are an opaque bitvector that can be manipulated with this API:

```
    fd_set fdset;
```

FD_ZERO (&fdset);

>Clear out the fd_set.

FD_SET (fd, &fdset);

>Add a file descriptor to the set.

FD_CLR (fd, &fdset);

>Remove a file descriptor from the set.

FD_ISSET (fd, &fdset);

>Test to see if a file descriptor is in the set.

Usually a fd_set holds 1024 items. If you try to put more than that into an fd_set, you could end up writing over memory after the fd_set's storage. You can alter this by putting a #define FD_SETSIZE before including <sys/types.h>. The getdtablesize() function will return the size of the file descriptor table for a process (but since it is a function call, it is not useful to send to FD_SETSIZE).

struct timeval is defined like this:

```
struct timeval {
    int32_t    tv_sec;          /* seconds */
    int32_t    tv_usec;         /* and microseconds */
```

```
};
```

You can specify the timeout in seconds and microseconds (but you are not
guaranteed of microsecond granularity). Specify zero for both values to have
`select()` return immediately. You can use this to have `select()` poll rather than
block.

The usual way to use select is like this (say for reading):

```
fd_set readfds;
int maxFd = -1, result;
FD_ZERO (&readfds);

// add the listen socket
FD_SET (myListenSocket, &readfds);
maxFd = MAX (maxFd, myListenSocket);

// walk your data structure that has your open sessions
for (i = 0; i < whatever; i++) {
    FD_SET (session->fd, &readfds);
    maxFd = MAX (maxFd, session->fd);
}

result = select (maxFd + 1, &readfds, NULL, NULL, NULL);

if (result == -1) {
    ... handle error
}

// see if our accept socket is there
if (FD_ISSET (myListenSocket, &readfds)) {
    // call accept(), make a new session
}

// walk the data structure again looking for activity
for (i = 0; i < whatever; i++) {
    if (FD_ISSET(session->fd, &readfds)) {
        result = read (session->fd, ...);
    }
}
```

Figure 13-1. select()

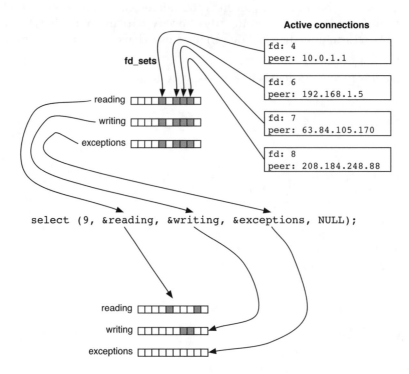

Note again that the first argument is one *more* than the largest file descriptor. A common mistake is to forget to do that. Also note that fd_sets can be copied and kept around. A common technique is to have a master fd_set that has all of the session file descriptors in it, then you can make a copy of it and pass the copy to select. This saves you from walking your data structures every time before a call to **select()**. It also means you have to keep that master set up to date when a session closes.

When a file descriptor is in the readfds set, it will appear in the set after **select()** returns when data is available. It will also appear when the connection closes (**read()** will return zero in that case). As seen above, you can also put the accept socket in there to know when new connections happen.

One thing you may notice is that **select()** does not tell you how much is available to read. If you just do a result = read (session->fd, buffer, bufferSize), the call to read will block until bufferSize data is read in, or an error happens. That is behavior you do not want in a busy server program. File descriptors can be put into a non-blocking mode. In this case, the **read()** will read however much data has appeared on the connection and then return. The return value from **read()** tells you how many bytes were read. To set a file descriptor to be non-blocking, use this **fcntl()** call:

```
result = fcntl (fd, F_SETFL, O_NONBLOCK);
```

(And of course error check the result. -1 is returned on error and errno set)

Message boundaries

Some networking protocols, like HTTP, are pretty easy to deal with. You can pretty much just read everything that comes on the socket, and then write out everything you need to. Other networking protocols are harder to deal with due to some of the "real world" issues regarding network communication and how the kernels on both sides of the connection buffer data.

Consider a little chat program where the client sends the server a message that looks like this:

length : one byte
message : length bytes of text

Here are some scenarios:

One message from a `read()`

This is pretty easy. Just look at the first byte for the length, and get the subsequent bytes of the message and send it out to the chat clients.

Multiple complete messages from a `read()`

Since read does not know where the messages begin and end you have to walk the read buffer: get a length byte, process subsequent bytes, get another length byte, process those bytes, until you run out

A message straddles a `read()` boundary

This is where things get complicated. Between calls to `read()` you need to remember that you only got half of a message. The first half waits around in a buffer until the second half gets in.

Generally you will keep a buffer large enough to hold two or more complete messages and read into that buffer. When processing messages, you need to know whether you are picking up a resumed message or are starting with a new one.

Figure 13-2. Worst-case Scenario for Messages

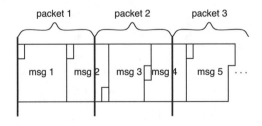

Here is the `Chatter` server side. The more interesting parts are the select loop, and `readMessage()`, which handles the various pathological cases of incoming messages.

Example 13-4. chatterserver.m

```
// chatterserver.m -- chat server using standard sockets API

/* compile with:
cc -g -Wall -o chatterserver chatterserver.m
*/

#import <sys/types.h>    // random types
#import <netinet/in.h>   // for sockaddr_in
#import <sys/socket.h>   // for socket(), AF_INET
#import <arpa/inet.h>    // for inet_ntoa
#import <errno.h>        // for errno
#import <string.h>       // for strerror
#import <stdlib.h>       // for EXIT_SUCCESS
#import <stdio.h>        // for fprintf
#import <unistd.h>       // for close
#import <arpa/inet.h>    // for inet_ntoa and friends
#import <fcntl.h>        // for fcntl()
#import <syslog.h>       // for syslog and friends
#import <sys/uio.h>      // for iovec

/* message protocol
 * first message is:
 *
 * 1 byte : length of message, no more than 8
 * length bytes : the nickname of the user
 *
 * 1 byte : length of message
 * length bytes : message, not zero-terminated
 *
 * therefore, maxmimum message size is 256 bytes
 */
#define MAX_MESSAGE_SIZE        256
#define READ_BUFFER_SIZE        4096

// there is one of these for each connected user

typedef struct chatterUser {
    int         fd;              // zero fd == no user
    char        username[9];     // 8 character name plus trailing zero byte
    int         gotNickname;     // have we gotten the nickname packet?

    // incoming data workspace

    // what the length byte says we should get
    unsigned int currentMessageSize;

    // what we have read (not including length)
    int         bytesRead;
    char        buffer[READ_BUFFER_SIZE];
} chatterUser;

#define MAX_USERS 50
chatterUser g_users[MAX_USERS];

#define PORT_NUMBER 2342
```

```
int g_listenFd;

// returns fd on success, -1 on error
// (this is cut-and-paste from main() of simpleserver.m)

int startListening ()
{
    int fd = -1, success = 0;
    int result;

    // cut and pasted from main() in simpleserver.m

    result = socket (AF_INET, SOCK_STREAM, 0);

    if (result == -1) {
        fprintf (stderr, "could not make a scoket.  error: %d / %s\n",
                 errno, strerror(errno));
        goto bailout;
    }
    fd = result;

    {
        int yes = 1;
        result = setsockopt (fd, SOL_SOCKET, SO_REUSEADDR, &yes, sizeof(int));
        if (result == -1) {
            fprintf (stderr,
                     "unable to setsockopt to reuse address. %d / %s\n",
                     errno, strerror(errno));
            goto bailout;
        }
    }

    // bind to an address and port
    {
        struct sockaddr_in address;
        address.sin_len = sizeof (struct sockaddr_in);
        address.sin_family = AF_INET;
        address.sin_port = htons (PORT_NUMBER);
        address.sin_addr.s_addr = htonl (INADDR_ANY);
        memset (address.sin_zero, 0, sizeof(address.sin_zero));

        result = bind (fd, (struct sockaddr *)&address, sizeof(address));
        if (result == -1) {
            fprintf (stderr, "could not bind socket.  error: %d / %s\n",
                     errno, strerror(errno));
            goto bailout;
        }
    }

    result = listen (fd, 8);

    if (result == -1) {
        fprintf (stderr, "listen failed.  error: %d /  %s\n",
                 errno, strerror(errno));
        goto bailout;
    }
```

```
        success = 1;

 bailout:
     if (!success) {
         close (fd);
         fd = -1;
     }

     return (fd);

 } // startListening

 // our listening socket appeared in a readfd from select.  That means
 // there is a connection there we can accept

 void acceptConnection (int listenFd)
 {
     struct sockaddr_in address;
     int addressLength = sizeof(address), result, fd, i;
     chatterUser *newUser = NULL;

     result = accept (g_listenFd, (struct sockaddr *)&address, &addressLength);

     if (result == -1) {
         fprintf (stderr, "accept failed.  error: %d / %s\n",
                  errno, strerror(errno));
         goto bailout;
     }
     fd = result;

     // set to non-blocking
     result = fcntl (fd, F_SETFL, O_NONBLOCK);
     if (result == -1) {
         fprintf (stderr, "setting nonblock failed.  error: %d / %s\n",
                  errno, strerror(errno));
         goto bailout;
     }

     // find the next free spot in the users array
     for (i = 0; i < MAX_USERS; i++) {
         if (g_users[i].fd == 0) {
             // found it
             newUser = &g_users[i];
             break;
         }
     }

     if (newUser == NULL) {
         const char *gripe = "too many users.  try again later";
         write (fd, gripe, strlen(gripe));
         goto bailout;
     }

     // ok, clear out the structure, and get it set up
     memset (newUser, 0, sizeof(chatterUser));
```

```
        newUser->fd = fd;

        // log where the connection is from

        syslog (LOG_NOTICE, "accepted connection from IP '%s' for fd %d",
                inet_ntoa (address.sin_addr), fd);
bailout:
        return;

} // acceptConnection


// send a message to all the signed-in users

void broadcastMessage (const char *username, const char *message)
{
        chatterUser *scan, *stop;  // use a pointer chase for fun
        struct iovec iovector[4];  // use scattered writes just for fun too
        const char *seperator = ": ";

        printf ("Broadcast message: %s: %s\n", username, message);

        scan = g_users;
        stop = scan + MAX_USERS;

        while (scan < stop) {
            if (scan->fd != 0) {
                iovector[0].iov_base = (char *)username;
                iovector[0].iov_len = strlen (username);
                iovector[1].iov_base = (char *)seperator;
                iovector[1].iov_len = strlen (seperator);
                iovector[2].iov_base = (char *)message;
                iovector[2].iov_len = strlen (message);

                writev (scan->fd, iovector, 3);
            }
            scan++;
        }

} // broadcastMessage

// user disconnected.  Do any mop-up

void cleanUpUser (chatterUser *user)
{
        syslog (LOG_NOTICE, "disconnected user on fd %d\n", user->fd);

        // broadcast 'user disconnected' message
        close (user->fd);
        user->fd = 0;

        broadcastMessage (user->username, "has left the channel\n");

} // cleanUpUser

// the first packet is the user's nickname.  Get it
```

```
void readNickname (chatterUser *user)
{
    int result;

    // see if we have read anything yet
    if (user->currentMessageSize == 0) {
        unsigned char length;
        // we need to get the size

        result = read (user->fd, &length, 1);

        if (result == 1) {
            // we got our length byte
            user->currentMessageSize = length;
            user->bytesRead = 0;

        } else if (result == 0) {
            // end of file
            cleanUpUser (user);
            goto bailout;

        } else if (result == -1) {
            fprintf (stderr, "error reading.  error is %d / %s\n",
                    errno, strerror(errno));
            cleanUpUser (user);
            goto bailout;
        }

    } else {
        int readLeft;

        // ok, try to read just the rest of the nickname
        readLeft = user->currentMessageSize - user->bytesRead;

        result = read (user->fd, user->buffer + user->bytesRead,
                    readLeft);

        if (result == readLeft) {
            // have the whole nickname
            memcpy (user->username, user->buffer,
                    user->currentMessageSize);
            user->username[user->currentMessageSize] = '\000';
            printf ("have a nickname! %s\n", user->username);
            user->gotNickname = 1;

            // no current message, so clear it out
            user->currentMessageSize = 0;

            syslog (LOG_NOTICE, "nickname for fd %d is %s",
                    user->fd, user->username);
            broadcastMessage (user->username, "has joined the channel\n");

        } else if (result == 0) {
            // other side closed the connection
            cleanUpUser (user);
            goto bailout;
```

```
        } else if (result == -1) {
            fprintf (stderr, "error reading.  error is %d / %s\n",
                    errno, strerror(errno));
            cleanUpUser (user);
            goto bailout;

        } else {
            // did not read all of it
            user->bytesRead += result;
        }
    }

bailout:
    return;

} // readNickname

// get message data from the given user

void readMessage (chatterUser *user)
{
    int result;
    char *scan, messageBuffer[MAX_MESSAGE_SIZE + 1];

    // read as much as we can into the buffer
    result = read (user->fd, user->buffer,
                    READ_BUFFER_SIZE - user->bytesRead);

    if (result == 0) {
        // other side closed
        cleanUpUser (user);
        // ok to skip message sending, since we have sent all complete
        // messages already
        goto bailout;

    } if (result == -1) {
        fprintf (stderr, "error reading.  error %d / %s\n",
                    errno, strerror(errno));
        goto bailout;

    } else {
        user->bytesRead += result;
    }

    // now see if we have any complete messages we can send out to
    // other folks the beginning of the buffer should have the length
    // byte, plus any subsequent message bytes

    scan = user->buffer;

    while (user->bytesRead > 0) {

        if (user->currentMessageSize == 0) {
            // start processing new message
            user->currentMessageSize = *scan++;
            user->bytesRead--;
        }
```

```
            if (user->bytesRead >= user->currentMessageSize) {
                // we have a complete message
                memcpy (messageBuffer, scan, user->currentMessageSize);
                messageBuffer[user->currentMessageSize] = '\000';
                user->bytesRead -= user->currentMessageSize;
                scan += user->currentMessageSize;

                // slide the rest of the data over
                memmove (user->buffer, scan, user->bytesRead);
                scan = user->buffer;

                broadcastMessage (user->username, messageBuffer);

                // done with this message
                user->currentMessageSize = 0;
            } else {
                break;
            }
        }
    }

bailout:
    return;

} // readMessage

// we got read activity for a user

void handleRead (chatterUser *user)
{
    if (!user->gotNickname) {
        readNickname (user);
    } else {
        readMessage (user);
    }

} // handleRead

int main (int argc, char *argv[])
{
    int programResult = EXIT_FAILURE;
    g_listenFd = startListening ();

    if (g_listenFd == -1) {
        fprintf (stderr, "could not open listening socket\n");
        goto bailout;
    }

    // block SIGPIPE
    signal (SIGPIPE, SIG_IGN);

    // wait for activity
    while (1) {
        fd_set readfds;
        int maxFd = -1, result, i;

        FD_ZERO (&readfds);
```

```
            // add our listen socket
            FD_SET (g_listenFd, &readfds);
            maxFd = MAX (maxFd, g_listenFd);

            // add our users;
            for (i = 0; i < MAX_USERS; i++) {
                if (g_users[i].fd != 0) {
                    FD_SET (g_users[i].fd, &readfds);
                    maxFd = MAX (maxFd, g_users[i].fd);
                }
            }


            // wait until something interesting happens
            result = select (maxFd + 1, &readfds, NULL, NULL, NULL);

            if (result == -1) {
                fprintf (stderr, "error from select(): error %d / %s\n",
                         errno, strerror(errno));
                continue;
            }

            // see if we have a new user
            if (FD_ISSET (g_listenFd, &readfds)) {
                acceptConnection (g_listenFd);
            }

            // handle any new incoming data from the users.
            // closes appear here too.
            for (i = 0; i < MAX_USERS; i++) {
                if (FD_ISSET(g_users[i].fd, &readfds)) {
                    handleRead (&g_users[i]);
                }
            }
        }

    programResult = EXIT_SUCCESS;

bailout:
    return (programResult);

} // main
```

The client program has a need for using **select()** as well. It needs to be able to read from both the terminal (the user typing their words) as well as the server's connection for messages sent by other users. The protocol from server to client in this case is much simpler, the server just returns a bolus of text without size information.

Example 13-5. chatterclient.m

```
// chatterclient.m -- client side of the chatter world

/* compile with:
cc -g -Wall -o chatterclient chatterclient.m
*/

/* message protocol
 * first message is:
 *
 * 1 byte : length of message, no more than 8
 * length bytes : the nickname of the user
 *
 * 1 byte : length of message
 * length bytes : message, not zero-terminated
 *
 * therefore, maxmimum message size is 256 bytes
 */

#import <sys/types.h>    // random types
#import <netinet/in.h>   // for sockaddr_in
#import <sys/socket.h>   // for socket(), AF_INET
#import <netdb.h>        // for gethostbyname, h_errno, etc
#import <errno.h>        // for errno
#import <string.h>       // for strerror
#import <stdlib.h>       // for EXIT_SUCCESS
#import <stdio.h>        // for fprintf
#import <unistd.h>       // for close
#import <fcntl.h>        // for fcntl()

#define PORT_NUMBER 2342

int writeString (int fd, const void *buffer, size_t length)
{
    int result;
    unsigned char byte;

    if (length > 255) {
        fprintf (stderr, "truncating message to 255 bytes\n");
        length = 255;
    }
    byte = (unsigned char)length;

    result = write (fd, &byte, 1);
    if (result <= 0) {
        goto bailout;
    }

    do {
        result = write (fd, buffer, length);
        if (result <= 0) {
            goto bailout;
        }
        length -= result;
        buffer += result;
```

```
    } while (length > 0);

bailout:
    return (result);

} // writeAll

int main (int argc, char *argv[])
{
    int programResult = EXIT_FAILURE;
    int fd = -1, result;
    struct sockaddr_in serverAddress;
    struct hostent *hostInfo;
    unsigned char length;

    if (argc != 3) {
        fprintf (stderr, "usage: chatterclient hostname nickname\n");
        goto bailout;
    }

    // limit nickname to 8 characters
    if (strlen(argv[2]) > 8) {
        fprintf (stderr, "nickname must be 8 characters or less\n");
        goto bailout;
    }

    hostInfo = gethostbyname(argv[1]);

    if (hostInfo == NULL) {
        fprintf (stderr, "unable to gethostbyname for '%s'\n",
                argv[1]);
        fprintf (stderr, "  error: %d / %s\n", h_errno, hstrerror(h_errno));
        goto bailout;
    }
    serverAddress.sin_len = sizeof (struct sockaddr_in);
    serverAddress.sin_family = AF_INET;
    serverAddress.sin_port = htons (PORT_NUMBER);
    serverAddress.sin_addr = *((struct in_addr *)(hostInfo->h_addr));
    memset (&(serverAddress.sin_zero), 0, sizeof(serverAddress.sin_zero));

    result = socket (AF_INET, SOCK_STREAM, 0);

    if (result == -1) {
        fprintf (stderr, "could not make a socket.  error: %d / %s\n",
                errno, strerror(errno));
        goto bailout;
    }
    fd = result;

    // no need to bind() or listen()

    // set standard in to non-blocking
    result = fcntl (STDIN_FILENO, F_SETFL, O_NONBLOCK);
    if (result == -1) {
        fprintf (stderr, "setting nonblock failed.  error: %d / %s\n",
                errno, strerror(errno));
        goto bailout;
```

```
    }

    result = connect (fd, (struct sockaddr *)&serverAddress, sizeof(serverAddr

    if (result == -1) {
        fprintf (stderr, "could not connect.  error: %d / %s\n",
                errno, strerror(errno));
        goto bailout;
    }

    // first, send the nickname
    length = strlen(argv[2]);
    result = write (fd, &length, 1);

    if (result == -1) {
        fprintf (stderr, "could not write nickname length.  "
                "error: %d / %s\n",
                errno, strerror(errno));
        goto bailout;
    }

    result = write (fd, argv[2], length);
    if (result == -1) {
        fprintf (stderr, "could not write nickname.  error: %d / %s\n",
                errno, strerror(errno));
        goto bailout;
    }

    // now set to non-block
    result = fcntl (fd, F_SETFL, O_NONBLOCK);
    if (result == -1) {
        fprintf (stderr, "setting nonblock on server fd failed.  "
                "error: %d / %s\n",
                errno, strerror(errno));
        goto bailout;
    }

    do {
        fd_set readfds;
        char buffer[255];

        FD_ZERO (&readfds);
        FD_SET (STDIN_FILENO, &readfds);
        FD_SET (fd, &readfds);


        result = select (fd + 1, &readfds, NULL, NULL, NULL);

        if (result == -1) {
            fprintf (stderr, "error from select(): error %d / %s\n",
                    errno, strerror(errno));
            continue;
        }

        if (FD_ISSET (STDIN_FILENO, &readfds)) {

            result = read (STDIN_FILENO, buffer, 254);
```

```
            if (result == -1) {
                fprintf (stderr, "error reading from stdin.  "
                        "Error %d / %s\n",
                        errno, strerror(errno));
                goto bailout;
            } else if (result == 0) {
                // closed
                break;
            }
            length = result; // lop off the CR
            result = writeString (fd, buffer, length);
            if (result == -1) {
                fprintf (stderr, "error writing to chatterserver.  "
                        "error %d / %s\n",
                        errno, strerror(errno));
                goto bailout;
            }
        }
    }
    if (FD_ISSET (fd, &readfds)) {
        char largeBuffer[4096];
        result = read (fd, largeBuffer, 4096);
        if (result == -1) {
            fprintf (stderr, "error reading from chatterserver.  "
                    "error %d / %s\n",
                    errno, strerror(errno));
            goto bailout;
        } else if (result == 0) {
            fprintf (stderr, "server closed connection\n");
            break;
        } else {
            largeBuffer[result] = '\000';
            printf ("%s", largeBuffer);
        }
    }
} while (1);

programResult = EXIT_SUCCESS;

bailout:
    close (fd);

    return (programResult);

} // main
```

The main thing of interest here is the writing of the string. Just calling **write()** is not sufficient. Once the buffer associated with the socket becomes full, **write()** is welcome to return a value smaller than what you told it to write. Here you have a loop that spins over **write()** until it completes.

For the More Curious:

Datagrams

What you have been talking about in this chapter have been "stream sockets." They are a connection-oriented, reliable form of network communication. Berkeley sockets also support "datagram sockets." These are a message-oriented, unreliable form of network communication. They are unreliable in the sense that datagrams may be lost in transit, and that the receiver might not get the datagrams in the same order in which they were sent. The data in the payload is checksummed, and so it will be correct. Stream sockets use the TCP protocol, and datagrams use the UDP protocol.

Figure 13-3. tcp vs. udp

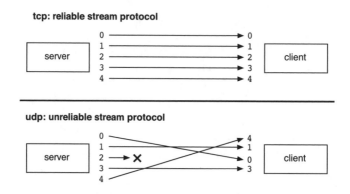

To create a datagram socket you use SOCK_DGRAM rather than SOCK_STREAM for the type parameter of **socket()**. For servers you would still **bind()** your address to the socket, but you do not call **listen()**. Clients do not have to **bind()**. They can just make a socket and then write through it.

To send and receive datagrams, you use **sendto()** and **recvfrom()**:

```
ssize_t sendto (int socket, const void *msg, size_t len, int flags,
                    const struct sockaddr *to, int tolen);
```

The arguments:

socket

> The socket to write to

msg, len

> The data and its length

flags

> Just pass zero

to, tolen

> a struct sockaddr_in of the destination and the size of the structure

The return value is the number of bytes sent, -1/`errno` on error.

```
ssize_t recvfrom (int socket, void *buf, size_t len, int flags,
                  struct sockaddr *from, int *fromlen);
```

The arguments:

`socket`

> The socket to read from

`buf, len`

> Where to deposit the incoming data

`flags`

> Just pass zero (you can pass in `MSG_PEEK` to peek at an incoming data)

`from, fromlen`

> The address of the machine that sent the message

The return value is the number of bytes read, or -1/`errno` on an error.

Challenge

1. There is a problem with the use of **write()** in the `chatterserver`. None of the writes check the number of bytes actually written, meaning that a partial write could happen. Any remaining bytes will be lost. This could happen with a busy server and lots of messages coming in and being broadcast out. To address this, a technique similar to the incoming read bytes needs to be used. Keep a buffer of outgoing data and put the `fd` into the `writefds` argument of **select()**.

2. Change `chatter` to use datagrams. The messages are small enough to fit into a single datagram. Given the quality of discussion in most chat rooms, a lost packet here or there probably is not too much of an issue. Since the messages fit into packet boundaries, and **recvfrom()** will not coalesce packets like socket streams, this should simplify a lot of the code.

Chapter 14. CFRunLoop

Unix networking is based on reading and writing with file descriptors. Using them in servers is pretty easy with the **select()** function. Using them in end-user GUI apps presents a problem. You cannot call **select()** to wait for network activity since that will cause the user interface to hang until there is something to be done on the network.

The solution lies in the *run loop*, which is an event loop that looks for events (mouse click, key press, timer firing), dispatches them to interested parties, and then waits for more. **NSRunLoop** from the Foundation libraries has a high-level API for watching for activity on mach ports, timers, and distributed object connections. **NSRunLoop** is built upon **CFRunLoop**.

Figure 14-1. The Run Loop

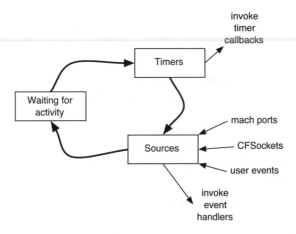

CFRunLoop is from the CoreFoundation, which has a hybrid Cocoa/Carbon flavor. You are dealing with CFReferences (which are like object pointers) and you need to retain and release them like Cocoa objects. Much of the work happens with C callbacks, which are more prevalent in the Carbon world. **CFRunLoop** is where you can put the socket file descriptors to react to network traffic and not gum up the GUI works. Note that there is one run loop per thread created with **NSThread**, so in a multithreaded application you can have multiple run loops, each handling multiple sockets.

CFSocket

CFSocket is the part of the **CFRunLoop** architecture you will be dealing with. CFSocketRef is a pointer to an opaque type, and is created with **CFSocketCreateWithNative()**:

```
CFSocketRef CFSocketCreateWithNative (CFAllocatorRef allocator,
                                      CFSocketNativeHandle sock,
                                      CFOptionFlags callBackTypes,
                                      CFSocketCallBack callout,
                                      const CFSocketContext *context);
```

There are lots of CF data types here. For `CFAllocatorRef` you can just pass NULL since you are not needing a custom allocator for this type (NULL says to use the default one).

The `CFSocketNativeHandle` is just the integer for your socket file descriptor.

`CFOptionFlags` for this call are one of these (which happens to be of an `enum` named `CFSocketCallBackType`):

kCFSocketNoCallBack

> No callback function is supplied.

kCFSocketReadCallBack

> Call the callback function when data can be read. The callback can get the data by calling **read()**.

kCFSocketAcceptCallBack

> Call the callback function when there is a new connection on a listening socket.

kCFSocketDataCallBack

> The data will be read and then packed into a **CFData** (similar to **NSData**). The callback will be called and be passed this **CFData**.

kCFSocketConnectCallBack

> The above 3 flags are mutually exclusive. This can be added if you want your socket to connect in the background. (**CFSocket** can be used also to connect to remote machines.)

`CFSocketContext` is a pointer to a struct that looks like this:

```
typedef struct {
    CFIndex        version;
    void *         info;
    const void    *(*retain)(const void *info);
    void           (*release)(const void *info);
    CFStringRef    (*copyDescription)(const void *info);
} CFSocketContext;
```

Set everything to zero or NULL for all of these. `info` is a pointer to whatever data you want (in the case of Cocoa, you can stick an object pointer there). You can see some of the Cocoa-flavored behavior in functions to perform retain and release on the context. Passing NULL for the function pointers indicates that the memory management for the item pointed to by `info` will be handled elsewhere, and that info will be valid at least as long as the life of the **CFSocket**.

The `CFSocketCallBack` is a function of the form

```
void (CFSocketRef s,
      CFSocketCallBackType type,
      CFDataRef address,
      const void *data,
      void *info);
```

The CFDataRef is what you get if you registered a kCFSocketDataCallBack. data can be ignored (it is used for the kCFSocketAcceptCallBack case), and info is the info pointer of the context structure given to **CFSocketCreateWithNative()**.

Here is some code that will register a socket, assuming you are in an object method:

```
CFSocketContext context = { 0, self, NULL, NULL, NULL };

runLoopSocket = CFSocketCreateWithNative (NULL,
                                          serverSocket,
                                          kCFSocketReadCallBack,
                                          socketCallBack,
                                          &context);
```

If runLoopSocket is NULL, something went wrong.

Once you have the CFSocketRef from this call, it is time to create a **CFRunLoopSource** with the socket. The **CFRunLoopSource** wraps the CFSocketRef such that it can be added to the run loop.

```
CFRunLoopSourceRef CFSocketCreateRunLoopSource (CFAllocatorRef allocator,
                                                CFSocketRef runLoopSocket,
                                                CFIndex order);
```

Like earlier, you can give allocator a NULL to use the default allocator. The CFSocketRef is what you got from **CFSocketCreateWithNative()** above. The order parameter can control the order in which multiple callbacks are invoked. If you do not care about the order (which is the usual case), pass zero.

Here it is in action:

```
CFRunLoopSourceRef rls;
rls = CFSocketCreateRunLoopSource (NULL, runLoopSocket, 0);
```

If the return value is NULL, something went wrong.

Finally you can add this RunLoopSourceRef to a runloop with **CFRunLoopAddSource()**:

```
void CFRunLoopAddSource (CFRunLoopRef rl,
                         CFRunLoopSourceRef source,
                         CFStringRef mode);
```

To get the current run loop, use **CFRunLoopGetCurrent()**. The source parameter is the **CFRunLoopSource** created above, and for the mode, use the constant kCFRunLoopDefaultMode. The run loop can run in other modes, like a modal panel mode.

After you add the socket to the run loop with

```
CFRunLoopAddSource (CFRunLoopGetCurrent(), rls, kCFRunLoopDefaultMode);
```

Since you created the run loop source, and the run loop itself retains the source, you need to use **CFRelease()** to keep the reference count correct.

GUI Chatter Client

The `chatterclient` from the networking chapter is all well and good if you are living on the command line. Most Mac users will understandably want to use GUI programs.

In `Project Builder`, create a new Cocoa Application project called `CFChatterClient`. Open up the `MainMenu.nib` file and layout the UI as shown:

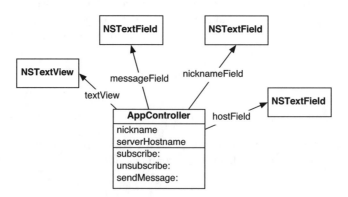

Create a subclass of **NSObject** called **AppController**. Add four outlets to the class:

- **NSTextField** *hostField
- **NSTextField** *messageField
- **NSTextField** *nicknameField
- **NSTextView** *textView

Add three actions: **sendMessage:, subscribe:, unsubscribe:**. Create files for the class and create an instance of it.

Set each outlet of the **AppController** to point to the appropriate view.

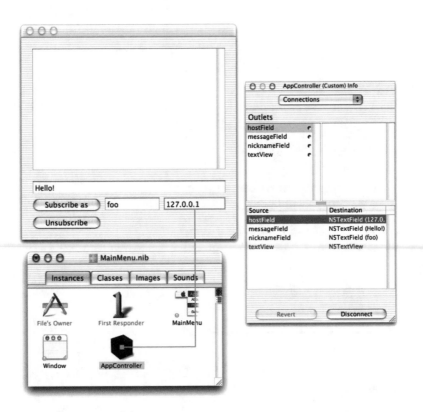

Make the **AppController** the target of the Subscribe button, the Unsubscribe button, and the message text field.

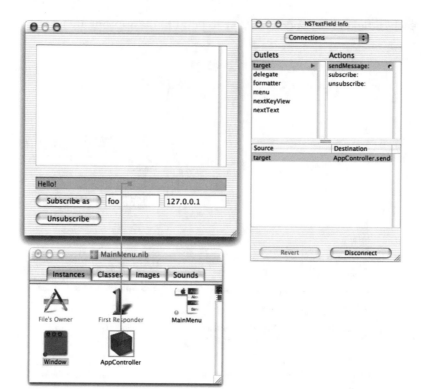

Save the nib file. Return to `Project Builder`.

Edit the class **AppController**:

Example 14-1. AppController.h

```objc
#import <Cocoa/Cocoa.h>

@interface AppController : NSObject
{
    IBOutlet    NSTextField     *hostField;
    IBOutlet    NSTextField     *messageField;
    IBOutlet    NSTextField     *nicknameField;
    IBOutlet    NSTextView      *textView;
                int              serverSocket;
                CFSocketRef      runLoopSocket;
}

- (IBAction)sendMessage:(id)sender;
- (IBAction)subscribe:(id)sender;
- (IBAction)unsubscribe:(id)sender;

@end // AppController
```

Example 14-2. AppController.m

```objc
#import "AppController.h"

#import <sys/types.h>    // random types
```

```
#import <netinet/in.h>   // for sockaddr_in
#import <sys/socket.h>   // for socket(), AF_INET
#import <netdb.h>        // for gethostbyname, h_errno, etc
#import <errno.h>        // for errno
#import <string.h>       // for strerror
#import <unistd.h>       // for close
#import <fcntl.h>        // for fcntl()

#define PORT_NUMBER 2342

int writeString (int fd, const void *buffer, size_t length)
{
    int result;
    unsigned char byte;

    if (length > 255) {
        fprintf (stderr, "truncating message to 255 bytes\n");
        length = 255;
    }
    byte = (unsigned char)length;

    result = write (fd, &byte, 1);
    if (result <= 0) {
        goto bailout;
    }

    do {
        result = write (fd, buffer, length);
        if (result <= 0) {
            goto bailout;
        }
        length -= result;
        buffer += result;

    } while (length > 0);

bailout:
    return (result);

} // writeString


@implementation AppController

- (id)init
{
    if (self = [super init]) {
        serverSocket = -1;
    }

    return (self);

} // init

- (void)updateUI
{
    // enable the message field if we are connected
```

```
        [messageField setEnabled: (runLoopSocket != NULL)];

    } // updateUI

    - (void)awakeFromNib
    {
        [nicknameField setStringValue: NSUserName ()];
        [self updateUI];
    } // awakeFromNib

    - (void)closeConnection
    {
        if (runLoopSocket != NULL) {
            CFSocketInvalidate (runLoopSocket);
            CFRelease (runLoopSocket);
        } else {
            close (serverSocket);
        }
        serverSocket = -1;
        runLoopSocket = NULL;

        [self updateUI];

    } // closeConnection

    - (void) dealloc
    {
        [self closeConnection];
        [super dealloc];
    } // dealloc

    - (void)showErrorMessage:(NSString *)message
                   sysError:(const char *)string
    {
        NSString *errnoString = @"";

        if (string != NULL) {
            errnoString = [[NSString alloc] initWithCString:string];
            [errnoString autorelease];
        }

        (void) NSRunAlertPanel (message, errnoString, @"OK", nil, nil);

    } // showErrorMessage

    - (IBAction)sendMessage:(id)sender
    {
        if (serverSocket != -1) {
            NSString *messageString;
            const char *message;
            unsigned char length;
            int result;

            // need to add newline to match behavior of the command-line client
            messageString = [[messageField stringValue]
                                            stringByAppendingString:@"\n"];
            message = [messageString cString];
```

```
            length = strlen (message);

            if (length > 1) {

                result = writeString (serverSocket, message, length);

                if (result == -1) {
                    NSLog (@"error writing: %s\n", strerror(errno));
                }
                [messageField setStringValue:@""];
            }
        }

} // sendMessage

- (void)appendMessage:(NSString *)string
{
    NSRange range;
    range = NSMakeRange ([[textView string] length], 0);

    [textView replaceCharactersInRange:range withString:string];

    range = NSMakeRange ([[textView string] length],
                         [[textView string] length]);

    [textView scrollRangeToVisible:range];

} // appendMessageAndScrollToEnd

- (void)readFromSocket
{
    int result;
    char buffer[5000];

    result = read (serverSocket, buffer, 5000 - 1);

    if (result == 0) {
        // other side closed
        [self closeConnection];
        NSLog (@"other side closed connection");
        [self showErrorMessage:@"Server closed the connection"
            sysError:NULL];

    } else if (result == -1) {
        [self showErrorMessage:@"Error reading from server"
            sysError:strerror(errno)];

    } else {
        [self appendMessage:[NSString stringWithCString:buffer
                                                 length:result]];
    }

} // readFromSocket

void socketCallBack (CFSocketRef socketref, CFSocketCallBackType type,
                     CFDataRef address, const void *data, void *info)
{
```

```
        AppController *me = (AppController *) info;

        [me readFromSocket];

    } // socketCallBack

    - (void)addSocketMonitor
    {
        CFSocketContext context = { 0, self, NULL, NULL, NULL };
        CFRunLoopSourceRef rls;

        runLoopSocket = CFSocketCreateWithNative (NULL,
                                                  serverSocket,
                                                  kCFSocketReadCallBack,
                                                  socketCallBack,
                                                  &context);
        if (runLoopSocket == NULL) {
            // something went wrong
            [self showErrorMessage:@"could not CFSocketCreateWithNative"
                    sysError:NULL];
            goto bailout;
        }

        rls = CFSocketCreateRunLoopSource (NULL, runLoopSocket, 0);
        if (rls == NULL) {
            [self showErrorMessage:@"could not create a run loop source"
                    sysError:NULL];
            goto bailout;
        }

        CFRunLoopAddSource (CFRunLoopGetCurrent(), rls,
                            kCFRunLoopDefaultMode);
        CFRelease (rls);

bailout:
        return;

    } // addSocketMonitor

    - (IBAction)subscribe:(id)sender
    {
        NSString *errorMessage = nil;
        char *sysError = NULL;
        int result;
        struct sockaddr_in serverAddress;


        if (serverSocket != -1) {
            [self closeConnection];
        }

        // sanity check our nick name before trying to connect
        if ([[nicknameField stringValue] length] == 0 ||
            [[nicknameField stringValue] length] > 8) {
            errorMessage = @"Nickname should be between 1 and 8 characters";
            goto bailout;
        }
```

```
{
    struct hostent *hostInfo;
    const char *hostname = [[hostField stringValue] cString];

    hostInfo = gethostbyname (hostname);
    if (hostInfo == NULL) {
        errorMessage = [NSString stringWithFormat:
                        @"Could not resolve host '%s'",hostname];
        sysError = hstrerror(h_errno);
        goto bailout;
    }

    serverAddress.sin_len = sizeof (struct sockaddr_in);
    serverAddress.sin_family = AF_INET;
    serverAddress.sin_port = htons (PORT_NUMBER);
    serverAddress.sin_addr = *((struct in_addr *)(hostInfo->h_addr));
    memset (&(serverAddress.sin_zero), 0, sizeof(serverAddress.sin_zero));
}

serverSocket = socket (AF_INET, SOCK_STREAM, 0);

if (serverSocket == -1) {
    errorMessage = @"Could not create server socket.  Error is %s.";
    sysError = strerror (errno);
    goto bailout;
}

result = connect (serverSocket, (struct sockaddr *)&serverAddress,
                  sizeof(serverAddress));
if (result == -1) {
    errorMessage = @"could not connect to server";
    sysError = strerror (errno);
    goto bailout;
}

// write out the nickname
{
    const char *nickname;
    unsigned char length;
    nickname = [[nicknameField stringValue] cString];
    length = strlen (nickname);

    result = write (serverSocket, &length, 1);
    if (result == -1) {
        errorMessage = @"Could not write nickname length";
        sysError = strerror (errno);
        goto bailout;
    }
    result = write (serverSocket, nickname, length);
    if (result == -1) {
        errorMessage = @"could not write nickname.";
        sysError = strerror (errno);
        goto bailout;
    }
}
}
```

```
    // set the serverSocket to non-blocking
    result = fcntl (serverSocket, F_SETFL, O_NONBLOCK);
    if (result == -1) {
        errorMessage = @"Could not set serverSocket to nonblocking mode.";
        sysError = strerror(errno);
        goto bailout;
    }

    // yay!  We are done.
    [self addSocketMonitor];

bailout:
    if (errorMessage != nil) {
        [self showErrorMessage: errorMessage  sysError: sysError];
        [self closeConnection];
    }

    [self updateUI];

} // subscribe

- (void)unsubscribe:(id)sender
{
    [self closeConnection];

} // unsubscribe

@end // AppController
```

Run the `chatterserver` from the networking chapter. Build and run this client.

The System Configuration Framework

The user is free to change aspects of the system configuration at any time, such as changing their network location from "Office" to "Home". Changing the network location could change a number of lower-level settings, such as which IP addresses the machine has available and which DNS servers to use. There are also system parameters that change dynamically, such as the battery level in laptops. In some situations, your application needs to be able to react to these changes. For example, if you have a network socket listening on a particular IP address (as opposed to listening on all of them), you'll need to listen on the new IP if the user changes it.

In Mac OS X 10.1, Apple introduced the system configuration framework which provides an architecture for storing configuration and run-time information. Currently it only supports network configuration and the powerbook battery monitor, but in the future more information will be supported.

Architecture

At the heart of the system configuration framework is `configd`, the system configuration daemon. `configd` holds the dynamic store, which is an online database of configuration information consisting of key/value pairs. These pairs are arranged in a hierarchy, like nested dictionaries, and are addressed by paths similar to the URLs used to identify web pages. There are two major spaces, one for "setup" information (what is set in configuration applications) and one for "State" information (what is actually configured and running). The keys look like `State:/Network/Service/serviceID/IPv4` for the current IP state, and like `Setup:/Network/Service/serviceID/PPP` for PPP configuration.

Much of the persistent configuration information is stored in the preferences file, which lives at `/var/db/SystemConfiguration/preferences.xml`. It is an xml file in preference list style. `configd` reads this file and places its contents into the dynamic store. There are also configuration agents, which are bundles that `configd` loads that provide configuration and notification services. Currently there are agents to monitor the preferences, to monitor the kernel and track the state of all network interfaces, as well as a PPP controller.

The documentation lives in `/Developer/Documentation/Networking`, which primarily describes the access paths and storage structure for the networking world. The API documentation lives in a couple of Apple tech notes (TN1145 and QA1133) and the header files in `/System/Library/Frameworks/SystemConfiguration.framework/`.

Basic API

The system configuration framework source code is included in Darwin, so you can poke around and see how things work. The API lives at the Core Foundation level, and so shares similarities to the rest of the Core Foundation API. The examples here that query the dynamic store will be primarily Cocoa based, and take advantage of the toll-free bridging between Core Foundation data structures and the equivalent Cocoa data structures. (toll-free bridging lets you cast `CF*` pointers to their equivalent `NS*` types, such as `CFString` and `NSString`, or `CFArray` and `NSArray`);

For querying the dynamic store, perform these steps:

1. Connect to `configd`'s dynamic store with **`SCDynamicStoreCreate()`**.

2. Construct some access keys, either by explicitly constructing the paths or by supplying a regular expression to **`SCDynamicStoreCopyKeyList()`**.

3. Iterate over the keys and call **`SCDynamicStoreCopyValue()`** to fetch the value. Or you can use **`SCDynamicStoreCopyMultiple()`** to fetch the values for all keys at once. This second call provides a read-consistent view to the data. Use the `CopyMultiple` version of the function when you can to prevent possible race conditions when performing multiple calls to `CopyValue`.

4. If you want to be notified when a particular value changes, call **`SCDynamicStoreSetNotificationKeys()`** and tell it which keys you are interested in.

Here are the calls in more detail.

```
SCDynamicStoreRef
SCDynamicStoreCreate (CFAllocatorRef allocator,
                      CFStringRef name,
                      SCDynamicStoreCallBack callback,
```

```
                    SCDynamicStoreContext *context);
```

Creates a new session to talk to `configd`. The parameters are:

allocator

> The allocator used to allocate memory for the local object and for any storage it may need. Just pass NULL to use the default allocator.

name

> A string (which can be cast from an NSString pointer) that names the calling process

callback

> A callback function that will get called when values change for the keys given to **SCDyanmicStoreSetNotificationKeys()**

context

> A structure just like CFSocketContext, where you give the version, a pointer, and some function pointers to retain and release functions. In Cocoa, you can make one of these like this:

```
        SCDynamicStoreContext context = {
            0, self, NULL, NULL, NULL
        };
```

CFArrayRef
SCDynamicStoreCopyKeyList (SCDynamicStoreRef store,
                            CFStringRef pattern);

Returns an array of string keys that match a given regular expression.

store

> The dynamic store reference that **SCDynamicStoreCreate()** returned

pattern

> A regular expression (not the simple shell globs used elsewhere) that matches the keys you're looking for. For instance, ".*" will match everything, and "State:/Network/Service/[^/]+/IPv4" will match IPv4 network service urls with for any service name.

CFPropertyListRef
SCDynamicStoreCopyValue (SCDynamicStoreRef store,
                            CFStringRef key);

Returns either a string or a dictionary with the value requested.

store

> The dynamic store reference from **SCDynamicStoreCreate()**.

key

> The key representing the data you want, either specified explicitly or taken from **SCDynamicStoreCopyKeyList()**.

```
CFDictionaryRef
SCDynamicStoreCopyMultiple (SCDynamicStoreRef store,
                            CFArrayRef keys,
                            CFArrayRef patterns);
```

Like **SCDynamicStoreCopyValue()**, but returns the values for a set of keys. It returns a dictionary containing the values.

store

The dynamic store reference from **SCDynamicStoreCreate()**.

keys

The set of keys that indicate the values to return.

patterns

Regular expression patterns to match keys in the dynamic store.

```
Boolean
SCDynamicStoreSetNotificationKeys (SCDynamicStoreRef store,
                                   CFArrayRef keys,
                                   CFArrayRef patterns);
```

This tells the dynamic store which keys and patterns of keys are interesting. When the values change, the callback function specified with **SCDynamicStoreCreate()** is called.

store

The dynamic store connection

keys

The keys of interest

patterns

regular expression indicating more keys of interest

The callback function should look like this:

```
void storeCallback (SCDynamicStoreRef store, CFArrayRef changedKeys,
                    void *info);
```

store

Is the dynamic store the callback has been associated with

changedKeys

An array of keys that have new values

info

The pointer specified in the second field of the context passed to **SCDynamicStoreCreate()**.

There are also some convenience functions like
`SCDynamicStoreCopyLocalHostName()` to get the current host name, and if you
want notifications on the current host name, you can call
`SCDyanmicStoreKeyCreateHostNames()` to get the key to pass to
`SCDynamicStoreSetNotificationkeys()`.

Seeing all values

Here is a foundation tool that will show all of the keys and values in `configd`'s
dynamic store:

Example 14-3. scf-dump.m

```
/* scf-dump.m -- show all the live entries from the
 *                SystemConfiguration.framework
 */

/* compile with:
cc -g -Wall -framework Foundation -framework SystemConfiguration \
   -o scf-dump scf-dump.m
*/

#import <Foundation/Foundation.h>
#import <SystemConfiguration/SystemConfiguration.h>

/* a little utility function to NSLog information, but without the
 * leading noise information like the current time and process ID
 */

void LogIt (NSString *format, ...)
{
    va_list args;
    va_start (args, format);

    NSString *string;
    // the string format stuff will expand %@, which regular v*printf
    // won't do
    string = [[NSString alloc] initWithFormat: format  arguments:args];

    va_end (args);

    printf ("%s\n", [string cString]);

    [string release];

} // LogIt

// print the contents of a dictionary (string keys, string values)

void dumpDictionary (NSDictionary *dictionary)
{
    NSArray *keys;
    NSArray *values;
    int i;

    keys = [dictionary allKeys];
```

```
    values = [dictionary objectsForKeys:keys  notFoundMarker:nil];

    for (i = 0; i < [keys count]; i++) {
        LogIt (@"    %@ : %@", [keys objectAtIndex:i],
               [values objectAtIndex:i]);
    }

} // dumpDictionary

int main (int argc, const char *argv[])
{
    NSAutoreleasePool *pool = [[NSAutoreleasePool alloc] init];

    // make a connection to the configd

    SCDynamicStoreRef store;
    SCDynamicStoreContext context = {
        0, NULL, NULL, NULL, NULL
    };

    store = SCDynamicStoreCreate (NULL,                    // allocator
                                  SCSTR("SCF Dumper"),  // name
                                  NULL,                   // callback
                                  &context);              // DynStore context
    if (store == NULL) {
        NSLog (@"oops!  can't SCDynamicStoreCreate");
        goto bailout;
    }

    // get a list of all the keys.  the .* regexp will match everything
    CFArrayRef keys;
    keys = SCDynamicStoreCopyKeyList (store, SCSTR(".*"));

    if (keys == NULL) {
        NSLog (@"oops!  can't SCDynamicStoreCopyKeyList");
        goto bailout;
    }

    // walk the set of keys.  It returns a CFArrayRef, which is
    // toll-free-bridged to an NSArray, so we can use the
    // NSArray enumerator

    CFStringRef key;

    NSEnumerator *enumerator;
    enumerator = [((NSArray*)keys) objectEnumerator];

    while ((key = (CFStringRef)[enumerator nextObject])) {

        LogIt (@"key is %@", key);

        // get the value from configd
        CFPropertyListRef value;
        value = SCDynamicStoreCopyValue (store, key);

        // some values are keys, others are dictionaries withricher
        // result values
```

```
            if ([(id)value isKindOfClass:[NSDictionary class]]) {
                dumpDictionary ((NSDictionary *) value);
            } else {
                LogIt (@"    %@", (id)value);
            }
            LogIt (@"\n");
        }

bailout:
    [pool release];

    return (EXIT_SUCCESS);

} // main
```

and part of a sample run:

```
% ./scf-dump
key is State:/Network/Global/DNS
    ServerAddresses : ("198.77.116.8", "198.77.116.12")

key is Setup:/Network/Service/5/DNS
    ServerAddresses : ("198.77.116.8", "198.77.116.12")

key is Setup:/System
    ComputerNameEncoding : 0
    ComputerName : iLamp

key is State:/Network/Service/4/IPv4
    Addresses : ("192.168.0.123")
    SubnetMasks : ("255.255.255.0")
    InterfaceName : en0

key is State:/Network/Interface
    Interfaces : (lo0, gif0, stf0, en0, en1)
...
```

SCFMonitor

The SCFMonitor application shows the current host name, the person logged in on the console, and the local IP address(es). Notifications are registered to keep the values up to date, although the console user won't change without a logout. The system configuration framework does not provide any notification or information about users logged in via the network.

Figure 14-2. SCFMonitor window

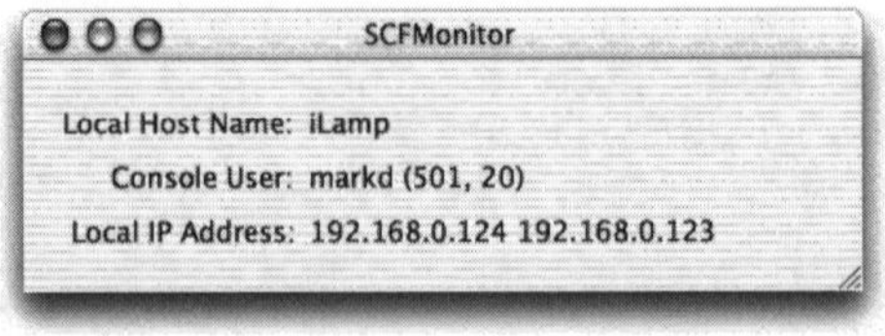

In `Project Builder`, create a new Cocoa Application project called `SCFMonitor`. Add the system configuration framework by choosing **Add Frameworks** from the **Project** menu and selecting `SystemConfiguration.framework`. Then open the `MainMenu.nib` file and layout the UI as shown with 6 static text labels:

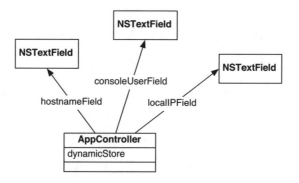

Create a subclass of **NSObject** called **AppController**. Add three outlets to the class:

- **NSTextField** *`hostnameField`
- **NSTextField** *`consoleUserField`
- **NSTextField** *`localIPField`

There is no direct user action in this program, so no need to add any actions.

Set each outlet of the **AppController** to point to the appropriate text field.

Save the nib file and return to `Project Builder`.

Edit the **AppController**.

Example 14-4. AppController.h

```
#import <Cocoa/Cocoa.h>
#import <SystemConfiguration/SystemConfiguration.h>

@interface AppController : NSObject
{
    IBOutlet    NSTextField    *hostnameField;
    IBOutlet    NSTextField    *consoleUserField;
    IBOutlet    NSTextField    *localIPField;

    SCDynamicStoreRef    dynamicStore;
```

```
    }

    - (void)refreshUI;

    - (NSString *)hostname;
    - (NSString *)consoleUser;
    - (NSString *)localIPs;

    @end // AppController
```

And then add the code to `AppController.m`:

Example 14-5. AppController.m

```
#import "AppController.h"

// result is a dictionary with Name, UID, and GID keys
#define CONSOLE_USER_KEY        (CFSTR("State:/Users/ConsoleUser"))

// result is a dictionary with a LocalHostName key.
// For illustration, this uses the convenience API for dealing
// with hostnames.  Change this by tweaking the Rendezvous Name
// in the Sharing preferences
#define HOSTNAME_KEY            (SCDynamicStoreKeyCreateHostNames(NULL))

// match any IPv4 service.  The "[^/]+" part of the pattern means
// "match one or more characters that are not slashes"
#define IP_PATTERN (CFSTR("State:/Network/Service/[^/]+/IPv4"))

// gets called when the dynamic store changes

void storeCallback (SCDynamicStoreRef store, CFArrayRef changedKeys,
                    void *info)
{
    NSLog (@"storeCallback: changedKeys is %@", changedKeys);

    AppController *controller = (AppController *)info;

    [controller refreshUI];

} // storeCallback


@implementation AppController

- (NSString *) hostname
{
    CFStringRef hostname;

    hostname = SCDynamicStoreCopyLocalHostName (dynamicStore);

    return ((NSString *) hostname);

} // hostname

- (NSString *) consoleUser
```

```
{
    NSArray *keyList;
    keyList =
        (NSArray *) SCDynamicStoreCopyKeyList (dynamicStore,
                                                CONSOLE_USER_KEY);

    CFStringRef consoleValueKey;
    consoleValueKey = (CFStringRef)[keyList objectAtIndex:0];

    NSDictionary *consoleUserDict;
    consoleUserDict =
        (NSDictionary *)SCDynamicStoreCopyValue (dynamicStore,
                                                consoleValueKey);

    NSMutableString *consoleUser;
    consoleUser = [[NSMutableString alloc] init];

    // make a string of the form "username (user-id, group-id)"
    [consoleUser appendString:[consoleUserDict objectForKey @"Name"]];
    [consoleUser appendFormat:@" (%@, %@)",
                [consoleUserDict objectForKey:@"UID"],
                [consoleUserDict objectForKey:@"GID"]];

    return (consoleUser);

} // consoleUser

- (NSString *) localIPs
{
    NSMutableString *localIPs;

    localIPs = [[NSMutableString alloc] init];


    // make an array of stuff so we can use SCDynamicStoreCopyMultiple
    // and get a consistent snapshot, since there may be several IP
    // addresses, rather than several calls to SCDynamicStoreCopyValue

    NSArray *patternList;
    patternList = [NSArray arrayWithObject:(NSString *)IP_PATTERN];

    NSDictionary *dictionary;
    dictionary =
        (NSDictionary*)SCDynamicStoreCopyMultiple (dynamicStore,
                            NULL,  // keys
                            (CFArrayRef)patternList);
    // now walk the dictionary.
    // the key is an identifier, like State:/Network/Service/5/IPv4
    // the value is another dictionary, which has a key of "Addresses"
    // that is an array strings, which are the actual IP addresses

    NSEnumerator *enumerator;
    enumerator = [dictionary keyEnumerator];

    NSString *key;
    while ((key = [enumerator nextObject])) {
        NSDictionary *oneConfig;
```

```
        oneConfig = [dictionary objectForKey: key];

        NSArray *addresses;
        addresses = [oneConfig objectForKey: @"Addresses"];

        // now walk the addresses
        NSEnumerator *addressesEnumerator;
        addressesEnumerator = [addresses objectEnumerator];

        NSString *address;
        while ((address = [addressesEnumerator nextObject])) {
            [localIPs appendString: address];
            [localIPs appendString: @" "];
        }
    }

    return (localIPs);

} // localIP

- (void) refreshUI
{
    [hostnameField setStringValue:[self hostname]];
    [consoleUserField setStringValue:[self consoleUser]];
    [localIPField setStringValue:[self localIPs]];

} // refreshUI

- (void) awakeFromNib
{
    // create the dynamic store
    SCDynamicStoreContext context = {
        0, self, NULL, NULL, NULL
    };

    dynamicStore = SCDynamicStoreCreate (NULL,              // allocator
                                CFSTR("SCFMonitor"), // name
                                storeCallback,       // callback
                                &context);        // context
    if (dynamicStore == NULL) {
        NSLog (@"could not create dynamic store reference");
    }

    // what are we interested in receiving notifications about?
    NSArray *noteKeys, *notePatterns;

    noteKeys = [NSArray arrayWithObjects:
                        (NSString *) HOSTNAME_KEY,
                        (NSString *) CONSOLE_USER_KEY,
                        nil];
    notePatterns = [NSArray arrayWithObject:
                            (NSString *) IP_PATTERN];
    // register those notifications
    if (!SCDynamicStoreSetNotificationKeys(dynamicStore,
                                (CFArrayRef) noteKeys,
                                (CFArrayRef) notePatterns)) {
        NSLog (@"could not register notification keys");
```

```
    }

    // create a run loop source
    CFRunLoopSourceRef runLoopSource;

    runLoopSource = SCDynamicStoreCreateRunLoopSource (NULL, // allocator
                                                       dynamicStore,
                                                       0);    // order
    // stick it into the current runloop

    CFRunLoopRef runLoop = CFRunLoopGetCurrent ();
    CFRunLoopAddSource (runLoop, runLoopSource, kCFRunLoopDefaultMode);

    CFRelease (runLoopSource);

    [self refreshUI];

} // awakeFromNib

@end // AppController
```

Build and run it. If you have two IP addresses, they should both show up in the window. If you have an airport card and built-in ethernet, they can each have their own IP (but you may need to plug in an ethernet cable for the OS to acknowledge that the interface should be used).

If you change an IP, you can see it disappear from the window for a couple of seconds, and then reappear as the network interface is taken down and is brought back up to effect the change. You can change the hostname by editing the **Rendezvous Name** in the Sharing preferences.

For the More Curious

You can hook more stuff into the run loop, such as an observer. A run loop observer has its callback function invoked at a number of well defined places:

- When the run loop is entered
- Before timers are fired
- After timers are fired
- Before sources (like the **CFSocket**) are checked
- Before the run loop waits for activity (blocking until it can do something)
- After it wakes up
- When the run loop exits

Figure 14-3. Run Loop Observation Points

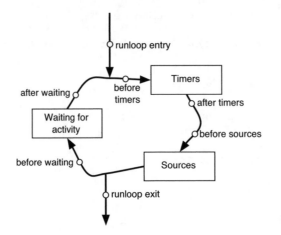

Here is a function that will register an observer:

```
void addRunLoopObserver ()
{
    CFRunLoopRef rl;
    CFRunLoopObserverRef observer;

    rl = CFRunLoopGetCurrent ();

    observer = CFRunLoopObserverCreate (NULL, // allocator
                        kCFRunLoopAllActivities, // activites
                        1, // repeats
                        0, // order
                        observerCallback,
                        NULL); // context

    CFRunLoopAddObserver (rl, observer, kCFRunLoopDefaultMode);

    CFRelease (observer);

} // addRunLoopObserver
```

This works in a very similar way to the `CFSocketRef`, except here you do not have to create an independent run loop source. You cannot use an observer for anything useful outside of a run loop, so the designers removed that step.

Here is an observer function which will print out what action is being observed:

```
typedef struct observerActivity {
    int          activity;
    const char *name;
} observerActivity;

observerActivity g_activities[] = {
    { kCFRunLoopEntry,          "Run Loop Entry" },
    { kCFRunLoopBeforeTimers,   "Before Timers" },
    { kCFRunLoopBeforeSources,  "Before Sources" },
    { kCFRunLoopBeforeWaiting,  "Before Waiting" },
```

```
    { kCFRunLoopAfterWaiting,    "After Waiting" },
    { kCFRunLoopExit,            "Exit" }
};

void observerCallback (CFRunLoopObserverRef observer,
                       CFRunLoopActivity activity,
                       void *info)
{
    observerActivity *scan, *stop;

    scan = g_activities;
    stop = scan + (sizeof(g_activities) / sizeof(observerActivity));

    while (scan < stop) {

        if (scan->activity == activity) {
            NSLog (@"%s", scan->name);
            break;
        }
        scan++;
    }

} // observerCallback
```

Challenge

1. Add the observer callback to your `CFChatterClient`.

2. If you run `scf-dump` on a powerbook, you'll probably see something like this:

   ```
   key is State:/IOKit/PowerSources/InternalBattery-0
       Max Capacity : 962
       Current Capacity : 962
       Name : InternalBattery-0
       Is Present : 1
       Is Charging : 0
       Time to Full Charge : 0
       Transport Type : Internal
       Time to Empty : 0
       Power Source State : AC Power
   ```

Extend the `SCFMonitor` application to monitor battery information, and display it in a tableview.

Chapter 15. Multiprocessing

All modern operating systems are multiprocessing, meaning that there are multiple independent programs running simultaneously and sharing the system's resources. The OS time-slices among the runnable programs, dividing the available CPU time among runnable processes (those that are not blocked by I/O). Using multiple processes allows multiple CPUs to be used as well.

Process Scheduling

The scheduler is the part of the OS that figures out what program should get the CPU next. It uses information such as process priority, how much CPU time a process has previously gotten, whether it has just completed an I/O operation, and other factors to decide what to run next.

Each process has a priority, an integer in the range from -20 to 20. Smaller values are actually higher priority than greater values. You can set the priority of a new program by running it with the `nice` command while the `renice` command changes the priority of a running process. You can "nice down" (using a larger number for the priority) your own programs, but you cannot "nice up" a program unless you have superuser privileges.

Internally, the scheduler has a list of processes with their individual priorities. Those that are not blocked are put into the run queue in order of priority. When it is time to run a new process, the scheduler pulls a process off the front of the queue, lets it run until it blocks for some reason or its time slice expires, then sticks it back in the queue.

Figure 15-1. The Scheduler

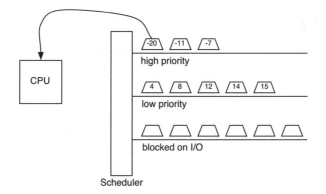

The load average shown by top and uptime:

```
2:10PM  up 6 days, 16:28, 5 users, load averages: 0.36, 0.39, 0.36
```

This is the average of the number of runnable processes (the depth of the run queue) over the last 1, 5, and 15 minutes. Here you can see that about a third of the time there is something in the run queue, and it is pretty constant over time. Mac OS X's load average just reports the depth of the run queue. It does not include the time blocked in disk I/O, which some Unix-like OSs (such as Linux) report.

A general rule of thumb is that a healthy machine, CPU-wise, has a load average at or less than two times the number of processors.

Convenience Functions

The easiest way to start another program is to use the **system()** function. This will start a program, wait until it finishes, and then return the result code. **system()** actually passes control to a new shell (/bin/sh) so you can use shell features like redirection.

```
int system (const char *string);
```

The return value is the result code from the program, or else -1 is returned and errno is set if there was an error before starting the shell. A return value of 127 means the shell failed for some reason (probably due to bad syntax in the command string). **system()** invokes the shell with the -c argument, passing in the command line. You can use this too if you get this error and want to experiment.

If you want to actually read or write to the program you start, use **popen()** to start the program and open a pipe to it. **pclose()** closes the connection:

```
FILE *popen (const char *command, const char *type);

int pclose (FILE *stream);
```

Like **system()**, **popen()** invokes a shell to run the command. Here is a little program that **popen**s the cal program to get a current calendar. Just for fun, the output from cal gets run through rev to reverse the lines (just to show that pipelines work in **popen()**). It does the equivalent of a head -9 by only reading the first nine lines.

Example 15-1. pcal.m

```
// pcal.m -- display a calendar using popen

/* compile with:
cc -g -Wall -o pcal pcal.m
*/

#import <stdio.h>        // for popen, printf
#import <stdlib.h>       // for EXIT_SUCCESS

#define BUFSIZE   4096
#define NUM_LINES 9

int main (int argc, char *argv[])
{
    int result = EXIT_FAILURE;
    FILE *pipeline = NULL;
    char buffer[BUFSIZE];
    int i;

    // reverse the lines just for fun
    pipeline = popen ("cal 2003 | rev", "r");
```

```
        if (pipeline == NULL) {
            fprintf (stderr, "error popening pipeline\n");
            goto bailout;
        }

        for (i = 0; i < NUM_LINES; i++) {
            if (fgets(buffer, BUFSIZE, pipeline) == NULL) {
                fprintf (stderr, "error reading from pipeline\n");
                goto bailout;
            }

            printf ("%s", buffer);
        }

        result = EXIT_SUCCESS;

bailout:

        if (pipeline != NULL) {
            pclose (pipeline);
        }

        return (result);

} // main
```

The man page for **popen()** says that you can use a bidirectional channel (meaning you can both write to and read from the pipeline), but it appears to be broken as of Mac OS X 10.2. Here is a sample run:

```
% ./pcal
                            3002

         hcraM                    yraurbeF                    yraunaJ
 S  F  hT W  uT M  S     S  F  hT W  uT M  S     S  F  hT W  uT M  S
 1                       1                       4  3  2  1
 8  7  6  5  4  3  2     8  7  6  5  4  3  2    11 01  9  8  7  6  5
51 41 31 21 11 01  9    51 41 31 21 11 01  9    81 71 61 51 41 31 21
22 12 02 91 81 71 61    22 12 02 91 81 71 61    52 42 32 22 12 02 91
92 82 72 62 52 42 32       82 72 62 52 42 32    13 03 92 82 72 62
```

fork

To create a new process in Unix you must first make a copy of an existing process. That copy can continue to execute as an independent entity, or it can then be replaced with another program. The **fork()** system call is used to make this copy:

```
pid_t fork (void);
```

fork() makes a copy of the running process. In the original process (known as the parent) **fork()** returns the process ID of the new process. In the child process, **fork()** returns zero. In the case of errors, it returns -1 and sets errno.

What is meant by making a copy of the process? All of the memory in the parent process is available to the child, as are open files, real and effective user and group IDs, the current working directory, the signal mask, the file mode creation mask (umasK), the environment, resource limits, and any attached shared memory segments.

Figure 15-2. Fork

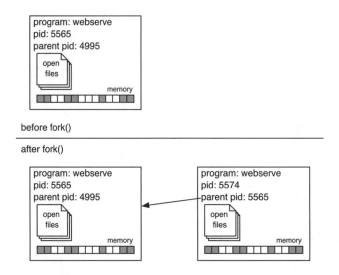

Note that Mac OS X does not really make a deep copy of the parent's memory space. It uses a technique called *copy on write* where all the physical pages that relate to this process are marked as read-only. If either process tries to modify something in memory, that particular page is then duplicated so that each process is given its own copy. This greatly reduces the amount of work the OS does on a `fork()`.

Figure 15-3. Copy On Write

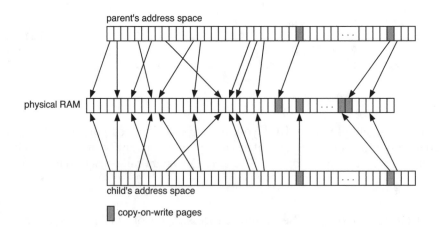

The convenience functions in the previous section (`system()` and `popen()`) call `fork()`, but for most purposes are rather heavy-weight and use more resources than a careful use of `fork()` would.

Here is a minimal program that makes a child:

Example 15-2. fork.m

```
// fork.m -- show simple use of fork()

/* compile with:
cc -g -Wall -o fork fork.m
*/

#import <sys/types.h>    // for pid_t
#import <unistd.h>       // for fork
#import <stdlib.h>       // for EXIT_SUCCESS
#import <stdio.h>        // for printf

int main (int argc, char *argv[])
{
    pid_t child;

    printf ("hello there");

    if ((child = fork())) {
        printf ("\nChild pid is %ld\n", (long)child);
        sleep (5);
    } else {
        printf ("\nIn the child.  My parent is %ld\n", (long)getppid());
        _exit (EXIT_SUCCESS);
    }

    exit (EXIT_SUCCESS);

} // main
```

and a sample run:

```
% ./fork
hello there
Child pid is 2870
hello there
In the child.  My parent is 2869
```

As with just about everything in Unix-land, there are some gotchas. The first involves race conditions between the parent and the child: you are not guaranteed which will run first. The other relates to how open files are shared between the two processes. Both the parent and child share the same file table entry in the kernel, which means that the current offset of the file is shared. This is commonly the desired behavior — when you want both child and parent to print to the same standard out, each process will increment the offset in the file when they print, so they'll avoid writing over each other. However, it can also be confusing when your file offsets move from underneath you and you weren't expecting them to.

Related to the file table issue is the state of the buffers for buffered I/O. Since these buffers are in the program's address space, these buffers get duplicated across the fork. If there is content in the buffer before the fork, both the child and the parent could print out the buffered data twice (like what happened in the sample above), which may not be what you want.

Figure 15-4. Files After Fork

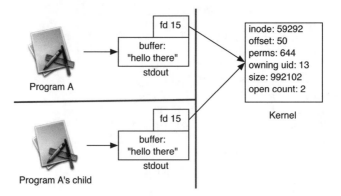

In the above program, note the use of **_exit()**. It behaves like **exit()**, closing file descriptors, generally cleaning up, but does not flush standard out, so you do not have to worry about **exit()** flushing a buffer with duplicate data. In this example, though, the newline in the subsequent **printf**s flushed the buffer for us.

Parent And Child Lifetimes

Due to the nature of **fork()**, every process has exactly one parent process, and a parent can have multiple child processes. When a process exits, it has a certain amount of state information (like its result code, system resource usage, etc.) that it wants to report to its parent. You use one of the **wait()** family of system calls to get this information (this is called *reaping the child process*).

```
pid_t wait (int *status);

pid_t waitpid (pid_t wpid, int *status, int options);

pid_t wait3 (int *status, int options, struct rusage *rusage);

pid_t wait4 (pid_t wpid, int *status, int options, struct rusage *rusage);
```

In general, calling a wait function will collect the result code from the child. **wait()** will block until there is an exited child waiting. If there are multiple child processes that have exited, **wait()** will return an arbitrary one of those. If you want to wait for a specific child process, use **waitpid()**. The options that **waitpid()** (and **wait3()** and **wait4()**) use are:

WNOHANG

Do not block waiting for a child. Return immediately if there are no exited children.

WUNTRACED

Report job-control actions on children (like being stopped or backgrounded).

wait3() is like **wait()**, and **wait4()** is like **waitpid()**, in that they either wait on an arbitrary child or a specific one, but they fill in a structure about resources

consumed by the child. You can find the full `struct rusage` in
`/usr/include/sys/resource.h`. The more interesting elements of this structure
are:

```
struct rusage {
    struct timeval ru_utime;        /* user time used */
    struct timeval ru_stime;        /* system time used */
    long    ru_maxrss;              /* max resident set size */
}
```

So you can see how much CPU was consumed as well as the child's high water
mark for memory usage.

The status value, along with a bunch of other useful bits of information, are encoded
in the status value returned by all the **wait()** functions. Use these macros to pull
them out:

WIFEXITED

> True if the process terminated normally via a call to **exit()** or **_exit()**.

WEXITSTATUS

> The low-order byte of the argument the child passed to **exit()** or **_exit()**.
> This assumes WIFEXITED(status) is true.

> WIFSIGNALED True if the process terminated due to receipt of a signal.

WTERMSIG

> The number of the signal that caused the termination of the process. This
> assumes that WIFSIGNALED(status) is true.

WCOREDUMP

> If true, the termination of the process was accompanied by the creation of a core
> dump.

WIFSTOPPED

> True if the process hasn't terminated, but was just job controlled.

WSTOPSIG

> The number of the signal that caused the process to stop. This assumes that
> WIFSTOPPED(status) is true.

Here are these macros in action:

Example 15-3. status.m

```
// status.m -- play with various child exiting status values

/* compile with:
cc -g -Wall -o status status.m
*/

#import <sys/types.h>           // for pid_t
```

```
#import <sys/wait.h>          // for wait()
#import <unistd.h>            // for fork
#import <stdlib.h>            // for EXIT_SUCCESS
#import <stdio.h>             // for printf
#import <sys/time.h>          // for ru_utime and ru_stime in rlimit
#import <sys/resource.h>      // for rlimit
#import <errno.h>             // for errno
#import <string.h>            // for strerror

void printStatus (int status)
{
    if (WIFEXITED(status)) {
        printf ("program exited normally.  Return value is %d",
                WEXITSTATUS(status));

    } else if (WIFSIGNALED(status)) {
        printf ("program exited on signal %d", WTERMSIG(status));
        if (WCOREDUMP(status)) {
            printf (" (core dumped)");
        }

    } else {
        printf ("other exit value");
    }
    printf ("\n");

} // printStatus

int main (int argc, char *argv[])
{
    int status;

    // normal exit
    if (fork() == 0) {
        _exit (23);
    }

    wait (&status);
    printStatus (status);

    // die by a signal (SIGABRT)
    if (fork() == 0) {
        abort ();
    }

    wait (&status);
    printStatus (status);

    // die by crashing
    if (fork() == 0) {
        int *blah = (int *)0xFeedFace;  // a bad address
        *blah = 12;
    }

    wait (&status);
    printStatus (status);
```

```
    // drop core
    if (fork() == 0) {
        struct rlimit rl;

        rl.rlim_cur = RLIM_INFINITY;
        rl.rlim_max = RLIM_INFINITY;

        if (setrlimit (RLIMIT_CORE, &rl) == -1) {
            fprintf (stderr,
                        "error in setrlimit for RLIMIT__COR: %d (%s)\n",
                        errno, strerror(errno));
        }
        abort ();
    }

    wait (&status);
    printStatus (status);

    return (EXIT_SUCCESS);

} // main
```

A sample run looks like this:

```
% ./status
program exited normally.  Return value is 23
program exited on signal 6
program exited on signal 11
program exited on signal 6 (core dumped)
```

For the period of time between when the child program exits and the parent performs a **wait()** on it, the kernel needs to store the status and resource information. It does so by keeping the process in the process table. The kernel disposes of much of what the child allocated (memory, files, etc.), but still keeps this last piece of information around. The child process is known as a *zombie* in this case, and shows up in ps in parentheses:

```
root    2832    0.0  0.0      0  0 con- Z+  31Dec69  0:00.00 (proctest)
markd   2834    0.0  0.0   4940  4 std  R+  10:42AM  0:00.00 grep 2832
```

Usually you do not have to worry too much about the occasional zombie, unless you get a whole bunch of them (usually due to a programming error). Uncontrolled zombie creation can fill up the process table and render the machine useless.

How do you know when to call **wait()**? You can call **waitpid()** occasionally, looking for children during idle time. Also, when a child exits, a SIGCHLD signal gets sent to the parent. You will not necessarily receive one SIGCHLD for each child process that exits, such as when two exit while the parent is waiting in the kernel's run queue.

One last issue dealing with parents and children: what happens to a child process when its parent goes away? Every child has to have a parent process ID, but now the original parent process is gone. init adopts it. The process with PID 1 in every Unix system is the init daemon, which is started by the kernel at the end of the bootstrap process, and is there (among other reasons) to be the parent of any orphaned children. So, when a parent dies, its children become children of init.

You can see the parent process ID by giving the `ppid` flag to the `-o` option of `ps` (more stuff added to make the output more useful):

```
% ps -axo user,pid,ppid,vsz,tt,state,start,time,command
USER     PID PPID    VSZ   TT  STAT  STARTED       TIME COMMAND
root       1    0   1308   ??  Ss    20Sep02    0:00.00 /sbin/init
root       2    1   1844   ??  Ss    20Sep02    0:01.52 /sbin/mach_init
root      51    1  15912   ??  Ss    20Sep02    0:02.45 kextd
root      73    1   1292   ??  Ss    20Sep02    0:20.98 update
...
root     429  397  14048   p2  Ss    21Sep02    0:00.84 login -pf markd
markd    430  429   5872   p2  S     21Sep02    0:00.05 -tcsh (tcsh)
markd    431  430  15840   p2  S+    21Sep02    2:34.63 emacs
markd    432  431   9952  std  Ss    21Sep02    0:01.10 -bin/tcsh -i (tcsh)
root    2894  432   5192  std  R+    11:18AM    0:00.00 ps -axo user pid pp
...
```

Here you can see some daemon processes with `/sbin/init` as the parent. There is also the login process (the parent pid 397 is `Terminal.app`), as well as some other programs like the shell and `emacs`.

exec

Most often after a fork you just want to run some other program. The **exec()** family of functions replace the current running process with a new one. You will typically hear of **fork()** and **exec()** spoken together since they are used a lot together.

There are number of variations of **exec()**, depending on how you specify the file to run, how you specify the program arguments, and how you specify the environment variables for the new program.

Table 15-1. Variations of exec()

	Finding the Executable	Program Arguments	Environment
execl	given path	separate arguments	environ variable
execlp	PATH search	separate arguments	environ variable
execle	given path	separate arguments	array of strings
execv	given path	array of strings	environ variable
execvp	PATH search	array of strings	environ variable
execve	given path	array of strings	array of strings

How to decipher the names:

p

If the given file name contains a slash, it is treated as a path to use. Otherwise, the call examines the PATH environment variable and locates the program.

v

Program arguments are an array of strings.

l

Program arguments are separate arguments in the **exec()** command.

e

Environment variables are an array of strings of the form `"VARIABLE=value"`.

Note that if you do not use an 'e' version of **exec()**, the global variable environ will be used to construct the environment for the new process. The **execve()** function is the actual system call that all the other functions are based on.

If you use an array argument, you provide it an array of strings with a NULL pointer as the last element of the array.

A number of attributes are inherited across the **exec()**, such as:

- Open files
- Process ID, parent process ID, process group ID
- Access groups, controlling terminal, resource usages
- Current working directory
- Umask, signal mask

Pipes

One thing to note is that open files are inherited across **exec()** (unless you explicitly tell the file descriptors to "close on exec"). This behavior is how pipelines between programs are built. A parent process calls **pipe()** to create the communications channel between two programs:

```
int pipe (int *fildes);
```

filedes is an array of two integers. **pipe()** fills in the filedes array with two file descriptors that are connected in such a way thatdata written to filedes[1] can be read from filedes[0]. So, if you wanted to **fork()** and **exec()** a command, and read that command's output, you would do something like this:

1. Create the pipe
2. **fork()**
3. In the child, use **dup2()** to move filedes[1] to become standard out.
4. **exec()** the program you want to run.
5. In the parent, read the program's output from filedes[0]. When the child program has finished, it will exit, and reads in the parent from filedes[0] will cease when the pipeline data runs out.
6. The parent calls **wait()** on the child.

Figure 15-5. Pipe and Fork

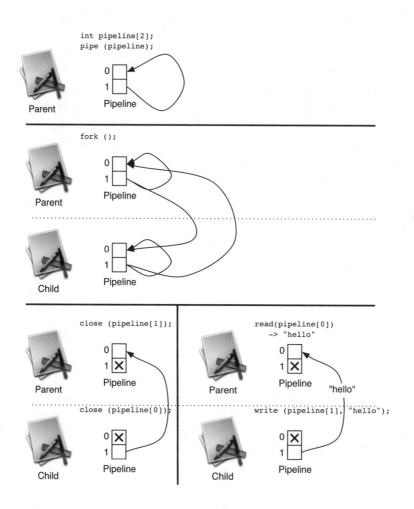

You can chain the input and output of multiple programs together using multiple pipes.

Here is a program that builds a pipeline equivalent to

```
% grep -i mail /usr/share/dict/words | tr '[:lower:]' '[:upper:]'
```

That is, get words that contain "mail," and translate them to uppercase.

Example 15-4. pipeline.m

```
// pipeline.m -- manually create a pipeline to run the command
//      grep -i mail /usr/share/dict/words | tr '[:lower:]' '[:upper:]'

/* compile with:
cc -g -Wall -o pipeline pipeline.m
*/

#import <sys/types.h>    // for pid_t
#import <sys/wait.h>     // for waitpid
```

```
#import <unistd.h>      // for fork
#import <stdlib.h>      // for EXIT_SUCCESS, pipe, exec
#import <stdio.h>       // for printf
#import <errno.h>       // for errno
#import <string.h>      // for strerror

#define BUFSIZE 4096

int main (int argc, char *argv[])
{
    int result;
    int status = EXIT_FAILURE;
    int pipeline1[2];     // write on 1, read on zero
    int pipeline2[2];
    pid_t grep_pid = 0;
    pid_t tr_pid = 0;

    result = pipe (pipeline1);
    if (result == -1) {
        fprintf (stderr, "could not open pipe\n");
        goto bailout;
    }

    // start the grep

    if ((grep_pid = fork())) {
        // parent

        if (grep_pid == -1) {
            fprintf (stderr, "fork failed.  Error is %d/%s\n",
                    errno, strerror(errno));
            goto bailout;
        }
        close (pipeline1[1]); // we are not planning on writing

    } else {
        // child

        char *arguments[] = { "grep", "-i",
                            "mail", "/usr/share/dict/words", NULL };

        close (pipeline1[0]); // we are not planning on reading

        // set the standard out to be the write-side of the pipeline1

        result = dup2 (pipeline1[1], STDOUT_FILENO);
        if (result == -1) {
            fprintf (stderr, "dup2 failed.  Error is %d/%s\n",
                    errno, strerror(errno));
            goto bailout;
        }
        close (pipeline1[1]);

        // exec the child
        result = execvp ("grep", arguments);
        if (result == -1) {
            fprintf (stderr, "could not exec grep.  Error is %d/%s\n",
```

```
                        errno, strerror(errno));
            goto bailout;
        }
    }

    // start the 'tr'

    result = pipe (pipeline2);
    if (result == -1) {
        fprintf (stderr, "could not open pipe\n");
        goto bailout;
    }

    if ((tr_pid = fork())) {
        // parent

        if (tr_pid == -1) {
            fprintf (stderr, "fork failed.  Error is %d/%s\n",
                    errno, strerror(errno));
            goto bailout;
        }
        close (pipeline2[1]); // we are not planning on writing

    } else {
        // child

        close (pipeline2[0]); // we are not planning on reading

        // set the standard out to be the write-side of the pipeline2

        result = dup2 (pipeline1[0], STDIN_FILENO);
        if (result == -1) {
            fprintf (stderr, "dup2 failed.  Error is %d/%s\n",
                    errno, strerror(errno));
            goto bailout;
        }
        close (pipeline1[1]);

        result = dup2 (pipeline2[1], STDOUT_FILENO);
        if (result == -1) {
            fprintf (stderr, "dup2 failed.  Error is %d/%s\n",
                    errno, strerror(errno));
            goto bailout;
        }
        close (pipeline2[1]);

        // exec the child

        result = execlp ("tr", "tr", "[:lower:]", "[:upper:]", NULL);

        if (result == -1) {
            fprintf (stderr, "could not exec tr.  Error is %d/%s\n",
                    errno, strerror(errno));
            goto bailout;
        }
    }
```

```
    // this is only in the parent.  read the results
    {
        FILE *blarg;
        char buffer[BUFSIZE];

        blarg = fdopen (pipeline2[0], "r");

        while (fgets(buffer, BUFSIZE, blarg)) {
            printf ("%s", buffer);
        }
    }

    // and wait
    {
        int childStatus;
        waitpid (grep_pid, &childStatus, 0);
        waitpid (tr_pid, &childStatus, 0);
    }

    // *whew*, we're done.

    status = EXIT_SUCCESS;

bailout:
    return (status);

} // main
```

A sample run:

```
% ./pipeline  | head
AIRMAIL
AUMAIL
BEMAIL
BLACKMAIL
BLACKMAILER
CAMAIL
...
UNMAIL
UNMAILABLE
UNMAILABLENESS
UNMAILED
```

Gotchas with Cocoa and fork()

There is one big huge issue involving **fork()** and Cocoa. Mac OS X is based on Mach, and Mach ports are used for a lot of interprocess communications and are important to Cocoa. These Mach ports (such as the connection to the window server) get closed on a **fork()**, and so you may run into problems if you use Cocoa calls after the **fork()**. Also, when you are using threads (which Cocoa programs use implicitly), only the thread that calls **fork()** is running in the child. Unfortunately, all of the other thread stuff (mutexes and other data structures) still exist, which can lead to mayhem. In general, if you are using threads or Cocoa, the only safe functions to call after a **fork()** are the **exec()** functions and any of the async-safe functions (the ones you can call in a signal handler). If you use any of the newer frameworks from Apple, be especially careful if you try to use them in the child program after a `fork()` without subsequently `exec()`ing. For example, the Disk Arbitration framework could do its work in a thread, and so could get confused in the child after a `fork()`.

For the More Curious

Despite the caveat with Cocoa and threaded programs, you can still do useful work after a `fork()`. For example, a web server could use `fork()` to do concurrent processing, especially if the processing is more than just I/O (such as CGI scripts for dynamic web pages).

The HTTP protocol

HTTP (the hypertext transport protocol) is what is used to exchange data between a web browser and the web server. In brief, the browser connects to a server listening on port 80 of whatever IP address is appropriate and sends a request that looks like this for the URL: `http://www.bignerdranch.com/Classes/Core.html`

```
GET /Classes/Core.html HTTP/1.1
Host: www.bignerdranch.com
User-Agent: Mozilla/5.0 (Macintosh; U; PPC Mac OS X; en-US; rv:1.0rc2) \
Gecko/20020510
Accept: text/xml,application/xml,application/xhtml+xml,text/html;q=0.9,\
text/plain;q=0.8,video/x-mng,image/png,image/jpeg,image/gif;q=0.2,\
text/css,*/*;q=0.1
Accept-Language: en, pdf;q=0.50
Accept-Encoding: gzip, deflate, compress;q=0.9
Accept-Charset: ISO-8859-1, utf-8;q=0.66, *;q=0.66
Keep-Alive: 300
Connection: keep-alive
```

The above is a request:

```
GET /Classes/Core.html HTTP/1.1
```

and a bunch of headers that influence server behavior. For instance, the Host header

```
Host: www.bignerdranch.com
```

has the name of the machine included in the URL. By inspecting the Host header, the web server can serve a bunch of domains off of a single IP address. Other headers can say what kind of data encoding (compressed or not) the browser supports, and what languages the user wants to see. Each line of the request is terminated with a \n, and a pair of \n's is the end of the request.

Pulling apart the request is a method, such as GET (get a page), POST (post data in a form you filled out), or HEAD (just return the headers), followed by the resource you want to see, and then the protocol supported by the browser.

The server then processes the request and sends a response that looks like this:

```
HTTP/1.1 200 OK
Date: Fri, 04 Oct 2002 16:43:55 GMT
Server: Apache
Last-Modified: Fri, 04 Oct 2002 14:50:19 GMT
Content-Length: 9023
```

```
Connection: close
Content-Type: text/html

<HTML>
<HEAD>
<title>Core Mac OS X and Unix Programming</title>
<link rel="stylesheet" type="text/css" href="/homepage_style.css">
...
```

The first line is the primary response, followed by a bunch of headers for the browser, followed by the actual data requested. The response

```
HTTP/1.1 200 OK
```

is the protocol the server will be talking in, the result code (200 for success, 404 for page not found, something in the 500s for an error) and a human-readable string whose actual value is ignored by the browser.

The headers have things like the time the server thinks it is, when the page was last modified (handy if you are caching pages), the content type (a MIME type that tells the browser how to handle the data), and how much data will be coming down the pipe. This last bit of data is optional. If no `Content-Length` header is returned, the browser will continually read new data from the network connection until it gets closed. Like the request, the header section is separated from the requested data by an extra \n.

The really nice thing about HTTP is that it is ubiquitous, and it is not that hard to write a serviceable web server. Having a web server embedded in some applications can make sense, particularly for things like application servers and middleware pieces in a big distributed system. Stick in a little web server listening to port 80 and you can have ordinary web browsers contact them to get status information, change configurations, or perform diagnostics. No need to cook up your own network protocol to do that kind of stuff.

Here is a little web server that uses **fork()** to handle the requests. In terms of efficiency, this is pretty bad, but it is simple and easy to write. The real life web servers will pre-fork a number of persistent children to handle requests and have a central process send the children requests to handle (like Apache), or will use threads to handle individual connections (like Apache 2 and AOLserver). In our example, we will **fork()**, handle the request in the new child process, then exit the child process. The parent process will begin waiting for another request immediately after forking off the child.

This architecture, though, has a couple of nice side benefits that simplify the implementation. There is no need for a select loop (and the resulting complexity) in either the parent or the child, but you still get parallel handling of requests. This is because the parent can block on the **accept()** call for a new connection while the child goes about its business. Setting system calls to be interruptible by signals makes **wait()**ing for children simple, because the SIGCHLD indicating a child process exiting will break out of the **accept()**.

Example 15-5. webserve.m

```
// webserve.m -- a very simple web server using fork() to handle requests

/* compile with:
```

```
cc -g -Wall -o webserve webserve.m
*/

#import <sys/types.h>          // for pid_t, amongst others
#import <sys/wait.h>           // for wait3
#import <unistd.h>             // for fork
#import <stdlib.h>             // for EXIT_SUCCESS, pipe, exec
#import <stdio.h>              // for printf
#import <errno.h>              // for errno
#import <string.h>            // for strerror
#import <sys/time.h>          // for struct timeval
#import <sys/resource.h>      // for struct rusage
#import <netinet/in.h>        // for sockaddr_in
#import <sys/socket.h>        // for socket(), AF_INET
#import <arpa/inet.h>         // for inet_ntoa
#import <unistd.h>            // for close
#import <arpa/inet.h>         // for inet_ntoa and friends
#import <assert.h>            // for assert

#define PORT_NUMBER 8080       // set to 80 to listen on the HTTP port

static int g_childSignaled;

// ----- child handling

// signal handler for SIGCHLD.  Just set a global value saying we have
// seen the signal.  We want to do more interesting stuff on child
// exits than are proper to do in a signal handler
// (runs in the parent)

void childExited (int signalNumber)
{
    g_childSignaled = 1;

} // childExited

// wait for children and print out some resource usage
// (runs in the parent)

void reapChildren ()
{
    pid_t childPid;
    int status;
    struct rusage resources;

    while (1) {

        childPid = wait3 (&status, WNOHANG, &resources);

        if (childPid < 0) {
            // even though the man page says that we shouldn't get this
            // with WNOHANG as an option to wait3, it sometimes happens
            if (errno != ECHILD) {
                fprintf (stderr, "wait3 returned an error: %d/%s\n",
                        errno, strerror(errno));
            }
            break;
```

```
        } else if (childPid == 0) {
            // we have run out of children
            break;

        } else {
            // otherwise print some stuff to our log

            fprintf (stderr, "child %ld terminated %s\n",
                        (long)childPid,
                        WIFEXITED(status) ? "normally" : "abnormally");
            fprintf (stderr, "    user time: %d seconds %d msec\n",
                    resources.ru_utime.tv_sec, resources.ru_utime.tv_usec);
            fprintf (stderr, "    system time: %d seconds %d msec\n",
                    resources.ru_stime.tv_sec, resources.ru_stime.tv_usec);
            fprintf (stderr, "    max RSS: %ld\n", resources.ru_maxrss);
        }
    }

    return;

} // reapChildren


// HTTP request handling

// these are some of the common HTTP response codes

#define HTTP_OK         200
#define HTTP_NOT_FOUND  404
#define HTTP_ERROR      500

// return a string to the browser

#define returnString(httpResult, string, channel) \
        returnBuffer((httpResult), (string), (strlen(string)), (channel))

// return a character buffer (not necessarily zero-terminated)
// to the browser (runs in the child)

void returnBuffer (int httpResult, const char *content,
                   int contentLength, FILE *commChannel)
{
    fprintf (commChannel, "HTTP/1.0 %d blah\n", httpResult);
    fprintf (commChannel, "Content-Type: text/html\n");
    fprintf (commChannel, "Content-Length: %d\n", contentLength);
    fprintf (commChannel, "\n");
    fwrite (content, contentLength, 1, commChannel );

} // returnBuffer

// stream back to the browser numbers being counted, with a pause between
// them.  The user should see the numbers appear every couple of seconds
// (runs in the child)

void returnNumbers (int number, FILE *commChannel)
{
```

```
    int min, max, i;
    min = MIN (number, 1);
    max = MAX (number, 1);

    fprintf (commChannel, "HTTP/1.0 %d blah\n", HTTP_OK);
    fprintf (commChannel, "Content-Type: text/html\n");

    // no content length as this is dynamic
    fprintf (commChannel, "\n");
    fprintf (commChannel, "<h2>The numbers from %d to %d</h2>\n",
             min, max);

    for (i = min; i <= max; i++) {
        sleep (2);
        fprintf (commChannel, "%d\n", i);
        fflush (commChannel);
    }

    fprintf (commChannel, "<hr>Done\n");

} // returnNumbers

// return a file from the file system, relative to where the webserve
// is running.  Note that this does not look for any nasty characters
// like '..', so this function is a pretty big security hole
// (runs in the child)

void returnFile (const char *filename, FILE *commChannel)
{
    FILE *file;
    const char *mimetype = NULL;

    // try to guess the mime type.
    // IE assumes all non-graphic files are HTML
    if (strstr(filename, ".m") != NULL) {
        mimetype = "text/plain";
    } else if (strstr(filename, ".h") != NULL) {
        mimetype = "text/plain";
    } else if (strstr(filename, ".txt") != NULL) {
        mimetype = "text/plain";
    } else if (strstr(filename, ".tgz") != NULL) {
        mimetype = "application/x-compressed";
    } else if (strstr(filename, ".html") != NULL) {
        mimetype = "text/html";
    } else if (strstr(filename, ".htm") != NULL) {
        mimetype = "text/html";
    }

    file = fopen (filename, "r");

    if (file == NULL) {
        returnString (HTTP_NOT_FOUND,
                      "could not find your file.  Sorry.\n",
                      commChannel);
    } else {
#define BUFFER_SIZE (8 * 1024)
        char *buffer[BUFFER_SIZE];
```

```
            int result;
            fprintf (commChannel, "HTTP/1.0 %d blah\n", HTTP_OK);
            if (mimetype != NULL) {
                fprintf (commChannel, "Content-Type: %s\n", mimetype);
            }
            fprintf (commChannel, "\n");
            while ((result = fread (buffer, 1, BUFFER_SIZE, file)) > 0) {
                fwrite (buffer, 1, result, commChannel);
            }
#undef BUFFER_SIZE
    }

} // returnFile

// using the method and the request (the path part of
// the url), generate the data for the user and send
// it back. (runs in the child)

void handleRequest (const char *method, const char
                    *originalRequest, FILE *commChannel)
{
    char *request = strdup (originalRequest);// strsep used to split this
    char *chunk, *nextString;

    if (strcmp(method, "GET") != 0) {
        returnString (HTTP_ERROR, "only GETs are supported",
                    commChannel);
        goto bailout;
    }

    nextString = request;
    chunk = strsep (&nextString, "/");
                    // urls start with slashes, so chunk is ""
    chunk = strsep (&nextString, "/");
                    // the leading part of the url

    if (strcmp(chunk, "numbers") == 0) {
        int number;

        // url of the form /numbers/5 to print numbers from 1 to 5
        chunk = strsep (&nextString, "/");
        number = atoi(chunk);
        returnNumbers (number, commChannel);

    } else if (strcmp(chunk, "file") == 0) {
        chunk = strsep (&nextString, ""); // get the rest of the string
        returnFile (chunk, commChannel);
    } else {
        returnString (HTTP_NOT_FOUND, "could not handle request.\n",
                    commChannel);
    }

bailout:
    fprintf (stderr, "child %ld handled request '%s'\n",
            (long)getpid(), originalRequest);

    free (request);
```

```
    } // handleRequest

    // read the request from the browser, pull apart the elements of the
    // request, and then dispatch it.  (runs in the child)

    void dispatchRequest (int fd, struct sockaddr_in *address)
    {
    #define LINEBUFFER_SIZE 8192
        char linebuffer[LINEBUFFER_SIZE];
        FILE *commChannel;

        commChannel = fdopen (fd, "r+");
        if (commChannel == NULL) {
            fprintf (stderr, "could not open commChannel.  Error is %d/%s\n",
                    errno, strerror(errno));
        }

        // this is pretty lame in that it only reads the first line and
        // assumes that is the request, subsequently ignoring any headers
        // that might be sent.

        if (fgets(linebuffer, LINEBUFFER_SIZE, commChannel) != NULL) {
            // ok, now figure out what they wanted
            char *requestElements[3], *nextString, *chunk;
            int i = 0;
            nextString = linebuffer;
            while ((chunk = strsep (&nextString, " "))) {
                requestElements[i] = chunk;
                i++;
            }
            if (i != 3) {
                returnString (HTTP_ERROR, "malformed request", commChannel);
                goto bailout;
            }

            handleRequest (requestElements[0], requestElements[1],
                        commChannel);
        } else {
            fprintf (stderr, "read an empty request.  exiting\n");
        }

    bailout:
        fclose (commChannel);
        fflush (stderr);

        _exit (EXIT_SUCCESS);

    } // dispatchRequest

    // sit blocking on accept until either it breaks out with a signal
    // (like SIGCHLD) or a new connection comes in.  If it is a new
    // connection, fork off a child to process the request

    void acceptRequest (int listenSocket)
    {
        struct sockaddr_in address;
```

```
        int addressLength = sizeof(address), result, fd;
        pid_t childPid;

        result = accept (listenSocket, (struct sockaddr *)&address,
                        &addressLength);

        if (result == -1) {
            if (errno == EINTR) {
                // system call interrupted by a signal.  maybe by SIGCHLD?
                if (g_childSignaled) {
                    // yes, we had gotten a SIGCHLD.  clean up after the kids
                    g_childSignaled = 0;
                    reapChildren();
                    // note that g_childSignaled is cleared before
                    // reapChildren is called, in case another SIGCHLD
                    // happened during reapChildren, we will not lose it
                    goto bailout;
                }
            } else {
                fprintf (stderr, "accept failed.  error: %d/%s\n",
                        errno, strerror(errno));
            }
            goto bailout;
        }
        fd = result;

        // fork off a child to do the work

        // child sends output to stderr, so make sure it is drained before
        // moving on
        fflush (stderr);

        if ((childPid = fork())) {
            // parent
            if (childPid == -1) {
                fprintf (stderr, "fork failed.  Error: %d/%s\n",
                        errno, strerror(errno));
                goto bailout;
            }
            // lose the new connection since the parent doesn't need it
            // Note: if we do not do this, the connection to the browser
            // will stay open after the child has handled and closed it
            close (fd);

        } else {
            // child
            dispatchRequest (fd, &address);
        }

bailout:
    return;

} // acceptRequest


// ----- network stuff
```

```
// this is 100% stolen from chatterserver.m
// start listening on our server port (runs in parent)

int startListening ()
{
    int fd = -1, success = 0;
    int result;

    result = socket (AF_INET, SOCK_STREAM, 0);

    if (result == -1) {
        fprintf (stderr, "could not make a socket.  error: %d / %s\n",
                    errno, strerror(errno));
        goto bailout;
    }
    fd = result;

    {
        int yes = 1;
        result = setsockopt (fd, SOL_SOCKET, SO_REUSEADDR,
                                &yes, sizeof(int));
        if (result == -1) {
            fprintf (stderr,
                "unable to setsockopt to reuseaddr. %d / %s\n",
                errno, strerror(errno));
            goto bailout;
        }
    }

    // bind to an address and port
    {
        struct sockaddr_in address;
        address.sin_len = sizeof (struct sockaddr_in);
        address.sin_family = AF_INET;
        address.sin_port = htons (PORT_NUMBER);
        address.sin_addr.s_addr = htonl (INADDR_ANY);
        memset (address.sin_zero, 0, sizeof(address.sin_zero));

        result = bind (fd, (struct sockaddr *)&address, sizeof(address));
        if (result == -1) {
            fprintf (stderr, "could not bind socket.  error: %d / %s\n",
                        errno, strerror(errno));
            goto bailout;
        }
    }

    result = listen (fd, 8);

    if (result == -1) {
        fprintf (stderr, "listen failed.  error: %d /  %s\n",
                    errno, strerror(errno));
        goto bailout;
    }

    success = 1;

bailout:
```

```
        if (!success) {
            close (fd);
            fd = -1;
        }
        return (fd);

} // startListening

int main (int argc, char *argv[])
{
    int listenSocket;

    // install a signal handler to reap any children that have exited
    (void) signal (SIGCHLD, childExited);
    siginterrupt (SIGCHLD, 1);

    listenSocket = startListening ();

    while (1) {
        acceptRequest (listenSocket);
    }

    return (EXIT_SUCCESS);

} // main
```

The code is set to listen on port 8080, since to listen to the port 80 HTTP port requires root access (using port 8080 makes it easier to run and to test).

Here is a sample run where the server is started, and these two requests are performed using a web browser: http://127.0.0.1:8080/file/webserve.m http://127.0.0.1:8080/numbers/23

```
% ./webserve
child 6514 handled request '/file/webserve.m'
child 6514 terminated normally
    user time: 0 seconds 0 msec
    system time: 0 seconds 0 msec
    max RSS: 0

child 6516 handled request '/numbers/23'
child 6516 terminated normally
    user time: 0 seconds 0 msec
    system time: 0 seconds 0 msec
    max RSS: 0
```

You can also use telnet to make requests. Type in the stuff in bold.

```
% telnet 127.0.0.1 8080
Trying 127.0.0.1...
Connected to localhost.
Escape character is '^]'.
GET /bork HTTP/1.0

HTTP/1.0 404 blah
Content-Type: text/html
Content-Length: 38
```

```
could not handle your request.  Sorry.
Connection closed by foreign host.
```

Challenge:

1. Add some more URL handling types. Some ideas are:
   `/upcase/some/file/name`: similar to returnFile, but uppercases everything.

2. Design and implement a scheme to allow programmers to write plug-ins to handle different URLs.

3. In `pipeline.m`, if the parent does not close `pipeline[1]` (the write end of the pipe), the program will hang in the loop that reads results from the children. Why does it behave like that?

4. Fix the security hole in **returnFile()** so that it does not allow anyone to use multiple slashes or dots to access files above the directory where the web server is running.

Chapter 16. Using NSTask

In this section, you will learn:

- How to create new processes using **NSTask**.
- How to send data to the new process's standard in and read data from its standard out and standard error using **NSPipe** and **NSFileHandle**.
- How **NSProcessInfo** supplies the program with information about itself.

NSProcessInfo

Your application can access its own process information using the **NSProcessInfo** object. Here are some of the commonly used methods on **NSProcessInfo**:

`+ (NSProcessInfo *)`**`processInfo`**

You will use this class method to get hold of the shared instance of **NSProcessInfo** for the current process.

`- (NSDictionary *)`**`environment`**

Returns a dictionary containing all the environment variables as keys and their values.

`- (NSString *)`**`hostName`**

The name of the computer upon which the program is running.

`- (NSString *)`**`processName`**

The name of the program. This is used by the user defaults system.

`- (NSString *)`**`globallyUniqueString`**

This method uses the host name, process ID, and a timestamp to create a string that will be unique for the network. It uses a counter to ensure that each time this method is invoked it will create a different string.

NSTask

The **NSTask** object is used to create and control new processes. When the process ends, the object will post an NSTaskDidTerminateNotification notification. Before creating (or *launching*) the new process, you will set the attributes of the new process with these methods:

`- (void)`**`setLaunchPath:`**`(NSString *)path`

Sets the path to the code that will be executed when the process is created.

`- (void)`**`setArguments:`**`(NSArray *)arguments`

Takes an array of strings that will be the arguments to the program.

`- (void)`**`setEnvironment:`**`(NSDictionary *)dict`

You can use this to set the environment variables. If unset, the environment variables of the parent process will be used.

- (void)**setCurrentDirectoryPath:**(NSString *)path

Every process has a directory from which all relative paths are resolved. This is known as the current directory. If unset, the current directory of the parent process is used.

- (void)**setStandardInput:**(id)input

You can provide an object (either an **NSPipe** or an **NSFileHandle**) to act as a conduit to the new process's standard input.

- (void)**setStandardOutput:**(id)output

You can provide an object (either an **NSPipe** or an **NSFileHandle**) to act as a conduit from the new process's standard output.

- (void)**setStandardError:**(id)error

You can provide an object (either an **NSPipe** or an **NSFileHandle**) to act as a conduit from the new process's standard error.

There are also methods you will use when the new process is running. Here are the most commonly used:

- (void)**launch**

Creates the new process.

- (void)**terminate**

Kills the new process by sending it a SIGTERM signal.

- (int)**processIdentifier**

Returns the new process's process ID.

- (BOOL)**isRunning**

Returns YES if the the new process is running.

NSFileHandle

When reading a file, Cocoa programmers usually read in an entire file and pack it into an **NSData** or **NSString** before parsing it. When writing a file, Cocoa programmers usually create a complete **NSData** or **NSString** which is then written to the file system. Sometimes you will want more control over reading from and writing to files. For example, you might read a file just until you find what you want and then close it. For more control over reading and writing from files, you will use **NSFileHandle**.

An **NSFileHandle** is used for reading and writing files. Some of the reading methods are blocking — that is, the application stops while the data is read— and others are non-blocking. We will discuss the non-blocking methods later in the chapter. Here are some commonly used methods for reading, writing, and seeking:

- (NSData *)**availableData**

```
- (NSData *)readDataToEndOfFile
- (NSData *)readDataOfLength:(unsigned int)length
```

These are blocking methods that read data from the file handle.

```
- (void)writeData:(NSData *)data;
```

A method for writing data to a file handle.

```
- (unsigned long long)offsetInFile
- (void)seekToFileOffset:(unsigned long long)offset
```

Methods for finding and changing your current location in a file.

```
- (void)closeFile
```

Closes the file.

NSPipe

The class **NSPipe** has two instances of **NSFileHandle**. One for input. The other for output.

```
- (NSFileHandle *)fileHandleForReading
- (NSFileHandle *)fileHandleForWriting
```

Creating an App that Creates a New Process

Unix systems have a program called sort that reads data from standard input, sorts it, and outputs it to standard output. You are going to write a program that invokes sort as a new process, writes data to its input and reads data from its output. The user will type in an **NSTextView**, click a button to trigger the sort, and read the result in another **NSTextView**. It will look like this:

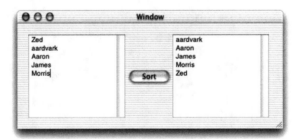

For the record, this is not how I would do a sort in a real application. The **NSArray** class has a couple of elegant ways to do sorting. This is just a simple example of using other processes. Here is an object diagram:

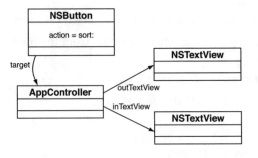

Create a new project of type **Cocoa Application** and name it SortThem. Open the MainMenu.nib file. Drop two **NSTextView** objects and an **NSButton** on the window. Make the text view on the right non-editable:

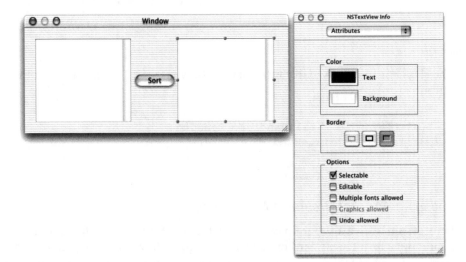

Under the **Classes** tab, create a new subclass of **NSObject** called **AppController**. Give it two outlets: inText and outText. Give it one action — **sort:**

Create the files for the class and create an instance.

Set the text view on the left to be inText.

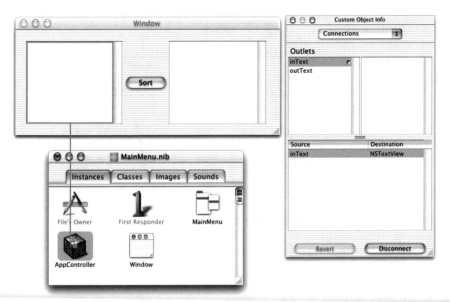

Set the text view on the right to be the `outText`. Set the target of the button to trigger `sort:`.

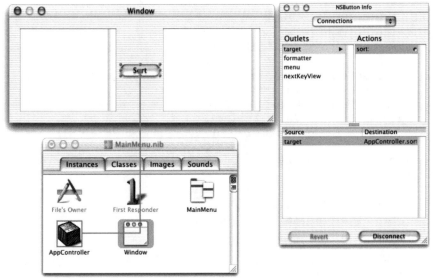

Before creating the code, here is an object diagram of the task:

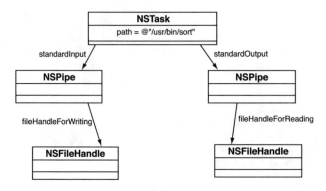

In Project Builder, edit the **sort:** method in `AppController.m`:

```
- (IBAction)sort:(id)sender
{
    NSData *data;
    NSPipe *inPipe, *outPipe;
    NSFileHandle *writingHandle;
    NSTask *task;
    NSString *aString;
    task = [[NSTask alloc] init];
    inPipe = [[NSPipe alloc] init];
    outPipe = [[NSPipe alloc] init];

    // Set attributes of new process
    [task setLaunchPath:@"/usr/bin/sort"];
    [task setStandardOutput:outPipe];
    [task setStandardInput:inPipe];
    [task setArguments:[NSArray arrayWithObject:@"-f"]];

    // Start the new process
    [task launch];

    // Write ASCII to its standard in
    writingHandle = [inPipe fileHandleForWriting];
    [writingHandle writeData:[
        [inText string] dataUsingEncoding:NSASCIIStringEncoding]];
    [writingHandle closeFile];

    // Read ASCII from its standard out
    data = [[outPipe fileHandleForReading] readDataToEndOfFile];
    aString = [[NSString alloc] initWithData:data
                            encoding:NSASCIIStringEncoding];
    [outText setString:aString];
    [aString release];
    [task release];
    [inPipe release];
    [outPipe release];
}
```

Build and run your application.

Non-blocking reads

If a process takes a long time to return output, like the program `traceroute`, you will not want your application to stop while waiting for output from the program. You will want to create a filehandle that does non-blocking reading. In particular, you will set up the file handle so that it posts a notification when there is data to be processed.

The notification created will be an `NSFileHandleReadCompletionNotification`. To start the file handle waiting for the data, you will send it the message **`readInBackgroundAndNotify`**.

In this example, you are going to create a task which runs `traceroute`. `traceroute` sends out packets to discover the routers between your machine and another host. The responses from the routers sometimes take a while to get back. You will read the data in the background and append it to the text view. The application will look like this:

Edit the nib file

Create a new project of type Cocoa Application. Name it TraceRoute. Open `MainMenu.nib` and create a new subclass of **NSObject** called **AppController**. Add three outlets to **AppController**: `button`, `hostField`, and `textView`. Add one action to `AppController` — `startStop:`.

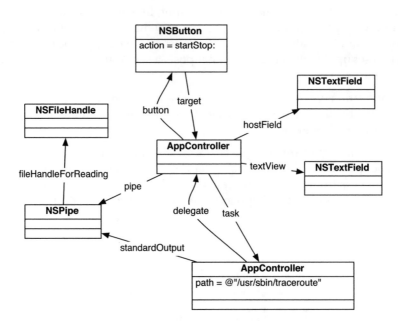

Create the files for **AppController**.

Create an instance of **AppController**. Drop a text field, a text view, and a button on the window. Make it look like this:

Connect the outlets of the **AppController** (button, hostField, textView) to the appropriate objects. Set the target of the button to point to the **AppController**, and set the action to be **startStop:**.

Edit the code

In Project Builder, edit AppController.h:

```
#import <Cocoa/Cocoa.h>
```

```
@interface AppController : NSObject
{
    IBOutlet NSButton *button;
    IBOutlet NSTextField *hostField;
    IBOutlet NSTextView *textView;
    NSPipe *pipe;
    NSTask *task;
}
- (IBAction)startStop:(id)sender;
- (void)dataReady:(NSNotification *)note;
- (void)taskTerminated:(NSNotification *)note;
- (void)appendData:(NSData *)d;
- (void)cleanup;
@end
```

Open `MainMenu.nib` and drag `AppController.h` into it.

Open the `AppController.m` and add these methods to it:

```
#import "AppController.h"

@implementation AppController

// Append the data to the string in the text view
- (void)appendData:(NSData *)d {
    NSRange endRange = NSMakeRange([[textView string] length],0);
    NSString *string = [[NSString alloc] initWithData:d
                                     encoding:NSASCIIStringEncoding];
    [textView replaceCharactersInRange:endRange
                            withString:string];
    [string release];
}

- (void)cleanup
{
    // Release the old task
    [task release];
    task = nil;

    // Release the pipe
    [pipe release];
    pipe = nil;

    // Change the title on the button
    [button setTitle:@"Trace the route"];

    // No longer an observer
    [[NSNotificationCenter defaultCenter] removeObserver:self];
}

- (void)taskTerminated:(NSNotification *)note
{
    NSData *leftInPipe;
    // Flush data still in pipe
    leftInPipe = [[pipe fileHandleForReading] readDataToEndOfFile];
    if (leftInPipe)
        [self appendData:leftInPipe];
    [self cleanup];
```

```objc
}

- (IBAction)startStop:(id)sender
{
    // Is the task already running?
    if ([task isRunning]) {
        // Stop it and tidy up
        [task terminate];
        [self cleanup];
    } else {
        // Create a task and pipe
        task = [[NSTask alloc] init];
        pipe = [[NSPipe alloc] init];

        // Set the attributes of the task
        [task setLaunchPath:@"/usr/sbin/traceroute"];
        [task setArguments:[NSArray arrayWithObject:
                                    [hostField stringValue]]];
        [task setStandardOutput:pipe];
        [task setStandardError:pipe];

        // Register for notifications
        [[NSNotificationCenter defaultCenter] addObserver:self
                    selector:@selector(dataReady:)
                        name:NSFileHandleReadCompletionNotification
                      object:[pipe fileHandleForReading]];
        [[NSNotificationCenter defaultCenter] addObserver: self
                    selector:@selector(taskTerminated:)
                        name:NSTaskDidTerminateNotification
                      object:task];
        // Launch the task
        [task launch];
        [button setTitle:@"Terminate"];
        [textView setString:@""];

        // Get the pipe reading in the background
        [[pipe fileHandleForReading] readInBackgroundAndNotify];
    }
}

- (void)dataReady:(NSNotification *)note
{
    NSData *data = [[note userInfo]
                valueForKey:NSFileHandleNotificationDataItem];
    if (data)
        [self appendData:data];
    // Must restart reading in background after each notification
    [[pipe fileHandleForReading] readInBackgroundAndNotify];
}

@end
```

Build and run the application.

Chapter 17. Accessing the Keychain

A *keychain* is a file that holds onto passwords and certificates and information about those passwords and certificates. (For the purposes of this chapter, I will use "password" to mean "password or certificate.") Each user can have several keychains, but most people only have one: `~/Library/Keychains/<username>`. In the Security framework, there is a set of functions and data structures that allow you to read and write passwords and their associated data. A password and its associated data is known as a keychain item.

The user can inspect their keychain using the application `Keychain Access`:

Some data inside the keychain is encrypted and can only be accessed if the keychain is unlocked. The user unlocks a keychain by typing a password into a keychain panel:

Access to keychain items can be controlled using the `Keychain Access` application.

Items and Attribute Lists

In a keychain, there are four types of items:

- *Internet* passwords are associated with some protocol, server, domain, and user.
- *AppleShare* passwords are used by the AppleShare system.
- *Certificate* items hold certificates, not passwords.
- *Generic* items are used for everything else.

The item has a password and a collection of attributes. The attributes are identified by a four-byte code. Here is a list of the four-byte codes:

`kSecCreationDateItemAttr`

> (`'cdat'`) Identifies the creation date attribute. You use this tag to set or get a value of type `UInt32` that indicates the date the item was created.

`kSecModDateItemAttr`

> (`'mdat'`) Identifies the modification date attribute. You use this tag to set or get a value of type `UInt32` that indicates the last time the item was updated.

`kSecDescriptionItemAttr`

> (`'desc'`) Identifies the description attribute. You use this tag to set or get a value of type string that represents a user-visible string describing this particular kind of item (For example, "disk image password").

`kSecCommentItemAttr`

> (`'icmt'`) Identifies the comment attribute. You use this tag to set or get a value of type string that represents a user-editable string containing comments for this item.

`kSecCreatorItemAttr`

> (`'crtr'`) Identifies the creator attribute.

`kSecTypeItemAttr`

> (`'type'`) Identifies the type attribute.

`kSecScriptCodeItemAttr`

> (`'scrp'`) Identifies the script code attribute. You use this tag to set or get a value of type ScriptCode that represents the script code for all strings. (Note: use of this attribute is deprecated; string attributes should be stored in UTF-8 encoding.)

`kSecLabelItemAttr`

> (`'labl'`) Identifies the label attribute. You use this tag to set or get a value of type string that represents a user-editable string containing the label for this item.

`kSecInvisibleItemAttr`

> (`'invi'`) Identifies the invisible attribute. You use this tag to set or get a value of type Boolean that indicates whether the item is invisible.

`kSecNegativeItemAttr`

> (`'nega'`)Identifies the negative attribute. You use this tag to set or get a value of type Boolean that indicates whether there is a valid password associated with this keychain item. This is useful if your application does not want a password for some particular service to be stored in the keychain, but prefers that it always be entered by the user. The item (typically invisible and with zero-length data) acts as a placeholder.

`kSecCustomIconItemAttr`

> (`'cusi'`) Identifies the custom icon attribute. You use this tag to set or get a value of type Boolean that indicates whether the item has an application-specific icon. To do this, you must also set the attribute value identified by the tag `kSecTypeItemAttr` to a file type for which there is a corresponding icon in the desktop database, and set the attribute value identified by the tag `kSecCreatorItemAttr` to an appropriate application creator type. If a custom icon corresponding to the item's type and creator can be found in the desktop database, it will be displayed by Keychain Access. Otherwise, default icons are used.

`kSecAccountItemAttr`

> (`'acct'`) Identifies the account attribute. You use this tag to set or get a string that represents the user account. It also applies to generic and AppleShare passwords.

`kSecServiceItemAttr`

('svce')Identifies the service attribute. You use this tag to set or get a string that represents the service associated with this item (For example, "iTools"). This is unique to generic password attributes.

`kSecGenericItemAttr`

('gena') Identifies the generic attribute. You use this tag to set or get a value of untyped bytes that represents a user-defined attribute. This is unique to generic password attributes.

`kSecSecurityDomainItemAttr`

('sdmn') Identifies the security domain attribute. You use this tag to set or get a value that represents the Internet security domain. This is unique to Internet password attributes.

`kSecServerItemAttr`

('srvr') Identifies the server attribute. You use this tag to set or get a value of type string that represents the Internet server name or IP address. This is unique to Internet password attributes.

`kSecAuthenticationTypeItemAttr`

('atyp') Identifies the authentication type attribute. You use this tag to set or get a value of type SecAuthenticationType that represents the Internet authentication scheme. This is unique to Internet password attributes.

`kSecPortItemAttr`

('port') Identifies the port attribute. You use this tag to set or get a value of type `UInt32` that represents the Internet port number. This is unique to Internet password attributes.

`kSecPathItemAttr`

('path') Identifies the path attribute. You use this tag to set or get a value that represents the path. This is unique to Internet password attributes.

`kSecVolumeItemAttr`

('vlme') Identifies the volume attribute. You use this tag to set or get a value that represents the AppleShare volume. This is unique to AppleShare password attributes.

`kSecAddressItemAttr`

('addr') Identifies the address attribute. You use this tag to set or get a value of type string that represents the AppleTalk zone name, or the IP or domain name that represents the server address. This is unique to AppleShare password attributes.

`kSecSignatureItemAttr`

('ssig') Identifies the server signature attribute. You use this tag to set or get a value of type SecAFPServerSignature that represents the server signature block. This is unique to AppleShare password attributes.

kSecProtocolItemAttr

> ('ptcl') Identifies the protocol attribute. You use this tag to set or get a value of type SecProtocolType that represents the Internet protocol. This is unique to AppleShare and Internet password attributes.

kSecCertificateType

> ('ctyp') Indicates a CSSM_CERT_TYPE type.

kSecCertificateEncoding

> ('cenc') Indicates a CSSM_CERT_ENCODING type.

kSecCrlType

> ('crtp') Indicates a CSSM_CRL_TYPE type.

kSecCrlEncoding

> ('crnc') Indicates a CSSM_CRL_ENCODING type.

kSecAlias

> ('alis') Indicates an alias.

Use a SecKeychainAttributeList to read and write these attributes:

```
struct SecKeychainAttributeList
{
    UInt32 count;
    SecKeychainAttribute *attr;
};
```

count is the number of attributes in the list. And attr is a pointer to the first one.

```
struct SecKeychainAttribute
{
    SecKeychainAttrType tag;
    UInt32 length;
    void *data;
};
```

The tag is the four-byte code listed above. The length is the number of bytes in the data buffer. Usually, the data buffer is just a string.

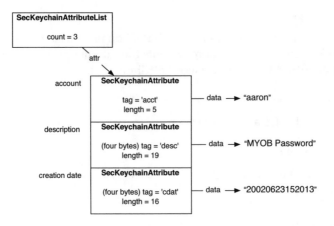

Searching for Items

Attribute lists are used in three ways:

1. To specify a search for items.
2. To read data from an item.
3. To set the data for an item.

For example, to create a search for all generic passwords that have *bignerdranch* as the account name, you would create an attribute list and invoke **SecKeychainSearchCreateFromAttributes()**.

```
OSStatus SecKeychainSearchCreateFromAttributes(CFTypeRef keychainOrArray,
               SecItemClass                      itemClass,
               const SecKeychainAttributeList  *attrList,
               SecKeychainSearchRef            *searchRef);
```

Most of the functions in the Security framework deal well with NULLs. They do what you would hope. For example, if you can pass NULL as the first argument, the search will check all the user's normal keychains. Usually, this is what you want. For the second argument, you will pass one of the following:

- kSecInternetPasswordItemClass
- kSecGenericPasswordItemClass
- kSecAppleSharePasswordItemClass
- kSecCertificateItemClass

If you pass NULL as the attribute list, all items of that class will be returned. The final argument is a pointer to a search-specifying structure.

So, here is a search that counts the number of internet passwords on your keychain where the account name is *bignerdranch*:

Example 17-1. dumpem.m

```
// dumpem.m -- poke inside the keychain

/*
compile with:
cc -g -Wall -framework Security -framework CoreFoundation \
                                    -o dumpem dumpem.m
*/

#import <Security/Security.h>
#import <CoreFoundation/CoreFoundation.h>

#import <stdlib.h>       // for EXIT_SUCCESS
#import <stdio.h>        // for printf() and friends
#import <string.h>       // for strncpy

int main (int argc, char *argv[])
{
    SecKeychainSearchRef search;
    SecKeychainItemRef item;
    SecKeychainAttributeList list;
    SecKeychainAttribute attribute;
    OSErr result;
    int i = 0;

    // create an attribute list with just one attribute specified
    // (You will want to change these to match a user name that you
    //  have on your key chain)
    attribute.tag = kSecAccountItemAttr;
    attribute.length = 12;
    attribute.data = "bignerdranch";

    list.count = 1;
    list.attr = &attribute;

    result = SecKeychainSearchCreateFromAttributes
                (NULL, kSecGenericPasswordItemClass,
                 &list, &search);

    if (result != noErr) {
        printf ("status %d from "
                "SecKeychainSearchCreateFromAttributes\n",
                result);
    }
    while (SecKeychainSearchCopyNext (search, &item) == noErr) {
        CFRelease (item);
        i++;
    }

    printf ("%d items found\n", i);
    CFRelease (search);

    return (EXIT_SUCCESS);

} // main
```

Before building and running the program, launch `Keychain Access`. It is located in `/Applications/Utilities/`. Add at least one keychain item with the account name set to "bignerdranch".

Reading Data From an Item

Of course, once you have fetched the item, you can do all sorts of nifty things with it. If you wanted to read the password, the account name, the description, and the modification date from an item, you would create an attribute list and call `SecKeychainItemCopyContent()`. Note that here the attribute list is specifying what data you want and is acting as a receptacle. Add these functions to dumpem.m:

```
// given a carbon-style 4-byte character identifier,
// make a C string that can be given to printf

const char *fourByteCodeString (UInt32 code)
{
    // sick-o hack to quickly assign an identifier
    // into a character buffer
    typedef union theCheat {
        UInt32 theCode;
        char theString[4];
    } theCheat;

    static char string[5];

    ((theCheat*)string)->theCode = code;
    string[4] = '\0';

    return (string);

} // fourByteCodeString

void showList (SecKeychainAttributeList list)
{
    char buffer[1024];
    SecKeychainAttribute attr;

    int i;

    for (i = 0; i < list.count; i++) {

        attr = list.attr[i];

        if (attr.length < 1024) {
                // make a copy of the data so we can stick on
                // a trailing zero byte
                strncpy (buffer, attr.data, attr.length);
                buffer[attr.length] = '\0';

            printf ("\t%d: '%s' = \"%s\"\n",
                        i, fourByteCodeString(attr.tag), buffer);
        } else {
            printf ("attribute %d is more than 1K\n", i);
        }
    }
}
```

```
} // showList

void dumpItem (SecKeychainItemRef item)
{
    UInt32 length;
    char *password;
    SecKeychainAttribute attributes[8];
    SecKeychainAttributeList list;
    OSStatus status;

    // list the attributes you wish to read
    attributes[0].tag = kSecAccountItemAttr;
    attributes[1].tag = kSecDescriptionItemAttr;
    attributes[2].tag = kSecLabelItemAttr;
    attributes[3].tag = kSecModDateItemAttr;

    list.count = 4;
    list.attr = attributes;

    status = SecKeychainItemCopyContent (item, NULL, &list, &length,
                            (void **)&password);

    // use this version if you don't really want the password,
    // but just want to peek at the attributes
    //status = SecKeychainItemCopyContent (item, NULL, &list, NULL, NULL);

    // make it clear that this is the beginning of a new
    // keychain item
    printf("\n\n");
    if (status == noErr) {
        if (password != NULL) {

            // copy the password into a buffer so we can attach a
            // trailing zero byte in order to be able to print
            // it out with printf
            char passwordBuffer[1024];

            if (length > 1023) {
                length = 1023; // save room for trailing \0
            }
            strncpy (passwordBuffer, password, length);

            passwordBuffer[length] = '\0';
            printf ("Password = %s\n", passwordBuffer);
        }
        showList (list);

        SecKeychainItemFreeContent (&list, password);

    } else {
        printf("Error = %d\n", (int)status);
    }

} // dumpItem
```

When you call **SecKeychainItemCopyContent()**, if the keychain requires authentication, it will automatically bring up an authentication panel. If you only read publicly available data, no authentication panel will appear. The code above will probably trigger the panel for each item. If you change one line so that you are no longer fetching the password, the panel will not appear at all:

```
SecKeychainItemCopyContent(item, NULL, &list, NULL, NULL);
```

Add a call to `dumpItem()` in `main()`:

```
while (SecKeychainSearchCopyNext (search, &item) == noErr) {
    dumpItem (item);
    CFRelease (item);
    i++;
}
```

Build and run the program. Note that if you choose **Always Allow**, the program will have access to the keychain item until you log out. However, if you recompile the program, you will have to re-authenticate. The security framework keeps checksums of the applications that have access.

Editing the Keychain

With the item, you can also make changes using an attribute list:

```
OSStatus SecKeychainItemModifyContent(SecKeychainItemRef itemRef,
                        const SecKeychainAttributeList *attrList,
                                        UInt32 newPasswordLength,
                                  const void *newPassword)
```

The new attribute values would go into the `attrList`. A new password would go into `data`.

To delete an item:

```
OSStatus SecKeychainItemDelete(SecKeychainItemRef itemRef)
```

Note that you would still have to call `CFRelease()` in the item to prevent a memory leak.

Getting Specific Keychains

As an argument to many of the keychain functions, you can specify a particular keychain. Usually, you will simply use the user's default keychain. For all of these functions, if you just supply NULL as the keychain, it will use the default keychain. However, if you want to explicitly get the default keychain you will use:

```
OSStatus SecKeychainCopyDefault(SecKeychainRef *keychain)
```

If you wanted to specify a different keychain (remember that it is just a file), you could use:

```
OSStatus SecKeychainOpen(const char *pathName,
                  SecKeychainRef *keychain)
```

When you are done with a keychain, make sure that you call `CFRelease()` to free it.

Keychain Access

Each keychain item defines how it may be accessed. The information about access privileges is kept in a SecAccessRef structure. To get the access structure for a particular keychain item, you will use the following function:

```
OSStatus SecKeychainItemCopyAccess(SecKeychainItemRef item,
                                   SecAccessRef *access);
```

To change the access on a keychain item, you edit the SecAccessRef and write it to the keychain item using:

```
OSStatus SecKeychainItemSetAccess(SecKeychainItemRef itemRef,
                                  SecAccessRef access);
```

What, then, is a SecAccessRef? You can get a list of access control lists (ACLs) from it. Each access list has a list of trusted applications that are allowed to access the keychain item. Some applications can access the keychain item only after the user types in the keychain password.

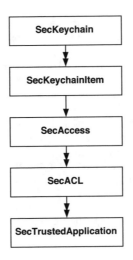

As an example of reading the ACLs for a keychain item, add the following code to **main()** in dumpem.m:

```
while (SecKeychainSearchCopyNext (search, &item) !=
            errSecItemNotFound) {
    dumpItem (item);
    // Get the SecAccess
    SecAccessRef access;
    SecKeychainItemCopyAccess(item, &access);
    showAccess(access);
    CFRelease(access);
    CFRelease(item);
    i++;
}
```

Add the following function:

```
void showAccess (SecAccessRef accessRef)
{
    int count, i;
    CFArrayRef aclList;
    CFArrayRef applicationList;
    SecACLRef acl;
    CFStringRef description;
    CSSM_ACL_KEYCHAIN_PROMPT_SELECTOR promptSelector;
    SecTrustedApplicationRef application;
    CFDataRef appData;

    // Get a list of access lists
    SecAccessCopyACLList(accessRef, &aclList);
    count = CFArrayGetCount(aclList);
    printf("%d access control lists\n", count);
    for (i = 0; i < count; i++) {
        char buffer[256];

        acl = (SecACLRef)CFArrayGetValueAtIndex(aclList, i);

        // Get the list of trusted applications
        SecACLCopySimpleContents(acl, &applicationList,
                            &description, &promptSelector);

        CFStringGetCString(description, buffer,
                                    256, kCFStringEncodingASCII);
        CFRelease(description);

        // Does the apps on this list require the user
        // to type in the keychain passphrase?
        if (promptSelector.flags &&
                CSSM_ACL_KEYCHAIN_PROMPT_REQUIRE_PASSPHRASE) {
            printf("\t%d: ACL %s - Requires passphrase\n",
                                        i, buffer);
        } else {
            printf("\t%d: ACL %s - Does not require passphrase\n",
                                        i, buffer);
        }
        // Sometimes there is no application list at all
        if (applicationList == NULL) {
            printf("\t\tNo application list\n");
            continue;
        }
        int j, appCount;
        appCount = CFArrayGetCount(applicationList);
        printf("\t\t%d trusted applications\n", appCount);
        for (j = 0; j < appCount; j++) {
            application = (SecTrustedApplicationRef)CFArrayGetValueAtIndex(
                                            applicationList, j);

            // Get the app data for the trusted application
            // (this is usually the path to the app)
            SecTrustedApplicationCopyData(application, &appData);
            printf("\t\t%s\n",CFDataGetBytePtr(appData));
            CFRelease(appData);
```

```
        }
        CFRelease(applicationList);
    }
    CFRelease(aclList);
}
```

If you are running Jaguar, you probably are missing the SecACL.h header file from your Security framework. You can download it from the Darwin sources online, or just declare the function you need:

```
extern OSStatus SecACLCopySimpleContents(SecACLRef acl,
                                    CFArrayRef *applicationList,
                                    CFStringRef *description,
                    CSSM_ACL_KEYCHAIN_PROMPT_SELECTOR *promptSelector);
```

Hopefully this will be fixed in later versions of Mac OS X.

Making a New Keychain Item

To create a new keychain item, you will use this function:

```
OSStatus SecKeychainItemCreateFromContent( SecItemClass   itemClass,
            SecKeychainAttributeList *attrList,
                        UInt32   lengthOfPassword,
                    const void *password,
                SecKeychainRef   keychainRef,
                SecAccessRef   initialAccess,
            SecKeychainItemRef *itemRef);
```

Where the itemClass is kSecInternetPasswordItemClass, kSecGenericPasswordItemClass, kSecAppleSharePasswordItemClass, or kSecCertificateItemClass. If you supply NULL as the keychainRef, the item will be added to the default keychain. itemRef will be set to point to the newly created item. To use the default access, just supply NULL as the initialAccess.

As an example, here is a short program that will insert a new item into your default keychain.

Example 17-2. add_item.m

```
/*
compile with
cc -g -Wall -framework Security -framework CoreFoundation
            -o add_item add_item.m
*/

#import <Security/Security.h>
#import <CoreFoundation/CoreFoundation.h>
#include <stdio.h> // for printf()

int main (int argc, const char * argv[]) {
    SecKeychainAttribute attributes[2];
    SecKeychainAttributeList list;
    SecKeychainItemRef item;
```

```
OSStatus status;

attributes[0].tag = kSecAccountItemAttr;
attributes[0].data = "fooz";
attributes[0].length = 4;

attributes[1].tag = kSecDescriptionItemAttr;
attributes[1].data = "No Girls Allowed";
attributes[1].length = 16;

list.count = 2;
list.attr = attributes;

status = SecKeychainItemCreateFromContent(
                  kSecGenericPasswordItemClass, &list,
                  5, "budda", NULL,NULL,&item);
if (status != 0) {
    printf("Error creating new item: %d",
                        (int)status);
}
return(0);
}
```

After running this program, look at the keychain item in `Keychain Access`.

Also, note what "default access" is: `Keychain Access`.

Convenience Functions

That is the whole story on keychains. There are some convenience functions that make common activities possible, but they simply use the functions that we have talked about already.

These functions allow you to create a new item without creating an attribute list:

```
OSStatus SecKeychainAddInternetPassword(SecKeychainRef keychain,
                    UInt32          serverNameLength,
                    const char    *serverName,
                    UInt32          securityDomainLength,
                    const char    *securityDomain,
                    UInt32          accountNameLength,
                    const char    *accountName,
                    UInt32          pathLength,
                    const char    *path,
                    UInt16          port,
                    SecProtocolType          protocol,
                    SecAuthenticationType authenticationType,
                    UInt32          passwordLength,
                    const void    *passwordData,
                    SecKeychainItemRef    *itemRef)


OSStatus SecKeychainAddGenericPassword(SecKeychainRef keychain,
                    UInt32          serviceNameLength,
                    const char    *serviceName,
                    UInt32          accountNameLength,
                    const char    *accountName,
                    UInt32          passwordLength,
                    const void    *passwordData,
                    SecKeychainItemRef *itemRef)
```

Note that neither of these can be used to change a password in an existing item. If you try this, the function will complain that the item already exists.

These methods allow you to find items without creating an attribute list:

```
OSStatus SecKeychainFindInternetPassword(CFTypeRef keychainOrArray,
                    UInt32        serverNameLength,
                    const char    *serverName,
                    UInt32        securityDomainLength,
                    const char    *securityDomain,
                    UInt32        accountNameLength,
                    const char    *accountName,
                    UInt32        pathLength,
                    const char    *path,
                    UInt16        port,
                    SecProtocolType protocol,
                    SecAuthenticationType authenticationType,
                    UInt32        *passwordLength,
                    void          **passwordData,
                    SecKeychainItemRef *itemRef)

OSStatus SecKeychainFindGenericPassword(CFTypeRef keychainOrArray,
                    UInt32        serviceNameLength,
                    const char    *serviceName,
                    UInt32        accountNameLength,
                    const char    *accountName,
                    UInt32        *passwordLength,
                    void          **passwordData,
                    SecKeychainItemRef *itemRef)
```

Notice that the protocol and authentication types are not strings. Here are the constants for the commonly used protocols:

- kSecProtocolTypeFTP

- kSecProtocolTypeFTPAccount

- kSecProtocolTypeHTTP

- kSecProtocolTypeIRC

- kSecProtocolTypeNNTP

- kSecProtocolTypePOP3

- kSecProtocolTypeSMTP

- kSecProtocolTypeSOCKS

- kSecProtocolTypeIMAP

- kSecProtocolTypeLDAP

- kSecProtocolTypeAppleTalk

- kSecProtocolTypeAFP

- kSecProtocolTypeTelnet

- kSecProtocolTypeSSH

There are several types of authentication, but you will almost certainly use kSecAuthenticationTypeDefault.

If you are writing a daemon or something else that should not be interrupting the user, you can prevent the authethentication panel from appearing:

```
SecKeychainSetUserInteractionAllowed(NO);
```

Challenge

1. Write an app that saves a username and password to the default keychain.

2. Write an app that can read and change the saved password.

Chapter 18. Authorization

When you are trying to make sure someone is who they say they are, you are dealing with *authentication*. When you are checking to make sure that they are allowed to do what they want to do, you are dealing with *authorization*. The Security framework has functions which make authentication and authorization easier. The framework is extensible so that you can create your own modules for retinal scans and smartcards. In this chapter, we are going to talk about how to use the Security framework, not how to extend it.

Let's say that you are writing an application called `Kama Sutra Coach`. You should only allow certain users in the household to run it. Even if one of those users is logged in, perhaps you should make the user re-authenticate when launching the app.

Here is the way the Security Server works: in your application, you ask for a right. A right is just a string, but it should relate to the task. In our example, you are writing the application for MegaCode Corporation. The name of the right might be `com.megacode.kamasutra.launch`.

The Security Server goes looking in its configuration file (`/etc/authorization`) for the right named `com.megacode.kamasutra.launch`. The configuration file is an XML property list containing one dictionary. The keys are rights, and the values are the rules by which those rights are authorized.

If you wanted everyone to have the right `com.megacode.kamasutra.launch`, you would add an entry like this:

```
<key>com.megacode.kamasutra.launch</key>
    <string>allow</string>
```

To prevent anyone from obtaining that right, you would change the entry:

```
<key>com.megacode.kamasutra.launch</key>
    <string>deny</string>
```

If you wanted to give the right to anyone who has authenticated as a member of the `parent` group within the last 700 seconds, you would make an entry like this:

```
<key>com.megacode.kamasutra.launch</key>
    <dict>
            <key>group</key>
            <string>parent</string>
            <key>shared</key>
            <true/>
            <key>timeout</key>
            <integer>700</integer>
    </dict>
```

You would also have to create a group called `parent` and add the user accounts of grown-ups in the house to that group.

In `/etc/authorization`, there is an entry with an empty key. This is the default that gets used for all unrecognized rights.

If the Security Server decides to grant the right, it returns a chunk of data to the application that requested the authorization. You can imagine this chunk of data as a ticket. Any process can present that ticket to the Security Server and ask, "Is this ticket good for the right `com.megacode.kamasutra.launch`?"

Notice the `shared` key in the entries in `/etc/authorization`. If that it is set to `true`, more than one ticket for the right can exist simultaneously.

The Security Framework API

The tickets representing rights that have been granted are held in an Authorization structure. To create an `AuthorizationRef` , you will use the function:

```
OSStatus AuthorizationCreate(const AuthorizationRights *rights,
                    const AuthorizationEnvironment *environment,
                            AuthorizationFlags flags,
                                AuthorizationRef *authorization);
```

Typically, this is used just to create an empty structure, like this:

```
AuthorizationRef authorizationRef;
OSStatus status;
status = AuthorizationCreate(NULL,  kAuthorizationEmptyEnvironment,
            kAuthorizationFlagDefaults, &authorizationRef);
if (status != errAuthorizationSuccess)  {
    NSLog(@"Unable to create an empty authorization object");
```

The real work of getting approved for a set of rights usually happens in `AuthorizationCopyRights()`:

```
OSStatus AuthorizationCopyRights(AuthorizationRef authorization,
                    const AuthorizationRights *rights,
                const AuthorizationEnvironment *environment,
                        AuthorizationFlags flags,
                            AuthorizationRights **authorizedRights);
```

To check for two rights, you would have a chunk of code like this:

```
OSStatus status;
AuthorizationItem rights[2];
rights[0] = { @"com.megacode.kamasutra.launch", 0, NULL, 0 };
rights[1] = { @"com.megacode.kamasutra.anotherright", 0, NULL, 0 };
AuthorizationRights rightSet = { 2, rights};
AuthorizationFlags flags = kAuthorizationFlagDefaults |
                        kAuthorizationFlagInteractionAllowed |
                        kAuthorizationFlagExtendRights;

status = AuthorizationCopyRights(authorizationRef, &rightSet,
                    kAuthorizationEmptyEnvironment, flags, NULL);

if (status != errAuthorizationSuccess)
    exit (EXIT_FAILURE);
```

If successful, the new rights are added to the `AuthorizationRef`.

Notice the flags. They say, "This is a preauthorization, bring up the authentication panel if necessary, and extend the rights of this user if possible. "

Notice that the policy is defined by `/etc/authorization`, so the code does not have to be recompiled if the policy is changed. In reality, of course, very few users are going to edit their `/etc/authorization` to create a policy for `com.megacode.kamasutra.launch` and put all the adults in the household into a group called `parent`, so you should assume that the default policy is what will actually be used.

To free the `AuthorizationRef`:

```
OSStatus AuthorizationFree(AuthorizationRef authorization,
                                AuthorizationFlags flags);
```

In the flags argument, you can supply `kAuthorizationFlagDestroyRights`. If you do, the function tells the Security server to revoke the ticket for the rights that have been authorized.

Passing authorization to a SUID tool

In Unix operating systems, if a process must be run with special privileges, the executable is owned by a privileged user and the SUID bit of the file permissions is set. When the SUID bit is set on an executable, the effective UID of a process created by running the executable is the UID of the owner of the file. (When the SUID bit is not set, the effective UID of the a process is the UID of the user that launched the executable.) So, for example, if you look at `passwd`, the SUID bit is set.

```
% ls -l /usr/bin/passwd
-r-sr-xr-x  1 root  wheel  30492 Jul 27 23:00 /usr/bin/passwd
```

Thus, when you run `passwd`, it is being run as `root`.

```
% whoami
rex

% passwd
Changing password for rex.
Old password:
^Z
Suspended

% ps -auxw | grep passwd
root  1309 0.0  0.1  1576   284 std  S  10:37AM  0:00.02 passwd
```

If you need to performed some privileged operation in your application, you will fork off a process and run an SUID tool. The tool can be embedded inside your app wrapper. All the dangerous stuff can be put into that tool. The tool should be as small, safe, and simple as possible.

But what keeps the bad people from going into my app wrapper and running the SUID tool. The answer is "Nothing!" So, we need to make sure that when the tool is run by an unauthorized user, it doesn't do anything.

Before launching your SUID tool from your application, you will preauthorize for a right and get a ticket. When the SUID tool is run, you will pipe the ticket to it. Before doing anything, the tool will check with the Security Server to make sure the ticket is good.

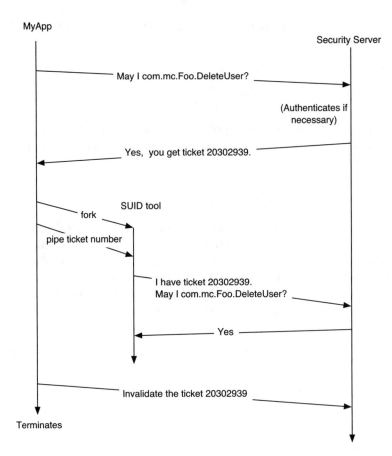

To pack the resulting ticket for sending to an external process, you will use:

```
OSStatus AuthorizationMakeExternalForm(AuthorizationRef authorization,
                                       AuthorizationExternalForm *extForm);
```

To unpack the ticket in the SUID tool, you will use :

```
OSStatus AuthorizationCreateFromExternalForm(const AuthorizationExternalForm
                                             AuthorizationRef *authorizat
```

Add Authentication to Remover

In this exercise, you will add the ability for Remover to read and delete any files on the system. Of course, you are going to make the user authenticate as a member of the admin group first.

Wrapping NSFileManager

You are going to write a replacement for **NSFileManager** called **AuthorizingFileManager** that will use **NSFileManager** when possible. If **NSFileManager**'s read or delete fails, **AuthorizingFileManager** will get authorization from the Security Server and run SUID tools to perform the forbidden operations.

(Notice that we could have subclassed **NSFileManager**, but the class uses a shared instance. This brings up many questions: Should we replace the shared instance with our own? Or should there be two shared instances: one for **AuthorizingFileManager** and one for **NSFileManager**? Instead we will skip the questions and just create a completely seperate class. This will also be an opportunity to use a couple of Objective-C tricks.)

You will also have to write three SUID tools: one that lists the contents of a directory, one that recursively deletes a directory and its contents, and one that determines if a path is a directory or a file.

So, open the Remover project and create a new subclass of **NSObject** called AuthorizingFileManager. We want it to be a drop-in replacement for **NSFileManager**, so it will have a shared instance. Alter your AuthorizingFileManager.m to look like this:

```
#import "AuthorizingFileManager.h"

static AuthorizingFileManager *_defaultAuthFileManager;

@implementation AuthorizingFileManager

+ (id)defaultManager
{
    if (!_defaultAuthFileManager) {
        _defaultAuthFileManager = [[self alloc] init];
    }
    return _defaultAuthFileManager;
}
```

The instance of **AuthorizingFileManager** will need a pointer to the **NSFileManager**, so add an instance variable to AuthorizingFileManager.h:

```
@interface AuthorizingFileManager : NSObject {
    NSFileManager *fileManager;
}
```

Initialize this in **init** and release it in **dealloc**:

```
- (id)init
{
    [super init];
    fileManager = [[NSFileManager defaultManager] retain];
    return self;
}

- (void)dealloc
{
    [fileManager release];
    [super dealloc];
}
```

You want any message not understood by **AuthorizingFileManager** to be forwarded on to the shared instance of **NSFileManager**. Objective-C makes this very easy. If a message is not recognized, it is bundled up into an **NSInvocation** object and the receiver is sent the message **forwardInvocation:**. So add the following methods to **AuthorizingFileManager**:

```
// This gets run before forwardInvocation:
- (NSMethodSignature *)methodSignatureForSelector:(SEL)aSelector
```

```
{
    NSMethodSignature *result;
    result = [super methodSignatureForSelector:aSelector];
    if (!result){
        result = [fileManager methodSignatureForSelector:aSelector];
    }
    return result;
}

- (void)forwardInvocation:(NSInvocation *)invocation
{
    SEL aSelector = [invocation selector];
    if ([fileManager respondsToSelector:aSelector])
        [invocation invokeWithTarget:fileManager];
    else
        [self doesNotRecognizeSelector:aSelector];
}
```

Now just replace **NSFileManager** with **AuthorizingFileManager** in
AppController.m and DirEntry.m. Build and run your app. It should work exactly
the same as before.

Preauthorizing

Now you will add the ability to delete directories that the user does not have write
access to.

First, add an instance variable to hold onto our authorization object. Also, declare
constants for the names of the rights. Make your AuthorizingFileManager.h file
start like this:

```
#define LIST_RIGHT "com.bignerdranch.remover.readforbiddendirectories"
#define DELETE_RIGHT "com.bignerdranch.remover.deleteforbiddendirectories"

#import <Foundation/Foundation.h>
#import <Security/Security.h>

@interface AuthorizingFileManager : NSObject {
    AuthorizationRef authorizationRef;
    NSFileManager *fileManager;
}
```

Open AuthorizingFileManager.m; initialize the AuthorizationRef in **init** and
free it in **dealloc**:

```
- (id)init
{
    OSStatus status;
    [super init];
    fileManager = [[NSFileManager defaultManager] retain];

    // Create an empty authorization structure
    status = AuthorizationCreate(NULL, kAuthorizationEmptyEnvironment,
                        kAuthorizationFlagDefaults, &authorizationRef);
    if (status != errAuthorizationSuccess) {
        NSLog(@"Failed to create the authref: %d.", status);
        [self release];
        return nil;
```

```
    }
    return self;
}

- (void)dealloc
{
    [fileManager release];
    AuthorizationFree(authorizationRef, kAuthorizationFlagDestroyRights);
    [super dealloc];
}
```

Create a method to preauthorize for a right:

```
- (BOOL)preauthorizeForRight:(const char *)rightName
{
    OSStatus status;
    AuthorizationItem right = { rightName, 0, NULL, 0 };
    AuthorizationRights rightSet = { 1, &right };
    AuthorizationFlags flags = kAuthorizationFlagDefaults |
                               kAuthorizationFlagPreAuthorize |
                               kAuthorizationFlagInteractionAllowed |
                               kAuthorizationFlagExtendRights;

    // This may cause the authorization panel to appear
    status = AuthorizationCopyRights(authorizationRef, &rightSet,
                        kAuthorizationEmptyEnvironment, flags, NULL);

    return (status == errAuthorizationSuccess);
}
```

Create a method that will pack your authorization ref into an **NSData**:

```
- (NSData *)authorizationAsData
{
    AuthorizationExternalForm extAuth;
    if (AuthorizationMakeExternalForm(authorizationRef, &extAuth))
        return nil;
    return [NSData dataWithBytes:&extAuth length:sizeof(extAuth)];
}
```

Create a method that will **alloc** and **init** an **NSTask**, set its launch path to an exectuable in the app wrapper, and connect pipes to its input and output:

```
// Create a task with pipes for input and output
- (NSTask *)taskForExecutable:(NSString *)execName
                     argument:(NSString *)arg
{
    NSString *executablePath;
    NSPipe *inPipe, *outPipe;
    NSTask *task;

    // Create a task for the requested executable
    task = [[NSTask alloc] init];
    executablePath = [[NSBundle mainBundle] pathForResource:execName
                                                ofType:@""];
    [task setLaunchPath:executablePath];
    [task setArguments:[NSArray arrayWithObject:arg]];

    // Set up the inPipe
```

```
        inPipe = [[NSPipe alloc] init];
        [task setStandardInput:inPipe];
        [inPipe release];

        // Set up the outPipe
        outPipe = [[NSPipe alloc] init];
        [task setStandardOutput:outPipe];
        [outPipe release];

        [task autorelease];
        return task;
    }
```

Now, create a method that tries to use **NSFileManager**'s **removeFileAtPath:handler:** method. If that fails, then create a task that will run an executable called remover_deletor.

```
- (BOOL)removeFileAtPath:(NSString *)path handler:handler
{
    BOOL successful = [fileManager removeFileAtPath:path handler:self];
    if (!successful) {
        NSFileHandle *inFile;
        NSTask *task;
        NSData  *authData;

        // preauthorize
        if (![self preauthorizeForRight:DELETE_RIGHT]) {
            NSLog(@"Unable to preauthorize delete");
            return NO;
        }

        // Pack authorization for piping to tool
        authData = [self authorizationAsData];

        // Create a task
        task = [self taskForExecutable:@"remover_deletor"
                             argument:path];
        if (!task) {
            NSLog(@"Unable to create task");
            return NO;
        }

        // Get filehandle for writing
        inFile = [[task standardInput] fileHandleForWriting];

        // Launch the task
        [task launch];

        // Pipe the authData to the tool and send EOF
        [inFile writeData:authData];
        [inFile closeFile];

        // Was it successful?
        [task waitUntilExit];
        successful = ([task terminationStatus] == 0);
    }

    return successful;
```

}

You may declare all these methods in `AuthorizingFileManager.h` if you wish.

Creating the SUID tools

Now, it is time to create the tool `remover_deletor`. First add a new target (using the **Project** menu in `Project Builder`) called **remover_deletor** of type **Tool** to your project. While you are at it, create targets for the other two tools also: **remover_lister** and **remover_statter**. `Remover` has a dependency on all three of the tools, so drag them under `Remover` in the target tab.

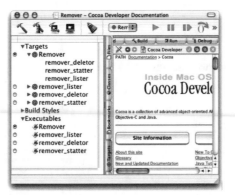

Create a C file called `remover_deletor.c`. This will be the tool that will remove the file or directory.

```c
#include <unistd.h>
#include <stdlib.h>
#include <sys/stat.h>
#include <stdio.h>
#include <Security/Security.h>
#include <dirent.h>

#define RIGHT "com.bignerdranch.remover.deleteforbiddendirectories"

void remove_tree(const char *path){
    DIR *dir;
    struct dirent *entry;
    char childPath[PATH_MAX];
    if (unlink(path) == 0)
        return;

    if (chdir(path) == -1) {
        fprintf(stderr, "Cannot cd to %s", path);
        return;
    }

    // Open the directory
    dir = opendir(path);
    if (!dir) {
        fprintf(stderr, "Cannot open %s\n", path);
        return;
    }
```

```
        // Read all the entries
        while (entry = readdir(dir)) {
            // Skip . and ..
            if (strcmp(entry->d_name, "..") == 0) {
                continue;
            }
            if (strcmp(entry->d_name, ".") == 0) {
                continue;
            }
            snprintf(childPath, PATH_MAX, "%s/%s", path, entry->d_name);
            remove_tree(childPath);
        }

        // Close the directory
        closedir(dir);

        // Delete the now-empty directory
        rmdir(path);
}

int main(int argc, char *argv[])
{
    OSStatus status;
    AuthorizationRef auth;
    char *path;

    AuthorizationExternalForm extAuth;

    // Is this process running as root?
    if (geteuid() != 0) {
        fprintf(stderr, "Not running as root\n");
        exit(-1);
    }

    // Was there one argument?
    if (argc != 2) {
        fprintf(stderr, "Usage: remove_deletor <dir>\n");
        exit(-1);
    }

    // Get the path
    path = argv[1];

    // Read the Authorization data from our input pipe.
    if (fread(&extAuth, sizeof(extAuth), 1, stdin) != 1)
        exit(-1);

    // Restore the externalized Authorization back
    // to an AuthorizationRef
    if (AuthorizationCreateFromExternalForm(&extAuth, &auth))
        exit(-1);

    // Create the rights structure
    AuthorizationItem right = { RIGHT, 0, NULL, 0 };
    AuthorizationRights rights = { 1, &right };
    AuthorizationFlags flags = kAuthorizationFlagDefaults |
                               kAuthorizationFlagExtendRights;
```

```
    fprintf(stderr, "Tool authorizing right %s for command.\n", RIGHT);

    // Check the authorization
    if (status = AuthorizationCopyRights(auth, &rights,
                    kAuthorizationEmptyEnvironment, flags, NULL)) {
        fprintf(stderr,
                "Tool authorizing command failed authorization: %ld.\n",
                status);
        exit(-1);
    }

    // Unlink the path
    remove_tree(path);

    // Terminate
    exit(0);
}
```

Make sure that the executables are part of the `Remover` application in the **Files** tab.

Before building the application, you will need to make sure that the file's owner is changed to `root` and the SUID bit is set on `remover_deletor` when it is installed. To do this, select the target **Remover**. We can set the SUID bit on install with some `Project Builder` tricks. Under the **Expert View** of the **Settings** pane, add the key `ALTERNATE_PERMISSIONS_FILES` and set it to

`Remover.app/Contents/Resources/remover_deletor`

(If you had multiple files to change the permissions on, you would separate their paths with spaces.)

Also add the key `ALTERNATE_MODE` and set it to `6555`. Also set the `ALTERNATE_OWNER` to `root` and `ALTERNATE_GROUP` to `admin`.

Go to the terminal and run

```
% sudo pbxbuild install
```

By using the `sudo` command to run `pbxbuild install`, the files for `Remover.app` are being created in the install location with `root` as the files' owner. Your application will appear in `/tmp/Remover.dst`, and `remover_deletor` will have its SUID bit set. Remember, even though the other files are owned by `root`, they will be executed as the user that launches them.

You could also set the SUID bit and the file's owner on the executables using Terminal commands:

```
% sudo -s
Password:
root# cd Remover/build/Remover.app/Contents/Resources
root# chmod 6555 remover_*
root# chown root:admin remover_*
```

Now run the application. If you try to delete a protected file or directory, the authorization panel should appear and force you to supply the username and password for a user in the admin group. After this, you should be able to delete protected directories for 300 seconds without reauthorizing. For testing purposes, I'd suggest that you create some protected directories as root in /tmp. Be careful with this application; an erroneous delete can cause much misery.

If that works, you are ready to add listing of protected files and directories. Add these two methods to AuthorizingFileManager.m:

```
- (NSArray *)directoryContentsAtPath:(NSString *)path
{
    NSFileHandle *inFile, *outFile;
    NSArray *result = nil;
    NSTask *task;
    NSData *output = nil, *authData = nil;
    NSString *outputAsString = nil;

    // Try to list the directory with using NSFileManager
    result = [fileManager directoryContentsAtPath:path];

    // Is there no result (because the file manager didn't have
    // permissions probably.
    if (!result) {

        // preauthorize
        if (![self preauthorizeForRight:LIST_RIGHT]) {
            NSLog(@"Unable to preauthorize");
            return nil;
        }

        // Pack authorization for piping to tool
        authData = [self authorizationAsData];

        // Create a task
        // Pass the path of the directory to the tool as argv[1]
        task = [self taskForExecutable:@"remover_lister" argument:path];
        if (!task) {
            NSLog(@"Unable to create task");
            return nil;
        }

        // Get filehandles for reading and writing
        inFile = [[task standardInput] fileHandleForWriting];
        outFile = [[task standardOutput] fileHandleForReading];

        // Launch the task
        [task launch];
```

```objc
        // Pipe the authData to the tool and send EOF
        [inFile writeData:authData];
        [inFile closeFile];

        // Read the listing of the directory from the tool's
        // standard output
        output = [outFile readDataToEndOfFile];

        if ([output length] == 0) {
            result = [NSArray array];
        } else {
            // Convert to an NSString
            outputAsString = [[NSString alloc] initWithData:output
                                  encoding:NSUTF8StringEncoding];

            // Break into components
            result = [outputAsString componentsSeparatedByString:@"\n"];

            // Release the string
            [outputAsString release];
        }
    }
    return result;
}

// This is sort of a cheap solution.  For the exercise,  we only
// need to know if it is a directory.  I should really put together
// an entire dictionary of file attributes.
// This is left as an exercise for the reader.

- (NSDictionary *)fileAttributesAtPath:(NSString *)path
                       traverseLink:(BOOL)willTraverse
{
    NSDictionary *result;
    // Try to use NSFileManager
    result = [fileManager fileAttributesAtPath:path
                              traverseLink:willTraverse];

    if (!result) {
        NSFileHandle *inFile, *outFile;
        NSTask *task;
        NSData *output, *authData;
        NSString *outputAsString;

        // preauthorize
        if (![self preauthorizeForRight:LIST_RIGHT]) {
            NSLog(@"Unable to preauthorize");
            return nil;
        }

        // Pack authorization for piping to tool
        authData = [self authorizationAsData];

        // Create a task
        task = [self taskForExecutable:@"remover_statter"
                          argument:path];
        if (!task) {
```

```
            NSLog(@"Unable to create task");
            return nil;
        }

        // Get filehandles for reading and writing
        inFile = [[task standardInput] fileHandleForWriting];
        outFile = [[task standardOutput] fileHandleForReading];

        // Launch the task
        [task launch];

        // Pipe the authData to the tool and send EOF
        [inFile writeData:authData];
        [inFile closeFile];

        // Read the listing of the directory from the tool's
        // standard output
        output = [outFile readDataToEndOfFile];

        // Convert to an NSString
        outputAsString = [[NSString alloc] initWithData:output
                                    encoding:NSUTF8StringEncoding];

        // Break into components
        result = [NSMutableDictionary dictionary];
        [(NSMutableDictionary *)result setObject:outputAsString
                                    forKey:NSFileType];

        // Release the string
        [outputAsString release];
    }
    return result;
}
```

Of course, you have to create the `remover_lister.c` and `remover_statter.c` files.
Here is `remover_lister.c`:

```
#include <unistd.h>
#include <stdlib.h>
#include <dirent.h>
#include <stdio.h>
#include <Security/Security.h>

#define RIGHT "com.bignerdranch.remover.readforbiddendirectories"

int
main(int argc, char * argv[])
{
    OSStatus status;
    AuthorizationRef auth;
    char *path;
    DIR *dir;
    struct dirent *entry;
    int firstTime = 1;

    AuthorizationExternalForm extAuth;

    // Is this process running as root?
```

```
if (geteuid() != 0) {
    fprintf(stderr, "Not running as root\n");
    exit(-1);
}

// Was there one argument?
if (argc != 2) {
    fprintf(stderr, "Usage: remove_lister <dir>\n");
    exit(-1);
}

// Get the path
path = argv[1];

// Read the Authorization "byte blob" from our input pipe.
if (fread(&extAuth, sizeof(extAuth), 1, stdin) != 1)
    exit(-1);

// Restore the externalized Authorization
// back to an AuthorizationRef
if (AuthorizationCreateFromExternalForm(&extAuth, &auth))
    exit(-1);

// Create the rights structure
AuthorizationItem right = { RIGHT, 0, NULL, 0 };
AuthorizationRights rights = { 1, &right };
AuthorizationFlags flags = kAuthorizationFlagDefaults |
                           kAuthorizationFlagExtendRights;

fprintf(stderr, "Tool authorizing right %s for command.\n", RIGHT);

// Check the authorization
if (status = AuthorizationCopyRights(auth, &rights,
                  kAuthorizationEmptyEnvironment, flags, NULL)) {
    fprintf(stderr, "Tool command failed authorization: %ld.\n",
                  status);
    exit(-1);
}

// Open the directory
dir = opendir(path);
if (dir == NULL) {
    fprintf(stderr, "Cannot open %s\n", path);
    exit(-1);
}

// Read all the entries
while (entry = readdir(dir)) {

    // Skip . and ..
    if (strcmp(entry->d_name, "..") == 0) {
        continue;
    }
    if (strcmp(entry->d_name, ".") == 0) {
        continue;
    }
```

```
        // Put \n before each line except the first
        if (firstTime) {
            firstTime = 0;
        } else {
            fputc('\n',stdout);
        }

        // Write out the filename
        fputs(entry->d_name,stdout);
    }

    // Close the directory
    closedir(dir);

    // Close output
    fclose(stdout);

    // Terminate
    exit(0);
}
```

Here is `remover_statter.c`:

```
#include <unistd.h>
#include <stdlib.h>
#include <sys/stat.h>
#include <stdio.h>
#include <Security/Security.h>

#define RIGHT "com.bignerdranch.remover.readforbiddendirectories"

int
main(int argc, char *argv[])
{
    OSStatus status;
    AuthorizationRef auth;
    char *path;
    struct stat statbuf;
    char *typeAsString;

    AuthorizationExternalForm extAuth;

    // Is this process running as root?
    if (geteuid() != 0) {
        fprintf(stderr, "Not running as root\n");
        exit(-1);
    }

    // Was there one argument?
    if (argc != 2) {
        fprintf(stderr, "Usage: remove_statter <dir>\n");
        exit(-1);
    }

    // Get the path
    path = argv[1];

    /* Read the Authorization "byte blob" from our input pipe.
```

```
    if (fread(&extAuth, sizeof(extAuth), 1, stdin) != 1)
    exit(-1);

    /* Restore the externalized Authorization back
    to an AuthorizationRef
    if (AuthorizationCreateFromExternalForm(&extAuth, &auth))
        exit(-1);

    // Create the rights structure
    AuthorizationItem right = { RIGHT, 0, NULL, 0 };
    AuthorizationRights rights = { 1, &right };
    AuthorizationFlags flags = kAuthorizationFlagDefaults |
                                kAuthorizationFlagExtendRights;

    fprintf(stderr, "Tool authorizing right %s for command.\n", RIGHT);

    // Check the authorization
    if (status = AuthorizationCopyRights(auth, &rights,
                        kAuthorizationEmptyEnvironment, flags, NULL)) {
        fprintf(stderr, "Tool failed authorization: %ld.\n",
                        status);
        exit(-1);
    }
    // Stat the path
    if (stat(path, &statbuf)) {
        fprintf(stderr, "Unable to stat %s", path);
        exit(-1);
    }

    // Write out stat info
    if (S_ISDIR(statbuf.st_mode))
        typeAsString = "NSFileTypeDirectory";
    else
        typeAsString = "NSFileTypeRegular";

    fprintf(stdout, "%s", typeAsString);
    fclose(stdout);

    // Terminate
    exit(0);
}
```

Once again, build it and set the SUID bit and owner for the tools. Run the application. You will now be able to browse protected directories.

For the More Curious: AuthorizationExecuteWithPrivileges()

Notice that in the case above, everything works nicely because the owner and the SUID bits are set on the tool. The question so many installers would have is, "How do I get the owner and SUID bits set?" (You can see the chicken-or-egg nature of the problem: you have no privileges with the SUID bit, and you can't set the SUID bit or change the owner to `root` without privileges.)

The solution is **AuthorizationExecuteWithPrivileges()**. It calls a tool in a manner that is similar to what you've done in this exercise. The difference is that the effective UID is changed *before* the tool is called. Actually, the way it works is that there is an SUID tool on every system called

/System/Library/CoreServices/AuthorizationTrampoline which reads the name of another tool (let's call it "Tool X") from its command line and reads an authorization from its standard input. It checks to make sure that the authorization includes the right system.privilege.admin. It then starts Tool X and pipes the authorization into the Tool X's standard input. Since Tool X was started by a process that has root's UID as its effective UID, Tool X also has root's UID as its effective UID.

This mechanism makes *self-repair* possible. If necessary, a self-repairing tool can set the owner and SUID bit on itself. Self-repair is suggested by Apple and the code here is mostly from their sample. If possible, I would avoid making self-repairing tools by using a good installer program to install the app and set the SUID bit where necessary. To me, this seems like a more secure way to handle things.

The flowchart for a self-repairing tool for deleting users might look like this:

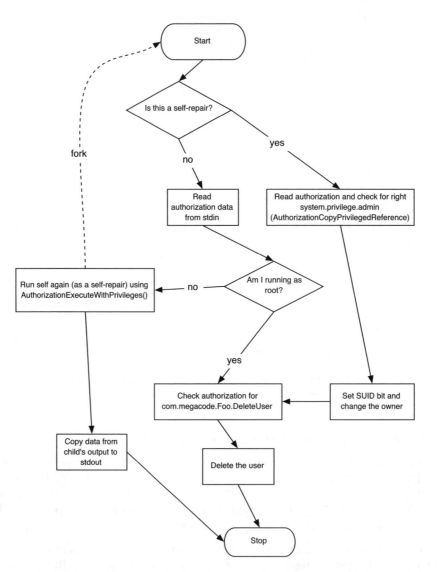

When you launch a tool from an application, you should supply the full path to the executable as argv[0] so that the tool knows the path to itself. (**NSTask** will handle this automatically.) Here is how the code for the above flowchart would look:

```
int
main(int argc, char *argv[])
{
    char *path_to_self;
    OSStatus status;
    AuthorizationRef auth;
    int bytesRead;
    MyAuthorizedCommand myCommand;

    path_to_self = argv[0];

    // Check to see if this is being called for self-repair
    if (argc == 2 && !strcmp(argv[1], "--self-repair")) {
        struct stat st;
        int fd_tool;

        // Recover the passed in AuthorizationRef and check for
        // the right system.privilege.admin.
        // This function only works if the tool was started by
        // AuthorizationExecuteWithPrivileges()
        if (AuthorizationCopyPrivilegedReference(&auth,
                                      kAuthorizationFlagDefaults))
            exit(kMyAuthorizedCommandInternalError);

        // Open tool exclusively, so noone can change it while we change
        // the owner and SUID bit it
        fd_tool = open(path_to_self, O_NONBLOCK | O_RDONLY | O_EXLOCK, 0);

        if (fd_tool == -1)
        {
            fprintf(stderr, "Exclusive open failed: %d.\n", errno);
            exit(-1);
        }

        if (fstat(fd_tool, &st))
            exit(-1);

        if (st.st_uid != 0)
            fchown(fd_tool, 0, st.st_gid);

        // Disable group and world writability and make setuid root.
        fchmod(fd_tool, (st.st_mode & (~(S_IWGRP | S_IWOTH))) | S_ISUID);

        close(fd_tool);

        fprintf(stderr, "Tool self-repair done.\n");

    } else {
        AuthorizationExternalForm extAuth;

        // Read the Authorization "byte blob" from our input pipe.
        if (read(0, &extAuth, sizeof(extAuth)) != sizeof(extAuth))
            exit(-1);

        // Restore the externalized Authorization back to an
```

```
              // AuthorizationRef
              if (AuthorizationCreateFromExternalForm(&extAuth, &auth))
                  exit(-1);

              // If we are not running as root we need to self-repair.
              if (geteuid() != 0)
              {
                  int status;
                  int pid;
                  FILE *commPipe = NULL;
                  char *arguments[] = { "--self-repair", NULL };
                  char buffer[1024];
                  int bytesRead;

                  // Set our own stdin and stdout to be the communication
                  // channel with ourself.
                  fprintf(stderr, "AuthorizationExecuteWithPrivileges\n");

                  if (AuthorizationExecuteWithPrivileges(auth, path_to_self,
                                      kAuthorizationFlagDefaults, arguments,
                                      &commPipe))
                      exit(-1);

                  // Read from stdin and write to commPipe.
                  for (;;)
                  {
                      bytesRead = read(0, buffer, 1024);
                      if (bytesRead < 1) break;
                      fwrite(buffer, 1, bytesRead, commPipe);
                  }

                  // Flush any remaining output.
                  fflush(commPipe);

                  // Close the communication pipe to let the child
                  // know we are done.
                  fclose(commPipe);

                  // Wait for the child of AuthorizationExecuteWithPrivileges
                  // to exit.
                  pid = wait(&status);
                  if (pid == -1 || ! WIFEXITED(status))
                      exit(-1);

                  // Exit with the same exit code as the child spawned
                  // by AuthorizationExecuteWithPrivileges()
                  exit(WEXITSTATUS(status));
              }
          }
          // You would check the authorization and actually
          // do the work of the tool here
      }
```

The right associated with **AuthorizationExecuteWithPrivileges()** is called
system.privilege.admin. The entry in /etc/authorization looks like this:

```
      <key>system.privilege.admin</key>
        <dict>
```

```
        <key>group</key>
        <string>admin</string>
        <key>shared</key>
        <false/>
        <key>allow-root</key>
        <true/>
        <key>timeout</key>
        <integer>300</integer>
</dict>
```

(The `allow-root` means "allow anyone running as root to have this right without authentication".)

Notice that `AuthorizationExecuteWithPrivileges()` is really easy to use. In one simple call it preauthorizes, forks, and packs up the authorization and sends it to the tool. The other end is easy, too. `AuthorizationCopyPrivilegedReference()` reads `stdin` and recreates the `AuthorizationRef`. In fact, it is too easy to use.

Because it is so easy to use, many programmers are using it anytime they need any sort of privilege. This is flawed because they are creating many apps and many types of operations that use the exact same right: `system.privilege.admin`. This is an invitation to evil doers to create trojan horses. A user may authenticate in an app that is supposed to do something relatively harmless. The generated ticket could be used to run a tool that does something much more violent.

Moral: Name your rights something unique. Do not use `AuthorizationExecuteWithPrivileges()` unless absolutely necessary.

It is necessary to use `AuthorizationExecuteWithPrivileges()` occasionally, so here is some information about it:

```
OSStatus AuthorizationExecuteWithPrivileges(AuthorizationRef authorization,
                                const char *pathToTool,
                        AuthorizationFlags options,
                            char * const *arguments,
                                FILE **communicationsPipe);
```

The first argument is an authorization structure. It will be filled in if necessary by bringing up the authentication panel. The second argument is the path to the tool. The third argument is always zero. The fourth argument is an `argv`-like array of command-line arguments to be passed to the tool. The final argument is a pointer. A new pipe that will be attached to the new process for bidirectional communcations will be created. This pointer will be set to point to it.

Chapter 19. Distributed Objects

Distributed Objects (or DO) is a technology that allows an object in one process to send a message to an object in another. In fact, the objects communicating may be on different machines. This is a rather nifty way to create client/server applications: the client sends messages to an object in the server process and gets back a response. It is also a way for one application to be informed of changes in another. Distributed Objects is part of Cocoa's Foundation framework.

DO integrates very neatly with the run loop that makes event handling work. Thus, while your app is waiting for messages to arrive from other processes, in can continue to handle user input. For this reason, DO is also used to send messages between threads in a single application.

Distributed Objects Concepts

Here is the basic idea: Let us say that there is a client process and a server process. The server process makes a server object available to the world. The client process asks for that server object, but gets an instance of **NSDistantObject**. The **NSDistantObject** is a proxy for the server object (it is, in fact, a subclass of **NSProxy**). When messages are sent to the proxy, the message (including the arguments) are packed up and sent across the network to the server object. The server object executes the method, and the result is packed up and sent back to the client process. The proxy returns the result as if it had done the computation.

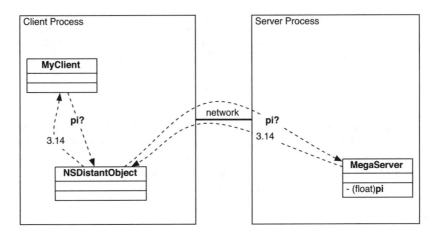

The dream, then, is that you get the proxy object and treat it just like you would the server object. The reality is not as simple because many things can go wrong with the client, the server, or the network in between. There are also performance issues to consider; you will want to keep the amount of data that you send across the network to a minimum.

Notice that when the client asks for the server, it gets a proxy. The proxy represents the server object. On the client side, the proxy is attached to an **NSConnection**, which handles its communications. On the server side, the corresponding server object is also attached to an **NSConnection**. You can ask a connection for its distant objects and it will return an array of the proxies for which it is responsible. You can ask a connection for its local objects, and it will return an array of server objects. More specifically, the local objects are objects which have been vended out as proxies in other processes.

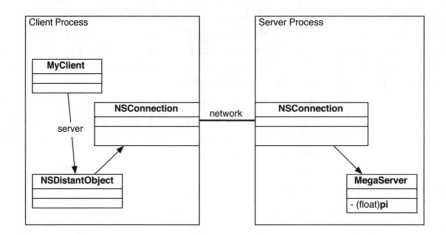

NSPort

An **NSConnection** object has two instances of **NSPort**: one receives data and the other sends data. There are several subclasses of **NSPort** which enable the connection to handle its communcations in different ways.

NSPort

> This is the superclass of all other ports. Concrete instances are only useful when the proxy and the object it represents are in the same process. Instances of **NSPort** are commonly used when DO is used for communications between two threads in the same process.

NSMachPort

> This port uses Mach messaging. Instances of **NSMachPort** are only useful when the proxy and the object it represents are on the same machine. Instances of **NSMachPort** are commonly used for communcations between two applications running on the same machine. If two mach ports are connected, when one stops working, the other is informed immediately.

NSSocketPort

> This port uses sockets. Instances can communicate even when the proxy and the object it represents are on different machines.

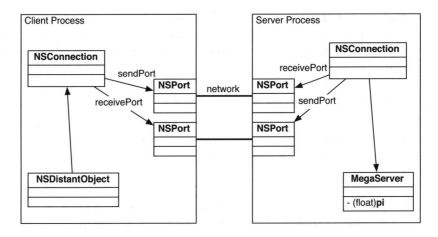

Create a DO Server

In this chapter, you will create a simple chat client and server using Distributed Objects. Create a new Foundation Tool Project. Name it **chatterd**. This is will be the server.

Clients will subscribe and unsubscribe with the server. Clients will send messages to be distributed to the server. The server will then send the message to the clients for display.

Whenever you are sending messages between two processes, it is a good idea to create a protocol that contains the messages that will be sent. This is an important step in design, and later you will see that the protocol can actually be used to increase performance.

Create an empty file called `ChatterServing.h`.

```objc
#import <Foundation/Foundation.h>

// Messages the client will receive from the server
@protocol ChatterUsing

- (oneway void)showMessage:(in bycopy NSString *)message
     fromNickname:(in bycopy NSString *)nickname;

- (bycopy NSString *)nickname;

@end

// Messages the server will receive from the client
@protocol ChatterServing

- (oneway void)sendMessage:(in bycopy NSString *)message
               fromClient:(in byref id <ChatterUsing>)client;

// Returns NO if someone already has newClient's nickname
- (BOOL)subscribeClient:(in byref id <ChatterUsing>)newClient;

- (void)unsubscribeClient:(in byref id <ChatterUsing>)client;

@end
```

Notice that this file has some Objective-C keywords that you may never have seen before. Remember when I said "packs up the message (including the arguments) and sends it to the server?" These keywords control specifically how the arguments and return values should be packed up.

`oneway void`

> If a method has a return type of `oneway void`, the client does not wait for a response. If the return type is anything else, the proxy blocks until the response comes from its corresponding object.

`in`

> If an argument has `in` in its type, it is assumed that the receiver is going to read the value, but not change it. The argument is thus sent from the requestor to the the receiver, but not returned. This minimizes network traffic.

`out`

> If an argument has `out` in its type, it is assumed that the reciever is going to change the value, but not read it. The argument is thus not sent from the requestor to the receiver, but is returned to requestor.

`inout`

> If an argument has `inout` in its type, it is assumed that the receiver is going to both read and change the value. This is the default if you supply neither `in` nor `out`.

`bycopy`

> If an argument has `bycopy` in its type, the argument is archived before it is sent to the receiver and unarchived in the receiver's process space.

`byref`

> If an argument has `byref` in its type, the argument is represented by a proxy in the receiver's process space.

That last keyword explains how our server will work: It will have an array of proxies. Each proxy will represent one client. When a client subscribes, its proxy will be added to the array. When the server receives a message, it will send that message to each of its proxies for display. When a client unsubscribes, it will be removed from the array of proxies.

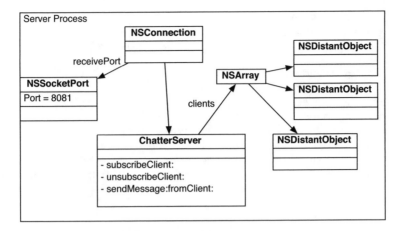

Create a new class called **ChatterServer**. Edit the header file:

Example 19-1. ChatterServer.h

```
#import <Foundation/Foundation.h>
#import "ChatterServing.h"

@interface ChatterServer : NSObject <ChatterServing> {
    NSMutableArray *clients;
}
@end
```

Implement the methods in the implementation file:

Example 19-2. ChatterServer.m

```
#import "ChatterServer.h"
@implementation ChatterServer

- (id)init
{
    [super init];
    clients = [[NSMutableArray alloc] init];
    return self;
}

// Private method
- (id)clientWithNickname:(NSString *)string
{
    id currentClient;
    NSEnumerator *enumerator;
    enumerator = [clients objectEnumerator];
    while (currentClient = [enumerator nextObject]) {
        if ([[currentClient nickname] isEqual:string]) {
            return currentClient;
        }
    }
    return nil;
}
```

```
// Methods called by clients
- (oneway void)sendMessage:(in bycopy NSString *)message
    fromClient:(in byref id <ChatterUsing>)client
{
    NSString *senderNickname;
    id currentClient;
    NSEnumerator *enumerator;
    senderNickname = [client nickname];
    enumerator = [clients objectEnumerator];
    NSLog(@"from %@: %@", senderNickname, message);
    while (currentClient = [enumerator nextObject]) {
        [currentClient showMessage:message fromNickname:senderNickname];
    }
}

- (BOOL)subscribeClient:(in byref id <ChatterUsing>)newClient
{
    NSString *newNickname = [newClient nickname];

    // Is this nickname taken?
    if ([self clientWithNickname:newNickname]) {
        return NO;
    }
    NSLog(@"adding client");
    [clients addObject:newClient];
    return YES;
}

- (void)unsubscribeClient:(in byref id <ChatterUsing>)client
{
    NSDistantObject *clientProxy = (NSDistantObject *)client;
    NSConnection *connection = [clientProxy connectionForProxy];
    [clients removeObject:client];
    [connection invalidate];
    NSLog(@"client removed");
}

- (void)dealloc
{
    [clients release];
    [super dealloc];
}
@end
```

Notice that in **unsubscribeClient:** you explicitly invalidated the connection. This ensures that the connection and its ports get freed. This is because for each client that subscribes, the server will create a proxy and a connection for that client.

Each connection can have a delegate. Each time the connection spawns a new "child" connection, the child will have its delegate outlet set to point to the parent's delegate. The delegate gets informed each time a new connection is spawned and when the connection dies. Create a new class to be the delegate of your connections. Create a class **ConnectionMonitor** to log these:

Example 19-3. ConnectionMonitor.m

```
#import "ConnectionMonitor.h"

@implementation ConnectionMonitor

- (BOOL)connection:(NSConnection *)ancestor
            shouldMakeNewConnection:(NSConnection *)conn
{
        NSLog(@"creating new connection: %d total connections",
                      [[NSConnection allConnections] count]);
        return YES;
}

- (void)connectionDidDie:(NSNotification *)note
{
    NSConnection *connection = [note object];
    NSLog(@"connection did die: %@", connection);
}
@end
```

Now edit `main.m` so that it creates a connection, a server, and a monitor before starting the runloop. Also, there is a bug in Foundation in Mac OS 10.2 that leaks instances of **NSSocketPort**. The magic fix is here.

Example 19-4. main.m

```
#import "ChatterServer.h"
#import "ChatterServing.h"
#import "ConnectionMonitor.h"
#include <sys/socket.h>

#import <Foundation/Foundation.h>

int main (int argc, const char * argv[]) {
    NSSocketPort *receivePort;
    NSConnection *connection;

    NSAutoreleasePool * pool = [[NSAutoreleasePool alloc] init];
    NSRunLoop *runloop = [NSRunLoop currentRunLoop];
    ConnectionMonitor *monitor = [[ConnectionMonitor alloc] init];
    ChatterServer *chatterServer = [[ChatterServer alloc] init];

    // Magic fix for socketPort/host leaks!
    if ([NSHost respondsToSelector:@selector(_fixNSHostLeak)]) {
        [NSHost _fixNSHostLeak];
    }
    if ([NSSocketPort respondsToSelector:@selector(_fixNSSocketPortLeak)]) {
        [NSSocketPort _fixNSSocketPortLeak];
    }

    NS_DURING
        // This server will wait for requests on port 8081
        receivePort = [[NSSocketPort alloc] initWithTCPPort:8081];
    NS_HANDLER
        NSLog(@"unable to get port 8081");
```

```
        exit(-1);
    NS_ENDHANDLER

    // Create the connection object
    connection = [NSConnection connectionWithReceivePort:receivePort
                                               sendPort:nil];

    // The port is retained by the connection
    [receivePort release];

    // When clients use this connection, they will
    // talk to the ChatterServer
    [connection setRootObject:chatterServer];

    // The chatter server is retained by the connection
    [chatterServer release];

    // Set up the monitor object
    [connection setDelegate:monitor];
    [[NSNotificationCenter defaultCenter] addObserver:monitor
            selector:@selector(connectionDidDie:)
                name:NSConnectionDidDieNotification
              object:nil];

    // Start the runloop
    [runloop run];

    // If the run loop exits (and I do not know why it would), cleanup
    [connection release];
    [monitor release];
    [pool release];
    return 0;
}
```

Build and run your server. It will not do much until you've created a client.

Create a Client Using DO

Create a new Cocoa Application project called **ChatterClient**. Open up the

`MainMenu.nib` file and layout the UI as shown:

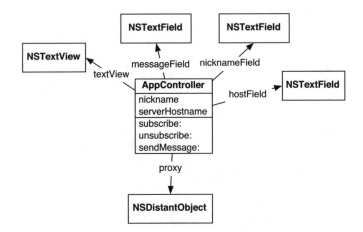

Create a subclass of **NSObject** called **AppController**. Add four outlets to the class: **NSTextField** *hostField, **NSTextField** *messageField, **NSTextField** *nicknameField, **NSTextView** *textView. Add three actions: **sendMessage:**, **subscribe:, unsubscribe:**. Create files for the class and create an instance of it.

Set each outlet of the **AppController** to point to the appropriate view.

Make the **AppController** the target of the Subscribe button, the Unsubscribe button, and the message text field.

Make the **AppController** the delegate of **NSApplication**.

Save the nib file. Return to `Project Builder`.

Add the file `ChatterServing.h` to the ChatterClient project.

Edit the class **AppController**.

Example 19-5. AppController.h

```
#import <Cocoa/Cocoa.h>
#import "ChatterServing.h"

@interface AppController : NSObject <ChatterUsing>
{
    IBOutlet NSTextField *hostField;
    IBOutlet NSTextField *messageField;
    IBOutlet NSTextField *nicknameField;
    IBOutlet NSTextView *textView;
    NSString *nickname;
    NSString *serverHostname;
    id proxy;
}
- (IBAction)sendMessage:(id)sender;
- (IBAction)subscribe:(id)sender;
- (IBAction)unsubscribe:(id)sender;
@end
```

Example 19-6. AppController.m

```
#import "AppController.h"

@implementation AppController

// Private method to clean up connection and proxy
// Seems to be leaking NSSocketPorts
```

```
- (void)cleanup
{
    NSConnection *connection = [proxy connectionForProxy];
    [[NSNotificationCenter defaultCenter] removeObserver:self];
    [connection invalidate];
    [proxy release];
    proxy = nil;
}

// Show message coming in from server
- (oneway void)showMessage:(in bycopy NSString *)message
       fromNickname:(in bycopy NSString *)n
{
    NSString *string = [NSString stringWithFormat:@"%@ says, \"%@\"\n",
                                                  n, message];

    NSTextStorage *currentContents = [textView textStorage];
    NSRange range = NSMakeRange([currentContents length], 0);
    [currentContents replaceCharactersInRange:range withString:string];
    range.length = [string length];
    [textView scrollRangeToVisible:range];
    // Beep to get user's attention
    NSBeep();
}

// Accessors
- (bycopy NSString *)nickname
{
    return nickname;
}

- (void)setNickname:(NSString *)s
{
    [s retain];
    [nickname release];
    nickname = s;
}

- (void)setServerHostname:(NSString *)s
{
    [s retain];
    [serverHostname release];
    serverHostname = s;
}

// Connect to the server
- (void)connect
{
    BOOL successful;
    NSConnection *connection;
    NSSocketPort *sendPort;

    // Create the send port
    sendPort = [[NSSocketPort alloc] initRemoteWithTCPPort:8081
                                        host:serverHostname];

    // Create an NSConnection
    connection = [NSConnection connectionWithReceivePort:nil
```

```
                                          sendPort:sendPort];

    // Set timeouts to something reasonable
    [connection setRequestTimeout:10.0];
    [connection setReplyTimeout:10.0];

    // The send port is retained by the connection
    [sendPort release];

    NS_DURING
        // Get the proxy
        proxy = [[connection rootProxy] retain];

        // Get informed when the connection fails
        [[NSNotificationCenter defaultCenter] addObserver:self
                              selector:@selector(connectionDown:)
                                  name:NSConnectionDidDieNotification
                                object:connection];

        // By telling the proxy about the protocol for the object
        // it represents, we significantly reduce the network
        // traffic involved in each invocation
        [proxy setProtocolForProxy:@protocol(ChatterServing)];

        // Try to subscribe with chosen nickname
        successful = [proxy subscribeClient:self];
        if (successful) {
            [messageField setStringValue:@"Connected"];
        } else {
            [messageField setStringValue:@"Nickname not available"];
            [self cleanup];
        }
    NS_HANDLER
        // If the server does not respond in 10 seconds,
        // this handler will get called
        [messageField setStringValue:@"Unable to connect"];
        [self cleanup];
    NS_ENDHANDLER
}


// Read hostname and nickname then connect
- (IBAction)subscribe:(id)sender
{
    // Is the user already subscribed?
    if (proxy) {
        [messageField setStringValue:@"unsubscribe first!"];
    } else {
        // Read the hostname and nickname from UI
        [self setServerHostname:[hostField stringValue]];
        [self setNickname:[nicknameField stringValue]];

        // Connect
        [self connect];
    }
}

- (IBAction)sendMessage:(id)sender
```

```
{
    NSString *inString;

    // If there is no proxy,  try to connect.
    if (!proxy) {
        [self connect];
        // If there is still no proxy, bail
        if (!proxy){
            return;
        }
    }

    // Read the message from the text field
    inString = [messageField stringValue];
    NS_DURING
        // Send a message to the server
        [proxy sendMessage:inString fromClient:self];
    NS_HANDLER
        // If something goes wrong
        [messageField setStringValue:@"The connection is down"];
        [self cleanup];
    NS_ENDHANDLER
}


- (IBAction)unsubscribe:(id)sender
{
    NS_DURING
        [proxy unsubscribeClient:self];
        [messageField setStringValue:@"Unsubscribed"];
        [self cleanup];
    NS_HANDLER
        [messageField setStringValue:@"Error unsubscribing"];
    NS_ENDHANDLER
}


// Delegate methods

//  If the connection goes down,  do cleanup
- (void)connectionDown:(NSNotification *)note
{
    NSLog(@"connectionDown:");
    [messageField setStringValue:@"connection down"];
    [self cleanup];
}

// If the app terminates,  unsubscribe.
- (NSApplicationTerminateReply)applicationShouldTerminate:
                                    (NSApplication *)app
{
    NSLog(@"invalidating connection");
    if (proxy) {
        [proxy unsubscribeClient:self];
        [[proxy connectionForProxy] invalidate];
    }
    return NSTerminateNow;
}
```

```
- (void)dealloc
{
    [self cleanup];
    [super dealloc];
}

@end
```

Add the magic leak fix to **main()**:

Example 19-7. main.m

```
#import <Cocoa/Cocoa.h>

int main(int argc, const char *argv[])
{
    if ([NSHost respondsToSelector:@selector(_fixNSHostLeak)]) {
        [NSHost _fixNSHostLeak];
    }
    if ([NSSocketPort respondsToSelector:@selector(_fixNSSocketPortLeak)]) {
        [NSSocketPort _fixNSSocketPortLeak];
    }
    return NSApplicationMain(argc, argv);
}
```

With your server running, build and run the client.

For the more curious: NSPortCoder

When a message is being sent to a remote object, the arguments are archived using an **NSPortCoder**. Each object that would be sent is first sent the message:

```
- (id)replacementObjectForPortCoder:(NSPortCoder *)aCoder
```

The object that comes back is the one that is put into the archive. This method is defined in **NSObject**. As defined in **NSObject**, the method returns an **NSDistantObject**. Thus, by default, proxies instead of objects are sent. In objects that would be willing to send copies of themselves (**NSString**, for example) **replacementObjectForPortCoder:** is overridden to return themselves.

An **NSPortCoder** knows whether the argument to the method is bycopy or byref, and you can ask it. Here is a reasonable way to override **replacementObjectForPortCoder:** in an object that conforms to the **NSCoding** protocol:

```
- (id)replacementObjectForPortCoder:(NSPortCoder *)c {
    if ([c isBycopy])
        return self;
    else
        return [NSDistantObject proxyWithLocal:self
                             connection:[encoder connection]];
}
```

Challenge

Make the server a true daemon.

```
    IBOutlet NSTextView *textView;
    NSString *nickname;
    id proxy;
    NSData *address;
    NSNetServiceBrowser *browser;
    NSMutableArray *services;
    IBOutlet NSComboBox *hostField;
}
- (IBAction)sendMessage:(id)sender;
- (IBAction)subscribe:(id)sender;
- (IBAction)unsubscribe:(id)sender;
- (void)cleanup;
// Combo box data source methods
- (int)numberOfItemsInComboBox:(NSComboBox *)aComboBox;
- (id)comboBox:(NSComboBox *)aComboBox
          objectValueForItemAtIndex:(int)index;
- (unsigned int)comboBox:(NSComboBox *)aComboBox
          indexOfItemWithStringValue:(NSString *)string;
@end
```

Save `AppController.h` and parse it into `MainMenu.nib`. Add a combo box and set its `datasource` to be the `AppController`. Set the `AppController`'s `hostField` to point at the combo box.

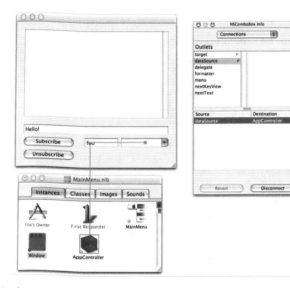

`AppController`'s `awakeFromNib`, create a browser and start the search:

```
(void)awakeFromNib

browser = [[NSNetServiceBrowser alloc] init];
services = [[NSMutableArray array] retain];
browser setDelegate:self];
browser searchForServicesOfType:@"_chatter._tcp" inDomain:@"local."];
NSLog(@"begun browsing: %@", browser);
```

using a discovered net service, you will want to resolve it — that is, look up address for it. This is another method that returns immediately but actually waits background for success.

Chapter 20. Rendezvous

Zeroconf is a very compelling idea. It extends the idea of DNS so that things on the network can declare their intentions. For example, when a zeroconf-compliant device is plugged into a network, it can declare "I am bozo.local, and my IP address is 168.254.32.1!" If another device already has that IP address, it can complain. The new device will then change its address. Thus, a network device can get in IP address without a DHCP server. This capability is known as *link local addressing*.

However, the beauty of Zeroconf does not end at devices and IP addresses. It also allows services to declare their name, type, address, and port number. Thus, the local network is informed of new devices and services as they are added. Furthermore, it adds the ability for the services to be browsed. That is, if you are looking for a type of service, you can ask for all the information about all the individual servers on a particular network.

The DNS standard actually already had a mechanism by which a service could be advertised. The idea was that, for example, to find all the ftp servers in the `bignerdranch.com` domain, your ftp client would ask for the SRV record for `_ftp._tcp.bignerdranch.com`. There are two why you have probably never heard of the SRV record:

1. No one uses it.
2. Only a DNS server can advertise the service.

To make it possible for many, many machines to advertise services on a network, Multicast DNS was created. Essentially, every machine is running a Multicast DNS server. This daemon is `/usr/sbin/mDNSResponder`.

Thus, Zeroconf is a clever marriage of link local addressing and multicast DNS. Zeroconf is a proposed standard, and Rendezvous is Apple's implementation of that standard. There are three different APIs for dealing with Rendezvous:

1. The mach-level API called DNSServiceDiscovery is what all the other APIs are based upon.
2. The C API in the CoreServices framework uses DNSServiceDiscovery but integrates more easily with the rest of Core Foundation.
3. The Objective-C classes **NSNetService** and **NSNetServiceBrowser** are part of the Foundation framework.

In this chapter, we will use the Objective-C API to let our chatter server declare its availability and let our chatter client browse for servers.

Publishing an NSNetService

In a server, you will advertise the availability of your service by creating an instance of **NSNetService** and publishing it. You will give the server a name, you will tell it

what service it provides, what port it runs on, and the name of the network it is part
of (the domain). The important methods are:

```
- (id)initWithDomain:(NSString *)domain
              type:(NSString *)type
              name:(NSString *)name
              port:(int)port
```

This is the initializer that you will use when creating a service to be published.
You may pass in @"" as the domain, and the host's default domain will be used.
The type is a string of the form "service_type.protocol.". As a convention,
host names are not prepended with an underscore, whereas service and
protocols are. The protocol is usually either _tcp or _udp. For our example, the
type will be @"_chatter._tcp.". You can use any Unicode string as the name.
The only tricky bit is that your name may conflict with another's. The port is
the port number upon which the server is waiting.

```
- (void)publish
```

This method advertises the service on the network. It returns immediately, and
the delegate is informed later if it was a failure.

The delegate can implement:

```
- (void)netService:(NSNetService *)sender
        didNotPublish:(NSDictionary *)errorDict
```

Notifies the delegate that the service offered by sender could not be published.
You can use the dictionary keys NSNetServicesErrorCode and
NSNetServicesErrorDomain to determine the cause of the error. A common
error is that the name of your server was already claimed by another server in
the same domain.

Make chatterd Zeroconf-compliant

Open the chatterd project. In main(), add the lines to read the first argument into a
string. Also, declare a variable for the NSNetService:

```
int main (int argc, const char * argv[]) {
    NSAutoreleasePool * pool = [[NSAutoreleasePool alloc] init];
    if (argc != 2) {
        NSLog(@"Usage: chatterd <servicename>");
        exit(-1);
    }
    NSString *serviceName = [NSString stringWithUTF8String:argv[1]];
    NSNetService *netService;
```

Immediately before the run loop starts, create and publish the NSNetService:

```
    netService = [[NSNetService alloc] initWithDomain:@""
                                            type:@"_chatter._tcp."
                                            name:serviceName
                                            port:8081];
    [netService setDelegate:monitor];
    [netService publish];
    NSLog(@"service published = %@", netService);
```

```
    [runloop run];
```

In ConnectionMonitor.m, add a method to indicate if the publish has failed

```
- (void)netService:(NSNetService *)sender
        didNotPublish:(NSDictionary *)errorDict
{
        NSLog(@"failed to publish = %@", errorDict);
}
```

Voila! A Rendezvous-aware server. Build and run it. It must be run with
argument -- the name of the service.

Browsing Net Services

When a client needs to find a service, it multicasts a message onto the
published servers respond. Notice, however, that with busy servers o
slow network, this might take some time. So a browser is told to star
then, as responses come in, the delegate is informed.

NSNetServiceBrowser has the following method:

```
- (void)searchForServicesOfType:(NSString *)type
                        inDomain:(NSString *)domainStri
```

This method kicks off the search for services of the given type in t
Once again, @"" can be supplied as the domain.

The delegate gets sent these messsages:

```
- (void)netServiceBrowser:(NSNetServiceBrowser *)aNe
            didFindService:(NSNetService *)aNetServi
               moreComing:(BOOL)moreComing
```

This method gets called as net services are discovered. If there
processed, the moreComing flag will be YES. Thus, you will kr
updating your user interface.

```
- (void)netServiceBrowser:(NSNetServiceBrowser *)
          didRemoveService:(NSNetService *)aNetSe
               moreComing:(BOOL)moreComing
```

This method gets sent if a server disappears.

Make ChatterClient browse for servers

Open the ChatterClient project.

First, we are going to replace the hostname text field wi
AppController.h. Change the type of the pointer, add
discovered services, and add an NSData to hold the ad

```
#import <Cocoa/Cocoa.h>
#import "ChatterServing.h"

@interface AppController : NSObject <Chatt
{
    IBOutlet NSTextField *messageField;
    IBOutlet NSTextField *nicknameField;
```

In A

```
- (v
{
    ...
}
```

Before
an add
in the b

If the net service has not resolved, when you ask it for its array of addresses (yes, there might be more than one) it will return an empty array.

Add these browser delegate methods to `AppController.m`:

```
- (void)netServiceBrowser:(NSNetServiceBrowser *)aNetServiceBrowser
         didFindService:(NSNetService *)aNetService
           moreComing:(BOOL)moreComing
{
    NSLog(@"Adding new service");
    [services addObject:aNetService];
    [aNetService setDelegate:self];
    [aNetService resolve];
    if (!moreComing) {
        [hostField reloadData];
    }
}


- (void)netServiceBrowser:(NSNetServiceBrowser *)aNetServiceBrowser
       didRemoveService:(NSNetService *)aNetService
           moreComing:(BOOL)moreComing
{
    NSLog(@"Removing service");
    NSEnumerator *enumerator = [services objectEnumerator];
    NSNetService *currentNetService;
    while (currentNetService = [enumerator nextObject]) {
        if ([[currentNetService name] isEqual:[aNetService name]] &&
            [[currentNetService type] isEqual:[aNetService type]] &&
            [[currentNetService domain] isEqual:[aNetService domain]]) {
            [services removeObject:currentNetService];
            break;
        }
    }
    if (!moreComing) {
        [hostField reloadData];
    }
}
```

Add methods for the combo box data source:

```
- (int)numberOfItemsInComboBox:(NSComboBox *)aComboBox
{
    return [services count];
}


- (id)comboBox:(NSComboBox *)aComboBox
          objectValueForItemAtIndex:(int)index
{
    NSNetService *item;
    item = [services objectAtIndex:index];
    return [item name];
}


- (unsigned int)comboBox:(NSComboBox *)aComboBox
             indexOfItemWithStringValue:(NSString *)string
{
    unsigned int k, max;
    NSNetService *item;
```

```
    max = [services count];
    for (k = 0; k < max; k++) {
        item = [services objectAtIndex:k];
        if ([string isEqual:[item name]]) {
            return k;
        }
    }
    return 0;
}
```

Create an accessor for the address instance variable:

```
- (void)setAddress:(NSData *)s
{
    [s retain];
    [address release];
    address = s;
}
```

In the **connect** method, use that address when you create the send port:

```
sendPort = [[NSSocketPort alloc]
              initRemoteWithProtocolFamily:AF_INET
                                socketType:SOCK_STREAM
                                  protocol:INET_TCP
                                   address:address];
```

To get these constants defined, add the following at the beginning of `AppController.m`:

```
#include <sys/socket.h>
```

In **subscribe:**, get the address from the selected service:

```
- (IBAction)subscribe:(id)sender
{
    NSNetService *currentService;
    NSArray *addresses;

    // Is the user already subscribed?
    if (proxy) {
        [messageField setStringValue:@"unsubscribe first!"];
    } else {

        // What is the selected service in the combobox?
        currentService = [services objectAtIndex:
                                    [hostField indexOfSelectedItem]];
        addresses = [currentService addresses];

        // Did it resolve?
        if ([addresses count] == 0) {
            [messageField setStringValue:@"Unable to resolve address"];
            return;
        }

        // Just take the first address
        [self setAddress:[addresses objectAtIndex:0]];
        [self setNickname:[nicknameField stringValue]];
```

```
        // Connect to selected server
        [self connect];
    }
}
```

That is it, build it and run it. If your server is running, its name should appear in the combo box. If you have several servers running, you should be able to choose among them.

Chapter 21. Directory Services

A network needs a database to hold information about host configuration (like IP addresses and shared directories) and user information (like the user's encrypted password). Other types of information (like contact information) might also be put into this database. We would call this database a *directory server*. This is a confusing name because it has nothing to do with filesystem directories, but rather relates to a directory that you would find in the lobby of a tall building.

In a perfect world, this database would:

- be an open standard

- be distributed and hierarchical (like DNS)

- use encryption to keep the data from prying eyes

- use public keys to ensure the users requesting the data and the returned data are both authentic

- have good performance and reliability

This is, however, the real world. As we have been slouching towards a real solution, different vendors have supplied us with half-baked ones. First, Unix systems used utilities like `rsync` to make copies of text files on every machine on the network. Then, Sun developed the Network Information Service (NIS) which was a very simple, reliable database. Then, NeXT developed NetInfo which was better than NIS in that it was hierarchical and distributed. Sun responded with NIS+, which was similar to NetInfo, but encrypted data before sending it across the network. With NT, Microsoft introduced its Primary Domain Controller. Novell built a company on its directory server. And the OSI gave us the Lightweight Directory Access Protocol (LDAP).

While most of OSI's ideas have been abandoned, LDAP is rapidly gaining popularity. It is also rapidly being revised to include the items on our dream list. It is likely that some mutation of LDAP is the future of directory servers.

The constant struggle for dominance in the directory server world makes a problem obvious: As a programmer, how do you create an application that reads from or writes to a directory server without having to make a new release of your application every time a new breed of directory server is introduced. The answer is Mac OS X's DirectoryServices framework -- one API that enables your app to access any sort of directory server.

This is a nice idea, but several things have gone wrong along the way. First problem: Mac OS X already had a way of dealing with files versus NIS versus NetInfo. In Mac OS X, every machine runs a local NetInfo server by default. There is also a daemon called `lookupd` that figures out where to get data from. There is also an API for dealing with `lookupd`.

For some reason, it was decided that these existing servers and the corresponding API could not be extended to deal with the future of directory servers. So, a new `lookupd`-like daemon was created: the `DirectoryService` daemon. And a new API was created: `DirectoryService.framework`. The source for both were released as part of the Darwin project. For backwards compatibility, by default your machine now runs a local NetInfo server, `lookupd`, and the `DirectoryService` daemon.

Second problem: It seems that Apple let the summer intern write the API. `DirectoryService.framework` is the most awkward-to-use framework in the entire system.

Directory Server Concepts

A directory server has nodes. Each node is identified by a path, and each node has some records. Each record has some attributes. An attribute is a key-value pair. For example, by default, the information about the users on your system are kept in a NetInfo directory server. The path to the node that holds this information is `/NetInfo/root`. This node has lots of records of different types: groups, aliases, mount points, and users. There is a user record for each user. Each record has serveral attributes like `realname`, `home`, and `shell`. The easiest way to browse this information is to use `NetInfo Manager`.

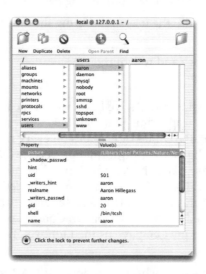

If you wanted your system to use an LDAP server instead of NetInfo, you could configure the system using the Directory Access application. You can list several different nodes (which can be different types of servers) to check for information.

To make this configuration invisible to the developer, the DirectoryServices server provides your application with several pseudo-nodes. `/Search`, for example, is the psuedo-node that you can query for authentication information: users, groups, and aliases.

Of course, editing user data is a privileged activity. Before you could edit the node, you would have to authenticate yourself with the node. After authenticating, you could edit the records in that node.

This introduces the idea of a Directory Service session. How long is your authentication good for? As long as the session lasts.

Open Directory Data Structures

All data structures in the DirectoryService framework have the following traits: The names of types are prefixed with 't'. The names of fields in a structure are prefixed with 'f'. Function names are prefixed with 'ds'. Any list-like data structure is one-based, not zero-based as nearly everything else in the C world.

tDirReference	A Directory Service Session
tDirNodeReference	/NetInfo/root
tRecordEntry	dsRecTypeStandard:Users = www
tAttributeEntry	dsAttrTypeStandard:RealName
tAttributeValueEntry	"World Wide Web Server"

tDirReference

A `tDirReference` structure keeps track of the information for your session. It is the first argument for many functions in the Open Directory APIs. You create one using the function **dsOpenDirService()** like this:

```
tDirReference dirRef;
dsOpenDirService(&dirRef);
```

And closing the session looks like this:

```
dsCloseDirService(dirRef);
```

During the session you can access many different nodes on different directory servers.

tDataBuffer

A `tDataBuffer` is used primarily as a string. It is actually defined like this:

```
typedef struct
{
```

```
    unsigned longfBufferSize;
    unsigned longfBufferLength;
    char     fBufferData[1];
} tDataBuffer;
```

The 1 is misleading. The buffer is often more than one character long.

You could initialize a 1k data buffer like this:

```
dataBuffer = dsDataBufferAllocate(dirRef, 1024);
```

And release it like this:

```
dsDataBufferDeAllocate(dirRef, dataBuffer);
```

(note the odd capitalization of DeAllocate)

tDataList

A tDataList is a list of tDataBuffers. For example, let's say you have a string that you want broken up into components. The following would put each component into a data buffer and put all the data buffers into a data list.

```
tDataListPtr nodeName;
char *myString;
myString = "/NetInfo/root";
nodeName = dsBuildFromPath(dirRef, myString, "/");
```

To free it, you would use **dsDataDeallocate()**:

```
dsDataListDeallocate(dirRef, nodeName);
```

tDirNodeReference

When you open a node, you will get a tDirNodeReference.

```
tDirNodeReference nodeRef;
long dirStatus;

dirStatus = dsOpenDirNode(dirRef, nodePath, &nodeRef);
if (dirStatus != eDSNoErr) {
    fprintf(stderr, "Unable to open node. Error %ld\n", dirStatus);
}
```

To close it:

```
dsCloseDirNode(nodeRef);
```

tRecordEntry and tAttributeList

When you get a record from a node, you will get a tRecordEntry and a list of attribute data in the form of a tAttributeList.

However, getting a record is a little tricky. You do a search based on the type of record, the name of the record, and which attributes you want. To do this search, you need to create a datalist of the names, types, and attributes.

```
tDataList recordNames;
tDataList recordTypes;
tDataList attributeTypes;
unsigned long recordCount;
tDataBufferPtr dataBuffer;
tContextData context = NULL;

// Specify fetch: get me all the attributes for all users named "www"
dsBuildListFromStringsAlloc (dirRef, &recordNames, "www", NULL);
dsBuildListFromStringsAlloc (dirRef, &recordTypes,
                             kDSStdRecordTypeUsers, NULL);
dsBuildListFromStringsAlloc (dirRef, &attributeTypes,
                             kDSAttributesAll, NULL);

// Create a buffer to hold the results of the fetch
dataBuffer = dsDataBufferAllocate(dirRef, 1024 * 32);

// Getting all the records may require multiple calls to dsGetRecordList()
do {

    // Do the fetch
    // dataBuffer gets the result
    // recordCount gets the number of records fetched
    // context is non-null if and only if there are more records to fetch
    dirStatus = dsGetRecordList(nodeRef, dataBuffer, &recordNames, eDSExact,
                        &recordTypes, &attributeTypes, 0,
                        &recordCount, &context);

    if (dirStatus != eDSNoErr) {
        fprintf(stderr, "Unable to read records:  Error %ld", dirStatus);
        exit(EXIT_FAILURE);
    }
    // Read the records
    for (i = 1; i <= recCount; i++) {
        tRecordEntry *recEntry;
        tAttributeListRef attrList;

        // Get record and list of attributes
        dirStatus = dsGetRecordEntry(nodeRef, dataBuffer, i,
                               &attrList, &recEntry);

        // Print record information
        printf("\tRecord %lu has %lu attributes\n", i,
                          recEntry->fRecordAttributeCount);

        // Process the attributes here (See next section)

        // Clean up
        dsCloseAttributeList(attrList);
        dsDeallocRecordEntry(dirRef, recEntry);
    }
} while (context != NULL)

dsDataListDeallocate(dirRef, &recNames);
dsDataListDeallocate(dirRef, &recTypes);
dsDataListDeallocate(dirRef, &attrTypes);
dsDataListDeallocate(dirRef, nodeName);
```

tAttributeValueList, tAttributeEntry, and tAttributeValueEntry

As mentioned above, each record can have several attributes. Each attribute has one name, but may contain many values. Once you have a `tRecordEntry` and `tAttributeList`, you will want to read the name of each attribute and its values. The attribute data (like its name) will be put into a `tAttributeEntry`, and the values will be put into a `tAttributeValueList`. When reading individual values, they will be put into a `tAttributeValueEntry`.

```
for (j = 1; j <= recEntry->fRecordAttributeCount; j++) {

    tAttributeEntry *attrEntry;
    tAttributeValueEntry *valueEntry;
    tAttributeValueListRef valueList;

    // Get the information for one attribute out of the data buffer
    dsGetAttributeEntry(nodeRef, dataBuffer, attrList, j,
                                &valueList, &attrEntry);

    // Print the name of the attribute
    printf("\t\t%s = ", attrEntry->fAttributeSignature.fBufferData);

    // Step through each value
    for (k = 1; k <= attrEntry->fAttributeValueCount; k++) {

        // Read the value
        dsGetAttributeValue(nodeRef, dataBuffer, k, valueList,
                                &valueEntry);

        // Print the value
        printf("%s, ", pValueEntry->fAttributeValueData.fBufferData);

        // Deallocate the value
        dsDeallocAttributeValueEntry(dirRef, pValueEntry);
    }
    // Put in a newline character before printing the next value
    fprintf(stderr,"\n");

    // Clean-up list
    dsCloseAttributeValueList(valueList);
    dsDeallocAttributeEntry(dirRef, attrEntry);
}
```

UserPictureBrowser

As a simple example of using the concepts that we have covered so far, you will create an application that will list the user name and real name of every user on your system. When you select a user name, you will see the image that appears on the login panel for that user.

Create a new Cocoa Application called **UserPictureBrowser**. Using the **Project** menu, add the framework `DirectoryService.framework`.

Open the `MainMenu.nib` file. Add a table view with two columns and an image view as shown:

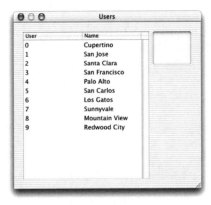

Set the identifier on the columns to be userName and realName. Create a subclass of
NSObject called **AppController**. **AppController** needs two outlets: imageView of
type **NSImageView**, and tableView of type **NSTableView**. Create the files for
AppController and create an instance of **AppController** in the nib file.

Make the **AppController** the dataSource and the delegate for the table view. Set
the **AppController**'s outlets to point to the table view and the image view. Save the
nib file.

In Project Builder, create a class called **User**. After fetching the data for a user
from the directory server, you will store it in a **User** object. **User** will have instance
variables for the userName, realName, and picturePath. All will be strings. After
fetching an image, the **User** will keep a reference to that image. The instance variable
will be _imageCache and it will be of type **NSImage**. User.h, then, will look like this:

```
#import <Cocoa/Cocoa.h>

@interface User : NSObject {
    NSString *userName;
    NSString *realName;
    NSString *picturePath;
    NSImage *_imageCache;
}

- (id)initWithUserName:(NSString *)un realName:(NSString *)rn
                                  picturePath:(NSString *)pp;
- (NSString *)userName;
- (NSString *)realName;
- (NSImage *)picture;
- (NSString *)picturePath;

@end
```

Implement these methods in User.m:

```
#import "User.h"

@implementation User

- (id)initWithUserName:(NSString *)un realName:(NSString *)rn
                                  picturePath:(NSString *)pp
{
    [super init];
    userName = [un copy];
```

```
        realName = [rn copy];
        picturePath = [pp copy];
        _imageCache = nil;
        return self;
    }

- (NSString *)userName
{
    return userName;
}

- (NSString *)realName
{
    return realName;
}

- (NSImage *)picture
{
    if (!_imageCache) {
        _imageCache = [[NSImage alloc] initWithContentsOfFile:picturePath];
    }
    return _imageCache;
}

- (NSString *)picturePath
{
    return picturePath;
}

- (void)dealloc
{
    [userName release];
    [_imageCache release];
    [picturePath release];
    [realName release];
    [super dealloc];
}
@end
```

In **AppController**, you are going to actually use the DirectoryService framework to fetch an array of **User** objects. Here is `AppController.h`:

```
#import <Cocoa/Cocoa.h>

@interface AppController : NSObject
{
    IBOutlet NSImageView *imageView;
    IBOutlet NSTableView *tableView;
    NSMutableArray *users;
}

- (void)fillUsersWithData;
- (void)tableViewSelectionDidChange:(NSNotification *)note;
- (int)numberOfRowsInTableView:(NSTableView *)tableView;
- (id)tableView:(NSTableView *)tableView
        objectValueForTableColumn:(NSTableColumn *)tableColumn
                              row:(int)row;
@end
```

Here is `AppController.m`:

```
#import "AppController.h"
#import "User.h"
#include <stdlib.h>
#include <stdio.h>
#include <DirectoryService/DirServices.h>
#include <DirectoryService/DirServicesUtils.h>
#include <DirectoryService/DirServicesConst.h>

@implementation AppController

- (void)fillUsersWithData
{
    long dirStatus;
    tDirReference dirRef;
    tDirNodeReference nodeRef;
    tDataListPtr nodeName;
    tDataList recNames;
    tDataList recTypes;
    tDataList attrTypes;
    tRecordEntry *recordEntry;
    unsigned long recCount, i, j;
    tAttributeListRef attributeList;
    tAttributeValueListRef valueList;
    tAttributeValueEntry *valueEntry;
    tAttributeEntry *attributeEntry;
    tDataBufferPtr dataBuffer;
    unsigned long bufferCount;
    tContextData context = NULL;
    char * pPath;

    // Start a directory service session
    dsOpenDirService(&dirRef);

    // Allocate a data buffer
    dataBuffer = dsDataBufferAllocate(dirRef, 32 * 1024);

    // Find the node for looking up users, pack the list in dataBuffer
    dirStatus = dsFindDirNodes(dirRef, dataBuffer, NULL,
            eDSAuthenticationSearchNodeName, &bufferCount, &context);

    if (dirStatus != eDSNoErr) {
        NSLog(@"Finding Authentication Node Failed: %d", dirStatus);
        return;
    } else {
        NSLog(@"Found %d nodes for authentication", bufferCount);
    }

    // Get the name of the first node in dataBuffer
    nodeName = dsDataListAllocate(dirRef);
    dirStatus = dsGetDirNodeName(dirRef, dataBuffer, 1, &nodeName);
    if (dirStatus != eDSNoErr) {
        NSLog(@"Getting Node Name Failed: %d", dirStatus);
        return;
    }
```

```
        // Display node name as path
        pPath = dsGetPathFromList(dirRef, nodeName, "/");
        NSLog(@"Node = %s", pPath);
        free(pPath);

        // Open the node and store in nodeRef
        dirStatus = dsOpenDirNode(dirRef, nodeName, &nodeRef);
        if (dirStatus != eDSNoErr) {
            NSLog(@"Opening Node Failed: %d", dirStatus);
            return;
        }

        // Describe what you are looking for as three lists of strings
        dsBuildListFromStringsAlloc (dirRef, &recNames,
                                     kDSRecordsAll, NULL);
        dsBuildListFromStringsAlloc (dirRef, &recTypes,
                                     kDSStdRecordTypeUsers, NULL);
        dsBuildListFromStringsAlloc (dirRef, &attrTypes,
                        "dsAttrTypeStandard:RecordName",
                        "dsAttrTypeStandard:RealName",
                        "dsAttrTypeStandard:Picture", NULL);
        do
        {
            // Get the list of all the records
            // Call this until context is null.
            dsGetRecordList(nodeRef, dataBuffer, &recNames, eDSExact,
                            &recTypes, &attrTypes, 0, &recCount, &context);
            printf("dsGetRecordList returned %lu entries\n", recCount);
            for (i = 1; i <= recCount; i++)
            {
                // Get a record from the list
                dsGetRecordEntry(nodeRef, dataBuffer, i, &attributeList,
                                 &recordEntry);

                NSString *userName = nil;
                NSString *realName = nil;
                NSString *picturePath = nil;
                for (j = 1; j <= recordEntry->fRecordAttributeCount; j++)
                {
                    NSString *key;
                    NSString *value;

                    // Read the attribute
                    dsGetAttributeEntry(nodeRef, dataBuffer,
                                        attributeList, j,
                                        &valueList, &attributeEntry);
                    key = [NSString stringWithUTF8String:
                            attributeEntry->fAttributeSignature.fBufferData];

                    // Read the first value for the attribute
                    dsGetAttributeValue(nodeRef, dataBuffer, 1, valueList,
                                        &valueEntry);
                    value = [NSString stringWithUTF8String:
                            valueEntry->fAttributeValueData.fBufferData];

                    // Tidy up attribute-level data
                    dsDeallocAttributeValueEntry(dirRef, valueEntry);
```

```objc
                valueEntry = NULL;
                dsDeallocAttributeEntry(dirRef, attributeEntry);
                attributeEntry = NULL;
                dsCloseAttributeValueList(valueList);

                // Put the data in the right variable
                if ([key isEqual:@"dsAttrTypeStandard:Picture"]) {
                    picturePath = value;
                }
                if ([key isEqual:@"dsAttrTypeStandard:RealName"]) {
                    realName = value;
                }
                if ([key isEqual:@"dsAttrTypeStandard:RecordName"]) {
                    userName = value;
                }


            }
            // Create a user object
            User *newUser = [[User alloc] initWithUserName:userName
                                             realName:realName
                                          picturePath:picturePath];

            [users addObject:newUser];

            // users will retain newUser
            [newUser release];

            // Tidy up record-level data
            dsCloseAttributeList(attributeList);
            attributeList = NULL;
            dsDeallocRecordEntry(dirRef, recordEntry);
            recordEntry = NULL;
        }
    // Loop until all of the data has been obtained.
    } while (context != NULL);

    // Tidy up node-level data
    dsDataListDeallocate(dirRef, &recNames);
    dsDataListDeallocate(dirRef, &recTypes);
    dsDataListDeallocate(dirRef, &attrTypes);
    dsDataListDeallocate(dirRef, nodeName);
    dsCloseDirNode(nodeRef);

    // Tidy up session-level data
    dsCloseDirService(dirRef);
}

- (id)init
{
    [super init];
    users = [[NSMutableArray alloc] init];
    [self fillUsersWithData];
    return self;
}

- (void)tableViewSelectionDidChange:(NSNotification *)notification
{
```

```
        int newSelection = [tableView selectedRow];
        if (newSelection >= 0) {
            NSImage *i = [[users objectAtIndex:newSelection] picture];
            [imageView setImage:i];
        }
}

- (int)numberOfRowsInTableView:(NSTableView *)tableView
{
    return [users count];          —
}

- (id)tableView:(NSTableView *)tableView
            objectValueForTableColumn:(NSTableColumn *)tableColumn
                               row:(int)row
{
    User *u = [users objectAtIndex:row];
    NSString *identifier = [tableColumn identifier];
    return [u valueForKey:identifier];
}
```

`@end`

Build it and run it. You should be able to browse users and see their login picture.

Authenticating

The exercise begs the question: I can see the user's picture, how do I change it? Before you can change important information like this, you need to authenticate yourself to the node.

There are many types of directory servers and each can be configured to require different types of authentication. When you want to authenticate with a node, you ask it what types of authentication it supports. Looking at the list of supported authentication methods, you will choose one and pack up a buffer with the required authentication data in the appropriate format. Then you will ask the node to authenticate with the preferred method using the supplied buffer. Depending on the method, you may get a buffer of data back from the node.

For most of the methods, you pack the buffer with the following:

- A 4-byte integer representing the length of username
- The username in UTF8 encoding
- A 4-byte integer representing the length of password
- The password in UTF8 encoding

Here are the currently supported authentication methods:

`dsAuthMethodStandard:dsAuthClearText`

Sends the user name and password as clear text.

`dsAuthMethodStandard:dsAuthCrypt`

> Run the password through crypt before sending.

`dsAuthMethodStandard:dsAuthSetPasswd`

`dsAuthMethodStandard:dsAuthChangePasswd`

> Used to change the password for a user. Does not require prior authentication. The buffer is packed as follows:
> - A 4-byte integer representing the length of username
> - The username in UTF8 encoding
> - A 4-byte integer representing the length of old password
> - old password in UTF8 encoding
> - A 4-byte integer representing length of new password
> - The new password in UTF8 encoding

`dsAuthMethodStandard:dsAuthSetPasswdAsRoot`

> Used to change the password for a user. Does not require prior authentication. The buffer is packed as follows:
> - A 4-byte integer representing the length of username
> - The username in UTF8 encoding
> - A 4-byte integer representing the length of the root password
> - old password in UTF8 encoding
> - A 4-byte integer representing length of new password
> - The new password in UTF8 encoding

`dsAuthMethodStandard:dsAuthNodeNativeCanUseClearText`

> Whatever authetication the node does most naturally.

`dsAuthMethodStandard:dsAuthNodeNativeCannotUseClearText`

> Whatever authentication excepting clear text that the node does most naturally.

`dsAuthMethodStandard:dsAuth2WayRandomChangePasswd`

> Change the password for a user using the two-way random method. The buffer is packed as follows:
> - A 4-byte integer representing the length of username
> - A username in UTF8 encoding
> - A 4-byte integer representing the length of old password encrypted with new (should be 8)
> - The old password encrypted with new
> - A 4-byte integer representing the length of new password encrypted with old (should be 8)

- The new password encrypted with old

dsAuthMethodStandard:dsAuthAPOP

dsAuthMethodStandard:dsAuth2WayRandom

kDSStdAuthSMB_NT_Key

kDSStdAuthSMB_LM_Key

kDSStdAuthCRAM_MD5

kDSStdAuthDIGEST_MD5

To figure out which are supported for a given node, you need to read the dsAttrTypeStandard:AuthMethod attribute of the node using **dsGetDirNodeInfo()**. (Yes, nodes and records can both have attributes.)

```
tDataList attributeTypes;
tDataBufferPtr dataBuffer;
unsigned long k;
tAttributeListRef attrListRef;
tContextData context;
tAttributeValueListRef valueList;
tAttributeValueEntry *valueEntry;
tAttributeEntry *attributeEntry;

// Create a buffer
dataBuffer = dsDataBufferAllocate(dirRef, 32 * 1024);

// Prepare to fetch the Authorization attributes
dsBuildListFromStringsAlloc (dirRef, &attributeTypes,
                                    kDSNAttrAuthMethod, NULL);

// Fetch the authorization attribute
dsGetDirNodeInfo(nodeRef, &attributeTypes, dataBuffer, 0,
                        &count, &attributeList, &context);

// There should be just one.  Read it into a value
// list and attribute entry
dsGetAttributeEntry(nodeRef, dataBuffer, attrList, 1,
                                    &valueList, attributeEntry);

// Print the name of the attribute
printf("\t%s = ", j, attributeEntry->fAttributeSignature.fBufferData);

// Iterate through its values
```

```
for (k = 1; k <= attributeEntry->fAttributeValueCount; k++) {

        // Read the value into valueEntry
        dsGetAttributeValue(nodeRef, dataBuffer, k,
                                        valueList, &valueEntry);

        // Print it
        printf("%s, ", valueEntry->fAttributeValueData.fBufferData);

        // deallocate the valueEntry
        dsDeallocAttributeValueEntry(dirRef, valueEntry);
}
printf("\n");
dsCloseAttributeValueList(valueList);
dsDeallocAttributeEntry(dirRef, attributeEntry);
dsDeallocList(dirRef, &attributeTypes);
```

Note that if you run this against the /Search node, it will return no authentication methods. Remember that it is a pseudo-node. You can not edit the /Search. Instead, you would fetch the dsAttrTypeStandard:AppleMetaNodeLocation when you fetch dsAttrTypeStandard:RecordName, dsAttrTypeStandard:RecordName and dsAttrTypeStandard:Picture. AppleMetaNodeLocation contains the name of the node where the record *really* lives.

Here is an example of how you might do node-native authentication. It assumes that you have already opened a directory services session and the node for which you want to authenticate:

```
int DoNodeNativeAuthentication (const tDirNodeReference nodeRef,
                                const char *username,
                                const char *password)
{
    tDataNodePtr authType;
    tDataBufferPtr dataBuffer;
    tDataBufferPtr responseBuffer;
    tDirStatus aDirErr;
    tContextData aContinueData;
    long aDataBufSize = 0;
    long aTempLength = 0;
    long aCurLength = 0;
    int result;

    // First, specify the type of authentication.
    authType = dsDataNodeAllocateString(dirRef,
                        kDSStdAuthNodeNativeClearTextOK);

    // Calculate the size and allocate a buffer
    // for the authentication data
    aDataBufSize += sizeof(long) + strlen(username);
    aDataBufSize += sizeof(long) + strlen(password);
    dataBuffer = dsDataBufferAllocate(dirRef, aDataBufSize);

    // Allocate a response buffer in case we get one from the
    // node when we try to authenticate
    responseBuffer = dsDataBufferAllocate(dirRef, 512);

    // Copy the length of the username into the buffer
```

```
        aTempLength = strlen(username);
        memcpy(dataBuffer->fBufferData, &aTempLength, sizeof(long));
        aCurLength += sizeof(long);

        // Copy the actual username into the buffer
        memcpy(&(dataBuffer->fBufferData[aCurLength]), username, aTempLength);
        aCurLength += aTempLength;

        // Copy the length of the password into the buffer
        aTempLength = strlen(password);
        memcpy(&(dataBuffer->fBufferData[aCurLength]), &aTempLength, sizeof(long));

        // Copy the actual password into the buffer
        aCurLength += sizeof(long);
        memcpy(&(dataBuffer->fBufferData[aCurLength]), password, aTempLength);

        // Tell the buffer how long it is
        dataBuffer->fBufferLength = aDataBufSize;

        // Do the authentication
        aDirErr = dsDoDirNodeAuth(nodeRef, authType, 0, dataBuffer,
                            responseBuffer, &aContinueData);

        // Were we successful?
        if (aDirErr == eDSNoErr) {
            result = 1;
        } else {
            printf("NodeAuth failed: %d\n", aDirErr);
            printf("response = %lu,%s\n", responseBuffer->fBufferLength,
                                        responseBuffer->fBufferData);
            result = 0;
        }

        // Clean up allocations.
        aDirErr = dsDataBufferDeAllocate(dirRef, dataBuffer);
        aDirErr = dsDataBufferDeAllocate(dirRef, responseBuffer);
        aDirErr = dsDataNodeDeAllocate(dirRef, authType);

        // Return the result of the authentication
        return result;
}
```

Editing Records

Once you have autheticated, you can insert, delete, and edit records. Deleting a record a simple. After you've opened the record, just call **dsDeleteRecord()**:

```
tRecordReference record;
tDataNodePtr recordName;
tDataNodePtr recordType;
recordName = dsDataNodeAllocateString(dirRef, "www");
recordType = dsDataNodeAllocateString(dirRef, kDSStdRecordTypeUsers);

// Open the record using its name and type
dirStatus = dsOpenRecord(nodeRef, recordType, recordName, &record);

if (dirStatus != eDSNoErr) {
```

```
        fprintf(stdout, "Unable to open record: %ld\n", dirStatus);
} else {
    dirStatus = dsDeleteRecord(recordEntry);

    if (dirStatus != eDSNoErr) {
        // Print a message to show failure
        fprintf(stdout, "Unable to delete record: %ld\n", dirStatus);

        // Close the record you were unable to delete
        dirStatus = dsCloseRecord(record);
    } else {
      printf("Deleted record\n");
    }
}
dsDataNodeDeAllocate(dirRef, recordType);
dsDataNodeDeAllocate(dirRef, recordName);
```

If you have an open node, here is how you would create a new record in that node and add an attribute to it:

```
void CreateRecord (const tDirNodeReference nodeRef)
{
    long dirStatus;
    tDataNodePtr recordName;
    tDataNodePtr recType;
    tDataNodePtr attrName;
    tDataNodePtr attrValue;
    tRecordReference record;

    // Create the name and type of the record to be created
    recordName = dsDataNodeAllocateString(dirRef, "NewUserRecordName");
    recType = dsDataNodeAllocateString(dirRef, kDSStdRecordTypeUsers);

    // Create and open the record
    dirStatus = dsCreateRecordAndOpen(nodeRef, recType,
                                recordName, &record);

    // Was it successful?
    if (dirStatus == eDSNoErr){
        printf("Successfully created and opened record\n");

        // Prepare an attribute to add to the record
        attrName = dsDataNodeAllocateString(dirRef,
                            kDS1AttrDistinguishedName);
        attrValue = dsDataNodeAllocateString(dirRef,
                            "User Record's Display Name");
        // Add the attribute to the record
        dirStatus = dsAddAttribute(record, attrName, NULL, attrValue);
        if (dirStatus != eDSNoErr) {
                printf("Error adding attribute:%ld\n", dirStatus);
        } else {
                printf("Successfully set attribute\n");
        }
        // Cleanup
        dsDataNodeDeAllocate(dirRef, attrValue);
        dsDataNodeDeAllocate(dirRef, attrName);
        dirStatus = dsCloseRecord(record);
    } else {
```

```
            printf("Unable to create record:%ld\n", dirStatus);
    }
    dsDataNodeDeAllocate(dirRef, recType);
    dsDataNodeDeAllocate(dirRef, recordName);
}
```

If you have an open record with an attribute that you would like to change, you could, theoretically, use **dsSetAttributeValue()**. I, however, have never actually gotten this to work. I recommend that you just remove the old attribute using **dsRemoveAttributeValue()** and then add a new value using **dsAddAttributeValue()**:

```
    long dirStatus;
    tDataNodePtr attrName;
    tDataNodePtr newValue;
    tRecordReference recRef;

    // Prepare an attribute to add to the record
    attrName = dsDataNodeAllocateString(dirRef, kDS1AttrDistinguishedName);

    // Remove the old value
    dirStatus = dsRemoveAttribute(recRef,attrName);
    if (dirStatus != eDSNoErr){
        printf("Uable to remove attribute info:%ld\n", dirStatus);
    }

    // Prepare a new value
    newValue = dsDataNodeAllocateString(dirRef, NEW_ATTRIBUTE_VALUE);

    // Put it in place
    dirStatus = dsAddAttribute(recRef, attrName, NULL, newValue);
    if (dirStatus != eDSNoErr) {
            printf("Error adding attribute:%ld\n", dirStatus);
    } else {
            printf("Successfully set attribute\n");
    }
    dsDataNodeDeAllocate(dirRef, attrName);
    dsDataNodeDeAllocate(dirRef, newValue);
```

Challenge

1. Extend UserPictureBrowser to allow the deletion of users.
2. Extend UserPictureBrowser to allow the picture to be changed.
3. Extend UserPictureBrowser to allow new users to be added to the system.

Chapter 22. Multithreading

Multithreading is another method for achieving concurrency in your application. While multiprocessing uses multiple independent processes with their own address spaces and resources, threads are multiple execution streams that all execute within a single application, with a single address space, all sharing the available resources.

Multithreading, like multiprocessing, can take advantage of multiple CPUs. You can also use it to simplify some kinds of programming. Each thread can go on its merry way, computing values and calling functions that block, while other threads can run independently and are unaffected. One very common use of threads is handling requests in a network server (like a web server). A new connection is `accept()`ed and a thread is created to handle the request. This thread can then use `read()` to get the request and `write()` to send data back. It can also open files and perform loops, so there is no need to multiplex the I/O using `select()`, and there is no need to go through contortions to do computations piecemeal.

Posix Threads

Mac OS X uses the Posix thread API, more commonly known as "pthreads," for its native threading model. Unfortunately, pthreads have a different convention for reporting error conditions than the rest of the Unix API. While it returns zero on success like you would expect, it returns the error code on error, rather than returning -1 and setting `errno`.

Creating threads

`pthread_create()` is used to create a new thread:

```
int pthread_create (pthread_t *threadID, const pthread_attr_t *attr,
                    void *(*startRoutine)(void *), void *arg);
```

which returns zero on success and an error value on failure. These are the arguments it takes:

threadID

> A pointer to a `pthread_t`. The thread ID for the new thread will be written here.

attr

> A set of attributes. Pass NULL to use the default attributes. Specific attributes are not discussed (they tend to confuse discussions about the basics of threaded programming).

startRoutine

> A pointer to a function with a signature of
>
> ```
> void *someFunction (void *someArg);
> ```
>
> This is where execution in the thread will start. The thread will terminate when this function returns. The someArg parameter is the value of the arg parameter passed to `pthread_create()`. The return value is some pointer to return status. You can pass whatever data structure you want for these two values.

```
arg
```

The argument given to the `startRoutine`.

The system allocates a private stack (similar to the main function call stack) for a thread when it gets created. The thread uses this stack for function call housekeeping and local variable storage.

Figure 22-1. Thread Stacks

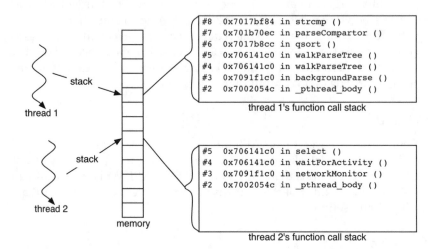

```
#8   0x7017bf84 in strcmp ()
#7   0x701b70ec in parseCompartor ()
#6   0x7017b8cc in qsort ()
#5   0x706141c0 in walkParseTree ()
#4   0x706141c0 in walkParseTree ()
#3   0x7091f1c0 in backgroundParse ()
#2   0x7002054c in _pthread_body ()
```
thread 1's function call stack

```
#5   0x706141c0 in select ()
#4   0x706141c0 in waitForActivity ()
#3   0x7091f1c0 in networkMonitor ()
#2   0x7002054c in _pthread_body ()
```
thread 2's function call stack

Threads are like processes in that they have a return value that could be of interest to whoever created the thread. Using a mechanism similar to **waitpid()** for processes you can use **pthread_join()** to rendezvous with a particular thread:

```
int pthread_join (pthread_t threadID, void **valuePtr);
```

pthread_join() will block until the indicated thread exits. The return value will be written into the `valuePtr`.

To determine your own `threadID`, use **pthread_self()**;

Sometimes you want to detach a thread so that you do not have to **pthread_join()** it. The thread will run to completion, and then exit. To do that, use **pthread_detach()**:

```
int pthread_detach (pthread_t threadID);
```

Detached threads are sometimes called "daemon threads", since they run independently of their parents like daemons.

A common idiom is for a thread function to call

```
pthread_detach (pthread_self());
```

to turn itself into a daemon thread.

Here is a little program that spins off a couple of threads that all count from zero to some value. Some are detached, and some are not and should be waited on:

Example 22-1. basics.m

```
// basics.m -- basic thread creation

/* compile with:
cc -g -Wall -o basics basics.m
*/

#import <stdio.h> // for printf
#import <pthread.h>        // for pthread_* calls
#import <string.h>         // for strerror()
#import <unistd.h>         // for usleep()
#import <stdlib.h>         // for exit

#define THREAD_COUNT 6

// information to tell the thread how to behave

typedef struct ThreadInfo {
    pthread_t    threadID;
    int          index;
    int          numberToCountTo;
    int          detachYourself;
    int          sleepTime;        // in microseconds (1/100,000,000)
} ThreadInfo;

void *threadFunction (void *argument)
{
    ThreadInfo *info = (ThreadInfo *) argument;
    int result, i;

    printf ("thread %d, counting to %d, detaching %s\n",
            info->index, info->numberToCountTo,
            (info->detachYourself) ? "yes" : "no");

    if (info->detachYourself) {
        result = pthread_detach (pthread_self());
        if (result != 0) {
            fprintf (stderr, "could not detach thread %d. %d/%s\n",
                     info->index, result, strerror(result));
        }
    }

    // now to do the actual "work" of the thread

    for (i = 0; i < info->numberToCountTo; i++) {
        printf ("  thread %d counting %d\n", info->index, i);
        usleep (info->sleepTime);
    }

    printf ("thread %d done\n", info->index);

    return (NULL);

} // threadFunction

int main (int argc, char *argv[])
```

```
{
    ThreadInfo threads[THREAD_COUNT];
    int result, i;

    // initialize the ThreadInfos:
    for (i = 0; i < THREAD_COUNT; i++) {
        threads[i].index = i;
        threads[i].numberToCountTo = (i + 1) * 2;
        threads[i].detachYourself = (i % 2); // detach odd threads
        threads[i].sleepTime = 500000 + 200000 * i;
        // (make subseuqent threads wait longer between counts)
    }

    // create the threads
    for (i = 0; i < THREAD_COUNT; i++) {
        result = pthread_create (&threads[i].threadID, NULL,
                                 threadFunction, &threads[i]);
        if (result != 0) {
            fprintf (stderr,
                     "could not pthread_create thread %d. %d/%s\n",
                     i, result, strerror(result));
            exit (EXIT_FAILURE);
        }
    }

    // now rendezvous with all the non-detached threads
    for (i = 0; i < THREAD_COUNT; i++) {
        void *retVal;
        if (!threads[i].detachYourself) {
            result = pthread_join (threads[i].threadID, &retVal);
            if (result != 0) {
                fprintf (stderr, "error joining thread %d. %d/%s\n",
                         i, result, strerror(result));
            }
            printf ("joined with thread %d\n", i);
        }
    }

    exit (EXIT_SUCCESS);

} // main
```

The sample run is much more interesting in real life. Here is a part of it:

```
% ./basics
thread 0, counting to 2, detaching no
  thread 0 counting 0
thread 1, counting to 4, detaching yes
  thread 1 counting 0
thread 2, counting to 6, detaching no
  thread 2 counting 0
...
  thread 2 counting 1
thread 0 done
joined with thread 0
  thread 3 counting 1
  thread 4 counting 1
```

```
. . .
    thread 4 counting 9
    thread 5 counting 8
thread 4 done
joined with thread 4
```

There are a couple of things to note. The first is there is no predefined order that the threads will run. They are at the mercy of the OS scheduler. The other is that the main thread (where **main()** runs) is special. Once the main thread exits, the program terminates immediately even if there are other threads still running. This is why thread five sometimes does not finish its work by the time the program exits.

Synchronization

Remember the discussion about race conditions and concurrency when talking about signals? Threads have the same kinds of problems. There is something mentioned above that bears repeating: There is no predefined order that the threads will run. They are at the mercy of the OS scheduler.

This can cause a lot of problems and introduces a lot of complexity to make sure that this (possibly) random order of execution will not corrupt data.

For example, in basics.m above, you made an array of the ThreadInfo structure and gave each thread a pointer to its own array element. Compare to this:

```
ThreadInfo info;

for (i = 0; i < THREAD_COUNT; i++) {
    info->index = i;
    info->numberToCountTo = (i + 1) * 2;
    . . .
    result = pthread_create (&threads[i].threadID, NULL,
                             threadFunction, &info);
}
```

Then threadFunction would copy the data it wanted.

There are three cases to consider:

1. *threadFunction starts executing immediately.* The thread copies the data out of its argument pointer and goes on its merry way. Things work OK in this mode.

2. *threadFunction starts executing a little later, like at the top of the loop.* The thread gets created when the i loop variable is 2. The loop then goes to index 3 and creates a thread, and now is about to do loop number 4. The "2 thread" finally gets scheduled and starts executing, looks at the memory for its control information, and uses the same config information intended for thread four.

3. *threadFunction starts executing a little later, in the middle of the loop.* This is the worst-case scenario: corrupted data. If the "2 thread" wakes up while index and numberToCountTo have been updated for i = 4, but detachYourself and sleepTime still have i = 3's values, it will get half the data of the "3 thread" and half from the "4 thread" info.

Along the same lines, unprotected manipulations to data structures in a threaded environment can lead to corruption. Imagine a linked list that is in the middle of the pointer manipulations for adding a new node. This thread gets preempted by another thread that tries to add something of its own to that list. Best case you will crash because a pointer being modified is pointing to a bad address. Worst case is that one or the other insertions gets lost and you have slightly corrupted data, an error that will only manifest itself later, far away from the race condition that caused it.

Getting synchronization right is hard to do, and can be very hard to debug. There is a fine line between safe data access and efficient data access, and this is the primary reason threaded programming is much harder than people think it is.

To help address these problems, the pthread API provides some synchronization mechanisms, specifically mutexes (mutual exclusion locks) and condition variables.

Mutexes

Mutexes are used to serialize access to critical sections of code, meaning that when mutexes are used properly, only one thread of execution can be executing that section of code. All other threads wanting to run there will be blocked until the original thread finishes. After that an arbitrary thread will be picked to run that piece of code.

Figure 22-2. A Mutex

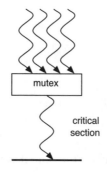

The use of a mutex over a section of code eliminates any concurrency that code may have (which is the general motivation for using threads), so you want the duration of a mutex lock to be as short as possible. Be aware that although mutexes control access to *code*, you are just using that to control access to *data*.

The datatype for a mutex is pthread_mutex_t. You can declare them as local variables, global variables, or **malloc()** memory for them. There is two ways to initialize a mutex. The first way is to use a static initializer, which is handy for a singleton mutex that you want to stick outside of a function:

```
static pthread_mutex_t myMutex = PTHREAD_MUTEX_INITIALIZER;
```

The other is to get a chunk of memory the size of pthread_mutex_t and use **pthread_mutex_init()** on that memory:

```
int pthread_mutex_init (pthread_mutex_t *mutex,
                        const pthread_mutexattr_t *attr);
```

Like with **pthread_create()**, specific attributes aren't discussed.

You would use `pthread_mutex_init()` when you have a mutex per data structure (like you create a new tree, and create a mutex just for that tree).

When you are done with a mutex you initialized with `pthread_mutex_init()`, use `pthread_mutex_destroy()` to release its resources:

```
int pthread_mutex_destroy (pthread_mutex_t *mutex);
```

To acquire a mutex use `pthread_mutex_lock`:

```
int pthread_mutex_lock (pthread_mutex_t *mutex);
```

If the mutex is unavailable, this call will block until it becomes free. When execution resumes after this call (with a zero return value), you know you have sole possession of the mutex.

To release a mutex, use `pthread_mutex_unlock()`:

```
int pthread_mutex_unlock (pthread_mutex_t *mutex);
```

If you do not want to block when acquiring a mutex, use `pthread_mutex_trylock()`:

```
int pthread_mutex_trylock (pthread_mutex_t *mutex);
```

If this returns with zero, you have locked the mutex. If it returns EBUSY, the mutex is locked by another party and you need to try again.

Here are mutexes in action.

Example 22-2. mutex.m

```
// copy basic.m to mutex.m first, then change threadFunction to this:

pthread_mutex_t g_mutex = PTHREAD_MUTEX_INITIALIZER;

void *threadFunction (void *argument)
{
    ThreadInfo *info = (ThreadInfo *) argument;
    int result, i;

    printf ("thread %d, counting to %d, detaching %s\n",
            info->index, info->numberToCountTo,
            (info->detachYourself) ? "yes" : "no");

    if (info->detachYourself) {
        result = pthread_detach (pthread_self());
        if (result != 0) {
            fprintf (stderr, "could not detach thread %d. Error: %d/%s\n",
                    info->index, result, strerror(result));
        }
    }

    // now to do the actual "work" of the thread

    pthread_mutex_lock (&g_mutex);

    for (i = 0; i < info->numberToCountTo; i++) {
```

```
        printf ("  thread %d counting %d\n", info->index, i);
        usleep (info->sleepTime);
    }

    pthread_mutex_unlock (&g_mutex);

    printf ("thread %d done\n", info->index);

    return (NULL);

} // threadFunction
```

And now see that execution has been serialized:

```
% ./mutex
  thread 0 counting 1
thread 0 done
  thread 1 counting 0
joined with thread 0
  thread 1 counting 1
  thread 1 counting 2
  thread 1 counting 3
thread 1 done
...
```

Also notice how much slower the entire program runs now that the critical section (the counting loop) is serialized.

Deadlocks

If you are dealing with multiple mutexes for a single operation (such as locking two data structures before manipulating them together) and you are not careful about acquiring the mutexes in the same order every time you use them, you could be open for a deadlock situation.

Suppose thread one has

```
    pthread_mutex_lock (mutexA);
    pthread_mutex_lock (mutexB);
```

and thread two has

```
    pthread_mutex_lock (mutexB);
    pthread_mutex_lock (mutexA);
```

And execution goes like this:

- Thread one locks A. It gets pre-empted.
- Thread two locks B. It gets pre-empted.
- Thread one attempts to lock B. It blocks.
- Thread two attempts to lock A. It blocks.

Figure 22-3. Deadlock

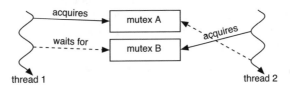

Both threads are now deadlocked, each waiting on the other to release its resource, and there is no way to break it. Each thread instead should do something like:

```
while (1) {
    pthread_mutex_lock (mutexA);
    if (pthread_mutex_trylock(mutexB) == EBUSY) {
        pthread_mutex_unlock (mutexA);
    }
}
```

That is, lock the first mutex and try locking the second. If it is locked, someone else has it, so release the first lock and try all over again, just in case someone has mutexB held and is waiting for mutexA.

Condition Variables

Mutexes are great for what they do, protecting critical regions of code. Sometimes, though, you have situations where you want to wait until some condition is true before locking your mutex (like a queue has an item in it before you process a request). If you use mutexes for this, you will end up writing loops to test the condition and then release the mutex. In other words, polling, which is wasteful of CPU time.

Condition variables (pthread_cond_t) address this problem. They let interested parties block on the variable, and they get waken up via a signal from another thread. (*Signal* is an unfortunate choice of words, since this signaling has no relation to the Unix signals that was discussed earlier.)

Like the mutex, you can initialize them statically with PTHREAD_COND_INITIALIZER, or use

```
int pthread_cond_init (pthread_cond_t *cond,
                       const pthread_condattr_t *attr);
```

Similarly, if you initialize a condition variable, release it with

```
int pthread_cond_destroy (pthread_cond_t *cond);
```

A mutex and a condition variable are associated. To use a condition variable, you lock the associated mutex, then while the condition you are interested in is false, call **pthread_cond_wait()**:

```
int pthread_cond_wait (pthread_cond_t *cond, pthread_mutex_t *mutex);
```

The mutex is automatically released and the call blocks. When another thread calls **pthread_cond_signal()**:

```
int pthread_cond_signal(pthread_cond_t *cond);
```

a single thread that is currently blocked on **pthread_cond_wait()** will wake up (use **pthread_cond_broadcast()** to wake up all blocked threads). Be aware that **pthread_cond_wait()** can spuriously return. You should always check the value of your condition before moving on.

OK, so what is this "value of your condition"? Consider the request queue for a web server:

Figure 22-4. Server Request Queue

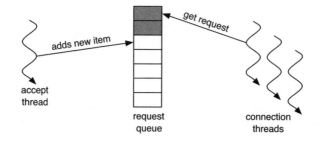

A single thread blocks on the **accept()** call waiting for new connections. When a new connection comes in, it gets put at the end of the request queue. At the same time, connection threads are hanging around, pulling the topmost entry off of the queue and processing them. (This is a version of the classic "producer/consumer" problem that just about every concurrent programming book talks about.)

For both the "accept" and "connection" threads, there are two states they can be in with respect to the queue. Accept thread accepts a new connection:

The queue has free space to put a new request

```
put request on queue
signal a connection thread to wake up
```

The queue is full:

```
block on a condition variable until there is space in the queue
when it wakes up, put the request in the queue
```

and in pseudo code:

```
pthread_mutex_lock (queueLock);
while (queue is full) {
    pthread_cond_wait (g_queueCond, queueLock);
}
put item on the queue;
pthread_mutex_unlock (queueLock);
signal a connection thread
go back to accept()
```

The **pthread_cond_wait()** will only happen when the queue is full, and you hang around in that loop until there is free space in the queue. The while loop is to protect against spurious returns.

Connection thread:

The queue has a request on it:

```
get the request from the queue
if the queue had been completely full, signal the accept() thread
that there is now space available, in case it is blocked waiting
for free space in the queue
```

The queue is empty:

```
block on a condition variable until there is space in the queue
when it wakes up, get the request from the queue
```

Likewise

```
pthread_mutex_lock (queueLock);
while (queue is empty) {
    pthread_cond_wait (g_queueCond, queueLock);
}
get item from the queue;
pthread_mutex_unlock (queueLock);
signal the accept thread
process the request.
```

If you do not want to block indefinitely, you can specify a timeout for waiting on a condition variable by using **pthread_cond_timedwait()**:

```
int pthread_cond_timedwait (pthread_cond_t *cond,
                            pthread_mutex_t *mutex,
                            const struct timespec *abstime);
```

The timeout is specified by filling out this structure:

```
struct timespec {
    time_t  tv_sec;         // seconds
    long    tv_nsec;        // nanoseconds
};
```

pthread_timed_condwait() differs from similar calls (like **select()**) in that the timeout is an absolute time, not a relative time. This makes it easier to handle the case of spurious wakeups since you do not have to recalculate the wait time each time.

This is the webserver program from the multiprocessing chapter modified to use threads instead of **fork()** (new or changed code is in bold). You will notice that all of the child process-handling code is gone, and that there is now a request queue that uses condition variables. The code to set up networking and to handle requests is identical to the previous version.

Example 22-3. webserve-thread.m

```
// webserve-thread.m -- a very simple web server using threads to
//                      handle requests

/* compile with:
```

```
cc -g -Wall -o webserve-thread webserve-thread.m
*/

#import <sys/types.h>       // for pid_t, amongst others
#import <sys/wait.h>        // for wait3
#import <unistd.h>          // for fork
#import <stdlib.h>          // for EXIT_SUCCESS, pipe, exec
#import <stdio.h>           // for printf
#import <errno.h>           // for errno
#import <string.h>          // for strerror
#import <sys/time.h>        // for struct timeval
#import <sys/resource.h>    // for struct rusage
#import <netinet/in.h>      // for sockaddr_in
#import <sys/socket.h>      // for socket(), AF_INET
#import <arpa/inet.h>       // for inet_ntoa
#import <unistd.h>          // for close
#import <arpa/inet.h>       // for inet_ntoa and friends
#import <assert.h>          // for assert
#import <pthread.h>         // for pthread_*

#define PORT_NUMBER 8080        // set to 80 to listen on the HTTP port

#define MAX_THREADS 5           // maximum number of connection threads

// ----- queue for handling requests

#define QUEUE_DEPTH 10

typedef struct Request {
    int                 fd; // file descriptor of the incoming request
    struct sockaddr_in  address;
} Request;

static Request g_requestQueue[QUEUE_DEPTH];
static int g_queueEnd = -1; // 0 is the head. end == -1 for empty queue
static pthread_mutex_t g_queueMutex = PTHREAD_MUTEX_INITIALIZER;
static pthread_cond_t g_queueCond = PTHREAD_COND_INITIALIZER;

void getRequest (int *fd, struct sockaddr_in *address)
{
    int doSignal = 0;

    pthread_mutex_lock (&g_queueMutex);
    while (g_queueEnd == -1) { // queue is empty
        pthread_cond_wait (&g_queueCond, &g_queueMutex);
    }

    // copy the request to the caller
    *fd = g_requestQueue[0].fd;
    memcpy (address, &g_requestQueue[0].address,
            sizeof(struct sockaddr_in));

    if (g_queueEnd == QUEUE_DEPTH - 1) {
        // going from full to not quite so full
        doSignal = 1;
    }
```

```
    // shift up the queue

    if (g_queueEnd > 0) {
        memmove (g_requestQueue, g_requestQueue + 1,
        sizeof(Request) * g_queueEnd);
    }
    g_queueEnd--;

    pthread_mutex_unlock (&g_queueMutex);

    if (doSignal) {
        pthread_cond_signal (&g_queueCond);
    }

} // getRequest

void queueRequest (int fd, struct sockaddr_in *address)
{
    pthread_mutex_lock (&g_queueMutex);

    assert (g_queueEnd <= QUEUE_DEPTH);

    while (g_queueEnd == QUEUE_DEPTH - 1) { // queue is full
        pthread_cond_wait (&g_queueCond, &g_queueMutex);
    }

    assert (g_queueEnd < QUEUE_DEPTH - 1);

    g_queueEnd++;
    g_requestQueue[g_queueEnd].fd = fd;
    memcpy (&g_requestQueue[g_queueEnd].address, address,
            sizeof(struct sockaddr_in));

    pthread_mutex_unlock (&g_queueMutex);

    pthread_cond_signal (&g_queueCond);

} // queueRequest

// HTTP request handling
// these are some of the common HTTP response codes

#define HTTP_OK        200
#define HTTP_NOT_FOUND 404
#define HTTP_ERROR     500

// return a string to the browser

#define returnString(httpResult, string, channel) \
    returnBuffer((httpResult), (string), (strlen(string)), (channel))

// return a character buffer (not necessarily zero-terminated) to
// the browser (runs in the child)

void returnBuffer (int httpResult, const char *content,
                   int contentLength, FILE *commChannel)
{
```

```
        fprintf (commChannel, "HTTP/1.0 %d blah\n", httpResult);
        fprintf (commChannel, "Content-Type: text/html\n");
        fprintf (commChannel, "Content-Length: %d\n", contentLength);
        fprintf (commChannel, "\n");
        fwrite (content, contentLength, 1, commChannel );

} // returnBuffer


// stream back to the browser numbers being counted, with a pause between
// them.  The user should see the numbers appear every couple of seconds
// (runs in the child)

void returnNumbers (int number, FILE *commChannel)
{
    int min, max, i;
    min = MIN (number, 1);
    max = MAX (number, 1);

    fprintf (commChannel, "HTTP/1.0 %d blah\n", HTTP_OK);
    fprintf (commChannel, "Content-Type: text/html\n");
    fprintf (commChannel, "\n");

    // no content length since this is dynamic

    fprintf (commChannel, "<h2>The numbers from %d to %d</h2>\n",
            min, max);

    for (i = min; i <= max; i++) {
        sleep (2);
        fprintf (commChannel, "%d\n", i);
        fflush (commChannel);
    }

    fprintf (commChannel, "<hr>Done\n");

} // returnNumbers


// return a file from the file system, relative to where the webserve
// is running.  Note that this does not look for any nasty characters
// like '..', so this function is a pretty big security hole
// (runs in the child)

void returnFile (const char *filename, FILE *commChannel)
{
    FILE *file;
    const char *mimetype = NULL;

    // try to guess the mime type.
    // IE assumes all non-graphic files are HTML
    if (strstr(filename, ".m") != NULL) {
        mimetype = "text/plain";
    } else if (strstr(filename, ".h") != NULL) {
        mimetype = "text/plain";
    } else if (strstr(filename, ".txt") != NULL) {
        mimetype = "text/plain";
    } else if (strstr(filename, ".tgz") != NULL) {
        mimetype = "application/x-compressed";
```

```
    } else if (strstr(filename, ".html") != NULL) {
        mimetype = "text/html";
    } else if (strstr(filename, ".html") != NULL) {
        mimetype = "text/html";
    } else if (strstr(filename, ".xyz") != NULL) {
        mimetype = "audio/mpeg";
    }

    file = fopen (filename, "r");

    if (file == NULL) {
        returnString (HTTP_NOT_FOUND,
                      "could not find your file. Sorry\n.",
                      commChannel);
    } else {
#define BUFFER_SIZE (8 * 1024)
        char *buffer[BUFFER_SIZE];
        int result;
        fprintf (commChannel, "HTTP/1.0 %d blah\n", HTTP_OK);
        if (mimetype != NULL) {
            fprintf (commChannel, "Content-Type: %s\n", mimetype);
        }
        fprintf (commChannel, "\n");
        while ((result = fread (buffer, 1, BUFFER_SIZE, file)) > 0) {
            fwrite (buffer, 1, result, commChannel);
        }
#undef BUFFER_SIZE
    }

} // returnFile

// using the method and the request (the path part of the url),
// generate the data for the user and send it back. (runs in
// the child)

void handleRequest (const char *method, const char *originalRequest,
                    FILE *commChannel)
{
 //strsep used to split this
    char *request = strdup (originalRequest);
    char *chunk, *nextString;

    if (strcmp(method, "GET") != 0) {
        returnString (HTTP_ERROR, "only GETs are supported",
                      commChannel);
        goto bailout;
    }

    nextString = request;
    chunk = strsep (&nextString, "/");
                    // urls start with slashes, so chunk is ""
    chunk = strsep (&nextString, "/");
                    // the leading part of the url

    if (strcmp(chunk, "numbers") == 0) {
        int number;
```

```
            // url of the form /numbers/5 to print numbers from 1 to 5
            chunk = strsep (&nextString, "/");
            number = atoi(chunk);
            returnNumbers (number, commChannel);

        } else if (strcmp(chunk, "file") == 0) {
            chunk = strsep (&nextString, ""); // get the rest of the string
                returnFile (chunk, commChannel);
        } else {
            returnString (HTTP_NOT_FOUND, "could not handle request.\n.",
                            commChannel);
        }

bailout:
    fprintf (stderr, "child %ld handled request '%s'\n",
            (long)pthread_self(), originalRequest);

    free (request);

} // handleRequest

// read the request from the browser, pull apart the elements of the
// request, and then dispatch it.  (runs in the child)

void dispatchRequest (int fd, struct sockaddr_in *address)
{
#define LINEBUFFER_SIZE 8192
    char linebuffer[LINEBUFFER_SIZE];
    FILE *commChannel;

    commChannel = fdopen (fd, "r+");
    if (commChannel == NULL) {
        fprintf (stderr, "could not open commChannel. Error:%d/%s\n",
                errno, strerror(errno));
    }

    // this is pretty lame in that it only reads the first line and
    // assumes that is the request, subsequently ignoring any headers
    // that might be sent.

    if (fgets(linebuffer, LINEBUFFER_SIZE, commChannel) != NULL) {
        // ok, now figure out what they wanted
        char *requestElements[3], *nextString, *chunk;
        int i = 0;
        nextString = linebuffer;
        while (chunk = strsep (&nextString, " ")) {
            requestElements[i] = chunk;
            i++;
        }
        if (i != 3) {
                returnString (HTTP_ERROR, "malformed request",
                                commChannel);
                goto bailout;
        }

            handleRequest (requestElements[0], requestElements[1],
                            commChannel);
```

```
    } else {
        fprintf (stderr, "read an empty request.  exiting\n");
    }

bailout:
    fclose (commChannel);
// removed fflush (stderr);  _exit EXIT_SUCCESS);

} // dispatchRequest

// sit blocking on accept until a new connection comes in.  queue the
// connection (which should eventually wake up a connection thread to
// handle it

void acceptRequest (int listenSocket)
{
    struct sockaddr_in address;
    int addressLength = sizeof(address), result, fd;

    printf ("before accept\n");
    result = accept (listenSocket, (struct sockaddr *)&address,
                     &addressLength);
    printf ("after accept\n");

    if (result == -1) {
        fprintf (stderr, "accept failed.  error: %d/%s\n",
                 errno, strerror(errno));
        goto bailout;
    }
    fd = result;

    queueRequest (fd, &address);

bailout:
    return;

} // acceptRequest

// ----- network stuff

// this is 100% stolen from chatterserver.m
// start listening on our server port (runs in parent)

int startListening ()
{
    int fd = -1, success = 0;
    int result;


    result = socket (AF_INET, SOCK_STREAM, 0);

    if (result == -1) {
        fprintf (stderr, "could not make a scoket.  error: %d / %s\n",
                 errno, strerror(errno));
        goto bailout;
    }
    fd = result;
```

```
        {
            int yes = 1;
            result = setsockopt (fd, SOL_SOCKET, SO_REUSEADDR,
                                 &yes, sizeof(int));
            if (result == -1) {
                fprintf (stderr,
                         "could not setsockopt to reuse address. %d / %s\n",
                         errno, strerror(errno));
                goto bailout;
            }
        }

        // bind to an address and port
        {
            struct sockaddr_in address;
            address.sin_len = sizeof (struct sockaddr_in);
            address.sin_family = AF_INET;
            address.sin_port = htons (PORT_NUMBER);
            address.sin_addr.s_addr = htonl (INADDR_ANY);
            memset (address.sin_zero, 0, sizeof(address.sin_zero));

            result = bind (fd, (struct sockaddr *)&address, sizeof(address));
            if (result == -1) {
                fprintf (stderr, "could not bind socket.  error: %d / %s\n",
                         errno, strerror(errno));
                goto bailout;
            }
        }

        result = listen (fd, 8);

        if (result == -1) {
            fprintf (stderr, "listen failed.  error: %d /  %s\n",
                     errno, strerror(errno));
            goto bailout;
        }

        success = 1;

bailout:
    if (!success) {
        close (fd);
        fd = -1;
    }
    return (fd);

} // startListening

// ----- thread functions

// there is just one of these. It is the producer of new requests

void *acceptThread (void *argument)
{
    int listenSocket = *((int *)argument);
```

```
        while (1) {
            acceptRequest (listenSocket);
        }

} // acceptThread

// there are N of these to handle requests

void *requestThread (void *argument)
{
    int fd;
    int result;

    // spin out on our own
    result = pthread_detach (pthread_self());

    if (result != 0) {
        fprintf (stderr, "could not detach connection thread.  "
                         "error %d/%s\n", result, strerror(result));
        return (NULL);
    }

    struct sockaddr_in address;

    while (1) {
        getRequest (&fd, &address); // this will block until request is queued
        dispatchRequest (fd, &address);
    }

} // requestThread

// ----- get things started in main
int main (int argc, char *argv[])
{
    int listenSocket, result;
    int i;
    pthread_t acceptThreadID;
    int status = EXIT_FAILURE;

    listenSocket = startListening ();

    if (listenSocket == -1) {
        fprintf (stderr, "startListening failed\n");
        goto bailout;
    }

    // block SIGPIPE so we do not croak if we try writing to a closed
    // connection
    if (signal (SIGPIPE, SIG_IGN) == SIG_ERR) {
        fprintf (stderr, "could not ignore SIGPIPE.  error is %d/%s\n",
                 errno, strerror(errno));
        goto bailout;
    }

    // start our accept thread
    result = pthread_create (&acceptThreadID, NULL, acceptThread,
                             &listenSocket);
```

```
    if (result != 0) {
        // pthread_* does not use errno :-|
        fprintf (stderr, "could not create accept thread. Error:%d/%s\n",
                result, strerror(result));
        goto bailout;
    }

    // start our connection threads
    for (i = 0; i < MAX_THREADS; i++) {
        pthread_t connThreadID;
        result = pthread_create (&connThreadID, NULL, requestThread, NULL);
        if (result != 0) {
            fprintf (stderr, "could not create connection thread.  "
                    "error is %d/%s\n", result, strerror(result));
            goto bailout;
        }
    }

    pthread_join (acceptThreadID, NULL);

    status = EXIT_SUCCESS;
bailout:
    return (status);

} // main
```

Cocoa and Threading

You can use multiple threads in a Cocoa program. As usual, Cocoa brings a nice set of clean APIs that provide the threading features. All of the caveats above regarding race conditions and performance apply when using Cocoa, as well as some additional gotchas.

NSThread

NSThread is the class that abstracts threads. To create a new thread, use the class method

```
+ (void) detachNewThreadSelector: (SEL) aSelector
                        toTarget: (id) aTarget
                      withObject: (id) anArgument;
```

aSelector is a selector that describes a method that aTarget can receive. The signature of aSelector should be

```
- (void) aSelector: (id) anArgument;
```

anArgument is what gets passed to this method. This call works just like **pthread_create()** in that the thread starts executing with the first instruction of aSelector and the thread terminates when the method exits. This is a daemon thread so there is no need to do any kind of waiting for it to finish.

When the first **NSThread** object is created the **NSThread** class posts an NSWillBecomeMultiThreadedNotification. Afterward, calls to [NSThread `isMultiThreaded]` will return YES. You can use this call and the notification to decide whether you need to use synchronization for your data structures. (If you are single threaded, using synchronization will just slow you down for zero benefit.) **pthread_create()** does not post this notification, nor does it cause **-isMultiThreaded** to return YES, so be aware of this if you mix pthreads and **NSThread**.

When you create an **NSThread**, you get an **NSRunLoop** along with it which you can use for event handling and DO operations. If you are going to be using any Cocoa calls in the thread, you should create an **NSAutoreleasePool**. **NSApplication**'s **+detachDrawingThread:toTarget:withObject** method is a convenience for making a new thread and setting up an autorelease pool. And you are not constrained to only doing drawing in that thread.

The **NSLock** class behaves very much like a `pthread_mutex_t`. You can lock and unlock it, try the lock, and have a lock timeout. Likewise, **NSConditionLock** fills the role of `pthread_cond_t`. The Cocoa condition lock API hides the loop that you had to use when using **pthread_cond_wait()**. Instead, it is a little state machine that keeps track of what state it is in (all programmer definable), and you can tell it to wait until a particular state occurs, as well as tell it what state to move to.

One of the nice things that Jaguar brought to the table was allowing drawing to Cocoa views from other threads. You need to call **- (BOOL)lockFocusIfCanDraw** before doing your drawing. You also have to explicitly flush the window before the window server will show the updated contents:

```
if ([drawView lockFocusIfCanDraw]) {
    // set colors, use NSBezierPath and NSString drawing functions
    [[drawView window] flushWindow];
    [drawView unlockFocus];
}
```

Here is a program that draws random colored lines into an **NSView** from multiple threads:

1. Create a new Cocoa Application project (call it `ThreadDraw`).

2. Create `AppController.h` and `AppController.m`:

Example 22-4. AppController.h

```
#import <Cocoa/Cocoa.h>

@interface AppController : NSObject
{
    IBOutlet NSView *drawView;
}

@end // AppController
```

Example 22-5. AppController.m

```
#import "AppController.h"
#import <unistd.h> // for sleep

@implementation AppController
```

```
- (NSPoint) randomPointInBounds: (NSRect) bounds
{
    NSPoint result;
    int width, height;
    width = round (bounds.size.width);
    height = round (bounds.size.height);
    result.x = (random() % width) + bounds.origin.x;
    result.y = (random() % height) + bounds.origin.y;
    return (result);

} // randomPointInBounds

- (void)threadDraw:(NSColor *)color
{
    NSAutoreleasePool *pool = [[NSAutoreleasePool alloc] init];
    NSPoint lastPoint = [drawView bounds].origin;

    while (1) {

        if ([drawView lockFocusIfCanDraw]) {
            NSPoint point;
            point = [self randomPointInBounds:[drawView bounds]];
            [color set];
            [NSBezierPath strokeLineFromPoint:lastPoint
                                      toPoint:point];
            [[drawView window] flushWindow];
            [drawView unlockFocus];
            usleep (random() % 500000); // up to 1/2 second
            lastPoint = point;
        }
    }
    [pool release];
} // threadDraw

- (void)awakeFromNib
{
    [drawView setNeedsDisplay:YES];

    [NSThread detachNewThreadSelector:@selector(threadDraw:)
             toTarget:self
             withObject:[NSColor redColor]];

    [NSThread detachNewThreadSelector:@selector(threadDraw:)
             toTarget:self
             withObject:[NSColor blueColor]];

    [NSThread detachNewThreadSelector:@selector(threadDraw:)
             toTarget:self
             withObject:[NSColor greenColor]];

    [NSThread detachNewThreadSelector:@selector(threadDraw:)
             toTarget:self
             withObject:[NSColor yellowColor]];

} // awakeFromNib
```

```
} // awakeFromNib

@end // AppController
```

3. Open `MainMenu.nib` in `Interface Builder`.

4. Drag over `AppController.h` and instantiate an **AppController** object.

5. Open the Window and drag over a plain **NSView**. Connect **AppController**'s `drawView` outlet to the view.

6. Build and run.

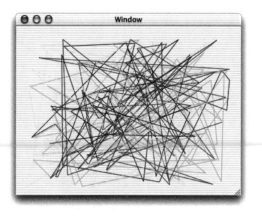

Cocoa and thread safety

Parts of the Foundation and AppKit frameworks are thread safe, and some are not. In general, immutable objects are thread safe and can be used by multiple threads. Mutable objects are not thread safe and should not be used by multiple threads. You have to be careful about how you create an object before making assumptions about mutability of an object — for instance, a method that takes an **NSString**. **NSStrings** are generally immutable. Given inheritance though, a caller can legally create an **NSMutableString** and give it to a method that takes an **NSString**. Similarly, immutable containers are safe to share amongt threads, but mutable containers are not. The file `/Developer/Documentation/Cocoa/TasksAndConcepts/ ProgrammingTopics/ Multithreading/Tasks/foundation.html` has a list of thread-safe and thread-unsafe functions.

For the More Curious: Thread Local Storage

Sometimes it is very handy to have storage that is private to a thread. In the `basics.m` program above, you could stash the contents of the `ThreadInfo` stack into thread local storage instead of on the function call stack. Thread local storage behaves like global variables, but are private to the thread. `errno` is stored in thread local storage so that every thread has its own `errno`.

To use thread local storage, initialize a `pthread_key_t` using `pthread_key_create()`:

```
int pthread_key_create (pthread_key_t *key, void (*destructor)(void *));
```

is called when the thread exits, so that dynamic memory (or other resources) can be cleaned up.

Set a thread-local value by using pthread_setspecific():

```
int pthread_setspecific (pthread_key_t key, const void *value);
```

and get the value by using **pthread_getspecific()**: void ***pthread_getspecific** (pthread_key_t key);

Figure 22-5. Thread Local Storage

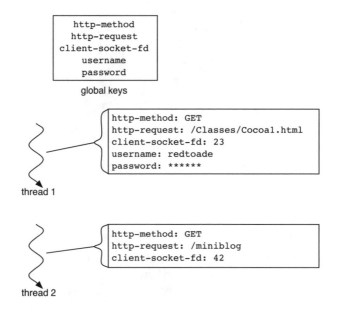

If you are using **NSThread**, you can use

```
- (NSMutableDictionary *)threadDictionary
```

To put stuff into thread local storage, just store stuff into the dictionary. This is an **NSThread** instance method, so you need to find your current **NSThread** object by using [NSThread currentThread].

For the More Curious: Read/Write Locks

Both Cocoa and pthreads provide read/write locks. These allow a data structure to be read by a number of readers simultaneously, but only allow one thread write access at a time.

pthread_rwlock_t works just like pthread_mutex_t, but with a couple of extra calls. Here are the details:

```
pthread_rwlock_init (pthread_rwlock_t *lock,
                     const pthread_rwlockattr_t *attr);
```

(OS X does not seem define PTHREAD_RWLOCK_INITIALIZER)

```
int pthread_rwlock_destroy (pthread_rwlock_t *lock);
```

Rather than use `lock()`, you specify which kind of locking you want:

- `int pthread_rwlock_rdlock (pthread_rwlock_t *rwlock);`
- `int pthread_rwlock_tryrdlock (pthread_rwlock_t *rwlock);`
- `int pthread_rwlock_wrlock (pthread_rwlock_t *rwlock);`
- `int pthread_rwlock_trywrlock (pthread_rwlock_t *rwlock);`

And unlock by using

```
int pthread_rwlock_unlock (pthread_rwlock_t *rwlock);
```

In general, using read/write locks is a bad idea, since the number of actual lock operations are doubled. (Read/write locks can be implemented with a mutex and two condition variables.) Unless you have some really expensive data structures, the overhead of the read/write lock operations will be more than the operation you are protecting. Given that caveat, there are some times when they are quite useful, especially when there are a lot of readers, not many modifications, and accessing the data structure is time consuming.

Challenge

1. Tweak `basics.m` to use Thread Local Storage to store the index, number to count to, and the sleep time.
2. Make `nodepool.m` from the Memory chapter thread safe so that multiple threads can allocate stuff out of the same pool.

Chapter 23. Using Distributed Objects Between Threads

In Chapter 19 (Distributed Objects), you used DO to communicate between two processes. Part of the reason DO is an elegant way to do this is because it plays nicely with the run loop -- messages coming in waited in the queue until the process was ready to handle them. This same mechanism can be very handy in multithreaded applications.

When a thread is created with **NSThread**, it gets its own runloop and its own autorelease pool stack. All messages sent via DO from another thread will be queued in the runloop until the thread is idle again. This queuing can often alleviate the need for locking. Many developers find that DO enables them to more easily create high-performance multithreaded applications.

"Each Server In Its Own Thread" Design

In Cocoa, drawing is usually done from the main thread. So a very common idiom is to create one or more server objects. Each server runs in its own thread and has its own run loop. The main thread communicates with these servers via DO. While the app is multithreaded, each object is only manipulated in a single thread. Thus, you can code them as if they are single threaded.

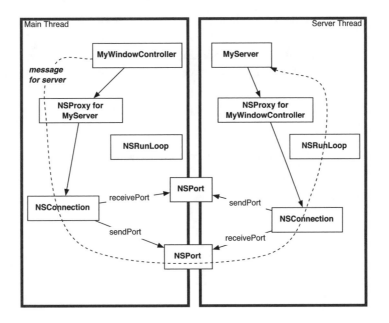

The server typically has a `oneway void` method that does some time-consuming operation. After dispatching the message via DO, the main thread immediately returns to doing whatever it would normally do (usually it sits around waiting for user events). The server calls back the client after it has completed the operation.

Generate the Mandelbrot set

The trickiest part of this design is getting the server, **NSConnection**, and **NSThread** objects set up correctly. The easiest way to demonstrate this is with an example. Our example will be an application that runs in five threads: the main thread and four server objects, each in its own thread. When a view in the main thread wants to fill a bitmap with the Mandelbrot set, it will ask each of the servers to fill in a quarter of the image. As each finishes, it will make a callback to the view. When all the servers are done, the view will composite the image map onto the window.

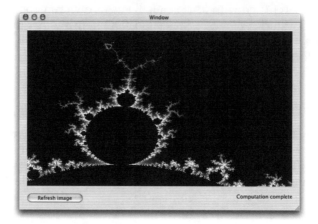

Notice the two benefits to this design:

- The main thread does not stop checking for events while the Mandelbrot set is being calculated. The user interface remains responsive and the user does not get the wait cursor.

- If the user has multiple processors, they will be fully utilized.

The view class will be called **MandelbrotView**. The server class will be called **MandelbrotServer**.

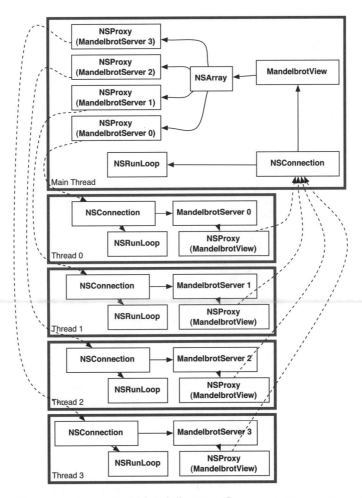

Create a new Cocoa project called **Mandelbrotter**. Open `MainMenu.nib` and create subclass of **NSView** called **MandelbrotView**. It should have one action (**refreshImage:**) and two outlets (`refreshButton` and `progressTextField`). Create an instance on the window. Also, drop a button and a textfield on the window. Set the button to be disabled.

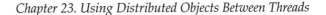

Make the view the target of the button. Set the view's outlets to point to the button and the text field. Create the files for **MandelbrotView**.

In `Project Builder`, create an empty file named `MandelbrotProtocols.h` to hold the protocols for the client and the server. The protocols act as hints to the DO system. I recommend that whenever possible, you define protocols for the messages sent over DO. Add the following to `MandelbrotProtocols.h`:

```
#import <Cocoa/Cocoa.h>

@protocol MandelbrotServerMethods

// Fill buffer with the colors for the region defined by
// minX, minY, maxX, and maxY.
// The buffer represents RBG data that is w pixels x h pixels
- (oneway void)fill:(uintptr_t)buffer
        minX:(float)minX minY:(float)minY
        maxX:(float)maxX maxY:(float)maxY
        width:(int)w height:(int)h;
@end


@protocol MandelbrotClientMethods

// Called when a new server object is created
- (void)addServer:(id)newServer;

// Called when a server reaches the end of
// fill:minX:minY:maxX:maxY:width:height:
- (oneway void)serverIsDone;

@end
```

Now the tricky part. Open up `MandelbrotView.h` and make it look like this:

```
#import <Cocoa/Cocoa.h>
#import "MandelbrotProtocols.h"

@class MandelbrotServer;

@interface MandelbrotView : NSView <MandelbrotClientMethods>
{
    // The array of Mandelbrot servers
    NSMutableArray *servers;

    // The imageRep that is displayed
    NSBitmapImageRep *imageRep;

    // This will be a count of all the servers
    // are done with their work
    int serversThatAreDone;

    // UI stuff
    IBOutlet NSTextField *progressTextField;
    IBOutlet NSButton *refreshButton;

    // Region to be drawn
    NSRect region;
}

- (id)initWithFrame:(NSRect)rect;
- (void)createServer;
- (IBAction)refreshImage:(id)sender;
@end
```

Now add the following to `MandelbrotView.m`:

```
#import "MandelbrotView.h"
#import "MandelbrotServer.h"
#define SERVER_COUNT 4

@implementation MandelbrotView

- (id)initWithFrame:(NSRect)frameRect
{
    [super initWithFrame:frameRect];

    // Create an retain an array to hold the servers
    servers = [[NSMutableArray alloc] init];
    imageRep = nil;

    // Start with a nice high-level view of the set
    region = NSMakeRect(-2.0, -1.2, 3, 2.4);
    return self;
}

- (void)awakeFromNib
{
    int i;

    // Create the servers
    for (i = 0; i < SERVER_COUNT; i++) {
        [self createServer];
    }
}

- (void)createServer
{
    NSPort *port1;
    NSPort *port2;
    NSArray *portArray;
    NSConnection *clientConnection;

    // Create two ports (one incoming, one out)
    // These actually create NSMachPort objects
    port1 = [NSPort port];
    port2 = [NSPort port];

    // Create an NSConnection on this end
    clientConnection = [[NSConnection alloc] initWithReceivePort:port1
                sendPort:port2];

    [clientConnection setRootObject:self];

    portArray = [NSArray arrayWithObjects:port2, port1, nil];

    // Create a new thread and send a message in the new thread
    [NSThread detachNewThreadSelector:@selector(connectWithPorts:)
                toTarget:[MandelbrotServer class] withObject:portArray];
}
```

So at this point, we have created a thread to send the message **connectWithPorts:** to the **MandelbrotServer** class with the array of **NSPort**. Before adding any more to

the **MandelbrotView** class, create the files for **MandelbrotServer**. Make
MandelbrotServer.h look like this:

```
#import <Cocoa/Cocoa.h>
#import "MandelbrotProtocols.h"

@interface MandelbrotServer : NSObject <MandelbrotServerMethods> {
    // This is a proxy that represents the view
    id client;
}
+ (void)connectWithPorts:(NSArray *)portArray;
- (id)initWithClient:(id)obj;
@end
```

In MandelbrotServer.m, implement the methods that will initialize the servers:

```
#import "MandelbrotServer.h"

void mandelbrot(double x, double y, unsigned char *buffer);

@implementation MandelbrotServer

// This is called when the new thread is created
+ (void)connectWithPorts:(NSArray *)portArray
{
    NSAutoreleasePool *pool;
    MandelbrotServer *serverObject;
    NSRunLoop *runLoop;
    NSConnection *serverConnection;
    id proxy;

    pool = [[NSAutoreleasePool alloc] init];

    // This connection uses the same ports as the client connection, but
    // reversed: the client's receive is the server's send.
    serverConnection = [[NSConnection
            connectionWithReceivePort:[portArray objectAtIndex:0]
            sendPort:[portArray objectAtIndex:1]] retain];

    // Get a proxy for the view
    proxy = [serverConnection rootProxy];

    // Create a new Mandelbrot server
    serverObject = [[self alloc] initWithClient:proxy];

    // Everything works better if you tell the proxy its protocol
    [proxy setProtocolForProxy:@protocol(MandelbrotClientMethods)];

    // Tell the view to add the new server to its list
    [(id)[serverConnection rootProxy] addServer:serverObject];

    // The server is retained by its connection
    [serverObject release];

    // Start up the run loop
    runLoop = [NSRunLoop currentRunLoop];
    [runLoop run];
    [pool release];
```

```
      return;
}

- (id)initWithClient:(id)obj
{
    [super init];
    client = [obj retain];
    return self;
}
```

Note that the client gets told to add the new server object.

Back in `MandelbrotView.m`, implement this method:

```
// This method will be called by the server via DO.
// anObject is really an NSProxy
- (void)addServer:(id)anObject
{
    [anObject setProtocolForProxy:@protocol(MandelbrotServerMethods)];
    [servers addObject:anObject];
    NSLog(@"added a server");

    // If all the servers are created,  generate the image
    if ([servers count] == SERVER_COUNT) {
        [self refreshImage:nil];
    }
}
```

Look over the code you've just typed in and the diagram for this application. You've already done everything that is necessary to get the servers, the threads, the **NSConnections**, and the proxies configured correctly. Build it and run it. You will get no pretty pictures, but you will see that instances of **MandelbrotServer** are created and proxies for them are added to the server's array of **MandelbrotView**.

What follows now is just the stuff to make pretty pictures.

We are going to need the C functions that calculate the value of the Mandelbrot set at any point and figure out the color for that value. Create a C file called `MandelbrotFunctions.c`:

```
#include <math.h>
#define LOOP 150
#define LIMIT 128

// Functions for doing complex math

_complex addComplex(_complex a, _complex b)
{
    _complex result;
    result.Real = a.Real + b.Real;
    result.Imag = a.Imag + b.Imag;
    return result;
}

_complex multiplyComplex(_complex a, _complex b)
{
    _complex result;
```

```
        result.Real = a.Real * b.Real - a.Imag * b.Imag;
        result.Imag = a.Real * b.Imag + a.Imag * b.Real;
        return result;
}


// gradient() determines what colors go with which values.
// I have set it up for a red scheme
void gradient(int value, unsigned char *buffer) {
        unsigned char *ptr = buffer;
        value = value * 4;
        if (value > 255)
            value = 255;
        *ptr++ = value;  // Red
        *ptr++ = 0;       // Green
        *ptr = 0;         // Blue
}


// (x, y) is the point to be dealt with
// buffer is a pointer to the three bytes that will hold
// the resulting color
void mandelbrot(double x, double y, unsigned char *buffer) {
        int i;
        _complex z,c;

        c.Real = x;
        c.Imag = y;
        z.Real = 0;
        z.Imag = 0;

        for (i = 0; i < LOOP; i++) {
            // Call the function iteratively
            z = addComplex(multiplyComplex(z, z),c);

            // Has it escaped?
            if ( cabs(z) > LIMIT) {
                gradient(i, buffer);
                return;
            }
        }
        // If z never escaped, color it as zero.
        gradient(0, buffer);
}
```

In `MandelbrotServer.m`, we are going to write the method that calls `mandelbrot()`:

```
// Notice that buffer is basically an int,  even though we know it is
// an unsigned char *.  DO cleverness caused trouble,  so we sent the
// pointer as an int.

- (oneway void)fill:(uintptr_t)buffer minX:(float)minX minY:(float)minY
            maxX:(float)maxX maxY:(float)maxY
            width:(int)w height:(int)h
{
    unsigned char *ptr;
    int x, y;
    float regionH, regionW;
    float regionX, regionY;
```

```
    NSLog(@"Server %p: starting", self);

    // What is the size of the region?
    regionW = maxX - minX;
    regionH = maxY- minY;

    ptr = (unsigned char *)buffer;

    // Loop through each row
    for (y = 0; y < h; y++) {
        // Calculate where on the set this y is
        regionY = maxY - (regionH * (float)y) / (float)h;

        // Loop through each column
        for (x = 0; x < w; x++) {
            // Calculate where on the set this x is
            regionX = minX + (regionW * (float)x) / (float)w;

            // Do the calculation and color the pixel.
            mandelbrot(regionX, regionY, ptr);

            // move the next pixel
            ptr += 3;
        }
    }
    NSLog(@"Server %p: done", self);

    // Tell the view that our part is done
    [client serverIsDone];
}
```

Note that the method is declared as `oneway void`. Thus, the client will not block waiting for this method to end. At the end of the method, we call back to the client via DO to tell it that the buffer of data is ready.

Add these methods to `MandelbrotView.m`:

```
- (void)drawRect:(NSRect)rect
{
    NSRect bounds = [self bounds];

    // Draw a white background
    [[NSColor whiteColor] set];
    [NSBezierPath fillRect:bounds];

    // If the image is ready,  draw it.
    if (serversThatAreDone == SERVER_COUNT) {
        [imageRep draw];
    }
}


- (IBAction)refreshImage:(id)sender
{
    unsigned long rowsPerServer;
    float maxY, maxX, deltaY;
    int i;
    unsigned char *ptr;
    [progressTextField setStringValue:@"Computation starting"];
```

```
    [refreshButton setEnabled:NO];

    // Clear the serversThatAreDone to show that
    // none of the servers are done
    serversThatAreDone = 0;
    NSRect bounds = [self bounds];
    int pixelsHigh = bounds.size.height;
    int pixelsWide = bounds.size.width;

    // The image maybe a few pixels shorter than the view.
    // Benefit:  all servers draw the same number of rows.
    int remainder = pixelsHigh % SERVER_COUNT;
    pixelsHigh = pixelsHigh - remainder;
    rowsPerServer = pixelsHigh / SERVER_COUNT;

    NSLog(@"Image will be %d x %d", pixelsWide, pixelsHigh);
    [imageRep release];

    // Create the image rep the servers will draw on
    imageRep = [[NSBitmapImageRep alloc]
                    initWithBitmapDataPlanes:NULL
                    pixelsWide:pixelsWide
                    pixelsHigh:pixelsHigh
                    bitsPerSample:8
                    samplesPerPixel:3
                    hasAlpha:NO
                    isPlanar:NO
                    colorSpaceName:NSCalibratedRGBColorSpace
                    bytesPerRow:NULL
                    bitsPerPixel:NULL];

    // Get the pointer to the raw data
    ptr = [imageRep bitmapData];
    maxY = NSMaxY(region);
    maxX = NSMaxX(region);
    deltaY = region.size.height / SERVER_COUNT;

    // Ask each server to draw a set of rows.
    for (i = 0; i < SERVER_COUNT; i++){
        // Assign a region to the server
        [[servers objectAtIndex:i] fill:(uintptr_t)ptr
            minX:region.origin.x minY:maxY - deltaY
            maxX:maxX maxY:maxY width:pixelsWide height:rowsPerServer];

        // Move down the image
        maxY = maxY - deltaY;

        // Move jump to next region in bitmapData
        ptr = ptr + (pixelsWide * rowsPerServer * 3);
    }
    [progressTextField setStringValue:@"Computation started"];
}

- (oneway void)serverIsDone
{
    serversThatAreDone++;
    [progressTextField setIntValue:serversThatAreDone];
```

```
    NSLog(@"%d servers are done", serversThatAreDone);
    if (serversThatAreDone == SERVER_COUNT) {
        [progressTextField setStringValue:@"Computation complete"];
        [refreshButton setEnabled:YES];
        [self setNeedsDisplay:YES];
    }
}
```

Build and run your application. You should see a lovely image. If you have multiple processors, you should see the image much faster than the people with single processors. Regardless, you should see that the menus are still useable while the image is being calculated.

Add Zooming

For those of you who want to be able to select regions to zoom in on, adding this to the **MandelbrotView** is quite easy. First, you will need a few more instance variables in MandelbrotView.h:

```
    BOOL dragging;
    NSPoint downPoint, currentPoint;
```

Also, you will need to override the **mouseDown:**, **mouseDragged:**, and **mouseUp:** methods:

```
- (void)mouseDown:(NSEvent *)event
{
    // Ignore drags while servers are working
    if (serversThatAreDone == SERVER_COUNT) {
        dragging = YES;
        NSPoint p = [event locationInWindow];
        downPoint = [self convertPoint:p  fromView:nil];
        currentPoint = downPoint;
    }
}

- (void)mouseDragged:(NSEvent *)event
{
    if (dragging) {
        NSPoint p = [event locationInWindow];
        currentPoint = [self convertPoint:p  fromView:nil];
        [self setNeedsDisplay:YES];
    }
}

- (void)mouseUp:(NSEvent *)event
{
    NSRect r, bounds;
    NSRect newRegion;
    if (dragging) {
        dragging = NO;
        NSPoint p = [event locationInWindow];
        currentPoint = [self convertPoint:p  fromView:nil];
        bounds = [self bounds];
        r = [self selectedRect];

        // Calculate newRegion as if in the unit square
```

```
        newRegion.origin.x = r.origin.x / bounds.size.width;
        newRegion.origin.y = r.origin.y / bounds.size.height;
        newRegion.size.width = r.size.width / bounds.size.width;
        newRegion.size.height = r.size.height / bounds.size.height;

        // Scale to region's size
        newRegion.origin.x = region.origin.x +
                            newRegion.origin.x * region.size.width;
        newRegion.origin.y = region.origin.y +
                            newRegion.origin.y * region.size.height;
        newRegion.size.width = region.size.width * newRegion.size.width;
        newRegion.size.height = region.size.height * newRegion.size.height;
        region = newRegion;
        [self refreshImage:nil];
    }
}


- (NSRect)selectedRect
{
    float minX = MIN(downPoint.x, currentPoint.x);
    float maxX = MAX(downPoint.x, currentPoint.x);
    float minY = MIN(downPoint.y, currentPoint.y);
    float maxY = MAX(downPoint.y, currentPoint.y);

    return NSMakeRect(minX, minY, maxX-minX,  maxY-minY);
}
```

Finally, let the user see the region they are selecting by adding the rectangle to the drawRect: method:

```
- (void)drawRect:(NSRect)rect
{
    NSRect bounds = [self bounds];

    // Draw a white background
    [[NSColor whiteColor] set];
    [NSBezierPath fillRect:bounds];

    // If the image is ready,  draw it.
    if (serversThatAreDone == SERVER_COUNT) {
        [imageRep draw];
    }
        // If the user is dragging,  show the selected rect
    if (dragging) {
        NSRect box = [self selectedRect];
        [[NSColor redColor] set];
        [NSBezierPath strokeRect:box];
    }

}
```

performSelectorOnMainThread:

In a multithreaded Cocoa application, it is common to have heavy computation going on in one thread while the main thread continues handling events and updating the screen. One way to communicate with the main thread is to use Distributed Objects as you did in this exercise. Another technique is to use the following method:

```
- (void)performSelectorOnMainThread:(SEL)aSelector
                         withObject:(id)obj
                      waitUntilDone:(BOOL)wait;
```

This method is defined on **NSObject**, so you can send it to any object. Basically, the method packs up an invocation (the receiver is the target and `obj` is the only argument) and queues it the run loop of the main thread to be executed as soon as possible. If `wait` is true, this method will block until the invocation has been executed.

In a single-threaded application, this method is used when you are thinking, "As soon as the current event has been handled and all the necessary redrawing has occurred, I'd like a message sent." Thus, if you call this method from the main thread with `wait` as NO, it will execute the invocation the next time through the run loop. If you call this method from the main thread with `wait` as YES, it will execute the invocation immediately.

Challenge 1

Make it so that if the user closes the window, the connections, proxies, servers and their run loops are destroyed.

Challenge 2

1. Make the **MandelbrotServer** run in a daemon that can be accessed from other machines. It will require that you change the protocol a bit. I suggest that this be the method on the server that begins the calculation:

```
- (oneway void)calculateMinX:(float)minX
                        minY:(float)minY
                        maxX:(float)maxX
                        maxY:(float)maxY
                       width:(int)w
                      height:(int)h
                         tag:(int)serverTag;
```

The callback to the client would be:

```
- (oneway void)doneWithData:(NSData *)calculatedData
                     forTag:(int)serverTag;
```

Notice that the client does not send the data buffer, but it will send a tag so that it knows which response came from with which server. Thus, the client will be able to assemble a single image from all the data that arrives.

2. Allow the server processes to be found via Rendezvous, and make your client utilize all the server processes on the local network.

Chapter 24. CVS

A *version control* system (also known as "source code control" and "revision control") keeps a history of the changes you make to a set of files, whether they are Objective-C or Java source files for a program, or HTML and CSS files for a website. After you make a change to a file, you tell the revision control system to remember that change. The system remembers all of your changes and when you made them, so you can (for instance) figure out what the file looked like at a particular instant in time, or figure out the changes in the file between two different dates.

Multiple people can interact with the same version control repository, which is the place where the system stores the past versions of the file, and these people can all contribute to the same body of work. The version control system keeps track of who changed files when, and what those changes were — in essence, an electronic paper trail. This is handy for figuring out who introduced a problem so you can re-educate them to not make this mistake again. Version control systems help multiple people contribute to the same project without stumbling on each other and losing people's work.

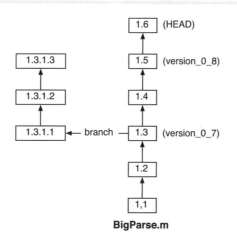

BigParse.m

For example, this is the revision tree for a file called `BigParse.m`. The main trunk of development (versions 1.1, 1.2, etc) is where the primary work happens on the file. Two releases of the product (versions 0.7 and 0.8) have been made and the revisions of `BigParse.m` that belong to those product versions have been labeled. A branch has been made off of revision 1.3. The head (most current) revision is 1.6.

CVS, the Concurrent Versions System (some people call it the Concurrent Versioning System), is an established open-source version control system that is really popular in the open-source community and also happens to come installed with the developer tools.

Version control systems usually work with one of two principles. The first is "lock, edit, unlock." If you want to change a file you first lock it, thereby preventing other people from editing the file. Make your changes (and test them, hopefully), and then tell the system to accept your changes and unlock the file. Then the next person can lock the file and make their changes.

The other model, which is what CVS uses, is an "edit, merge" model. The idea is that every person is toiling on their own personal copy of the program (or website, or whatever). They are free to edit any file there. Once they are done editing, they ask the version control system to merge the changes into the original. If there are no conflicts, the changes are added. If there are conflicts (like you change a word to Tomato, and someone else changes it to Tomahto), the person checking in the new version is asked to resolve the conflict. This model scales up much better with larger, more distributed teams. Plus you do not have the problem of someone locking a file and then flying to Aruba for a couple of weeks.

CVS Commands and Environment

CVS commands take the form of

```
cvs <global-options> <command> <command-options> <file-name(s)>
```

The global options are command-line flags that apply to all the specific CVS commands. Command flags apply to just the specific command.

Use `cvs --help-commands` to see the different commands available. The common ones you will use regularly are

- `add` Add a new file/directory to the repository.
- `checkout` Checkout sources for editing.
- `commit` Check files into the repository.
- `diff` Show differences between revisions.
- `log` Print out history information for files.
- `tag` Add a symbolic tag to checked out version of files.
- `update` Bring work tree in sync with repository.

`cvs --help-options` shows you the global flags. Here are some common ones:

- `-n` Do not execute anything that will change the disk.
- `-q` Cause CVS to be somewhat quiet.
- `-d` *CVS_root* Overrides $CVSROOT as the root of the CVS tree.
- `-z` # Use compression level # for network traffic.

In particular, the `-n` flag is very useful when experimenting with stuff. CVS will not change anything on disk and potentially mess up your work.

Then to see the flags available for a command, use the `-H` global command flag:

```
% cvs -H commit
```

There are a couple of environment variables that affect how commands operate:

- `CVSROOT` Where to look for the CVS repository. Individual source trees can have their own CVS root which overrides the environment variable.
- `CVSEDITOR` Sometimes you need to edit stuff, like writing check-in comments. This variable controls which editor is used.

- CVSIGNORE A list of file names and expressions to describe the files CVS should ignore (like .depend, *.o, core, etc.).

Creating a Repository

The repository is where CVS stores the revision history for projects (there can be many projects in a single repository), and each project can have a collection of files. Use cvs init to create the repository:

```
% cvs -d /usr/local/cvsroot init
```

This creates a new repository at /usr/local/cvsroot. You can have multiple repositories on a single machine. They are just directories that contain a hierarchy of revisions, along with a couple of control files.

The -d flag tells CVS to use the indicated path as the repository. You can choose between multiple repositories by giving different paths to this flag. You can also set the CVSROOT environment variable. Once you check out a project, it remembers which repository it came from, so you do not need to explicitly set the CVSROOT very often.

CVS Keywords

Before you put files into the repository, there is bit of overhead work that needs to be done so that a CVS feature does not destroy some of the binary files. You can put tags in your files like $Date: $ (which will expand to the date and time of a change to the file) and $Id: $ (which shows who checked in a file, when it was checked in, and the file's revision number). CVS searches for those strings and expands them with the check-in information, which is great when you walk up to a file and want to know what revision it is.

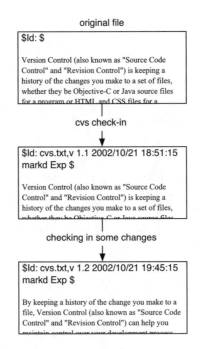

Unfortunately if you have an mp3, jpeg, or nib file which coincidentally has $Id: $ in it, CVS will happily expand that, thereby corrupting your file. Perform these steps to tell CVS not to expand keywords in certain binary files for any project added to the repository. (You only need to do this once per repository you create, and only if you will be adding binary files, which for a typical Mac OS X app, will be "always.")

1. `cd` to a directory to hold some scratch files

2. `cvs -d /usr/local/cvsroot checkout CVSROOT`

3. `cd CVSROOT`

4. Edit the `cvswrappers` file and these lines:

```
*.gif -k 'b'
*.jpg -k 'b'
*.jpeg -k 'b'
*.pdf -k 'b'
objects.nib -k 'b'
*.tiff -k 'b'
*.class -k 'b'
*.icns -k 'b'
*.pbxproj -k 'b'
*.strings -k 'b'
(and any other binary types you will be using, like .mp3 or .png)
```

5.

```
% cvs commit -m "added binary file types" cvswrappers
Checking in cvswrappers;
```

```
/usr/local/cvsroot/CVSROOT/cvswrappers,v  <--  cvswrappers
new revision: 1.2; previous revision: 1.1
done
cvs commit: Rebuilding administrative file database
```

6. `cd ..`

7. `rm -rf CVSROOT` (note that it is directory name CVSROOT, *not* the environment variable `$CVSROOT`!)

Importing Files

The usual way to create a new project in CVS is to import an existing set of files, such as the source tree for a program or a source distribution from a vendor. `cvs import` walks a directory and adds all of the files contained therein to a new project.

```
% cd /directory/with/code
% cvs -d /usr/local/cvsroot import -m "initial revision" \
project-name vendor-tag release-tag
```

For example, using the Big Nerd Ranch's BigShow slide show program:

```
% cd ~/projects/BigShow
% rm -rf build
```

You do not want to keep track of transient stuff like the build directory.

```
% cvs -d /usr/local/cvsroot import -m "initial revision" \
BigShow BigNerdRanch start
```

You will see output like this:

```
N BigShow/AppController.h
N BigShow/AppController.m
N BigShow/BigElement.h
...
N BigShow/English.lproj/Prefs.nib/info.nib
N BigShow/English.lproj/Prefs.nib/objects.nib

No conflicts created by this import
```

The `project-name` (`BigShow`) will be the name used for the project in the repository. The values of the `vendor-tag` and `release-tag` are not really important for most projects, and can be anything. Typically either use your username or the name of the project again. The `release-tag` is used when you get a pile of code from a vendor, and you want to remember what version it came from. If you do not care, you can put any name there. Some programmers just use "start." The `-m "initial revision"` is the comment to be added to the activity log for the file.

Now that you've created the project (you can poke around in `/usr/local/cvsroot` and see what is there), there is still another step that needs to be done before you can use CVS on these files. CVS needs some housekeeping information (which is kept in subdirectories named CVS), but it does not add these directories when importing a file hierarchy. You need to tell CVS to check out these files into a new directory hierarchy:

```
% cd somewhere
% cvs -d /usr/local/cvsroot checkout BigShow
cvs checkout: Updating BigShow
U BigShow/AppController.h
U BigShow/AppController.m
U BigShow/BigElement.h
...
U BigShow/English.lproj/Prefs.nib/info.nib
U BigShow/English.lproj/Prefs.nib/objects.nib
```

The U means that CVS is "updating" the files. If you go into the BigShow directory now, you will see the CVS directory and all the source files.

Seeing Other People's Changes

Part of CVS's power is that multiple people can make changes to files independently, where the other people make their changes locally and then commit them to the repository. You can pick up other people's changes by using cvs update. If you do cvs update at the top of your source tree, the update will happen recursively. Any changes made to files will be merged into your local copies. The -n global flag to CVS (to not mess with the disk) comes in very handy here to see what is going to happen before you actually pull over the new files.

For instance, Bork and markd are working on some tweaks to BigShow. Bork checked in some changes, and markd made some local changes. markd does cvs -n update to see what state things are in:

```
% cvs -n update
cvs update: Updating .
M AppController.h
C BigParse.m
U Show.h
```

The letters on the side mean:

- M The file is modified locally. There are uncommitted changes.

- U The file will be updated. Someone else's changes will be merged in.

- C The file needs to be updated. Someone made changes, and you have made modifications locally. These two changes conflict so you need to manually fix the conflict.

By doing cvs -n update, you can see what files you need to check in, what files other folks have changed, and what will have problems when you go to check stuff in.

Now, markd goes ahead and does the update:

```
% cvs update
cvs update: Updating .
M AppController.h

RCS file: /usr/local/cvsroot/BigShow/BigParse.m,v
retrieving revision 1.1.1.1
retrieving revision 1.2
Merging differences between 1.1.1.1 and 1.2 into BigParse.m
```

```
rcsmerge: warning: conflicts during merge
cvs update: conflicts found in BigParse.m
C BigParse.m

U Show.h
```

Show.h has been updated with the new changes, and BigParse.m has had a conflict, specifically between revision 1.1.1.1 (the one I have) and revision 1.2 (the new one).

Looking in the file you will see some markers:

```
<<<<<<< BigParse.m
// Use the dataTypeID to determine what to print.
// !!! verfiy XML frobulation
=======
// Use the dataTypeID to determine what to print
>>>>>>> 1.2
```

The text between <<<<<<<< and ======= are what you have done to the file. The text afterward is what the other person did. Remove either one or the other branches (or remove the whole thing) to resolve the conflict.

If you are just interested in picking up one file (like your buddy has made changes to a header that you need), you can explicitly update that one file:

```
% cvs update Show.h
U Show.h
```

CVS by default does not bring in new directories, so if someone has added an entire subdirectory of stuff to the project, you will need to add the -d flag to cvs update (this is a command flag, not the -d global flag), using a command like this:

```
% cvs update -d testCases
cvs update: Updating testCases
U testCases/elementtest.m
U testCases/parsetest.m
U testCases/printtest.m
```

Making Changes

Since CVS works on the "edit, merge" model, you are free to edit any file in your source tree. Say you edit AppController.h and add a comment to the top

```
/* AppController.h : central controller that controls the Big Show
 * (C) Forever Big Nerd Ranch
 */
```

and you want to commit your change. First you need to make sure that the file is up to date regarding changes other programmers have made, via cvs update. CVS only lets you commit changes if the file you are working on has the same revision number as the head of the revision tree. If not, you will get an error like this:

```
% cvs commit -m "tweaked horizontal alignment element" BlockElement.m
cvs commit: Up-to-date check failed for 'BlockElement.m'
cvs [commit aborted]: correct above errors first!
```

Before I commit a change, I like to remind myself what I did, as well as take an opportunity to remove any bad comments or caveman debugging code. cvs diff will show the difference between this file and the original revision it was based on.

```
% cvs diff BigParse.m
Index: BigParse.m
===========================================================
RCS file: /usr/local/cvsroot/BigShow/BigParse.m,v
retrieving revision 1.2
diff -r1.2 BigParse.m
15c15,17
< // Use the dataTypeID to determine what to print
---
>
> // Use the dataTypeID to determine what to print.
> // !!! verify XML frobulation
>
18a21
>
106a110
>
119a124
>
```

This shows stuff in "diff" format. It is machine readable, and human readable if the humans spend enough time looking at it. It says a comment was changed and a little whitespace was added. You can see the changes in context by using the -c flag (for "context diff"):

```
% cvs diff -c BigParse.m
...
*** BigParse.m 2002/10/18 17:02:08 1.2
--- BigParse.m 2002/10/18 17:34:45
***************
*** 12,22 ****
  CFStringRef myDataStr;
  CFMutableStringRef theText;

- // Use the dataTypeID to determine what to print

  switch (CFXMLNodeGetTypeCode(node)) {
      const CFXMLElementInfo *elementInfo;
!     case kCFXMLNodeTypeDocument:
          return NULL;
          break;
      case kCFXMLNodeTypeElement:
--- 12,25 ----
  CFStringRef myDataStr;
  CFMutableStringRef theText;


+ // Use the dataTypeID to determine what to print.
+ // !!! verify XML frobulation
+
+
  switch (CFXMLNodeGetTypeCode(node)) {
      const CFXMLElementInfo *elementInfo;
```

```
!
!          case kCFXMLNodeTypeDocument:
              return NULL;
              break;
          case kCFXMLNodeTypeElement:
```

- indicates a line removed, + a line added, and ! a line changed. If you do not care about horizontal whitespace differences (like when you are arguing with your cubemate over code indentation), you can use the -b flag to suppress diff report of whitespace.

Once you've checked over the differences, you commit the file with:

```
% cvs commit -m "added flag to comment" BigParse.m
Checking in BigParse.m;
/usr/local/cvsroot/BigShow/BigParse.m,v  <--  BigParse.m
new revision: 1.3; previous revision: 1.2
done
```

cvs log will show you the edit history of a file along with a lot of other information:

```
% cvs log BigParse.m
RCS file: /usr/local/cvsroot/BigShow/BigParse.m,v
Working file: BigParse.m
head: 1.3
branch:
locks: strict
access list:
symbolic names:
 start: 1.1.1.1
 BigNerdRanch: 1.1.1
keyword substitution: kv
total revisions: 4; selected revisions: 4
description:
----------------------------
revision 1.3
date: 2002/10/18 17:52:43;  author: markd;  state: Exp;  lines: +7 -2
added flag to comment
----------------------------
revision 1.2
date: 2002/10/18 17:02:08;  author: bork;  state: Exp;  lines: +1 -1
tweaked a comment
----------------------------
revision 1.1
date: 2002/10/18 16:13:41;  author: markd;  state: Exp;
branches:  1.1.1;
Initial revision
----------------------------
revision 1.1.1.1
date: 2002/10/18 16:13:41;  author: markd;  state: Exp;  lines: +0 -0
initial revision
============================================================
```

By the way, revision 1.2 by Bork is what caused the conflict earlier on.

You can tell cvs diff to get the differences between two revisions:

```
% cvs diff -r 1.2 -r 1.1 BigParse.m
```

If you want to retrieve a specific revision, `cvs update` will do that for you. You can do

```
% cvs update -r 1.2 BigParse.m
```

which will update `BigParse.m` to be the same contents as revision 1.2. From now on, `BigParse.m` in this source tree will refer to revision 1.2, and subsequent updates will not bring down new versions (this is useful if someone has introduced instabilities to a file and you need a stable version to work on). This command will re-point the file to the head revision:

```
% cvs update -A BigParse.m
```

If you just want to look at a file, you can bring the file's contents out through `stdout`, but using the `-p` (pipe) flag:

```
% cvs update -p 1.2 BigParse.m > somefile
```

Adding New Files

Projects grow over time and new source files get added. To add a new source file, create the initial revision of the file and then add it with `cvs add`:

```
% cvs add SuperAboutBox.m
cvs add: scheduling file 'SuperAboutBox.m' for addition
cvs add: use 'cvs commit' to add this file permanently
```

Then commit it to tell CVS to actually keep track of it:

```
% cvs commit SuperAboutBox.m
cvs commit -m "initial revision" SuperAboutBox.m
RCS file: /usr/local/cvsroot/BigShow/SuperAboutBox.m,v
done
Checking in SuperAboutBox.m;
/usr/local/cvsroot/BigShow/SuperAboutBox.m,v  <--  SuperAboutBox.m
initial revision: 1.1
done
```

If you are adding a binary file and you want to suppress keyword expansion, use the `-kb` (keyword, binary) flag when adding it:

```
% cvs add -kb BigNerdTheme.mp3
cvs add: scheduling file 'BigNerdTheme.mp3' for addition
cvs add: use 'cvs commit' to add this file permanently
```

Then commit it as before.

You can remove obsolete files as well. `cvs remove` will "remove" the file from the repository. It does not actually wipe out the revision history from the repository. Instead, CVS moves it to the "Attic" in case you need to look at an older revision of the file, or decide you really needed it.

```
% rm SuperAboutBox.m
% cvs remove SuperAboutBox.m
cvs remove: scheduling 'SuperAboutBox.m' for removal
cvs remove: use 'cvs commit' to remove this file permanently
```

```
Removing SuperAboutBox.m;
/usr/local/cvsroot/BigShow/SuperAboutBox.m,v   <--   SuperAboutBox.m
new revision: delete; previous revision: 1.1
done
```

If you need it back, you can recreate it like this:

```
% cvs update -r 1.1 -p SuperAboutBox.m > SuperAboutBox.m
=========================================================

Checking out SuperAboutBox.m
RCS:  /usr/local/cvsroot/BigShow/Attic/SuperAboutBox.m,v
VERS: 1.1
***************

% cvs add SuperAboutBox.m
cvs add:re-adding file SuperAboutBox.m(in place of dead revision 1.2)
cvs add:use 'cvs commit' to add this file permanently

% cvs commit -m "back from the dead" SuperAboutBox.m
Checking in SuperAboutBox.m;
/usr/local/cvsroot/BigShow/SuperAboutBox.m,v   <--   SuperAboutBox.m
new revision: 1.3; previous revision: 1.2
done
```

Tags

CVS tags (also called labels) are symbolic names given to a collection of specific revisions. Tagging your source code after a major release is a good idea since you can go back and recreate a source tree with those revisions. cvs tag will walk a CVS-controlled tree and add tags for each revision as it exists in the tree.

```
% cvs tag "version_0_7"
cvs tag: Tagging .
T AppController.h
T AppController.m
T BigElement.h
T BigElement.m
T BigParse.h
T BigParse.m
...
T testCases/parsetest.m
T testCases/printtest.m
```

If you cvs log a file, you will see the tag information there:

```
% cvs log BigParse.m | head -10

RCS file: /usr/local/cvsroot/BigShow/BigParse.m,v
Working file: BigParse.m
head: 1.3
branch:
locks: strict
access list:
symbolic names:
  version_0_7: 1.3
```

```
    start: 1.1.1.1
```

So, suppose you are happily working on version 0.8 of the product, and an "important user" has a big show stopper that you need to fix. You can check out a new source tree based on that revision:

```
% cvs checkout -r version_0_7 -d BigShow0.7 BigShow
cvs checkout: Updating BigShow0.7
U BigShow0.7/AppController.h
U BigShow0.7/AppController.m
...
U BigShow0.7/testCases/parsetest.m
U BigShow0.7/testCases/printtest.m
```

(Yes, yet another -d flag. This one says to put the checkout in a directory called BigShow0.7, rather than using the name of the project as the checkout directory.)

If you make a change to a file and try to check it in, you will get an error like this:

```
% cvs commit -m "fixed image problem" BigParse.m
cvs commit: sticky tag 'version_0_7' for file 'BigParse.m'
            is not a branch
cvs [commit aborted]: correct above errors first!
```

CVS draws a distinction between regular tags, which just label a particular revision, and branch tags, which would let you create an offshoot of an older revision of a file.

Branch Tags

A branch tag is a special kind of tag that CVS can use as the starting point for a new line of revisions.

When using cvs tag, add the -b flag:

```
% cvs tag -b "version_0_7_branch"
```

(The "_branch" is just a naming convention.)

If you already have a non-branch tag, you can create a branch tag based on it and not have to tag an existing source tree. The cvs rtag command operates solely on the repository, not on a particular source tree.

You can make a new tag off the 0.7 tag by using

```
% cvs rtag -b -r version_0_7 version_0_7_branch BigShow
```

and check out a new tree, or you can re-point a source tree to a new tag by doing

```
% cvs update -r version_0_7_branch
```

and then check-in your change.

To point your source tree back to the head revision, use cvs update -A:

```
% cvs commit -m "fixed image problem" BigParse.m
Checking in BigParse.m;
/usr/local/cvsroot/BigShow/BigParse.m,v  <--  BigParse.m
new revision: 1.3.2.1; previous revision: 1.3
```

```
done
```

Note the revision number now. It is gone from two numbers to four numbes. The first two numbers represent the "parent" revision and the second two digits are a unique, ascending sequence.

Here is part of the `cvs log` for the file:

```
% cvs log BigParse.m

RCS file: /usr/local/cvsroot/BigShow/BigParse.m,v
Working file: BigParse.m
head: 1.3
branch:
...
----------------------------
revision 1.3
date: 2002/10/18 17:52:43;  author: markd;  state: Exp;  lines: +7 -2
branches:  1.3.2;
added flag to comment
----------------------------
revision 1.2
date: 2002/10/18 17:02:08;  author: markd;  state: Exp;  lines: +1 -1
tweaked a comment
...
revision 1.3.2.1
date: 2002/10/18 21:14:00;  author: markd;  state: Exp;  lines: +1 -1
fixed image problem
============================================================
```

Remote Repositories

CVS is a useful tool that has applications for the developer working alone on a project. It really becomes powerful, though, when multiple developers are using CVS to collaborate on the same project, sharing the same repository and project. Unless all development occurs on a shared machine, some network access is necessary so that the interested parties can communicate with the repository. That brings along questions of convenience (how complicated is the setup and day-to-day use of the tools?) and security (do you care if someone can see the network traffic and see your source code?).

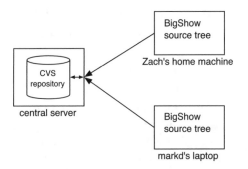

Here, two developers are working on the same project using a CVS repository on a central server machine.

The method described here (using ssh and having Unix account logins) is the easiest to set up and use for small teams, in that programmers who have CVS access need logins to the machine that holds the repository. It has the advantage of using secure communication for both passwords and the transport of data.

Another available method is *pserver*, which uses cleartext communication so passwords and source are sent in the clear but users are not required to have logins (CVS maintains its own user and password file). For an internal network or for an opensource project, this should be OK. *gserver* uses the GSS (Generic Security Services) API and has hooks into Kerberos, so you have user authentication and encryption. To use password authentication, it is necessary to apply some patches to CVS and rebuild it.

You can mix and match these as well. One open source project I am involved with (OpenACS) uses pserver for anonymous (public) CVS access. The people who have commit rights have a login to the repository box and use the ssh mechanism. That way the public has read access, but write access (particularly the passwords) is authenticated and encrypted.

Here are the steps for using ssh access:

1. Make sure you have a login on the box with the CVS repository, and you have the repository path. In this case, the remote machine is on my local network, called "ilamp" (my G4 iMac) and the repository is at /usr/local/cvsroot.

2. Set your CVS_RSH environment variable to ssh, otherwise CVS will try to use rsh which is all cleartext and insecure. You may want to put this in a login config file.

   ```
   % setenv CVS_RSH ssh
   ```

3. The CVSROOT you want to use (whether set in an environment variable or as the argument to the -d global option to CVS) is hostname:/path/to/repository, or for my case, ilamp:/usr/local/cvsroot

4. Check out the project you are interested in:

   ```
   % cvs -d ilamp:/usr/local/cvsroot checkout BigShow
   markd@ilamp's password:
   cvs server: Updating LampShow
   U LampShow/AppController.h
   U LampShow/AppController.m
   ...
   U LampShow/English.lproj/Prefs.nib/info.nib
   U LampShow/English.lproj/Prefs.nib/objects.nib
   ```

You can now look at file logs, update and get new revisions of files, and commit your work.

Passwordless authentication

There is one drawback using this remote access method: ssh asks for your password every time you issue a command. Depending on your temperament, this could get annoying quickly. ssh has a feature where you can generate an authorization key on one machine and then place it on the remote machine that contains the repository. When you then ssh to the repository machine (or use a CVS command that uses ssh), the two sides will exchange authorization keys and bypass having to ask for the password. This can also be a security concern. If your machine gets compromised, someone can log into the repository machine without requiring a password. As with all things, it is good to balance the convenient with the secure.

With that caveat, here is how you do it:

1. On your machine (say your desktop machine), run `ssh-keygen` with an empty passphrase:

   ```
   % ssh-keygen -t rsa
   Generating public/private rsa key pair.
   Enter file in which to save the key (/Users/markd/.ssh/id_rsa):
   Enter passphrase (empty for no passphrase):
   Enter same passphrase again:
   Your identification has been saved in /Users/markd/.ssh/id_rsa.
   Your public key has been saved in /Users/markd/.ssh/id_rsa.pub.
   The key fingerprint is:
   9b:51:90:95:d9:40:65:ff:6a:fe:f7:15:06 markd@borkopolis.local.
   ```

2. Copy the public key to the repository machine:

   ```
   % scp ~/.ssh/id_rsa.pub ilamp:
   markd@ilamp's password:
   id_rsa.pub     100% |****************************|   233    00:00
   ```

3. Log into the repository machine.

4. Move the `id_rsa.pub` file into the `.ssh` directory and name it `authorized_keys`:

   ```
   % hostname
   iLamp.local.
   % mv ~/id_rsa.pub ~/.ssh/authorized_keys
   ```

Mac OS X Specific Weirdness

File wrappers

OS X is unique in that it has file wrappers (also called bundles), those directories that get treated as single files. `Project Builder` projects and `Interface Builder` nib files are file wrappers. There are two ways to deal with these. One is to use `cvswrappers` (the file described earlier when adding the binary files that shouldn't have keyword expansion). `/Developer/Tools/cvswrappers` has some sample wrappers that use `tar` to pack and unpack a file wrapper into a single file, and then CVS deals with this tar file. This works great with CVS 1.10 (which comes with Mac OS X), but is broken in CVS 1.11 and beyond (which is what most of the rest of the world, including SourceForge, uses).

The main reason these CVS wrappers were necessary was because `Interface Builder` did not handle the CVS directories well, which made CVS interactions difficult. Luckily `Interface Builder` (and `Project Builder`) behave nicely these days and you can just check in these file wrappers as if they were ordinary directories of files. Just be aware that when you roll back a nib or a `.pbproj` file, you need to roll back all the files contained therein.

CVS and Project Builder

If your source tree is under CVS control, `Project Builder` will give you a front end to some CVS operations. The **CVS** menu lets you **Compare With Base** (`cvs diff`, using the `FileMerge` program to display a graphical view of the file differences), and **Commit Changes** does a `cvs commit`. If you have locally modified files, `Project Builder` notes them with an "M" in the **Files** window:

To see the `cvs log` information, you need to see the info window for the file:

This shows `BigParse.m`'s revision history, and the tag and branch (this is from a project checked out on the branch).

For the More Curious

Backing up repositories

The CVS repository can be one of your most valuable corporate assets since it contains the current version of your product, the history of all the changes, and if you've used tags, it carries the ability to regenerate the product at any given point in time. Luckily the repository is just a bunch of files, all easily backed up. The only problem is if someone is in the process of doing something (like checking in files or tagging revisions) while the backup takes place. This could lead to those files becoming inconsistent (which can usually be patched up manually; the way CVS stores revisions is well documented). The ideal situation is to do the backups when nobody is using them (in the middle of the night), or to let your developers know that the repository backup happens every night from 3 to 4 a.m. If they pull an all-nighter, they should be aware not to do any CVS activity during those times.

The CVSROOT project

Recall earlier when setting up CVS that you checked out the CVSROOT project and edited the cvswrappers file. The CVSROOT project has all of the administrative controls for the repository. The standard procedure is to check out CVSROOT, make changes, and then commit the files. CVS will then rebuild its configuration database (so do not edit the files in /usr/local/cvsroot/CVSROOT directly). Of particular interest are the cvswrappers file (as seen earlier), and the cvsignore file to tell it what files and patterns to ignore (for instance, you can have CVS ignore the build directory inside a Project Builder project).

Chapter 25. Performance Tuning

It is happened to all of us: We have our program written, subject it to real world data, and discover that performance is sub-optimal (ranging from "could be faster" to "locks up instantly"). Finding out where the performance problem is can be tough. A lot of times we think we know where the problem is, but that turns out to be wrong. That is when it is time to turn to some of the tools available to give definite metrics of where the program spends its time, and what kind of pressure it put on the OS in general.

Major Causes of Performance Problems

Performance problems typically come from one or more of 5 major areas: algorithms, memory usage, CPU, usage, disk usage, and graphics.

Memory

Even thought modern machines have large amounts of memory, it is still a scarce resource. Given that current Macintoshes have slower memory busses than their PC brethren makes memory operations seem slow. Typically, when optimizing, if you optimize to reduce your memory usage (optimizing for space), you will also get speedups as well since the processor is not waiting for data to arrive from memory. Also, since Mac OS X is a shared system, with each user running lots of programs, and potentially multiple users, it is good to be conservative with your memory usage. This can be a tough discipline, since each process has its own wide-open address space to play in.

Locality of Reference

Locality of reference means that memory accesses happen near each other. Reading a hundred bytes off of one 4k page is faster than reading one byte from a hundred different pages scattered across the address space.

This program creates a large two dimensional array and accesses it in two different ways. The first loop follows the way that C has the array's memory organized, that is, accessing adjacent bytes. As the loop works through the array it has good locality of reference. Memory pages are accessed only once, and after the loop has stopped manipulating memory on a page that page is no longer used. The second loop works "across the grain". It ends up hitting a different page every time through the loop. This puts a lot of pressure on the virtual memory system and causes it to waste time manipulating its internal data structures.

Example 25-1. locality.m

```
// locality.m -- time the effect of locality of reference

/* compile with
cc -g -Wall -o locality locality.m
*/

#include <stdio.h>    // for printf
#include <time.h>     // for time_t, time()
#include <stdlib.h>   // for EXIT_SUCCESS
```

```
#define ARRAYSIZE (10000)
int a[ARRAYSIZE][ARRAYSIZE]; // make a huge array

int main (int argc, char *argv[])
{
    int i = 0, j = 0;
    time_t starttime;
    time_t endtime;

    starttime = time(NULL);

    // walk the array in row-major order, so that once we're done
    // with a page we never bother with it again

    for (i = 0; i < ARRAYSIZE; i++){
        for(j = 0; j < ARRAYSIZE; j++){
            a[i][j] = 1;
        }
    }

    endtime = time(NULL);

    printf("%d operations in %d seconds.\n", i * j,
            (int)(endtime - starttime));

    starttime = time(NULL);

    // walk the array in column-major order. We end
    // up touching a bunch of pages multiple times

    for (j = 0; j < ARRAYSIZE; j++){
        for(i = 0; i < ARRAYSIZE; i++){
            a[i][j] = 1;
        }
    }

    endtime = time(NULL);

    printf("%d operations in %d seconds.\n", i * j,
            (int)(endtime - starttime));

    return (EXIT_SUCCESS);

} // main
```

And a sample run:

```
% ./locality
100000000 operations in 21 seconds.
100000000 operations in 106 seconds.
```

Showing that a simple reversal the for loops can give you a 5x performance penalty.

Caches

One technique that is often suggested when there are performance problems (especially disk problems) is to perform aggressive caching. The thought is that you can save on disk I/O by doing it once and keeping the results in memory. The section below on Disk Usage will show that this technique has some drawbacks in Mac OS X. But if you choose to cache information, it is best to split up your caches so that all your metadata about the cached objects is together. You will have good locality of reference when walking your cache looking for expired objects. So, you do not want to do this:

Figure 25-1. Bad Locality of Reference

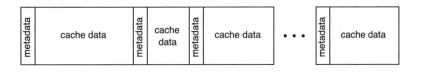

instead, organize your data like this:

Figure 25-2. Good Locality of Reference

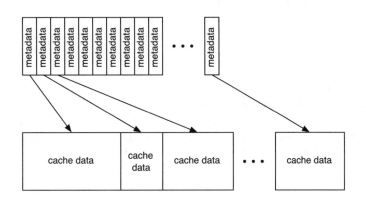

CPU

CPU usage is the metric that most folks think of first when confronted with an optimization issue. "My app is pegging the CPU and I need to speed it up". Typically when CPU usage issues happen they are caused by a bad algorithm, whether it is fundamentally bad, or just a poor implementation. In almost all cases changing your algorithm will give you more speedups than most other kinds of code tweaking. The classic example is changing from a bubble-sort (an order $O(N^2)$ algorithm) to a quicksort or merge sort ($O(n \log n)$).

Sometimes a bad implementation of an algorithm can wreak havoc. A programming error turned `strstr()` on SunOS 4.1.x from an $O(N)$ operation to a worthless $O(N^2)$ one:

```
while (c < strlen(string)) {
    // do stuff with string[c]
}
```

Recall that `strlen()` has to traverse the entire string counting characters. In this particular case, the length of the string will not change, so there is no reason to take the length every time through the loop.

Luckily high CPU usage can be pretty obvious to discover (by noticing that the CPU meter is pegged, or `top` is showing your app consuming 99% of the available CPU power). The sampling and profiling tools discussed later are ideal for tracking down the cause of these problems.

Disk

Disk access is very slow, many orders of magnitude slower than accessing memory. In general, if you can avoid disk I/O, do so. One thing to watch out for is that the virtual memory system also uses the disk, so if you cache a huge amount of data you could end up causing the VM system to do disk I/O. This is a very bad situation since you have now exchanged one disk read (from disk into memory) into a read, a write (paging it out), and another read (paging it back in from the disk into memory).

Recall earlier about locality of reference. That plays a part in optimizing disk access when there is VM paging involved. With bad locality of reference you end up touching lots of pages. These pages cause other pages to "age out" of the VM cache and get sent to disk. Eventually you will touch them again which could cause disk I/O to retrieve the data on those pages.

You can avoid some of the expense of I/O by not doing the work at all. Such as putting windows into different `.nib` files and loading them on demand. If you have a large database of information, accessing it piecemeal can yield significant speedups over loading the whole thing into memory. Similarly, using memory mapped files can avoid disk activity. The VM system will only pull into memory the chunks of the file you actually touch.

Graphics

The Quartz graphics engine in Mac OS X puts a lot of pressure on the memory system, due to the large graphic buffers sitting around, and the compositing operations that happen with those buffers. Quartz also puts a lot of pressure on the CPU to do all of the fancy drawing effects.

The key to optimizing drawing is to avoid doing drawing when you can. Use the `Quartz Debug` program to see where you are doing unnecessary drawing. You can hit-test the rectangle that is passed to `NSView`'s `drawRect:` method and only perform drawing calls for items that live in that rectangle. Unfortunately this isn't not as good of an optimization as it could be since the Apple versions of Cocoa tend to union dirty rectangles, leading to much larger areas that need drawing, which somewhat defeats the purpose of calls like `setNeedsDisplayInRect:`. If your application lends itself to small self-contained updates when drawing, it can be more efficient for you to lock focus and invoke `drawRect:` yourself when doing small-area updates.

One aspect of Quartz drawing that catches some programmers off-guard is that overlapping lines in a single path are very expensive. A lot of work happens at line crossing, such as anti-aliasing the intersections, as well as making sure that transparent colors do not get "painted" multiple times at the crossings and appear darker. If you need to do lots of overlapping lines, especially if you are using opaque colors and don not care about antialiasing, you can get much better performance by drawing a bunch of small paths.

Before using any of the profiling tools

When doing optimizations, forget any assumptions you may have about where the problems may be. Programmers are notoriously bad about predicting where performance problems are, otherwise they would have already fixed them.

Also, keep good notes on what you do and the measurements you, so you can possibly apply the optimizations to other situations. By keeping a record of execution times (for instance) you can tell if your optimization attempts are actually making the problem worse.

When tracking down performance problems, throw a large data set at your application. If you think you have a problem with the speed of your file loading routines, using a 5K file that a second to load will not show the problem, plus it gives you too small a window in which to use your profiling tools. If your application is designed to edit 50 page research papers then throw a 500 or 5000 page document at it. If you have an order N^2 in there, the larger data set should make it stand out like the proverbial sore thumb. Sometimes using larger data can tell you that the problem is not where you think it is. It could be the setup of an NSOutlineView after you get the data loaded, for instance. If you can make your program responsive with 5000 page documents, it should give the user a really nice experience when they are just using it to edit the 50 page documents.

There is some debate over when you should optimize. One school of thought is "premature optimization is the root of all evil", where you should wait until the end of your development cycle to identify and fix performance problems. Unfortunately that can require re-enginering large chunks of the product if it is a deeply rooted bottleneck. Another school of thought is to act like you are on a diet, and have a constant discipline about performance. The down side to that is that premature optimization can obscure the design and the code, and make it harder to track down program errors before shipping.

As with everything in programming, the middle ground is a good place to live. Keep an eye out for algorithms that can be improved, but do not obfuscate code to early in the development process. Throw large datasets at your program often. Do not wait until right before launch to subject your program to what the customer is going to be throwing at it. Keep an eye on your memory usage so that it does not grow too large too quickly. Also be sure to often run the program in the user's environment. If you are writing a desktop app, be sure to have a web browser and iTunes running, since the user probably will have those apps running. If your application is a memory pig and makes iTunes skip, you will definitely get some user complaints.

Command-Line Tools

Mac OS X comes with a number of command line tools for tracking down some types of performance problems. The nice thing about the command line tools is that you can remotely log into a machine and watch things, and not bother with having the tool's interface interfere with the user interface or the system in general.

time

The simplest tool is `time`. It times command execution and shows you clock time, CPU time in userspace, and CPU time spent in the kernel. Here is a run of `/usr/bin/time` on `BigShow`, the Big Nerd Ranch slide show program (which will be the unfortunate victim of many of the tools here). The time measured was the time starting `BigShow` up, loading a big set of slides, and then paging through them.

```
% /usr/bin/time build/BigShow.app/Contents/MacOS/BigShow
       128.35 real            3.07 user            0.80 sys
```

This is 128 seconds of clock time, three seconds in user space, and less than a second in the kernel. All in all, pretty good performance characteristics.

The C shell has its own version of time that gives some more information:

```
% time build/BigShow.app/Contents/MacOS/BigShow
3.300u 0.800s 1:44.78 3.9% 0+0k 0+22io 0pf+0w
```

3.3 seconds in user space, 0.8 seconds in kernel space, one minute, 44 seconds clock time. The 3.9% is a utilization percentage : ratio of user + system times to real time. After the time information is memory information: shared + unshared memory usage, input + output operations, number of pagefaults and swaps. OS X seems not to report the shared + unshared memory usage.

`time` is very handy when comparing optimizations. Run a baseline or two with `time`, make the optimization, then try `time` again. If you are optimizing CPU, and the CPU time figures go up, then the optimization is not a good one, or it could use some work.

ktrace

Many Unix systems have a utility that will show all of the system calls a program makes. On Solaris it is called `truss`, on Linux it is `strace`. Darwin has `ktrace` (kernel tracing). In versions of Mac OS X prior to Jaguar, kernel tracing was disabled, requiring you to rebuild your kernel before using it. Jaguar has tracing enabled by default.

The tracing of system calls is a two-stage process. Run your program with `ktrace` (or tell `ktrace` to attach to a program and start logging system calls). `ktrace` writes this information out to a file named `ktrace.out`. The `kdump` program takes this file and turns it into something readable.

For example:

```
% ktrace ls
% kdump
```

This generates a couple hundred lines of output. Stuff like this:

```
17477 ktrace   CALL   execve(0xbffff7b0,0xbffffd9c,0xbffffda4)
17477 ktrace   NAMI   "/bin/ls"
17477 ktrace   NAMI   "/usr/lib/dyld"
```

```
17477 ls        RET    execve 0
17477 ls        CALL   open(0x1460,0,0)
17477 ls        NAMI   "/usr/lib/libSystem.B.dylib"
17477 ls        RET    open 3
```

The columns are process ID, program name, action performed, and the system call +
arguments.

The first three lines are ktrace doing an **exec()** of the ls program. The CALL is the
system call invocation. NAMI are certain interesting arguments being printed out.
RET is the return code. Following the **exec()**, ktrace turns into ls, and **open()** is
called on a system shared library. The return value of **open()** is 3, file descriptor
number three. This is the correct value, since file descriptors 0, 1, 2 are used for the
standard streams.

A little later on is something like this;

```
17477 ls        CALL   write(0x1,0x48000,0x4b)
17477 ls        GIO    fd 1 wrote 75 bytes
       "CVS            objectalloc-bs.pdf      sampler-bs-default.pdf
       "
17477 ls        RET    write 75/0x4b
```

This is a **write** system call. The arguments to write are 0x1 (file descriptor number
1), which is standard out. The last argument 0x4b is the number of bytes written (75
bytes). GIO is the input/output data. Just by looking at the string you can tell this is
one line of ls's output.

You can watch a ktrace trace in real time. Either background the traced program or
open a new window, then run kdump -l. This acts like tail -f in that kdump will
continually read from kdump.out and display the results. Seeing the system call
traffic can be a great debugging aid, as well as a performance tuning aid. For
instance, you discover a lot of one-byte writes, or you give a bad timeout to select so
that it returns a lot sooner than you expect, or your program blocks unexpectedly.

fs_usage and sc_usage

fs_usage and sc_usage are programs run as the root user which also show system
call activity. fs_usage shows file system information. Here is BigShow about to start
paging through slides:

```
18:38:06 open   /Preferences/com.apple.dock.plist 0.00005    BigShow
18:38:06 fstat                                     0.00000    BigShow
18:38:06 read                                      0.00029    BigShow
18:38:06 close                                     0.00002    BigShow
18:38:06 open   com.apple.dock.0003931024a6.plist  0.00015    BigShow
18:38:06 PAGE_IN                                    0.00070 W  BigShow
18:38:06 open   /Library/Preferences/Network        0.00008    BigShow
18:38:06 open   com.apple.systempreferences.plist  0.00005    BigShow
```

Part of Cocoa is looking at the plist for the dock (presumably for getting size and
location information so that it can place a window). You can see the open, the stat
(to get the size of the file), the read of the file, and its close. Unlike ktrace, there is
not an easy way to correlate specific calls (like a **read()**) and the file descriptor it is
using, but fs_usagedoes show you how much time it took. fs_usage can be run on

a system-wide basis, which can be handy if you have a problem that is slowing the entire machine down.

One really snazzy feature of `fs_usage` is when it is used with Carbon applications. If you set the environment variable `DYLD_IMAGE_SUFFIX` to `_debug`, `fd_usage` will show the Carbon calls being made. Here is a peek at Mozilla running:

```
18:34:38 GetCatInfo                                    0.000174   LaunchCFMApp
18:34:38 PBMakeFSSpec   (0, 0x0, 0x0, 0x0)                        LaunchCFMApp
18:34:38 getattrlist    .vol/280763/Mozilla.app 0.000032         LaunchCFMApp
18:34:38 PBMakeFSSpec                                  0.000064   LaunchCFMApp
18:34:38 GetCatInfo     (-100, 0x0, 0x0, 0x0)                     LaunchCFMApp
18:34:38 getattrlist    .vol/280763/Mozilla.app 0.000046         LaunchCFMApp
```

`sc_usage` shows system calls for a program in a manner like `top`, a continually updating display. Here is a snapshot from BigShow:

```
BigShow        0 preemptions  0 context switches  1 thread   18:41:43
               0 faults       0 system calls                  0:00:52

TYPE                       NUMBER    CPU_TIME   WAIT_TIME
-----------------------------------------------------------------------
System         Idle                            0:37.893(0:00.019)
System         Busy                            0:07.969(0:01.118)
BigShow        Usermode              0:01.333

zero_fill                    1549    0:00.045   0:00.000
pagein                         16    0:00.005   0:00.329
cache_hit                     174    0:00.005   0:00.000

mach_msg_trap                4398    0:00.113   0:27.360(0:01.137) W
vm_deallocate                1100    0:00.054   0:00.000
vm_allocate                   105    0:00.002   0:00.000
vm_copy                        99    0:00.020   0:00.000
getattrlist                    18    0:00.000   0:00.000
mk_timer_arm                  105    0:00.003   0:00.000
mach_port_insert_member       103    0:00.001   0:00.000
write                           2    0:00.000
```

The CPU_TIME is the amount of cpu time consumed, and WAIT_TIME is the absolute time the process waits.

If you think you have I/O performance problems, these two programs can help you track down the specific calls that could be causing problems.

gprof

`gprof` is a profiler. A profiler instruments your code and records function entries and exits. You give `-pg` flag to the compiler and the linker so that it will include this instrumentation (you have to do this manually because `Project Builder` does not include the `-pg` flag everywhere it needs to be). After the program exits normally, it will leave a file named `gmon.out` which can then be run through `gprof`. `gprof` builds a table of functions called, sorted in order of CPU time consumed (useful to see if there is an obvious bad function). It also builds a call graph of the program, showing which functions call what other functions, and how many times. You can use this to see if the number of function calls involved is in line with what you expect. If reading a five slide XML file results in 500,000 string allocations and deallocations, then you know there is a problem.

Unfortunately, `gprof` does not seem to behave well in the face of threads or with Cocoa programs. `gprof` also needs profiling versions of the libraries found in the standard system frameworks. Unfortunately, software updates don't install new profiling versions of the libraries, so if you upgrade to a 0.0.x release you'll lose the ability to profile. With that said, `gprof` can be be effective with single-threaded command-line programs, and some daemons.

Stochastic profiling

To wrap up the command-line tools, one of my favorite low-tech tools is stochastic profiling. Basically, you run the program in the debugger, interrupt it every now and then, and notice what is on your stack. If you see the same function(s) on the stack over and over again, you know you have a place to start looking. This technique is handy if you are on a platform or in a situation where traditional performance tools are not available or do not work. Plus it is fast and easy.

GUI Tools

The GUI performance tools live in `/Developer/Applications/`.

ObjectAlloc

Memory issues are frequently performance hot spots. Too many allocations and deallocations can chew up time that could be saved by reusing the same memory or reusing some objects. The ObjectAlloc tool can be used for Objective-C programs to keep a tally of allocations and deallocations of objects, along with the stack traces of each of these operations. If you see a couple million allocs/deallocs when opening a small file, you have a good idea where to start looking.

You can set a "mark" at a point in time to restrict the allocations you are evaluating (this is used to screen out all the overhead work that happens on program startup).

Here is BigShow with a mark set after program start, showing the result of loading a really big slide show (a couple hundred slides) XML File. Artificially inflating the data you are processing can make performance issues stand out more.

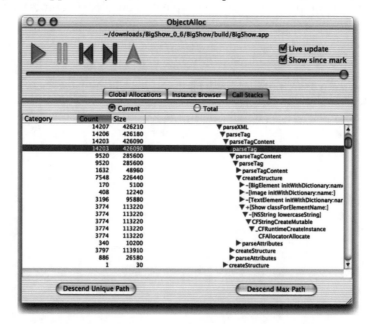

You can see that a lot of `CFString` action has gone on. Looking at CFString (immutable), there are currently 10,667 of them floating around. At the high point, there were 12,676 in existence, with a total of 22,895 allocations.

If you see a particular kind of allocation that looks interesting, the Call Stacks tab will give you an opportunity to see who was responsible for allocations.

Here the CFString (mutable) entry has been expanded. The count column is a cumulative summation of the number of `CFString`s that have been allocated. Note the difference between the selected line and the next line. `parseTag` was responsible for 4683 (14203 - 9520) allocations. Likewise, **parseAttributes** contributed 2911 (3797 - 886) allocations.

Sampler

Sampling is a profiling technique where the program being sampled is interrupted periodically and the stack traces of the threads are recorded. Once the sampling stops, the sampler program accumulates the data it recorded and determines which functions were most active during the sampling period. One of the nice things about sampling is that it shows time spent blocked in system calls. Profiling will not calculate that time. `Sampler` is one such utility.

Here is a sampling of `BigShow` after paging through a hundred or so slides:

The tree browser portion of the window lets you navigate stack traces to see where the samples are distributed. Unfortunately the browser portion is not easily resizable, so function call names get cut off. In this case, **mach_msg_send()** was on the top of the stack for 48% of the samples. If you want to see who called all those **mach_msg_send**s, you can re-root the call tree. Select the **mach_msg_send** and set the root. You will then see something like this:

So the calls **SendFontM***, **_CGSynch**, **__CFRunLoop** are the big callers. The first two imply that there is a lot of text (font stuff) and graphics (CG for Core Graphics).

QuartzDebug

`QuartzDebug` is a utility to show where drawing is happening on the screen, as well as any drawing the program does that does not actually change what is already on the screen. It will show excessive or wasteful graphics operations. The autoflush drawing option will flush each drawing operation to the screen, which will also show unnecessary drawing.

CHUD

CHUD is Apple's new profiling framework. Apple says that CHUD means "Computer Hardware Understanding Development kit," but it is probably just a fun code name that stuck. CHUD is a kernel extension plus a framework that gives access to the Performance Monitor Counters (PMC) of the CPU, the memory controller (for machines 133mhz or faster), and certain OS counters. There are a number of pre-built programs that are useful for getting performance metrics both system wide and for a particular program. The framework those programs are built on are available for your use as well.

The `Shikari` program (included with the CHUD distribution) can be used to get a profile of your program execution. It does not gather stack traces, but will show you the functions that appeared most often at the top of the stack.

Here is `BigShow` after loading an XML file:

The dark bars are supervisor (kernel) functions, while others are application-space functions. In this case, you can see that obtaining memory from the OS is high up there, as are string functions and Objective-C method dispatch. Double-clicking on a line will show a disassembly of the function, with the hot spots colorized.

In addition to collecting function names, you can use any of the PMC registers for accumulating counts, such as altivec instructions, instruction counts, unaligned data access, and lots of very esoteric metrics.

Shikari will also show a chart of the metrics it accumulates:

Clicking on a sample on the chart will highlight it in the main window. The other metrics it can accumulate tend to be more interesting when charted.

Option-escape is a hot key to turn on and off Shikari's sampling, and you can also do that under your program control. If you have performance problems in a very specific part of your program (like opening a document), you can limit the sampling to exactly that part of the program and not worry about noise introduced by program startup, nor noise from drawing the document window.

You do this by including the CHUD framework in your application, and performing these calls at startup:

```
#import <CHUD/chud.h>
```

```
chudInitialize ();
chudSetErrorLogFile (stderr);
chudUmarkPID (getpid(), TRUE);
chudAcquireRemoteAccess ();
```

Then before your code of interest, invoke:

```
result = chudStartRemotePerfMonitor ("SomeIdentifier");
// zero for success, a code on error
```

Do your code, then call:

```
chudStopRemotePerfMonitor ();
chudReleaseRemoteAccess ();
```

Before running this part of your code, tell Shikari to go into Remote Monitoring Mode. Once you execute **chudStartRemotePerfMonitor()**, Shikari turns on the counters and starts sampling your program.

CHUD also includes programs like MONster, which shows many details of system-wide performance; amber, which captures the entire instruction and data streams from a program; and acid, which takes the trace from amber and analyzes it. There are also some examples living in /Developer/Examples/CHUD/.

For the More Curious:Top

As systems get more complex, they tend to be composed of multiple programs interacting. Sometimes performance problems manifest themselves as overall system slowness while each program looks fine in isolation. The fs_usage and sc_usage utilities are useful for monitoring system calls. The top program can be used to monitor all the programs on the system. Running top without arguments will show the familiar OS information (memory distributions, load average). By default, it orders programs by launch order (most recent program listed first). This is useful if you are monitoring a particular program. The -u flag will sort things by CPU usage.

top can also count and show system-wide events. top -e shows VM (virtual memory), network activity, disk activity, and messaging stats:

```
% top -e

Processes:  74 total, 3 running, 71 sleeping... 198 threads
Load Avg: 0.52, 0.57, 0.58  CPU usage:  9.4% user, 5.9% sys, 74.7% idle
Networks:    967607 ipkts/552961K      1198784 opkts /445769K
Disks:       318661 reads/3531419K      464932 writes/5488572K
VM:           89751 pageins            99649 pageouts

  PID COMMAND %CPU    TIME     FAULTS PAGEINS COW_FAULTS MSGS_SENT MSGS_
17550 top      1.8%  0:00.52   4180   0       72         21555     21504
17536 tcsh     0.0%  0:00.06   271    0       24         54        50
17535 login    0.0%  0:00.75   281    0       51         145       135
17534 ssh      0.0%  0:00.61   300    14      20         60        49
17533 tcsh     0.0%  0:00.05   267    0       24         53        49
17532 login    0.0%  0:00.68   565    0       50         145       135
17526 Preview  0.0%  0:02.78   5741   29      169        8114      5338
17523 tcsh     0.0%  0:00.03   283    0       22         45        44
```

```
17520 emacs    0.9%  0:17.94  2680   125  536   59       54
17494 tcsh     0.0%  0:00.09  337    0    24    60       56
17493 login    0.0%  0:00.80  385    0    52    145      135
17436 iCal     0.0%  0:05.12  4725   27   184   4979     4188
17428 Mozilla  4.6%  8:41.23  57963  38   317   477036   40587
17231 tcsh     0.0%  0:00.04  267    2    24    53       49
17230 login    0.0%  0:00.69  488    10   53    145      135
```

`top -e` is a cumulative output. `top -d` will show things in a delta mode. The update interval is one second. That can be changed by using the `-s` flag to control the number of seconds between intervals.

Index

putchar(), 221
puts(), 221
putw(), 225
Quartz Debug tool, 528
race conditions, 194, 211, 230, 345, 463
raise(), 186
read(), 25, 208
read/write locks, 482
readir(), 247
readlink(), 254
readv(), 213
real user ID, 237
realloc(), 120, **124**
reaping children, 346
recursion, 24
recvfrom(), 313
reentrancy, 191, 463
remote debugging, 172
removing files, 226, 270
removing open files, 227
rename(), 265
Rendezvous, 288, 433
    browsing services, 435
    publishing services, 433
renice command, 341
reportException:, 198
repository, 499, 501
resident set, 116
resource forks, 262
resource limits, **141**, 174, 343
reusing network addresses, 289
revision control, 499
revision tree, 499
rewind(), 224
rewinddir(), 247
Ritchie, Dennis, 1
RLIMIT_* constants, 141
rmdir(), 247
rot-13, 244
run loop, 315
run loop observers, 337
Sampler tool, 527
saved set user ID, 237
scanf(), 225
scatter / gather I/O, 213
SCDynamicStoreCopyKeyList(), 327
SCDynamicStoreCopyMultiple(), 327
SCDynamicStoreCopyValue(), 327
SCDynamicStoreCreate(), 327
SCDynamicStoreSetNotificationKeys(), 327
sc_usage command, 524

SecAccessCopyACLList(), 389
SecACLCopySimpleContents(), 389
SecKeychainAddGenericPassword(), 391
SecKeychainAddInternetPassword(), 391
SecKeychainAttributeList, 381
SecKeychainCopyDefault(), 386
SecKeychainFindGenericPassword(), 392
SecKeychainFindInternetPassword(), 392
SecKeychainItemCopyAccess(), 387
SecKeychainItemCopyContent(), 384
SecKeychainItemDelete(), 386
SecKeychainItemModifyContent(), 386
SecKeychainItemSetAccess(), 387
SecKeychainOpen(), 386
SecKeychainSearchCopyNext(), 382
SecKeychainSearchCreateFromAttributes(), 382
SecKeychainSearchRef, 382
SecKeychainSetUserInteractionAllowed(), 393
SecTrustedApplicationCopyData(), 389
SecTrustedApplicationRef, 389
Security Framework, 395
seekdir(), 247
seeking, 210, 224
SEEK_* constants, 210
select(), 295, 307, 315, 459
sendto(), 312
set-uid, 237
setenv, 108
SetFile command, 267
setjmp(), **182**, 196
setrlimit(), 143, 175, 349
setsockopt(), 289
sexual reproduction, 1
shared libraries, 83
Shikari tool, 528
SIGABRT(), 201
sigaction(), 190
sigaddset(), 187
SIGBUS, 184
SIGCHLD, 184, 349, 357
sigdelset(), 188
sigemptyset(), 187
sigfillset(), 187
SIGHUP, 184
sigismember(), 188
SIGKILL, 186

To order another copy of *Core Mac OS X and Unix Programming*:

Web: http://www.devdepot.com/
Phone: 805-494-9797
Fax: 805-494-9798

Dev Depot
PO Box 5200
Westlake Village, CA 91359-5200